D1474399

COMPREHENSIVE REVIEW GUIDE FOR HEALTH INFORMATION

RHIA & RHIT EXAM PREP

SECOND EDITION

Carla Tyson-Howard
EdD, MHA, RHIA

Chair, Health Information
Technology Department
Houston Community College

Shirlyn C. Thomas
MEd, RHIA

Executive Director, Holistic
Community Development
Corporation
Adjunct Instructor, Health
Information Technology
Department
Houston Community College

JONES & BARTLETT
LEARNING

World Headquarters
Jones & Bartlett Learning
5 Wall Street
Burlington, MA 01803
978-443-5000
info@jblearning.com
www.jblearning.com

Jones & Bartlett Learning books and products are available through most bookstores and online booksellers. To contact Jones & Bartlett Learning directly, call 800-832-0034, fax 978-443-8000, or visit our website, www.jblearning.com.

Copyright © 2016 by Jones & Bartlett Learning, LLC, an Ascend Learning Company

Substantial discounts on bulk quantities of Jones & Bartlett Learning publications are available to corporations, professional associations, and other qualified organizations. For details and specific discount information, contact the special sales department at Jones & Bartlett Learning via the above contact information or send an email to specialsales@jblearning.com.

All rights reserved. No part of the material protected by this copyright may be reproduced or utilized in any form, electronic or mechanical, including photocopying, recording, or by any information storage and retrieval system, without written permission from the copyright owner.

The content, statements, views, and opinions herein are the sole expression of the respective authors and not that of Jones & Bartlett Learning, LLC. Reference herein to any specific commercial product, process, or service by trade name, trademark, manufacturer, or otherwise does not constitute or imply its endorsement or recommendation by Jones & Bartlett Learning, LLC and such reference shall not be used for advertising or product endorsement purposes. All trademarks displayed are the trademarks of the parties noted herein. *Comprehensive Review Guide for Health Information: RHIA & RHIT Exam Prep, Second Edition* is an independent publication and has not been authorized, sponsored, or otherwise approved by the owners of the trademarks or service marks referenced in this product.

There may be images in this book that feature models; these models do not necessarily endorse, represent, or participate in the activities represented in the images. Any screenshots in this product are for educational and instructive purposes only. Any individuals and scenarios featured in the case studies throughout this product may be real or fictitious, but are used for instructional purposes only.

This publication is designed to provide accurate and authoritative information in regard to the Subject Matter covered. It is sold with the understanding that the publisher is not engaged in rendering legal, accounting, or other professional service. If legal advice or other expert assistance is required, the service of a competent professional person should be sought.

Production Credits

Executive Publisher: William Brottmiller
Publisher: Michael Brown
Associate Editor: Chloe Falivene
Editorial Assistant: Nicholas Alakel
Associate Production Editor: Rebekah Linga
Senior Marketing Manager: Sophie Fleck Teague
Manufacturing and Inventory Control Supervisor: Amy Bacus

Composition: Cenveo Publisher Services
Cover Design: Kristin E. Parker
Manager of Photo Research, Rights & Permissions: Amy Rathburn
Cover Image: Green square: © saicle/ShutterStock, Inc.; Bokeh green: © Ghenadie/ShutterStock, Inc.
Title Page Image: © saicle/ShutterStock, Inc.
Printing and Binding: Edwards Brothers Malloy
Cover Printing: Edwards Brothers Malloy

To order this product, use ISBN: 978-1-284-04532-1

Library of Congress Cataloging-in-Publication Data
Tyson-Howard, Carla.
  Comprehensive review guide for health information : RHIA & RHIT exam prep / Carla Tyson-Howard and Shirlyn C. Thomas. — Second edition.
      pages cm
  Includes bibliographical references and index.
  ISBN 978-1-284-02764-8 (paper)
  1. Medical records—Management—Examinations, questions, etc.   2. Information resources management—Examinations, questions, etc.   I. Thomas, Shirlyn C.   II. Title.
  RA976.T97 2015
  610.76—dc23
                                    2014021651

6048

Printed in the United States of America
18 17 16 15 14   10 9 8 7 6 5 4 3 2 1

Contents

Contents

CHAPTER 4

Healthcare Statistics, Research, and Epidemiology 147

CHAPTER 5

Quality Management and Performance Improvement 189

iv

CHAPTER 6

Information Technology and Systems   259

CHAPTER 7

Biomedical Sciences   303

CHAPTER 8

Clinical Classification Systems   339

Contents

CHAPTER 9

Organization and Management: Human and Financial Resources   437

vi

About the Authors

Carla Tyson-Howard, EdD, MHA, RHIA
Chair, Health Information Technology Department
Houston Community College
Houston, Texas

Shirlyn C. Thomas, MEd, RHIA
Executive Director, Holistic Community Development Corporation (CDC)
Galveston, Texas
Adjunct Instructor, Health Information Technology Department
Houston Community College
Houston, Texas

CONTRIBUTING AUTHORS

Fannie C. Hawkins, EdD, CPHQ, RHIA
(Chapter 8: Clinical Classification Systems)
Program Director, Health Information Management Department
Texas Southern University
Houston, Texas

Jeannie Helton, RHIT
(Chapter 8: Clinical Classification Systems)
Adjunct Faculty, Health Information Technology Department
Houston Community College
Houston, Texas

Casandra Johnson, RHIT, CCS
(Chapter 8: Clinical Classification Systems)
Health Information Manager
Park Plaza Hospital
Houston, Texas

Bunmi Ogunleye, MSHEd, CHES, RHIA
(Chapter 3: Healthcare Privacy, Confidentiality, Legal, and Ethical Issues; Chapter 5: Quality
Management and Performance Improvement)
Health Information Manager
Harris Health System
Adjunct Instructor, Houston Community College
Houston, Texas

Irma Rodriguez, MEd, RHIA, CCS
(Chapter 2: Health Data Management, Health Services Organization, Delivery and Reimbursement Methodologies)
Chair, Health Information Technology Department
South Texas College
McAllen, Texas

Acknowledgments

I am grateful to G-d for giving me the idea, inspiration, and energy to co-develop this review guide with my sister-partner, Shirlyn Thomas. It is a labor of love to my students and health information students around the world. I hope that this review guide brings clarity and focus to your studies and exam preparation.

I express gratitude to my mentors, Linda Johnson and Tella Williams, for guiding me in the health information field. Thank you also to Debora Butts for reviewing and providing input on the text while under construction. I thank the co-authors for sharing their knowledge, wisdom, and expertise. I acknowledge Houston Community College for supporting faculty in the use of technology to make the teaching and learning process easier.

In memory of my father, Carl, I thank him and my mother, Odell Tyson, for instilling in me the importance of education. Thanks to my sister, Cassandra Tyson, and my friend Elizabeth Hoover for countless hours of reviewing and referencing material.

Finally, I acknowledge my handsome husband, John Howard, whose encouragement and endless love are priceless.

—Carla Tyson-Howard

No one is or becomes without the help of others. I would like to express my sincere gratitude to the others in my life who have contributed in various ways to make this product a living instrument to help others.

To God and my Lord and Savior, for creating me in your image and your likeness and for equipping me with all that was needed to complete your idea.

To Carla, for being a conduit of the idea and allowing me to share a part of making the lives of others better and for being one of my greatest teachers.

To my mother, who has given me a genetic transfer of determination and tenacity.

To my wonderful and precious husband, who became whatever I needed in the toughest parts of the process and is always a source of strength.

To my children, LaToya, T.K., and Trae, who are my inspirations and whose faces I reflect on when the going gets tough. To my grandson Prince Manuel, who is the joy of my heart.

To my sisters, Deborah and Kim, who are parts of the foundation on which I stand. Thanks for your never-ending support.

To all of the contributing authors, thank you for co-laboring with Carla and I to make this a superior learning tool.

—Shirlyn Thomas

Introduction

HOW TO USE THIS REVIEW GUIDE

Congratulations on your choice to use the *Comprehensive Review Guide for Health Information: RHIA and RHIT Exam Prep*. It is an invaluable resource for navigating through school and preparing for the national exams. This comprehensive review of health information is designed to assist students in passing the national examination for Registered Health Information Administrators (RHIA) and Registered Health Information Technicians (RHIT) and with navigating through coursework.

We are excited about the added revisions and updates to this edition of the *Comprehensive Review Guide for Health Information: RHIA and RHIT Exam Prep*. These revisions reflect major renovations in the curriculum and the industry of health information. The inclusion of these additions provides the user with a more superior guide for test success. Namely, the new material covers the following topics:

- The electronic health record and reimbursement methodologies
- The Health Information Technology for Economic and Clinical Health (HITECH) legislation
- ICD-10-CM/PCS
- New additions to the *Information Technology and Systems* chapter from the *HITECH curriculum* chapter
- New practice tests questions added to each chapter
- A Test Prep product that provides multiple online mock exams with item analysis
- A companion website that provides online learning opportunities consisting of a series of gradable activities, including matching and sequencing excrcises

The *Comprehensive Review Guide* was created to accommodate the various learning styles:

- **Visual (spatial):** Learn best using pictures, images, and spatial understanding.
- **Aural (auditory–musical):** Learn best using sound and music.

- **Verbal (linguistic):** Learn best using words, both in speech and writing.
- **Physical (kinesthetic):** Learn best using your body, hands, and sense of touch.
- **Logical (mathematical):** Learn best using logic, reasoning, and systems.
- **Social (interpersonal):** Learn best within groups or with other people.
- **Solitary (intrapersonal):** Learn best working alone and utilizing self-study.

This review series is not intended to teach or introduce new information, but rather highlights major areas of study that you have learned about or are learning during your coursework.

This unique guide contains all the components needed for a comprehensive strategy for test success. Each of the nine chapters is organized as follows:

- An extensive review of the subject area
- Practical Application of Your Knowledge exercises (short-answer, fill-in-the-blank, and matching questions)
- Test Your Knowledge opportunities (multiple-choice chapter questions)

To assure maximum strength of your knowledge, answers for the Practical Application of Your Knowledge exercises are not provided (with the exception of the classification systems section). If you do not know the answers in a given chapter, reread the review section or reference your textbooks. However, answers and references are provided for the Test Your Knowledge sections.

All test questions have been created utilizing the Domains and Subdomains structure dictated by the American Health Information Management Association. To maximize this learning tool, we recommend the following:

1. Review the content areas in the review section of the book. Begin with your challenging areas first (visual, social, solitary, verbal, logical learning).
2. Complete the Practical Application of Your Knowledge exercises related to the content area of study (physical, logical, solitary).
3. Evaluate your comprehension of the content area by taking the "Test Your Knowledge" exam on the relevant content area.
4. Repeat this process until you have completed all of the content areas.
5. After completion of all areas of content in the review book section and workbook, take a mock examination. Take advantage of the multiple mock exams via the online Test Prep product. It is designed to decrease your test anxiety and build confidence that you have the knowledge capacity to succeed on the national examination.
6. Repeat steps 1 through 4 for areas of weakness as indicated by the mock exam results.

In addition, utilize your textbooks to provide more support for challenging areas. Remember the steps in your study process (Figure 1-1). Information about the exams may change. Be sure you consult with the American Health Information Management Association (AHIMA) to obtain the latest information. Their website is www.ahima.org.

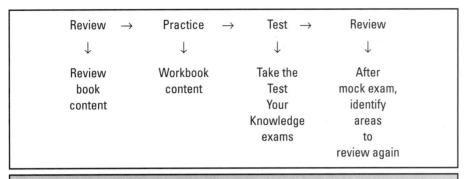

Figure 1-1 Study Process Steps

The RHIA and RHIT national exams of the AHIMA are based on an explicit set of competencies. The RHIA exam is 4 hours in duration and has 180 test questions. The RHIT exam is 3.5 hours and consists of 150 questions. Please see the following comptency domains outline and the percentage of each domain area on the RHIA and RHIT exams.

Registered Health Information Administrator (RHIA) Examination Content Outline

Number of Questions on Exam: 180 Multiple Choice   **Exam Time: 4 hours**

Domain I

Health Data Management (20%)

1. Manage health data elements and/or data sets
2. Develop and maintain organizational policies, procedures, and guidelines for management of health information
3. Ensure accuracy and integrity of health data and health record documentation
4. Manage and/or validate coding accuracy and compliance
5. Manage the use of clinical data required in reimbursement systems and prospective payment systems (PPS) in healthcare delivery
6. Code diagnosis and procedures according to established guidelines
7. Present data for organizational use (e.g., summarize, synthesize, and condense information)

Domain II

Health Statistics and Research Support (11%)

1. Identify and/or respond to the information needs of internal and external healthcare customers
2. Filter and/or interpret information for the end customer
3. Analyze and present information for organizational management (e.g., quality, utilization, risk)
4. Use data mining techniques to query and report from databases

Reproduced with permission from the Commission on Certification for Health Informatics and Information Management (CCHIM). Copyright © 2014 by the Commission on Certification for Health Informatics and Information Management (CCHIM). All rights reserved. No part of this may be reproduced, reprinted, stored in a retrieval system, or transmitted, in any form or by any means, electronic, photocopying, recording, or otherwise, without the prior written permission of the association.

(continues)

Registered Health Information Administrator (RHIA) Examination Content Outline (*continued*)

Number of Questions on Exam: 180 Multiple Choice	Exam Time: 4 hours

Domain III

Information Technology and Systems (20%)

1. Implement and manage use of technology application
2. Develop data dictionary and data models for database design
3. Manage and maintain databases (e.g., data migration, updates)
4. Apply data and functional standards to achieve interoperability of healthcare information systems
5. Apply data/record storage principles and techniques associated with the medium (e.g., paper-based, hybrid, electronic)
6. Evaluate and recommend clinical, administrative, and specialty service applications (e.g., financial systems, electronic record, clinical coding)
7. Manage master person index (e.g., patient record integration, customer/client relationship management)

Domain IV

Organization and Management (30%)

1. Develop and support strategic and operational plans for facility-wide health information management (HIM)
2. Monitor industry trends and organizational needs to anticipate changes
3. Perform human resource management activities (e.g., recruiting staff, creating job descriptions, resolve personnel issues)
4. Conduct training and educational activities (e.g., HIM systems, coding, medical and institutional terminology, documentation and regulatory requirements)
5. Establish and monitor productivity standards for the HIM function
6. Optimize reimbursement through management of the revenue cycle (e.g., chargemaster maintenance)
7. Develop, motivate, and support work teams and/or individuals (e.g., coaching, mentoring)
8. Prepare and manage budgets
9. Analyze and report on budget variances
10. Determine resource needs by performing analyses (e.g., cost–benefit, business planning)
11. Evaluate and manage contracts (e.g., vendor, contract personnel, maintenance)
12. Organize and facilitate meetings
13. Advocate for department, organization, and/or profession
14. Manage projects
15. Prepare for accreditation and licensing processes (e.g., Joint Commission, Medicare, state regulators)

Domain V

Privacy, Security, and Confidentiality (13%)

1. Design and implement security measures to safeguard Protected Health Information (PHI)
2. Manage access, disclosure, and use of Protected Health Information (PHI) to ensure confidentiality
3. Investigate and resolve healthcare privacy and security issues/problems
4. Develop and maintain healthcare privacy and security training programs

Registered Health Information Administrator (RHIA) Examination Content Outline (*continued*)

Number of Questions on Exam: 180 Multiple Choice	Exam Time: 4 hours

Domain VI

Legal and Regulatory Standards (6%)

1. Administer organizational compliance with healthcare information laws, regulations, and standards (e.g., audit, report and/or inform; legal health record)
2. Prepare for accreditation and licensing processes (e.g., Joint Commission, Medicare, state regulators)

Registered Health Information Technician (RHIT) Content Outline

Number of Questions on Exam: 150 Multiple Choice	Exam Time: 3.5 hours

Domain I

Data Analysis and Management (20%)

1. Abstract information found in health records (e.g., coding, research, physician deficiencies)
2. Analyze data (e.g., productivity reports, quality measures, health record documentation, case mix index)
3. Maintain filing and retrieval systems for health records
4. Identify anomalies in data
5. Resolve risks and/or anomalies of data findings
6. Maintain the master patient index (e.g., enterprise systems, merge/unmerge medical record numbers)
7. Eliminate duplicate documentation
8. Organize data into a useable format
9. Review trends in data
10. Gather/compile data from multiple sources
11. Generate reports or spreadsheets (e.g., customize, create)
12. Present data findings (e.g., study results, delinquencies, conclusion/summaries, gap analysis, graphical)
13. Implement workload distribution
14. Design workload distribution
15. Participate in the data management plan (e.g., determine data elements, assemble components, set time frame)
16. Input and/or submit data to registries
17. Summarize findings from data research/analysis
18. Follow data archive and backup policies
19. Develop data management plan
20. Calculate healthcare statistics (e.g., occupancy rates, length of stay, delinquency rates)
21. Determine validation process for data mapping
22. Maintain data dictionaries

Reproduced with permission from the Commission on Certification for Health Informatics and Information Management (CCHIM). Copyright © 2014 by the Commission on Certification for Health Informatics and Information Management (CCHIM). All rights reserved. No part of this may be reproduced, reprinted, stored in a retrieval system, or transmitted, in any form or by any means, electronic, photocopying, recording, or otherwise, without the prior written permission of the association.

(*continues*)

Registered Health Information Technician (RHIT) Content Outline (*continued*)

Number of Questions on Exam: 150 Multiple Choice	Exam Time: 3.5 hours

Domain II

Coding (18%)

1. Apply all official current coding guidelines
2. Assign diagnostic and procedure codes based on health record documentation
3. Ensure physician documentation supports coding
4. Validate code assignment
5. Abstract data from health record
6. Sequence codes
7. Query physician when additional clinical documentation is needed
8. Review and resolve coding edits (e.g., correct coding initiative, outpatient code editor, national coverage determination, local coverage determination)
9. Review the accuracy of abstracted data
10. Assign present on admission (POA) indicators
11. Provide educational updates to coders
12. Validate grouper assignment (e.g., MS-DRG, APC)
13. Identify hospital-acquired condition (HAC)
14. Develop and manage a query process
15. Create standards for coding productivity and quality
16. Develop educational guidelines for provider documentation
17. Perform concurrent audits

Domain III

Compliance (16%)

1. Ensure patient record documentation meets state and federal regulations
2. Ensure compliance with privacy and security guidelines (e.g., HIPAA, state, hospital)
3. Control access to health information
4. Monitor documentation for completeness
5. Develop a coding compliance plan (e.g., current coding guidelines)
6. Manage release of information
7. Perform continual updates to policies and procedures
8. Implement internal and external audit guidelines
9. Evaluate medical necessity (clinical documentation management program [CDMP])
10. Collaborate with staff to prepare the organization for accreditation, licensing, and/or certification surveys
11. Evaluate medical necessity (outpatient services)
12. Evaluate medical necessity (data management)
13. Responding to fraud and abuse
14. Evaluate medical necessity (ISSI utilization review)
15. Develop forms (e.g., chart review, documentation, EMR)
16. Evaluate medical necessity (case management)
17. Analyze access audit trails
18. Ensure valid healthcare provider credentials

Registered Health Information Technician (RHIT) Content Outline (*continued*)

Number of Questions on Exam: 150 Multiple Choice   **Exam Time: 3.5 hours**

Domain IV

Information Technology (12%)

1. Train users on software
2. Maintain database
3. Set up secure access
4. Evaluate the functionality of applications
5. Create user accounts
6. Troubleshoot HIM software or support systems
7. Create database
8. Perform end-user audits
9. Participate in vendor selection
10. Perform end-user needs analysis
11. Design data archive and backup policies
12. Perform system maintenance of software and systems
13. Create data dictionaries

Domain V

Quality (12%)

1. Audit health records for content, completeness, accuracy, and timeliness
2. Apply standards, guidelines, and/or regulations to health records
3. Implement corrective actions as determined by audit findings (internal and external)
4. Design efficient workflow processes
5. Comply with national patient safety goals
6. Analyze standards, guidelines, and/or regulations to build criteria for audits
7. Apply process improvement techniques
8. Provide consultation to internal and external users of health information on HIM subject matter
9. Develop reports on audit findings
10. Perform data collection for quality reporting (e.g., core measures, PQRI, medical necessity)
11. Use trended data to participate in performance improvement plans/initiatives
12. Develop a tool for collecting statistically valid data
13. Conduct clinical pertinence reviews
14. Monitor physician credentials to practice in the facility

Domain VI

Legal (11%)

1. Ensure confidentiality of the health records (paper and electronic)
2. Adhere to disclosure standards and regulations (e.g., HIPAA privacy, HITECH Act, breach notifications) at both state and federal levels

(*continues*)

Registered Health Information Technician (RHIT) Content Outline (*continued*)

Number of Questions on Exam: 150 Multiple Choice   **Exam Time: 3.5 hours**

3. Demonstrate and promote legal and ethical standards of practice
4. Maintain integrity of legal health record according to organizational bylaws, rules, and regulations
5. Follow state-mandated and/or organizational record retention and destruction policies
6. Serve as the custodian of the health records (paper or electronic)
7. Respond to release of information (ROI) requests from internal and external requestors
8. Work with risk management department to provide requested documentation
9. Identify potential health record–related risk management issues through auditing
10. Respond to and process patient amendment requests to the health record
11. Facilitate basic education regarding the use of consents, healthcare power of attorney, advanced directives, DNRs, etc.
12. Represent the facility in court-related matters as it applies to the health record (e.g., subpoenas, depositions, court orders, warrants)

Domain VII

Revenue Cycle (11%)

1. Communicate with providers to discuss documentation deficiencies (e.g., queries)
2. Participate in clinical documentation improvement programs to ensure proper documentation of health records
3. Collaborate with other departments on monitoring accounts receivable (e.g., unbilled, uncoded)
4. Provide ongoing education to healthcare providers (e.g., regulatory changes, new guidelines, payment standards, best practices)
5. Identify fraud and abuse
6. Assist with appeal letters in response to claim denials
7. Monitor claim denials/overpayments to identify potential revenue impact
8. Prioritize the work according to accounts receivable, patient type, etc.
9. Distribute the work according to accounts receivable, patient type, etc.
10. Maintain the charge-master
11. Ensure physicians are credentialed with different payers for reimbursement

Cognitive Levels of the RHIA and RHIT National Examinations

The RHIA and RHIT computer-based national examinations consist of four-option, multiple-choice questions written at three different cognitive levels: recall, application, and analysis. These levels represent an organized way to identify the performance that practitioners will utilize on the job. The three cognitive levels are defined as follows:

Cognitive Level	Purpose	Performance Required
Recall (RE)	Primarily measuring memory.	Identify terms, specific facts, methods, procedures, basic concepts, basic theories, principles, and processes.
Application (AP)	To measure simple interpretation of limited data.	Apply concepts and principles to new situations; recognize relationships among data; apply laws and theories to practical situations; calculate solutions to mathematical problems; interpret charts and translate graphic data; classify items; interpret information.
Analysis (AN)	To measure the application of knowledge to solving a specific problem and the assembly of various elements into a meaningful whole.	Select an appropriate solution for responsive action; revise policy, procedure, or plan; evaluate a solution, case scenario, report, or plan; compare solutions, plans, ideas, or aspects of a problem; evaluate information or a situation; perform multiple calculations to arrive at one answer.

Reproduced with permission from the Commission on Certification for Health Informatics and Information Management (CCHIM). Copyright © 2014 by the Commission on Certification for Health Informatics and Information Management (CCHIM). All rights reserved. No part of this may be reproduced, reprinted, stored in a retrieval system, or transmitted, in any form or by any means, electronic, photocopying, recording, or otherwise, without the prior written permission of the association.

Please check the AHIMA website regularly for the most up-to-date competencies: http://ahimafoundation.org/education/curricula.aspx.

A WORD ABOUT SOFT SKILLS

As educators, we take a holistic approach to student success. This guide has been designed to assist in the achievement of passing the National Exams for Registered Health Information Administrators and Technicians. The test accomplishment is an outcome that validates your knowledge base and skill sets. It prepares you to enter the world of health information as a credentialed professional. Securing proof that you possess the entry-level required hard skills (technical skills that relate to a specific profession or industry) to become employable is step 1. The degree and the credential will get your foot in the door, but the remaining doors that lead to upward mobility, promotion, and sustainability will be opened to you through soft skills. Soft skills, it is suggested, will be the new hard skills of the future. Every industry is seeing a deterioration in what was wrongly assumed would be innate skills in a new hired professional. Employers are often shocked to learn that educated and credentialed professionals lack communication skills, do not know how to extend courtesy and respect to others in the workplace, inappropriately text and use cell phones, create e-mails with tactless tones, and lack sound emotional intelligence, resulting in an inability to manage conflict and maintain balance of work and home life.

So what are soft skills? Soft skills can be defined as personal attributes that enhance an individual's interactions, job performance, and career prospects. Unlike hard skills, which focus on a person's skill set and ability to perform a certain type of task or activity, soft skills are interpersonal and applicable on a broader scale. Soft skills can also be defined as people skills, social skills, and interpersonal skills that, when well developed, enrich the quality of our interactions with others. They are displayed in our personality, attitudes, and behavior. Although they are intangible and challenging to measure, they have a tremendous influence on our personal and professional development and on the culture of any organization.

For this reason, soft skills are increasingly being pursued by employers in addition to standard qualifications. The following is an abbreviated list of soft skills desired by employers:

- Ability to communicate verbally and in writing
- Ability to work with others
- Impulse control
- Common sense
- Possess manners
- Problem solving
- Initiative
- Self-discipline
- Respectful
- Loyalty
- Commitment
- Enthusiasm
- Motivation
- Adaptability
- Honesty and integrity
- Pride in personal appearance
- Ability to deal with pressure
- Ability to deal with conflict
- Reliability

- Emotionally intelligent
- A balanced attitude toward work and home life.

As you proceed to a future with endless possibilities, to secure your ultimate goals, you need to perfect your entire self by conducting an inventory of your soft skills. Make a commitment to yourself to cultivate the areas where you are lacking. This investment will lead to greater success returns.

Best wishes on your professional journey!

STUDY TIPS

You are either navigating your way through your HIM program or preparing to take your national RHIA or RHIT exam. Either way, the *Comprehensive Review Guide for Health Information: RHIA and RHIT Exam Prep* is an excellent tool in your arsenal for success. Because everyone is different and our learning styles vary, different methods work for different people. The following are only suggestions for improving your current study techniques to help launch your achievement in the field of HIM.

1. **Make a study schedule.** Use a calendar to plan the days and times to study specific courses or subject areas. Space out your studying; review class materials at least several times a week, focusing on one topic at a time.
2. **Set a standard place to study** such as your office, library, kitchen table, or wherever is comfortable and conducive for focused and concentrated learning. Make sure you have adequate lighting and that you are not distracted by noises.
3. **Place all of your study material in front of you:** lecture notes, course textbooks, study guides, and any other relevant material.
4. **Take notes** and write down a summary of the important ideas as you read through your study material. Make notes in your books. There is nothing wrong with writing in your books; they are your books.
5. **Take short breaks frequently.** Your memory retains the information that you study at the beginning and the end better than what you study in the middle.
6. **Make sure that you understand the material well.** Do not just read through the material and try to memorize everything. Use the review guide to test your knowledge. Make an exam for yourself and answer the questions. The more times you test yourself, the more you increase your chance of scoring higher on your exam.
7. **Use the review guide** to review the main information of the knowledge clusters quickly. You also may use the review guide to rewrite the main ideas, information, and formulas to reinforce your comprehension of the material. This may make it easier to retain the key concepts that will be on the test.
8. If you choose to study in a group, **only study with others who are serious** about the test. Study groups are not social gatherings for happy hour. At the end of the predetermined study period you may want to end with snacks and fellowship. However, the latter is not the main purpose of coming together; stay focused.

TEST-TAKING TIPS

Studying is only a part of getting good results on your exam. You also have to master test taking so that you will score the most points.

1. Familiarize yourself with the AHIMA knowledge clusters. Know what is expected for you to know and master. Read the candidate application book and know what is allowed in the testing center and take the resources you will need with you.
2. Many colleges and state and local associations offer review sessions for mastering the national exams. Go to the reviews and incorporate the testing hints that are relevant to you. Take careful notes and ask questions about items you may be confused about.
3. Do not try to cram the night before the exam. You have studied hard and have retained as much information as you possibly can. Get at least eight hours of sleep the night before the exam.
4. Eat before the exam. You will need the energy that having food in your stomach will provide, and it will help you stay focused on the task at hand. Avoid heavy foods that can make you groggy.
5. Use your alarm clock to assure that you do not oversleep for the exam. Try to show up at least 15 minutes before the test will start. Use this time to acquaint yourself with bathroom and water fountain locations. This also is a good time to pray or meditate and calm yourself.
6. Time is of the essence. Whether you are taking a test in class or the national RHIA or RHIT exams, you have a limited amount of time. Schedule your time accordingly. If you notice yourself spending too much time on one question, come back to it later if you have time. Pace yourself.
7. The RHIA and RHIT are multiple-choice tests. Multiple-choice test-taking tips include the following:
   a. Read the question before you look at the answer.
   b. Try to come up with the answer in your head before looking at the possible answers. This will cut down the distractions of the choices given.
   c. Eliminate answers you know are not correct.
   d. Read all the choices before choosing your answer.
   e. There is no guessing penalty, so always take an educated guess if you do not know the answer.
   f. Do not keep changing your answer. Usually your first choice is the right one unless you misread the question.

8. Keep a positive attitude throughout the whole test and try to stay relaxed; if you start to feel nervous, take 10 deep breaths and relax.

9. When you are finished and if you have time left, look over your test and make sure that you have answered all the questions. Only change an answer if you misread or misinterpreted the question, because your first answer is usually the correct one.

It is our hope that this guide helps you to achieve your goal of becoming a credentialed professional in the field of health information. Good studying to you and may your success be great!

© saicle/ShutterStock, Inc.

Health Data Management, Health Services Organization, Delivery and Reimbursement Methodologies

1. **Definition, Purpose, Uses, and Users of the Health Record**
   a. Health Record Defined
      i. Also referred to as the medical record, patient record, resident record, or client record
      ii. Identifies the patient, the diagnosis, treatments rendered, and documentation of all results
      iii. Used as a documentation tool for continuous patient care
      iv. Serves as a communication tool for healthcare professionals
      v. Serves as a data and information collection tool for all healthcare services
      vi. Combination of discrete data elements and narrative in various media, including paper, electronic, voice, images, and waveforms
      vii. Electronic health record
         1. Healthcare information managed by electronic system(s) used to capture, transmit, receive, store, retrieve, link, and manipulate multimedia data
   b. Purpose of Health Record
      i. Primary source of health data and information for the healthcare industry
      ii. Created as a direct by-product of healthcare delivered in a health setting and is the legal documentation of care provided by the healthcare professionals
      iii. A valuable source of aggregate data for research and program evaluation
      iv. Healthcare reimbursement
   c. Uses of Patient Record
      i. Documenting healthcare services provided to an individual to support ongoing communication and decision making among healthcare providers
         1. Planning and managing diagnostic, therapeutic, and nursing services
      ii. Establishing a record of healthcare services provided to an individual that can be used as evidence in legal proceedings
         1. Protects the legal interest of the patient, healthcare provider, and healthcare organization

       iii. Assessing the efficiency and effectiveness of the healthcare services provided

         1. Evaluating the adequacy and appropriateness of care

       iv. Documenting healthcare services provided to support reimbursement claims that are submitted to payers

       v. Supplying data and information that support the strategic planning, administrative decision making, and research activities as well as support the public policy development related to health care (regulations, legislation, and accreditation standards)

    d. Five Unique Roles of a Patient's Health Record

       i. A record of the patient's health status and the health services provided over time

       ii. Provides a method for clinical communication and care planning among the individual healthcare practitioners serving the patient

       iii. Serves as the legal document describing the healthcare services provided

       iv. A source of data for clinical, health services, and outcomes research

       v. Serves as a major resource for healthcare practitioner education

    e. Users of Patient Record and Health Data

       i. Patient

       ii. Healthcare practitioners

       iii. Healthcare providers and administrators

       iv. Third-party payers

       v. Utilization managers

       vi. Quality of care committees

       vii. Accrediting, licensing, and certifying agencies

       viii. Governmental agencies

       ix. Attorneys and the courts in the judicial process

       x. Planners and policy developers

       xi. Educators and trainers

       xii. Researchers and epidemiologists

       xiii. Media reporters

2. Format of the Health Record

    a. Source-Oriented Health Record

       i. Documents are organized into sections according to the practitioners and departments that provide treatment.

         1. Example

            a. Laboratory records are grouped together, radiology records are grouped together, clinical notes are grouped together, and so on.

    b. Problem-Oriented Health Record

       i. Developed by Dr. Lawrence L. Weed in the 1960s, in response to the lack of clarity of the patient's problems in the source-oriented record

       ii. Divided into four parts

         1. Database

         2. Problem list

         3. Initial plan

         4. Progress notes (SOAP)

            a. Subjective

               i. Patient states the problem to healthcare provider.

            b. Objective

               i. What the practitioner identifies

      c. Assessment

          i. Combines the subjective and objective to make a conclusion

      d. Plan

          i. The approach to be taken to resolve the patient's problem

  c. Integrated Health Records

      i. Documentation from various sources is intermingled and organized in strict chronological or reverse chronological order.

      ii. Advantage is that it is easy to follow the course of the patient's diagnosis and treatment.

      iii. Disadvantage is that the format makes it difficult to compare similar information.

3. Basic Principles of Health Record Documentation

  a. General Documentation Guidelines of the American Health Information Management Association (AHIMA)

      i. Uniformity of both the content and format of the health record

      ii. Organized systematically to facilitate data retrieval and compilation

      iii. Only authorized individuals should be allowed to document in the record.

      iv. Policies must identify which individuals may receive and transcribe verbal physician's orders.

      v. Documentation should occur when the services were rendered.

      vi. Entries should identify authors clearly.

      vii. Individuals making entries should use only abbreviations and symbols approved by the organization and/or medical staff.

      viii. All entries in the record should be permanent.

      ix. Error correction for paper-based records

          1. Never obliterate errors; original entry should remain legible, and corrections should be entered in chronological order.

          2. Draw a single line in ink through the incorrect entry. Print "error" or "correction" at the top of the entry along with a legal signature or initials, date, time, reason for change, and the title and discipline of the individual making the correction. Add correct information to the entry.

          3. Late entries should be labeled as such.

      x. Any corrections on information added to the record by the healthcare provider from verbal corrections from the patient should be inserted as an addendum or a separate note with no changes in the original entries in record.

      xi. Health information department should develop, implement, and evaluate policies and procedures related to the quantitative and qualitative analysis of the health record.

  b. Common Time Frames for Completion of Health Record Documents

      i. History and physical: within 24 hours of admission

      ii. Operative report: immediately following surgery

      iii. Verbal orders: cosigned within 24 hours

      iv. Discharge summary: immediately after discharge of patient

  c. The Joint Commission (TJC) Type I Recommendation

      i. Too many delinquent records may cause the hospital to receive a Type I Recommendation, which must be resolved to retain accreditation.

      ii. Guidelines that indicate a Type I Recommendation

          1. The number of delinquent records is greater than 50% of the average number of discharged patients per quarter, over the previous 12 months.

      2. All medical records must have a history documented within 24 hours.

      3. All medical records, including a surgery, must have an immediate postoperative note documented, and the operative report must be dictated immediately after surgery.

4. **Content of the Acute Care Health Record**

    a. Administrative Data (includes demographic and financial information as well as various consent and authorization forms related to the provision of care and the handling of confidential patient information)

      i. Registration record

      ii. Consent to treatment

      iii. Consent to release information

      iv. Consent to special procedures

      v. Advanced directives

      vi. Patient rights acknowledgment

      vii. Property and valuables list

      viii. Birth and death certificates

    b. Clinical Data (documents the patient's medical condition, diagnosis, and treatment as well as the healthcare services provided)

      i. Medical history and review of systems

      ii. Physical examination

      iii. Interdisciplinary patient care plan

      iv. Physician's orders

      v. Progress notes (clinical observations)

      vi. Reports and results of diagnostic and therapeutic procedures

      vii. Consultation reports

      viii. Discharge and interval summary that includes final instructions given to patient upon discharge

      ix. Operative data

        1. Anesthesia report

        2. Recovery room record

        3. Operative report

        4. Pathology report

      x. Obstetric data

        1. Antepartum record

        2. Labor and delivery record

        3. Postpartum record

      xi. Neonatal data

        1. Birth history

        2. Neonatal identification

        3. Neonatal physical examination

        4. Neonate progress notes

      xii. Nursing data

        1. Nursing notes

        2. Graphic sheet

        3. Medication sheet

        4. Special care units

      xiii. Ancillary data

        1. Electrocardiographic reports

        2. Laboratory reports

        3. Radiology and imaging reports

        4. Radiation therapy

        5. Therapeutic services

6. Case management and social service record
7. Patient and family teaching and participation
8. Discharge and follow-up plan

5. **Record Content for Alternative Healthcare Sites**
  a. Ambulatory Care
    i. Patient data items
    ii. Patient care provider data items
    iii. Encounter data items
  b. Emergency Room
    i. Identification
    ii. History of the present disease or injury
    iii. Physical findings and vital signs
    iv. Laboratory and radiology reports if needed
    v. Diagnosis
    vi. Treatment
    vii. Disposition of the case
  c. Long-Term Care
    i. Socio-demographic information
    ii. Database
    iii. Patient care plans
    iv. Ancillary reports
    v. Activities of facility-community living
    vi. Correspondence and third-party information
  d. Home Health Care
    i. Initial database
      1. Diagnoses and problems
      2. History and physical condition
      3. Current medication and treatment
      4. Activity limitations
      5. Dietary information
      6. Suitability of residence
    ii. Plan of treatment contains
      1. Identified patient problems and needs
      2. Goals and objectives for patient care
      3. Services provided, including type, frequency, and duration
      4. Plan implementation
    iii. Progress notes
    iv. Discharge summary
    v. Consent forms
    vi. Service agreement
  e. Hospice Care
    i. Initial database
    ii. Interdisciplinary team documentation
    iii. Ongoing documentation
    iv. Discharge/transfer record
    v. Bereavement record
    vi. Consents
  f. Mental Health Care
    i. Identification/face sheet
    ii. Evaluation for admission
    iii. Problem-asset list
    iv. Comprehensive evaluation
    v. Periodic summaries

   vi. Transfer and/or discharge summary
   vii. Death summary
   viii. History and physical examination
   ix. Consultations
   x. Diagnostic tests, including X-rays or other operations or procedures
   xi. Physician orders
   xii. Record of medication administered
   xiii. Progress notes
   xiv. Flow sheets
   xv. Electroshock observations documentation
   xvi. Seizures
   xvii. Issues related to infectious disease control
   xviii. Legal and administrative
   xix. Previous admissions
  g. Rehabilitative Care
   i. Identification data
   ii. Pertinent history
   iii. Disability diagnosis, rehabilitation problems, goals, and prognosis
   iv. Assessments
   v. Ancillary reports
   vi. Program manager information
   vii. Decision-making information
   viii. Evaluations
   ix. Staff conferences reports
   x. Program plans
   xi. Progress notes
   xii. Relative correspondence
   xiii. Release forms
   xiv. Discharge report
   xv. Follow-up report
  h. Personal Health Record
   i. Electronic lifelong resource of health information needed by individuals to make health decisions
   ii. Individuals own and manage the information that comes from healthcare providers and individuals

6. **Data Quality Monitoring**
 a. The accuracy of data depends on the manual or computer information system design for collecting, recording, storing, processing, accessing, and displaying data, as well as the ability and follow-through of the individuals involved in each phase of the activities.
  i. Systems should be developed to ensure the accuracy and timeliness of documentation at the point of care, to monitor output, and to take appropriate correction action when needed.
  ii. Health information technicians may perform a quality improvement (QI) study to evaluate data quality of paper or computerized patient records; the study may assess the presence of reports and authentications as well as the quality of the information documented in the entries.
 b. Quantitative Analysis Ensures
  i. Patient identification on the front and back of every paper form or on every screen is correct.
  ii. All necessary authorizations or consents are present and signed or authenticated by the patient or legal representative.

    iii. Documented principal diagnosis on discharge, secondary diagnoses, and procedures are present in the appropriate form or location within the record.

    iv. Discharge summary is present when required, and authenticated.

    v. History and physical report are present, documented within the time frame required by appropriate regulations, and authenticated as appropriate.

    vi. When a consultation request appears in the listing of physician or practitioner orders, a consultation report is present and authenticated.

    vii. All diagnostic tests ordered by the physician or practitioner are present and are authenticated by comparing physician orders, financial bill, and the test reports documented in the patient's health record.

    viii. An admitting progress note, a discharge progress note, and an appropriate number of notes documented by physicians or clinicians throughout the patient's care process are present.

    ix. Each physician or practitioner order entered into the record is authenticated.

        1. Admitting and discharge physician or practitioner orders are present.

        2. Orders are present for all consultations, diagnostic tests, and procedures, when these reports are found in the record.

    x. Operative, procedure, or therapy reports are present and authenticated, when orders, consent forms, or other documentation in the record indicates they were performed.

    xi. A pathology report is present and authenticated when the operative report indicates that tissue was removed.

    xii. Preoperative, operative, and postoperative anesthesia reports are present and authenticated.

    xiii. Nursing or ancillary health professionals' reports and notes are present and authenticated.

    xiv. Reports required for patients treated in specialized units are present and authenticated.

    xv. Preliminary and final autopsy reports on patients who have died at the facility are present and authenticated.

c. Qualitative Analysis Involves Checks

    i. Review for obvious documentation inconsistencies related to diagnoses found on admission forms, physical examination, operative and pathology reports, care plans, and discharge summary.

    ii. Analyze the record to determine whether documentation written by various healthcare providers for one patient reflects consistency.

    iii. Compare the patient's pharmacy drug profile with the medication administration record to determine consistency.

    iv. Review an inpatient record to determine whether it reflects the general location of the patient at all times or whether serious time gaps exist.

    v. Determine whether the patient record reflects the progression of care, including the symptoms, diagnoses, tests, treatments, reasons for the treatments, results, patient education, location of patient after discharge, and follow-up plans.

    vi. Interview the patient and/or family.

        1. Review recorded patient demographic information and medical history with the patient several hours or days after admission to determine completeness and accuracy.

        2. A patient may be too physically ill or mentally confused at admission or the family may be too preoccupied with the patient to provide valid data.

     vii. Compare written instructions to the patient that are documented in the record with the patient's or family's understanding of those instructions.

     viii. Review for other documentation as determined by the facility.

  d. AHIMA-Identified Characteristics of Data Quality

     i. Accuracy: data are the correct values and are valid.

     ii. Accessibility: data items should be easily obtainable and legal to collect.

     iii. Comprehensiveness

         1. All required data items are included.

         2. The entire scope of the data is collected and intentional limitations are documented.

     iv. Consistency: the value of the data should be reliable and consistent across applications.

     v. Currency

         1. Data should be up to date.

         2. A datum value is up to date if it is current for a specific point in time.

         3. It is outdated if it was current at some preceding time yet incorrect at a later time.

     vi. Definition

         1. Clear definitions should be provided so that current and future data users will know what the data mean.

         2. Each data element should have clear meaning and accepted values.

     vii. Granularity: the attributes and values of data should be defined at the correct level of detail.

     viii. Precision: data values should be just large enough to support the application or process. To collect data precise enough for application, acceptable values or value ranges for each data item must be defined (e.g., values for sex should be limited to male, female, or unknown).

     ix. Relevance: the data are meaningful to the performance of the process or application for which they are collected.

     x. Timeliness: determined by how the data are being used and their context

7. Forms Design

  a. Well-designed and controlled forms or computer views (information on screens) are important to reduce errors and recopying of data and to increase efficiency.

  b. Forms team (view team, forms committee) is charged to work on administrative and patient information applications and become involved in the selection of data collection technology.

     i. Forms team forwards its patient-related recommendations to the clinical information committee for approval, and its administrative recommendations follow the organizational chain of command.

     ii. Team members include

         1. Health information management

         2. Information systems

         3. Materials management

        4. Patient care services

        5. Quality improvement

        6. Others as needed

c. General Forms and Views Design Principles

  i. Need of users

    1. Forms should be designed to meet needs of all users (patients, healthcare providers, government agencies, healthcare facility staff).

  ii. Purpose of form or view

    1. Standardize, identify, instruct, and facilitate documentation and decision making, as well as promote consistency in data collection, reporting, and interpretation.

    2. Identify patients and practitioners and instruct them step by step in what data items to gather, where to obtain them, and how to record them.

    3. Good instructions that facilitate complete and accurate documentation should be provided for forms.

  iii. Selection and sequencing of items

    1. Construct a list or grid of required data to ensure the collection of all required data and elimination of unnecessary items.

    2. Flow should be logical and take into consideration the order of data collection or transfer.

    3. Numbering items makes references to both items and written instructions on completion of forms faster and easier.

  iv. Standard terminology, abbreviations, and format

    1. Words, numbers, and abbreviations should be standardized.

    2. A master format or template should be developed by the forms team or committee.

  v. Instructions

    1. Instructions should briefly identify who should complete the data items and provide guidance to the user of the form.

    2. Computer views typically provide this information on introductory screens and as needed throughout data entry.

  vi. Simplification

    1. Forms or views should be created only when there is an established need that is not being met by an existing form.

    2. All forms or views are documented and available.

  vii. Paper forms design

    1. Header and footer

    2. Introduction and instructions

    3. Body and close

    4. Other production considerations

      a. Only approved forms should be used in the healthcare record.

      b. There should be a master for each paper form and all copies should be made from the original or master.

      c. Using standardized paper size (8.5 by 11 inches) keeps cost low and facilitates copying and filing.

      d. Multipart forms may require carbon sheets or NCR paper.

      e. Duplicating methods include in-house and commercial printing.

  viii. Computer-view or screen-format design considerations

    1. Needs of user

    2. Purpose of view

             3. Selection and sequencing of essential data items

             4. Standardization of terminology, abbreviations, and formats

             5. Provision of instructions

             6. Attention to simplification

             7. Views require the development of menus of alternatives and screen or window formats that may include spots to touch with a finger or light pen

          ix. Online system interfaces make it possible to

             1. Organize the data entry fields in logical format

             2. Include field edits

             3. Include passwords to add, delete, or modify data

             4. Allow simultaneous entry or updating in many tables at one time

             5. Include brief instructions on the screens or provide more lengthy help screens

             6. Make the screens attractive through the use of color, lines, and borders

             7. Use default values in a field to eliminate the need to key repeated data

             8. Allow automatic sequential numbering

             9. Show data on the screen from a different table when the key field is entered (e.g., for the master patient index (MPI), where the doctor's number, name, address, etc. can automatically appear on the screen)

            10. Develop or customize menus or submenus to add, delete, or change data

8. Healthcare Data Sets and Databases

  a. The purpose of a minimum data set (MDS) is to promote comparability and compatibility of data by using standard data items with uniform definitions.

  b. The National Committee on Vital and Health Statistics has promulgated data sets that have influenced both the conditions of participation and claim forms on which Medicare and Medicaid data sets are based.

  c. Data sets facilitate uniformity in collection and analytical techniques of hospital data.

    i. Uniform Hospital Discharge Data Set (UHDDS): uniform collection of data on inpatients

    ii. Uniform Ambulatory Core Data Set (UACDS): improve ability to compare data in ambulatory care settings.

    iii. Minimum Data Set (MDS) for Long-Term Care (LTC) and Resident Assessment Instrument (RAI): comprehensive functional assessment of long-term care patients

    iv. Outcome and Assessment Information Set (OASIS): comprehensive assessment for adult home care patient and forms the basis for measuring patient outcomes

    v. Uniform Clinical Data Set (UCDS): data collection utilized by peer review organizations to determine the quality of patient care

9. Data Quality and Technology

  a. Electronic Health Record (EHR) or Computer-Based Patient Record (CPR)

    i. CPR defined by Institute of Medicine (IOM) as a record that resides in a system specifically designed to support users by providing accessibility to complete and accurate data, alerts, reminders, clinical decision support systems, links to medical knowledge, and other aids.

        1. 2003 core functionalities
           a. Health information and data
           b. Results management
           c. Order entry management
           d. Decision support
           e. Electronic communication and connectivity
           f. Patient support
           g. Administrative processes
           h. Reporting and population health management

      ii. The EHR has the ability to capture data from multiple electronic sources and is the primary source of information at the point of care.

      iii. Information is maintained online indefinitely, immediately retrievable, and continuously backed up.

      iv. Point-of-care clinical information system
        1. Allows caregivers to capture and input data where healthcare service is provided and may be at the time of patient care

      v. Electronic data exchange
        1. Provides the ability to edit, submit, and pay healthcare claims by way of electronic transfer

      vi. Health information exchange (HIE)
        1. Sharing of health information electronically among two or more entities, plus an organization that provides services to accomplish the exchange

      vii. Decision support system
        1. Computerized system that gathers information from various sources and uses analytical models to assist providers in making clinical decisions regarding administrative, clinical, and cost issues

      viii. National Health Information Infrastructure or Network (NHII or NHIN) that encompasses an EHR system for all providers and the ability to communicate electronically so that an EHR is assembled at the point of care

  b. Data Versus Information
      i. Data
        1. A collection of elements on a given subject
        2. Raw facts and figures expressed in text, numbers, symbols, and images
        3. Facts, ideas, or concepts that can be captured, communicated, and processed, either manually or electronically

      ii. Information
        1. Data that have been processed into meaningful form, either manually or by computer, to make them valuable to the user
        2. Adds to a representation and tells the recipient something that was not known before

  c. Database Structure and Model
      i. Data model: a plan or pattern for an information system, including the database structure, known as a conceptual model, and the translation of the concept to the computer, known as the physical model

      ii. Entities: persons, locations, things, or concepts about which data can be collected and stored

      iii. Attribute: describes an entity or distinct characteristic about it

      iv. Relationship: associations between entities

      v. Character, field, record, and file

         1. Character: collection of bits make up a byte; a byte is a character such as a number, letter, or symbol.

         2. Field: made up of several characters such as name, age, or gender

         3. Record: made up of a series of fields about one person or thing

         4. File

            a. Made up of fields (columns) and records (rows) about an entity such as a patient

            b. Table is another word for file or entity

      vi. Database models

         1. Relational model

         2. Hierarchical model

         3. Network model

         4. Object-oriented model

d. Data Quality and Computer Systems

      i. Edits, rules, or validation checks are added to the database, along with a message to be displayed when the data do not satisfy the condition.

         1. Checks look at the who, what, when, where, and why of transactions.

         2. Transaction is an event that takes place during the routine course of business.

            a. Event validation

            b. Transaction validation

            c. Sequence checks

            d. Batch tools

            e. Audit trail

            f. Duplicate processing

            g. Format checks

            h. Reasonableness checks

            i. Check digits

      ii. Data characteristics

         1. Validity

         2. Reliability

         3. Completeness

         4. Recognizability

         5. Timeliness

         6. Relevance

         7. Accessibility

         8. Security

         9. Legality

e. Architecture

      i. Open system: hardware, software, transmission, media, and database industry standards allow different computer vendor systems to communicate to each other.

      ii. Closed system: communication is possible on only one vendor's system.

      iii. Hardware

         1. Physical equipment that makes up computers and computer systems

         2. Mainframes, minicomputers, microcomputers

        iv. Electronic data-entry technology

          1. Keyed-entry devices

            a. Keyboard and mouse

            b. Light pen

            c. Touch-sensitive screen

            d. Graphics tablet

          2. Portable and hand-held terminals

            a. Point-of-care applications are well suited to this technology.

          3. Scanned entry

            a. Optical scanners

            b. Bar code readers

            c. Optical character readers

            d. Mark-sense readers

            e. Magnetic-ink character readers

          4. Other entry devices

            a. Magnetic strips

            b. Voice recognition

            c. Biomedical devices

            d. Electronic data interchange

      v. Output

          1. Terminal or workstation

          2. Printers

      vi. Software

          1. Operating systems software

          2. Application software

  f. Communications Technology

      i. Local area network (LAN): multiple devices connected via communications media and located in a small geographical area

      ii. Wide area network (WAN): a computer network that connects separate institutions across a large geographical area

      iii. Internet

          1. Similar to a WAN in that it serves multiple users and connects with various communication channels, but structure is different

          2. Consists of thousands of loosely connected network servers (LANs and WANs), and no single group is responsible for it

          3. Web-based healthcare information systems make it possible for healthcare workers to search for and quickly find huge amounts of information on virtually any health-related topic

      iv. Intranet

          1. Private network that has its servers located inside a firewall

10. Data Access and Retention

  a. Assignment of Health Record Identification and Numbering

      i. Alphabetic identification: the patient's name identifies the patient's record.

      ii. Numeric identification

          1. Serial numbering: a new number is assigned to the patient for each new encounter at the facility.

          2. Unit numbering: the patient retains the same number for every encounter at the facility.

          3. Serial-unit numbering: a new number is assigned to the patient for each new encounter at the facility, but the former records are brought forward and filed under the new number.

Table 2-1   Alphabetic Filing Records

Last	First	Middle
Burns	Linda	Cooper
James	Annie	
James	Kiesha	
James	Kiesha	T.
Ramirez	Juan	
Zen	Lee	M.

b. Filing Equipment
    i. Filing cabinets
    ii. Open-shelf files (least expensive option)
    iii. Motorized revolving units
    iv. Compressible units
c. Space Management
    i. Centralized filing: records filed in one location
    ii. Decentralized filing: records filed in multiple locations
d. Filing Methodologies
    i. Alphabetic filing starts with last names and then includes first name and middle initial (see Table 2-1).
    ii. Straight numeric filing: filing charts in sequential order; the records start with the chart with lowest number value and end with the chart with highest number value.
    iii. Terminal digit filing
        1. Numeric filing is divided into three parts.
        2. It is read from right to left instead of left to right (see Table 2-2).

Table 2-2   Illustration of Terminal Digital Filing

	←		
Record 1	15	35	86
Record 2	16	35	86
Record 3	00	36	86
Record 4	01	00	87
	Tertiary Digits	**Secondary Digits**	**Primary Digits**

This table indicates how to read records (charts) in terminal digital filing. The arrow illustrates that the numbers on the record are read from right to left. In filing or retrieving records, follow these steps:

1. Go to the primary section (terminal section). In the case of records 1, 2, and 3, the section is 86. In the case of record 4, the section is 87.
2. Within the primary digits, go to the subdivision of the secondary digits. In records 1 and 2, this is 35. In record 3, it is 36. In record 4, it is 0.
3. Lastly, go to the subdivision of the tertiary digits. Record 1 is subdivision 15, record 2 is subdivision 16, record 3 is subdivision 00, and record 4 is subdivision 01.

e. Calculating Storage Requirements

    i. Consider filing system, numbering system, filing equipment, average size of individual records, volume of patients, and the number of readmissions

    ii. Example: A hospital has 6000 discharges per year, uses the TDO unit numbering filing system, with open shelves. The open shelves have 8 shelves per unit that are 36 inches wide with 34 inches of actual filing space. The average record is 3 inches thick. The hospital requires 18,000 inches (6000 discharges at 3 inches each) of filing space. Each open shelf unit has 272 linear filing inches available (8 shelves with 34 inches each). Therefore, the hospital needs 67 open shelf units (18,000 inches divided by 272 filing inches per unit). Although 18,000 divided by 272 is 66.17, the hospital cannot purchase a fraction of a unit; therefore, it must purchase 67 units to file 6000 records.

f. Health Record Retrieval

    i. Audit filing area periodically to assure files are in order and all records are accounted for

    ii. Requested records are located, checked out, and tracked.

        1. Calculating retrieval rate

            a. Statistics are maintained to determine the accuracy, quantity, and quality of the filing and retrieval system.

            b. The ratio of the number of records located to the number of records requested

            c. Example: The ambulatory care clinic requested 9043 records during the month of March. The filing area retrieved 9039 of the requested records. Therefore, the department had a 99.96% retrieval rate ([9039/9043] × 100).

g. Record Retention

    i. State statutes and regulations

        1. Statute of limitations

            a. Varies by state and determines the period of time in which a legal action can be brought against a facility

            b. It begins at the time of the event, or at the age of majority if the patient was treated as a minor.

            c. Retention schedule

                i. The American Hospital Association recommends retaining records for a minimum of 10 years.

                ii. If minor, 10 years past age of majority

    ii. Facility closure

        1. If the facility is sold to a healthcare provider, the record is an asset of the sale.

        2. If the buyer is not a healthcare provider, the record is not to be sold, but other arrangements should be made.

        3. The state department of health may assume responsibility for the records.

    iii. Disasters such as fires, broken water pipes, blocked drains, malfunctioning equipment, environmental storms and floods

h. Image-Based Records Storage

    i. Magnetic disk

    ii. Optical disk platters

    iii. Optical scanning (Paper, X-rays, MRIs, or microfilm is scanned and converted into a computer-readable digital format.)

    iv. Jukebox device

    v. Micrographics

      1. Creating miniature pictures on film

      2. Microfilm, roll, jacket, microfiche

      3. Computer-assisted retrieval of microfilm

        a. Scanner

        b. Optical character recognition

11. **Secondary Health Information Data Sources**

  a. Indexes

    i. Listing or arrangement of data in a designated order; contains special types of information

    ii. Purpose is to assist in the location of desired information

    iii. Master patient index (MPI)

      1. Identifies all patients admitted to a healthcare facility for treatment, along with their identifying information

      2. Also referred to as master person index, master population index, master name file, enterprise-wide master person or patient index, regional master patient index, and master patient database

    iv. Number index: list of patient identification numbers issued to patients

    v. Physician index: provides every physician with a list of identifying medical cases

    vi. Disease index: list of diseases and conditions according to the classification system used in the facility

    vii. Procedure or operation index: list of surgical and procedural codes

  b. Registries

    i. Created to monitor various diseases and health problems with different goals and objectives

    ii. Each register serves a different purpose or is maintained for different outcomes (goals). As with the index outline, the register is identified and its purpose follows.

    iii. Admission and discharge register: kept permanently and in chronological order

    iv. Operating room register

      1. Maintained for 10 years

      2. Provides statistical data for caseload analysis and administrative reports

    v. Births and deaths registers: provide accessible information about births and deaths

    vi. Emergency room register: monitors the patients who enter the emergency room for services

    vii. Cancer or tumor registry

      1. System that monitors all types of cancer diagnosed or treated in an institution

      2. Database components

        a. Reference date: beginning date of data collection

        b. Case eligibility: cases that meet the eligibility criteria for inclusion into the database

        c. Patient eligibility: inpatients and outpatients diagnosed and/or treated for cancer who are eligible for inclusion in the database

        d. Patient index: permanent alphabetic file that identifies patients who have been entered into the registry database

Table 2-3 Accession Register

Accession Number	Patient's Name	Primary	Site	Date of Diagnosis
xx-0001/00	Smith, Robert	Liver	C22	01/02/xx
xx-0002/02	Williams, Joe	Colon	C18	01/03/xx
xx-0245/02	Chavez, Juan	Lung	C34	01/03/xx
xx-0004/01	Cruz, Tom	Prostate	C61	01/04/xx
xx-0004/02	Cruz, Tom	Colon	C18	01/04/xx

      e. Case finding: method for locating and identifying every reportable case in the database

      f. Accession register

        i. List of numbers assigned by the facility to the patient

        ii. First two digits of accession number indicate the year when patient was eligible and added to the registry (Table 2-3)

      g. Abstracting: preparation of a brief summary on the patient

      h. Coding: code assigned to cancer diagnosis

      i. Staging: recording the extent of the spread of the disease for every case entered into the registry database

      j. Primary site file: permanent file that contains an abstract of every primary neoplasm site for each patient

   3. Quality control: process of ensuring the completeness, accuracy, and timeliness of the data collected

   4. American College of Surgeons requires annual lifetime follow-up of the patient

   5. Patient information is confidential and protected from unauthorized access

   6. Use of cancer registry data

      a. Annual report

      b. Quality outcome and improvement

      c. Administrative reports

      d. Cancer conferences

      e. Marketing

      f. Request log or file

   7. Staffing includes certified tumor registrar (CTR)

   8. Cancer committee

      a. Policymaking body that meets at least quarterly

      b. Responsible for planning, initiating, stimulating, and assessing all cancer-related activities in the institution

viii. Other registry subjects

   1. National and state cancer registries

   2. HIV/AIDS

   3. Birth defects

   4. Diabetes

   5. Implant

   6. Organ

   7. Trauma

12. Health Information Management Organizations and Professionals
  a. Healthcare Information and Management Systems Society (HIMSS) provides leadership in health care for the management of technology and management systems.
    i. Certified Professional in Health Information Management Systems (CPHIMS)
    ii. Certified in Healthcare Security (CHS)
  b. International Federation of Health Record Organizations (IFHRO) supports national associations and health record professionals to improve health records.
  c. International Medical Informatics Association (IMIA) promotes informatics in health care and biomedical research.
  d. National Cancer Registrars Association (NCRA) supports quality cancer data management.
    i. Certified Tumor Registrar (CTR)
  e. American Medical Informatics Association (AMIA) supports information technology professionals to improve health care.
  f. American Association for Medical Transcription (AAMT) is the largest association for medical transcription.
  g. College of Healthcare Information Management Executives (CHIME) serves the needs of healthcare chief information officers and advocates for more effective use of information management in health care.
  h. American Health Information Management Association (AHIMA)
    i. Association for HIM practitioners
    ii. This association sets guidelines and standards for patient records and health information systems.
      1. Accreditation of education programs
        a. AHIMA accredits coding certificate programs.
        b. Commission on Accreditation of Health Information and Informatics Management (CAHIIM) accredits professional education programs at the associate, baccalaureate, and post-baccalaureate certificate levels at college and universities across the nation.
      2. Certification and registration programs
        a. Processes whereby the public can be assured that certified individuals have met or maintain a level of competency required to deliver quality health information
          i. Registered health information administrator (RHIA) has achieved a baccalaureate in HIM with 30 hours of continuing education within a 2-year cycle.
          ii. Registered health information technician (RHIT) has achieved an associate degree in HIM with 20 hours of continuing education within a 2-year cycle.
          iii. Certified coding specialist (CCS) must complete a formal self assessment process annually to maintain credentialed status.
          iv. Certified coding specialist-physician (CCS-P) must complete a formal self-assessment process annually to maintain credentialed status.
          v. Certified coding associate (CCA)
          vi. Certified in healthcare privacy and security (CHPS) designation signifies advanced competency in designing, implementing, and administering comprehensive privacy and security protection programs.

          vii. Clinical Documentation Improvement Practitioner (CDIP)

          viii. Certified Health Data Analyst (CHDA)

13. **Health Services Organization and Delivery**

  a. Definitions

      i. Accreditation

          1. The professional organizations such as TJC and the AOA regulate and review the standards of healthcare organization.

      ii. Alternative delivery systems: health care provided by methods other than the traditional inpatient care, including home health, ambulatory, hospice, and other types of health care

      iii. Care: the management of, responsibility for, or attention to the safety and well-being of another person or other persons

      iv. Client: individual who is receiving professional services

      v. Inpatient: patient who is receiving healthcare services such as room, board, and continuous nursing service in a hospital

      vi. Health: defined by World Health Organization as a person who is in a state of complete physical, mental, and social well-being

      vii. Healthcare services: services such as hospital, ambulatory care, home setting, or other health-related services

      viii. Health information management (HIM): a health profession that is responsible for the uses of health information, accuracy, and protection of clinical information

      ix. Hill-Burton Act: legislation enacted in 1946 that provided funding for the construction of hospitals and other healthcare facilities

      x. Hospital: healthcare institution with an organized medical and professional staff and with inpatient beds available around the clock whose primary function is to provide inpatient medical, nursing, and other health-related services to patients for both surgical and nonsurgical conditions and that usually provides some outpatient services, particularly emergency care

      xi. Hospital inpatient: a patient who stays in the hospital overnight and is provided room, board, and nursing service in a unit or area of the hospital

      xii. Hospital patient: a patient who receives or is utilizing healthcare services for which the hospital is liable or held accountable

      xiii. Outpatient: patient who is receiving ambulatory care services in a hospital or hospital-based clinic or department

      xiv. Patient: individual who is receiving healthcare services

      xv. Payer: individual or organization who pays for healthcare services

      xvi. Primary patient record: healthcare professionals use this record to review the patient data or documents

      xvii. Provider: any entity that provides healthcare services to patients, such as a hospital or clinic

      xviii. Resident: a patient who resides in a long-term care facility.

      xix. Secondary patient record: a record used for selected data elements to aid in research conducted by clinical and nonclinical people

  b. Historical Development

      i. People who are ill have always gone to people with reputations as healers.

      ii. Earliest written health record dates back to 2700 B.C. and is from an Egyptian physician and dentist.

      iii. Greek medicine became the forerunner of modern medicine 2500 years ago.

iv. The concept of hospital is rooted in medieval Christendom, when religious orders cared for the sick.

v. Term *hospital* originated in 5th century, from the Latin word *hospitium*.

vi. During Middle Ages, the hospitium evolved from a Christian tradition of offering weary travelers a place to rest (called hospice); such places were funded by the churches and wealthy individuals.

vii. Cortez founded the first permanent hospital in North America in 1554, which was the Jesus of Nazareth Hospital in Mexico.

viii. First school in America dedicated to training physicians was founded in 1765 in Philadelphia.

ix. To assure the quality of American medical education, the American Medical Association (AMA) was formed in 1847.

x. The American Hospital Association (AHA) was established in 1848 to promote public welfare by providing better health care in hospitals.

xi. In late 19th century, state governments established mental institutions for the confinement of the mentally ill rather than housing them in prisons and poorhouses.

xii. In mid 1800s, plantation owners in Hawaii, mining companies in Pennsylvania and Minnesota, and lumber companies tried to attract and keep immigrant workers by offering medical care to the workers.

xiii. In early 1900s, hospitals were funded by private beneficiaries, endowments, and donations.

    1. Hospitals were viewed as boarding houses for the poor and sick.

    2. Private sector had little interest in serving the population as a whole, assuming that the local government would pay for the poor.

    3. Physicians did not do history and physicals on the patients and seldom documented diagnoses, care, and treatment.

xiv. Between 1870s and 1920s, the number of American hospitals increased from fewer than 200 to more than 6000.

    1. Private benevolence was responsible for establishing hundreds of new hospitals that were not interested in providing care to the poor.

    2. By 1910, there were as many hospitals per 1000 population as there are today.

    3. Not all of the population was being served.

    4. Hospitals operated on the principle that the more expensive the care, the more valuable the service, which resulted in the escalation of healthcare cost.

xv. The Flexner Report of 1910 identified serious problems and inconsistencies in medical education.

    1. This resulted in the closing of many proprietary schools.

    2. Remaining schools underwent curriculum revision.

    3. AMA initiated accreditation process for medical education.

xvi. In 1913, the American College of Surgeons (ACS) was founded to develop a system of hospital standardization to improve patient care and recognize hospitals that had the highest ideals.

    1. The ACS collected data from the health record to establish standards and improve quality of care.

2. Upon analysis of the data, the ACS realized that the documentation was inadequate.

3. In 1917, the ACS established the Hospital Standardization Program, which laid the groundwork for establishing standards of care.

4. In 1919, the ACS adopted the minimum standards, which identified the standards that were essential for the "proper care and treatment of patients in any hospital."

xvii. Due to the need for more hospitals and high-quality health care that was accessible to all Americans, in 1946 the Hill-Burton Act provided funding for the construction of hospitals and other healthcare facilities based on state need.

xviii. The early 1950s saw an increase in the number and complexity of hospitals and nonsurgical specialties, which burdened the hospital standardization program.

1. As a result, the Joint Commission on Accreditation of Hospitals (JCAH) (currently referred to as TJC) was founded in 1952 and adopted the hospital standardization program.

xix. The 1950s experienced an increase in biomedical advances, technology, and patient demand for more healthcare services.

1. Medical advances extended life expectancy, which resulted in an increasing elderly population.

2. Hospitals became more expensive, and the uninsured and underinsured (primarily the poor and elderly) could not access the healthcare system.

3. The federal and state government did little to control hospital costs.

xx. In 1965, Congress amended the Social Security Act of 1935, establishing both Title XVIII (Medicare) and Title XIX (Medicaid).

1. Medicare is a federally funded program that provides health insurance for the elderly and certain other groups.

2. Medicaid supports the states in paying for health care for people who are indigent.

xxi. The 1960s saw a proliferation of various healthcare facilities, including long-term care, psychiatric and substance abuse, and programs for people with developmental disabilities.

1. JCAH redefined standards to reflect the optimal achievable as opposed to minimum acceptable and began to develop standards for various types of healthcare facilities.

a. In the late 1980s, JCAH changed its name to the Joint Commission on Accreditation of Healthcare Organizations (JCAHO) to reflect its broader scope (currently TJC).

xxii. Occupational Safety and Health Act was passed in 1970, which mandated that employers provide a safe and healthy workplace.

xxiii. In 1977, the AMA founded the Committee on Allied Health Education and Accreditation (CAHEA) for the purpose of accrediting allied health programs, but the Committee was disbanded in 1994.

xxiv. The federal Department of Health, Education and Welfare (HEW) was reorganized in 1980 to become the Department of Health and Human Services (DHHS). It is a federal, cabinet-level department responsible for health issues, including health care and cost, welfare of various populations, occupational safety, and income security plans.

    1. DHHS oversees but is not limited to the following: Centers for Disease Control and Prevention (CDC); Food and Drug Administration (FDA); Office of Inspector General; Substance Abuse and Mental Health Services Administration (SAMHSA); National Institutes of Health (NIH); Indian Health Service (IHS); and the Centers for Medicare and Medicaid Services (CMS), formerly the Health Care Financing Administration (HCFA).

xxv. In 1982, the Tax Equity and Fiscal Responsibility Act (TEFRA) established a mechanism for controlling the cost of the Medicare program, set limits on reimbursement, and required the development of the prospective payment system.

xxvi. The Consolidated Omnibus Budget Reconciliation Act (COBRA) of 1985, known as the antidumping statute, established criteria for the transfer and discharge of Medicare and Medicaid patients.

xxvii. The Patient Self-Determination Act of 1990 gave patients the right to set advance directives.

xxviii. In 1992, the Computer-Based Patient Record Institute was created for the purpose of developing strategy that supports the development and adoption of the computer-based patient record.

xxix. In 1996, the Health Insurance Portability and Accountability Act (HIPAA) provided for continuity of health coverage and attempted to control fraud and abuse in health care, reduce healthcare cost, and guarantee the security and privacy of health information.

xxx. The healthcare delivery system has evolved into a complex system composed of various and multiple types of facilities, providers, payers, and regulators.

    1. In 1990s, health care was costly and not accessible to all citizens, yet consumers demanded more and better care.

    2. The advances in technology and scientific developments have increased life expectancy.

    3. Alternative medicine includes unconventional therapies that may or may not have been proven to be effective, such as herbal remedies, massage therapy, natural food diets, acupuncture, and biotherapy.

    4. Due to the escalating cost of health care, the rising number of uninsured and underserved in both urban and rural areas, reform of the healthcare delivery system is ongoing.

        a. Plans for healthcare reform address issues such as universal coverage, healthcare cost, and the quality of care provided.

xxxi. American Recovery and Reinvestment Act (2009)

    1. HITECH (2009) provided funding for the national adoption of the Electronic Health Record (EHR) by 2014.

xxxii. Affordable Care Act (2010) attempts to provide healthcare coverage for all Americans.

c. Healthcare occupations licensed by states and/or certified or registered by accrediting agencies include but are not limited to the following

    i. Physicians: doctor of medicine (MD) and doctor of osteopathy (DO)

    ii. Nurses

        1. Registered nurse (RN)

        2. Licensed practical nurse (LPN)

        3. Nurse practitioner

        4. Clinical nurse specialist

        5. Certified nurse midwife

        6. Certified nurse anesthetist

  iii. Dentist

  iv. Pharmacist

   v. Podiatrist

  vi. Chiropractor (DC)

 vii. Optometrist (DO)

viii. Healthcare administrators

  ix. Allied health personnel

        1. Laboratory technologist and technicians

          a. Radiologic technologist

          b. Nuclear medicine technologist

          c. Histologic technician

          d. Diagnostic medical sonographer

          e. Cytotechnologist

          f. Clinical laboratory technician

          g. Cardiovascular technologist

          h. Ophthalmic laboratory technician

        2. Therapeutic science practitioners

          a. Physical therapist and physical therapist assistant

          b. Occupational therapist and occupational therapist assistant

          c. Speech–language pathologist

          d. Physician assistant

          e. Surgeon assistant

          f. Respiratory therapist

          g. Music therapist

          h. Therapeutic recreation specialist

          i. Paramedic

        3. Behavior scientist

          a. Social worker

          b. Rehabilitation counselor

        4. Support services

          a. Health information managers

          b. Dental laboratory technologist

          c. Electroencephalographic technologist

          d. Food service administrator

          e. Surgical technologist

          f. Environmental health technologist

d. Hospitals (may be classified by ownership, population served, number of beds, length of stay, type, patients, or organization)

    i. Ownership

        1. Government (federal, state, or local)

          a. Federally owned hospitals receive funding as well as administrative direction from the branch of the government that owns them.

            i. Native Americans and native Alaskans

           ii. Facilities for active and retired military personnel and their dependents

         iii. Veterans (Department of Veteran Affairs medical centers)

         iv. Merchant marines

     b. State facilities for mental illness, mental retardation, chronic disease, and medical education

     c. County, district, and city hospitals: local facilities established to meet the healthcare needs of the community that are governed by elected officials

  2. Nongovernmental

     a. For-profit

         i. Proprietary

         ii. Private

         iii. Investor

     b. Not-for-profit

         i. Churches and religious orders

         ii. Industries

         iii. Unions

         iv. Fraternal organizations

ii. Population served (based on the group to whom services are provided); examples include pediatric, women's, psychiatric, cancer, burn

iii. Bed size

  1. Total number of inpatient beds with which the facility is equipped and staffed for patient admissions

  2. A facility is licensed by the state for a specific number of beds.

iv. Length of stay

  1. If average length of stay is less than 25 days, hospital is a short-term or acute-care facility.

  2. If average length of stay is more than 25 days, hospital is a long-term care facility.

v. Types

  1. General: provides patient with diagnostic and therapeutic services for a variety of medical conditions, including radiographic, clinical, laboratory, and operating room services

  2. Special: provides diagnostic and therapeutic services for patients with a specific medical condition such as diabetes, cancer, burns, sports injuries, or eye injuries or diseases

  3. Rehabilitation and chronic disease: provides diagnostic and therapeutic services to patients who are disabled or handicapped and require restorative and adjustive services

  4. Psychiatric: provides diagnostic and therapeutic services for patients with mental illness, including psychiatric, psychological, and social work services

  5. Critical access hospital (CAH): certified by the state as necessary to residents in the community, or no hospital or other CAH within 35 miles; no more than 25 beds, with an average length of stay of 96 hours

vi. Patients

  1. Inpatients

  2. Observation patients

  3. Ambulatory care patients

  4. Emergency patients

  5. Newborn patients

vii. Organization (typical of traditional acute-care facility)
   1. Composition and structure
      a. Governing board
         i. Also called governing body, board of trustees, board of governors, or board of directors
         ii. Has ultimate legal authority and responsibility for the operation of the hospital, including the quality and cost of care
         iii. Functions according to bylaws established by the board, has regular meetings with documented minutes, and has subcommittees (standing and special) that assist in the responsibilities of the board
            1. Standing committees may include executive, finance, medical staff, nominating, personnel, physician recruitment, or long-range planning.
            2. Special committees may be created for specific projects or tasks and are disbanded upon completion.
      b. Administration
         i. Chief executive officer (CEO) is a hospital administrator or president who is selected by the governing board and is the principal administrative official of the healthcare facility.
         ii. Chief operating officer (COO) is also called the vice president or executive vice president and is an associate administrator who oversees the operation of specific departments.
         iii. Chief information officer (CIO) is responsible for information resources management, which includes design, integration, and implementation of health information systems (administrative, financial, and clinical).
         iv. Chief financial officer (CFO), sometimes called director of finance or fiscal affairs director, directs the financial operations.
      c. Medical staff
         i. Formally organized staff or licensed physicians, and other licensed providers as permitted by law (dentist, podiatrist, midwives)
         ii. Governed by its own bylaws, rules, and regulations, which must be approved by the hospital's governing board
         iii. TJC states the primary responsibility of the medical staff is the quality of the professional services provided by the members with clinical privileges and the responsibility of being accountable to the governing board
         iv. Recommends staff appointments and reappointments, delineates clinical privileges and continuing medical education, and maintains a high quality of patient care
         v. Medical staff is organized to include officers, committees, and clinical services.
         vi. Clinical services include, but not limited to, the following:
            1. Medicine (cardiology, dermatology, oncology, pediatrics, psychiatry, radiology)
            2. Surgery (anesthesiology, gynecology, obstetrics, orthopedics, urology)
      d. Essential services
         i. Nursing
         ii. Diagnostic radiology

       iii. Nuclear medicine
       iv. Dietetics
       v. Pathology and clinical laboratory
       vi. Emergency
       vii. Pharmaceutical
       viii. Physical rehabilitation
       ix. Respiratory care
       x. Social services
       xi. Other services
         1. Pastoral care
         2. Ethics
         3. Patient representatives (advocates)
         4. Patient escort
         5. Plant technology
         6. Safety management
         7. Central supply
       xii. Health information management (medical records department)
         1. Responsible for management of all paper and electronic patient information
         2. Develops and maintains an information system
         3. Responsible for the organization, maintenance, production, and dissemination of information, including data security, integrity, and access
         4. Functions include transcribing, coding, release of information, retrieving and storing health information, managing databases, and filing information

2. Hierarchical form
  a. Historical model for hospitals
  b. Individuals at the top have authority that passes downward through a chain of command.

3. Vertical operation
  a. The governing board has ultimate authority, followed by the CEO.
  b. The organization includes a governing board, administration, medical staff, department directors, supervisors, and numerous subordinates.

4. Matrix organizational scheme
  a. Flexible and supports multidimensional organization
  b. This scheme supports general managers who focus on managing people and processes, as opposed to strategy and structure.
  c. Horizontal information communication that embraces individual capabilities
  d. Employees have dual responsibilities and may have two or more supervisors, but they have a shared vision that supports the organization as a whole.

5. Product line management
  a. Hospital may be organized around product line categories, such as obstetrics/gynecology, rehabilitation, or cardiology, as opposed to departments such as nursing, pharmacy, or respiratory therapy.

e. Ambulatory Care
   i. Comprehensive term for all types of health care provided in an outpatient setting
   ii. Patient travels to and from the facility on the same day and is not hospitalized
   iii. Two major types
      1. Freestanding medical centers
         a. Physician solo practices
         b. Partnerships
         c. Group practices
         d. Public health departments
         e. Neighborhood and community health centers (NHCs, CHCs)
            i. Serve the needs of a catchment area (defined geographic area that is served by a healthcare program, project, or facility)
            ii. Funded by grants, DHHS, local and state health departments
            iii. Services provided at low or no cost to patients
      2. Organized settings (function independently of the physician providing the care)
         a. Hospital-owned clinics
            i. Satellite clinics: clinics located at a distance from the hospital
            ii. Observation units for patients who need assessment and monitoring but do not require admission to hospital
         b. Outpatient departments
            i. Outpatient departments provide primary or specialized care, including preadmission testing, pediatrics, obstetrics, gynecology, psychiatry, surgery, neonatal care, sports medicine, oncology.
         c. Ambulatory treatment units
         d. Emergency rooms (emergency departments, emergency care areas)
            i. Provide care for urgent, life-threatening, or potentially disabling conditions
            ii. Patients are triaged (rapid assessment to determine urgency and type of care needed).
            iii. Ranked from level I (most comprehensive) to level IV (not required to operate 24 hours a day), based on the center's hours of operation, availability of physicians, nurses, and other trained staff, access to laboratory, radiology surgery, anesthesia, equipment and drugs
            iv. Mortality trauma center
               1. Specialized staff and equipment
               2. Air transport system
         e. Ancillary services
            i. Hospital diagnostic and therapeutic services that are provided to both outpatients and inpatients; exclude room and board
            ii. Hospital is able to charge patients or third parties directly.
         f. Health maintenance organizations (HMOs)
            i. Managed health care that integrates healthcare delivery with insurance for health care

        ii. Subscribers voluntarily enroll in plan.

        iii. Providers voluntarily agree to participate in plan.

        iv. HMO assumes an explicit contractual responsibility for providing care.

        v. Subscriber to HMO makes a fixed periodic payment that is independent of utilization of healthcare services.

        vi. HMO bears financial risk.

        vii. Four basic models

            1. Staff

                a. HMO employs salaried physicians to provide care to HMO subscribers.

                b. HMO owns and operates ambulatory care facilities (ancillary services and physician offices).

                c. Inpatient care is under contract with local healthcare facilities.

            2. Group

                a. HMO contracts with group practices and hospitals to provide care to subscribers

            3. Network

                a. HMO contracts with various providers to treat the HMO clients.

                b. Providers' clients may be HMO subscribers and non-HMO patients.

            4. Independent practice association (IPA)

                a. Legal, separate entity of healthcare providers that contract with HMO for provision of services and compensation for those services

                b. Patient population is HMO and non-HMO patients.

    g. Surgicenters: freestanding minor surgical facilities

    h. Urgent care centers

        i. Serve patients who need routine care or have minor but urgent healthcare problems

        ii. Patients may walk in, and appointments are not required.

f. Home Healthcare Services

    i. Provision of medical and nonmedical care in the home or place of residence to promote, maintain, or restore health or to minimize the effect of disease or disability

    ii. Mainly provide post-acute care and rehabilitation therapies

g. Long-Term Care

    i. Care provided over a long period of time (30 days or more) to patients who have chronic diseases or disabilities

    ii. Care includes personal, social, recreational, dietary, and skilled nursing services.

    iii. Patients are usually referred to as residents.

    iv. Historically, two types of facilities include skilled-nursing facilities (SNFs), which provide a higher level of care to sicker patients, and intermediate-care facilities (ICFs).

        1. In 1987, the Nursing Home Reform Act reduced the differences between the two types of facilities by mandating that ICFs provide the same level of care and staffing as SNFs.

    v. Several types of long-term care facilities

        1. Nursing: comprehensive term that describes nursing care and related services for residents who need medical, nursing, or rehabilitative care; sufficient number of nursing personnel employed on a 24-hour basis to provide care to residents according to the care plan

2. Independent living: apartments and condominiums that allow residents to live independently; assistance includes dietary, healthcare, and social services

3. Domiciliary (residential)
   a. Supervision, room, and board are provided for people who are unable to live independently.
   b. Most residents need assistance with activities of daily living (bathing, dressing, eating).

4. Life care centers (retirement communities)
   a. Provide living accommodations and meals for a monthly fee
   b. Other services include housekeeping, recreation, health care, laundry, and exercise programs.

5. Assisted living: offers housing and board with a broad range of personal and supportive care services

vi. To be certified as a Medicare or Medicaid provider, a nursing facility must comply with the conditions of participation.

vii. Facility is licensed by state to provide a designated level of care, which may be personal care, room and board, or skilled nursing care.

h. Hospice Care
   i. Literally means "given to hospitality"
   ii. Provides palliative and supportive care to terminally ill patients and their families, with consideration for their physical, spiritual, social, and economic needs
   iii. Respite care: an intervention in which the focus of care is on giving the caregiver time off while continuing the care of the patient

i. Adult Day Care
   i. Provides supervision, medical, and psychological care and social activities for older adult clients who reside at home
   ii. Clients either cannot stay alone or prefer social interaction during the day.
   iii. Services include intake assessment, health monitoring, occupational therapy, personal care, transportation, and meals.

j. Sub-acute Care
   i. Transitional level of care that may be necessary immediately after the initial phase of an acute illness
   ii. Commonly used with patients who have been hospitalized and are not yet ready for return to long-term care or home care
   iii. May be located in a designated area of the hospital or nursing facility, or provided by a home health agency

k. Mobile Diagnostic Services
   i. Healthcare services are transported to the patients, especially diagnostic procedures (mammography, magnetic resonance) and preventive services (immunizations, cholesterol screening).

l. Contract Services
   i. Healthcare organizations contract for services that include food, laundry, waste disposal, transcription, and housekeeping.

m. Multi-hospital Systems
   i. Healthcare systems composed of two or more hospitals that are owned, contractually managed, sponsored, or leased by a single organization

           ii. Include acute, sub-acute, long-term, pediatric, rehabilitation, or psychiatric facilities; may provide diagnostic services

14. Regulatory Agencies

  a. Agencies review patient information to provide public assurance that quality health care is being provided and monitored.

  b. Data serve as evidence in assessing compliance with standards of care.

  c. Licensure

      i. Gives legal approval for a person to practice within his or her profession

      ii Gives legal approval for a facility to operate

      iii. Sets minimal standards for a facility to operate

      iv. Virtually every state requires hospitals, sanatoria, nursing homes, and pharmacies to be licensed to operate, even though requirements and standards for licensure may vary by state.

      v. Addresses staffing, credentialing, physical aspects of facility, services provided, and review of health records

      vi. Typically reviewed annually

  d. Nongovernmental Agencies

      i. Accreditation Association for Ambulatory Health Care, Inc. (AAAHC)

      ii. AHIMA

        1. Established the *Professional Practice Standards for Health Information Management Services*, which provides a structured model of standards, guidelines, and measures of quality and quantity

      iii. American Medical Association (AMA)

        1. Involved in accreditation of medical schools, residency programs, and some allied health programs

        2. Collaborates with the Commission on Accreditation of Allied Health Education Programs (CAAHEP) in the accreditation of allied health programs

      iv. American Osteopathic Association (AOA)

        1. Bureau of Professional Education accredits osteopathic medical education.

        2. Has a voluntary program that accredits osteopathic hospitals

        3. DHHS recognizes accredited hospitals as eligible for receiving Medicare funds.

      v. Commission on Accreditation of Rehabilitation Facilities (CARF)

        1. Accredits rehabilitation facilities

        2. Sets quality standards to improve care, shares aggregate data, identifies competent organizations that provide rehabilitation services, and provides an organized forum in which people served, providers, and others can participate in quality improvement

      vi. Community Health Accreditation Program (CHAP)

        1. Accredits home health agencies

        2. Subsidiary of the National League for Nursing

        3. More emphasis on patient perspectives than on clinical care

      vii. The Joint Commission (TJC)

        1. Develops accreditation standards for various types of healthcare facilities

      viii. National Committee for Quality Assurance (NCQA)

        1. Accrediting agency for managed care organizations

2. Mission is to improve quality of patient care and health plan performance in conjunction with managed care plans, purchasers, consumers, and the public.
3. Healthcare Effectiveness Data and Information Set (also known as 'The Health Plan Employer Data Information Set', HEDIS), a component of the NCQA, is a standardized set of performance measures designed to allow purchasers and consumers to compare the performance of managed care plans.

ix. National League of Nursing (NLN)
1. Accredits nursing schools from diplomas to doctorate degrees
2. Establishes standards for nursing curriculum

e. Federal Regulatory Agencies
i. DHHS is the branch of federal government primarily responsible for numerous healthcare regulatory programs and agencies.
1. Administration for Children and Families administers and funds state grants to support activities that improve the development of children, youth, and families.
2. Administration on Aging (AoA) advocates for older persons.
3. Agency for Healthcare Research and Quality (AHRQ) established by Omnibus Budget Reconciliation Act of 1989; purpose is to produce and disseminate scientific and policy relevant information that improves the quality, reduces cost, and enhances effective health care.
4. Agency for Toxic Substances and Disease Registry (ATSDR) protects workers and the public from exposure to adverse effects of hazardous substances.
5. CDC is concerned with communicable diseases, environmental health, and foreign quarantine activities.
   a. National Center for Health Statistics (NCHS)
      i. Under management of CDC
      ii. Federal government's principal vital and health statistics agency
      iii. Provides data to monitor the nation's health
6. CMS (formerly the Health Care Financing Administration, or HCFA) is responsible for the Medicare and Medicaid programs, with special emphasis on quality and utilization control.
7. FDA is responsible for the safety of foods, drugs, medical devices, cosmetics, and radiation-emitting equipment, and for proper labeling, product information, safety, and efficacy.
8. Health Resources and Services Administration (HRSA) distributes major grant funding to state governments and the private sector, especially funding for community-based health services.
9. IHS is responsible for providing health care through a network of hospitals, health centers, health stations, and school health centers, and through contracts with private providers to eligible Native Americans.
10. National Committee on Vital and Health Statistics (NCVHS)
    a. Statutory public advisory body on health data, statistics, and national health information policy
    b. Encourages the evolution of shared, public–private national health information infrastructure that will promote the availability of valid, credible, timely, and comparable health data
    c. Advises on HIPAA

    d. Standardizes health information by formalizing uniform data sets
        i. Data sets promulgated by the NCVHS
            1. UHDDS
            2. UACDS
            3. Minimum Data Set for Long-Term Care (MDS)
            4. OASIS

11. NIH

    a. Major research center composed of numerous departments and divisions

    b. Major source of funding for health-related research

12. Occupational Safety and Health Administration (OSHA)

    a. Created by the Occupational Safety and Health Act of 1970, which mandated that employers provide a safe and healthy work environment

    b. Responsible for developing standards and regulations and conducting inspections and investigations to determine compliance, and proposes corrective actions for noncompliance

13. Office of Inspector General is responsible for conducting and monitoring audits, inspections, and investigations regarding programs or projects sponsored by the DHHS.

14. SAMHSA is concerned with the effective prevention and treatment of addictive and mental disorders.

15. Clinical Vocabularies

    a. Nomenclature

        i. International Standards Organization (ISO) defines nomenclature as a system of clinical terms of preferred terminology.

        ii. Classification and nomenclature often used interchangeably.

    b. Clinical Terminology

        i. Provides for the proper use of clinical words as names or symbols

        ii. Equated with a nomenclature by AHIMA's Coding Policy and Strategy Committee

    c. Clinical Vocabularies

        i. A list or collection of clinical words or phrases, with their meanings

        ii. Used to represent concepts and to communicate these concepts; include symptoms, diagnoses, procedures, and health status

        iii. *Controlled vocabularies* refers to a code or classification system that requires information to be presented using a preestablished term.

        iv. Classification and nomenclature systems

            1. International Classification of Diseases, Ninth Revision Clinical Modification (ICD-9-CM); only used in United States; developed by World Health Organization (WHO) to code and classify diagnoses and procedures
                i. Will be replaced in 2014 by ICD-10-CM and ICD-10-PCS

            2. International Classification of Diseases, 10th Revision, Clinical Modification contains substantial increases in content over ICD-9-CM.

            3. International Classification of Diseases, 10th Revision, Procedural Coding System replaces tabular list of procedures, volume 3 of ICD-9-CM.

4. International Classification of Diseases for Oncology (ICD-O-3) is used for coding neoplasms in tumor or cancer registries.
5. International Classification on Functioning, Disability, and Health (ICF) is used to describe body functions, structures, activities, and participation.
6. Current Procedural Terminology (CPT) describes medical, surgical, and diagnostic services and was adopted by CMS as level I of the Healthcare Common Procedure Coding System (HCPCS).
7. Healthcare Common Procedure Coding System (HCPCS) is administered by CMS and includes two levels of codes.
   a. Level 1: current procedural terminology (CPT).
   b. Level 2: alphanumeric procedure and modifier codes represent items, supplies, and non-physician services not covered by the CPT codes.
   c. Level 3: were local procedure and modifier codes used prior to 2003. They are no longer used; additional Level 2 codes to compensate for the loss of the Level 3 codes.
8. *Diagnostic and Statistical Manual of Mental Diseases* (DSM-IV) is a five-axis coding system.
9. Diagnosis-related groups (DRG) are used to bill for inpatient services rendered.
   i. 2007 became Medicare Severity diagnosis-related groups (MS-DRGs)
10. Ambulatory Payment Classification (APC) is used to bill for outpatient services and is based on the grouping procedures by CPT/HCPCS.
11. International Classification of Primary Care (ICPC-2) is a coding classification of primary care.
12. Current Dental Terminology is a national standard for reporting dental services by the federal government under HIPAA and is recognized by third-party payers.
13. Galen Common Reference Model is a computer-based clinical terminology developed in Europe for representing medical concepts.
14. National Drug Codes (NDC) were developed by the FDA as universal product identifiers for drugs used in humans.
15. ABC codes were created by Alternative Link; they describe alternative medicine, nursing, and other integrative healthcare interventions.
16. **Financing Healthcare Services: Reimbursement Methodologies and Systems**
    a. DHHS is the largest purchaser of health care in the United States.
    b. Private prepaid health plans or federal healthcare programs cover about 85% of Americans.
    c. Prior to prospective payment system (PPS), individuals, insurance companies, and government plans reimbursed providers on a retrospective fee-for-service basis.
    d. Patient Payment Methods
       i. Direct pay (out-of-pocket): patient pays provider directly.
       ii. A prepaid health plan (insurance) is considered indirect pay; it is a purchased policy in which the insured may pay a deductible and

is protected from loss by the insurer's agreement to reimburse for such loss.

1. In 1860, the Franklin Health Assurance Company of Massachusetts became the first commercial insurance company in the United States to provide healthcare coverage.
2. In 1929, Baylor University Hospital in Dallas, Texas, agreed to provide healthcare services to Dallas schoolteachers, which was the birth of Blue Cross.
3. In the 1950s, Blue Cross and Blue Shield began to offer major medical insurance coverage for catastrophic illnesses and injuries.
4. Healthcare insurance coverage expanded through the 1950s, and more Americans were covered by a major medical plan or indemnity plan (insurance coverage in the form of cash payment).
5. Types of insurance
   a. Commercial
      i. Private health insurance plans; financed through the insured person's payment of premiums
      ii. Employer-based insurance; group health insurance coverage, in which companies contract with private insurers to provide coverage to employees
   b. Blue Cross Blue Shield
      i. Blue Cross (1929) covered hospital care.
      ii. Blue Shield (1939) covered physician services.
      iii. In 1982, Blue Cross and Blue Shield merged.
         1. First prepaid healthcare plan in the United States
         2. One of the largest nonprofit insurance companies in the United States
      iv. Offers health insurance to individuals, small businesses, seniors, and large employer groups
      v. Federal employees offered
         1. Preferred provider organizations (PPOs): healthcare services provided to members at a discounted rate.
         2. Point-of-service plan: subscribers select providers from a network, but allowed to use out-of-network providers at a higher copayment rate.
   c. Government-sponsored healthcare programs
      i. Medicare (1965)
         1. Title XVIII of the Social Security Act
         2. Part A: hospitalization insurance for those eligible for Social Security benefits
         3. Part B: voluntary supplemental insurance to help pay for physician services, medical services, and medical and surgical supplies
         4. Part C: Medicare advantage plans run by private companies
            a. Similar to HMOs and PPOs
            b. Provides all of Part A and Part B benefits
            c. Copayments, coinsurance, and deductibles are charged to recipients.
            d. Vision, hearing, dental, wellness, and prescription medications provided at extra cost to beneficiary.
         5. Part D: prescription drug coverage through private insurance companies

        ii. Medicaid (1966)

            1. Title XIX of the Social Security Act

            2. Medical assistance for individuals and families with low incomes

            3. Managed at the state level

        iii. Civilian Health and Medical Program–Veterans Administration (CHAMPVA): provides healthcare services for dependents and survivors of disabled veterans, survivors of veterans who die from service-connected conditions, and survivors of military personnel who died in the line of duty

        iv. TRICARE (formerly CHAMPUS): provides coverage for dependents of armed forces personnel and retirees receiving care outside a military treatment facility

        v. Indian Health Service: provides federal health services to American Indians and Alaska natives

        vi. State Children's Health Insurance Program (SCHIP): Title XXI of the Social Security Act provides federal funds to states; these funds allow states to expand existing insurance programs to cover children up to age 19, thus expanding coverage to a greater number of children.

    e. Reimbursement Methodologies

      i. Fee for service

        1. Third-party payers and/or patients issue payments to healthcare providers based on charges assigned to each service performed for each patient.

          a. Traditional fee for service: third-party payers and/or patients pay healthcare providers after services have been rendered.

          b. Managed fee for service: costs are controlled by the managed care plan's management of members' uses of services; providers are reimbursed by fee schedules.

      ii. Episode of care

        1. Healthcare plan compensates providers with a lump-sum payment to compensate them for all services delivered to a patient for a specific illness and over a specific period of time.

        2. Also referred to as bundled payments, which cover multiple services and providers

        3. Capitation

          a. Based on per-person premiums instead of itemized for each procedure or service

          b. Calculated on projected cost per patient per month

        4. Global payment

          a. Utilized with procedures that involve professional and technical components (e.g., radiological services)

          b. Lump-sum payments distributed to healthcare providers and facilities that provided services, equipment, and supplies

        5. Prospective payment

          a. Tax Equity and Fiscal Responsibility Act (1982) modified Medicare's retrospective hospital inpatient payment system to a prospective payment system (PPS).

          b. In 1983, CMS implemented PPS for hospital care provided to Medicare patients.

          c. DRGs are a system used to control Medicare spending; DRG determines payment to facility.

    d. Omnibus Budget Reconciliation Act (1986) mandated CMS to develop a prospective system for hospital-based outpatient services rendered to Medicare beneficiaries.

    e. Effective October 2007, CMS implemented Medicare Severity diagnosis-related groups (MS-DRGs).

      i. Expanded DRGs from 538 to 745

      ii. Revised complications and comorbidities list

      iii. Redistributed cardiac cases into lower-weighted DRGs

      iv. Instituted a 1.2% reduction in overall payments to offset any coding and documentation improvements, which drew the ire of many hospital associations

      v. Payment penalties proposed for complications that occur while a patient is in the hospital

6. Resource-based relative value scale (RBRVS): implemented in 1992 by CMS for reimbursement of physician services of beneficiaries covered under Medicare Part B

7. Medicare SNF PPS

    a. System was mandated by Balanced Budget Act and implemented in 1998.

    b. SNF paid according to a per-diem PPS based on case-mix-adjusted payment rates.

8. Medicare/Medicaid outpatient PPS

    a. Implemented in 2001 with authorization of Balanced Budget Act and applies to the following:

      i. Hospital outpatient services, including partial hospitalization

      ii. Certain Part B services to beneficiaries who have no Part A coverage

      iii. Partial hospitalization services provided by CHCs

      iv. Vaccines, splints, casts, and antigens provided by home health agencies (HHAs) that provide medical- and health-related services

      v. Vaccines provided by comprehensive outpatient rehabilitation facilities (CORFs)

      vi. Splints, casts, and antigens provided to hospice patients for the treatment of nonterminal illnesses

      vii. CPT/HCPCS codes used to calculate payment

9. Home health PPS

    a. Balanced Budget Act called for development and was implemented in 2001 for covered services to Medicare beneficiaries.

    b. OASIS data set and Home Assessment Validation and Entry (HAVEN) data entry software are used to conduct patient assessments.

    c. Home health resource groups (HHRGs) are the classification system for Home Health PPS.

10. Ambulance fee schedule

    a. Included in 2002 as part of the BBA

    b. Ambulance services are reported using HCPCS codes.

11. Inpatient rehabilitation facility (IRF) PPS

    a. Implemented in 2002 with authorization of BBA

    b. Patient Assessment Instrument (PAI) completed for all patients.

      c. Inpatient Rehabilitation Validation and Entry (IRVEN) system collects PAI and transmits it to national IRF-PAI database.

          i. Patients are classified into case-mix groups (CMG).

          ii. The CMG relative weight is used to calculate payment.

   12. Long-term care hospitals (LTCHs) PPS: Balanced Budget Refinement Act of 1999, amended by Benefits Improvement Act of 2000, mandated a 2002 implementation of a DRG-based PPS for LTCHs.

   13. Inpatient psychiatric facilities (IPFs): Balanced Budget Refinement Act of 1999 mandated a per-diem PPS that became effective in 2005 and utilizes DRGs.

f. Reimbursement Claims Processing

   i. Patient accounts department is responsible for billing third-party payers, processing accounts receivable, monitoring payments, and verifying insurance.

   ii. Explanation of benefits (EOB) statement is sent to patient to explain services provided, amounts billed, and payments made by health plan.

   iii. Remittance advice (RA) sent to provider to explain payments made by third-party payers.

   iv. Either CMS-1500 (physician office visit) or UB-04 (CMS-1450) (inpatient, outpatient, home health, hospice, long-term care) claim form is submitted to third-party payer for reimbursement.

   v. Medicare carriers process Part B claims for services by physicians and medical suppliers, while Medicare fiscal intermediaries process Part A claims and hospital-based Part B claims for institutional services (Blue Cross and Blue Shield).

   vi. Support processes

      1. Management of fee schedules (MFS)

         a. Third-party payers update fee-for-service fee schedules (list of healthcare services and procedures using CPT/HCPCS codes) on an annual basis.

         b. Healthcare providers notify Medicare at the end of each year whether they are willing to participate in program.

         c. Nonparticipating providers may or may not accept assignment; if assignment is accepted, provider is paid 95% of MFS (5% less than participating providers).

      2. Charge-master

         a. Also called charge description master (CDM); contains information about healthcare services and transactions provided to a patient

         b. Allows provider to accurately charge routine services and supplies to the patient

         c. Services, supplies, and procedures included on charge-master generate reimbursement for approximately 75% of UB-04 claims submitted for outpatient service.

         d. Routinely updated and maintained by representatives from health information management, clinical services, finance, business office/patient financial services, compliance, and information systems

         e. HIM professionals provide expertise concerning CPT codes updates.

3. Revenue cycle

    a. Assures facility is properly reimbursed for services provided

    b. Major functions include

        i. Admitting, patient-access management

        ii. Case management

        iii. Charge capture

        iv. Health information management

        v. Patient financial services, business office

        vi. Finance

        vii. Compliance

        viii. Information technology

    c. Revenue cycle indicators

        i. Value and volume of discharges

        ii. Number of accounts-receivable days

        iii. Number of bill-hold days

        iv. Percentage and amount of write-offs

        v. Percentage of clean claims

        vi. Percentage of claims returned to providers

        vii. Percentage of denials

        viii. Percentage of accounts missing documents

        ix. Number of query forms

        x. Percentage of late charges

        xi. Percentage of accurate registrations

        xii. Percentage increased point-of-service collections for elective procedures

        xiii. Percentage of increased DRG payments due to improved documentation and coding

4. Documentation and coding quality

    a. Accurate coding is contingent upon complete, accurate, legible, and timely documentation.

    b. ICD-9-CM and CPT coding drives reimbursement and is a mechanism used to determine utilization of services and the quality of care rendered to patients.

    c. HIPAA authorizes the Office of the Inspector General (OIG) to investigate cases of healthcare fraud, which includes unnecessary services, upcoding, unbundling, and billing for services not provided.

g. Healthcare Reform

    i. Due to increased healthcare expenditures in mid-1990s, hospitals and practitioners formed alliances, networks, systems, and joint ventures that made them more competitive.

        1. Integrated delivery networks

        2. Healthcare systems

        3. Healthcare organizations

    ii. Comprehensive care models offer full range of healthcare services, including hospitals, primary care physicians, specialty care physicians, and other pertinent healthcare providers.

        1. Accountable health plans

        2. Coordinated care networks

        3. Community care networks

        4. Integrated health systems

h. HMOs
- **i.** Oldest of managed healthcare plans
- **ii.** Integrates healthcare delivery with insurance for health care

i. PPOs
- **i.** Network of physicians who enter into agreement to provide healthcare services on a discounted fee schedule
- **ii.** Patients pay a penalty fee for using nonparticipating physicians.

j. National Health Insurance
- **i.** In 1915, the American Association of Labor Legislation drafted model health insurance legislation that was never adopted into law.
- **ii.** In the 1930s, the Committee on the Cost of Medical Care was formed to address access to medical care; however, its recommendations were not followed.
- **iii.** In 1939, the Tactical Committee on Medical Care drafted the Wagner National Health Act, which supported a federally funded national health program that the state and local governments would manage; it was not enacted.
- **iv.** In 1945, President Truman introduced a universal comprehensive national insurance plan that was not adopted into law.
- **v.** In 1946, Hill-Burton Act initiated healthcare facility construction program under Title VI of the Public Health Service Act; it provided federal grants for modernizing hospitals, and in return, hospitals would provide free or reduced-cost medical services to those unable to pay.
- **vi.** In 1965, Title XVIII of the Social Security Act established Medicare, which covered most Americans over age 65.
  - **1.** Overseen by CMS
  - **2.** Health insurance to complement retirement, survivors, and disability insurance benefits
  - **3.** Groups added in 1973 included
    - **a.** Those entitled to Social Security or railroad retirement disability cash benefits for at least 24 months
    - **b.** Most persons with end-stage renal disease
    - **c.** Certain individuals over 65 who were not eligible for paid coverage but elected to pay for Medicare benefits
- **vii.** In 1966, Title XIX of the Social Security Act established Medicaid.
  - **1.** Overseen by CMS
  - **2.** Healthcare coverage was added to states' public assistance programs for low-income groups, families with dependent children, aged, and the disabled.
  - **3.** Currently the program covers approximately 40% of indigent population.
- **viii.** Patient Protection and Affordable Care Act of 2010 (Obamacare)
  - **1.** Reduces health insurance premium costs by providing tax relief
  - **2.** Caps out-of-pocket expenses and requires preventive care to be fully covered without any out-of-pocket expense
  - **3.** Those with healthcare insurance can keep their coverage if it meets the minimum standards set by the legislation
  - **4.** Those without healthcare insurance choose the coverage that works best for them

5. Establishes an insurance exchange for purchase of private insurance plans
   a. Small business owners will not only be able to choose insurance coverage through the insurance exchange, but will also receive a tax credit to help offset the cost of covering their employees.

PRACTICAL APPLICATION OF YOUR KNOWLEDGE

1. Define the following terms:

  a. Accreditation

  b. Inpatient

  c. Hospital

  d. Outpatient

  e. Patient

  f. Primary patient record

  g. Provider

  h. Resident

  i. Secondary patient record

2. In 1913 the American College of Surgeons was founded. What did it do to improve patient care?

3. What was the result of the Hill-Burton Act of 1946?

4. Describe Title XVIII of the Social Security Act.

5. Describe Title XIX of the Social Security Act.

6. Discuss the following:
   a. DHHS

   b. CMS

   c. TEFRA

   d. COBRA

   e. HIPAA

7. State the various ways that a hospital may be classified.

8. State the responsibilities of the following administrative leaders:

Governing Board	
CEO	
COO	
CIO	
CFO	

9. How is the medical staff managed?

10. Compare the following healthcare facilities:

Acute-Care	
Ambulatory Care	
Home Health Care	
Hospice	
Long-Term Care	
Urgent Care Center	
Adult Day Care	

11. Discuss the following regulatory agencies and organizations:

TJC (formerly JCAHO)	
AAAHC	
AMA	
AoA	
CARF	
CHAP	
NCQA	
NLN	

12. Match the government agency with its mission or purpose.

a. CDC   **e.** IHS   **h.** DHHS
b. NCHS   **f.** OSHA   **i.** AHRQ
c. CMS   **g.** FDA   **j.** ATSDR
d. OIG

    i. _____ Responsible for numerous healthcare regulatory programs and encompasses various agencies

    ii. _____ Produces and disseminates relevant scientific and policy information that improves the quality and reduces the cost of effective health care

    iii. _____ Protects workers and the public from exposure to adverse effects of hazardous substances

    iv. _____ Concerned with communicable diseases, environmental health, and foreign quarantine activities

    v. _____ Federal government's principal vital and health statistics agency

    vi. _____ Responsible for the safety of foods, drugs, medical devices, cosmetics, and radiation-emitting equipment

    vii. _____ Responsible for Medicare and Medicaid programs

    viii. _____ Responsible for providing health care to Native Americans

    ix. _____ Responsible for developing standards and regulations concerning safe and healthy work environments

    x. _____ Conducts and monitors audits, inspections, and investigations sponsored by DHHS

13. What are the purposes of the health record?

14. Who uses the health record?

15. Distinguish between the source-oriented health record and the problem-oriented health record.

Source Oriented	Problem Oriented

16. Match the formats of the paper-based medical records:

    a. Source-oriented medical record

    b. Problem-oriented medical record

    c. Integrated medical record

        i. _____ Most common paper-based health record

        ii. _____ Medical record is organized into sections according to treatment and data collection.

        iii. _____ Developed by Dr. Lawrence L. Weed

        iv. _____ Recorded in strict chronological order without any divisions by source

        v. _____ Medical record divided into database, problem list, initial plan, and progress notes

        vi. _____ Progress notes written in SOAP format

17. State general documentation guidelines.

18. Compare the contents of the various healthcare records:

Acute-Care	
Ambulatory Care	
Emergency Room	
Long-Term Care	
Home Health Care	
Hospice	
Mental Health	

19. Calculate the following:

    a. Out of 2694 records requested from the health information management department, 2588 were located. What is the record retrieval rate?

    b. City General Hospital has been in operation for 20 years. It has 15,000 admissions per year. The healthcare facility has expanded, which will allow for 500 more admissions per year from now on. Currently, the hospital is using 3000 megabytes for MPI storage. If storage of one patient's data in the MPI averages 1 KB of space, how many additional megabytes are needed to store information for the new patients for next year?

20. Contrast quantitative and qualitative analysis.

21. Describe the following data sets:
    a. UHDDS

    b. UACDS

    c. MDS Long-Term Care and RAI

    d. OASIS

    e. UCDS

22. What is the difference between a LAN and a WAN?

23. Describe the following indexes and registries:
  a. MPI

  b. Number index

  c. Physician index

  d. Disease index

  e. Procedure index

  f. Admission and discharge register

  g. Operating room register

  h. Birth register

  i. Death register

  j. Emergency room register

  k. Cancer or tumor registry

24. How did TEFRA affect the reimbursement of health care?

25. How has the Balanced Budget Act affected the reimbursement of health care?

26. What are the purposes of the following classification systems?
   a. ICD-9-CM

   b. CPT

   c. HCPCS

   d. ICD-O

   e. APC

   f. DRG

   g. RBRVS

27. Discuss the charge-master.

28. Explain the revenue cycle.

29. Mark these statements as True or False.

    a. _____ The primary criterion used to evaluate a filing system is the satisfaction of the file clerks.

    b. _____ Movable open shelving saves a lot of filing space.

    c. _____ In a centralized filing system, record control and security are easier to maintain than in a decentralized system.

    d. _____ Color coding of medical record folders assists with the control of misfiles.

    e. _____ A hospital with limited filing space should retain all records in hard copy indefinitely.

    f. _____ The master patient index is the best source for locating patients with an ICD-9-CM diagnostic code of 250.01.

    g. _____ According to the American Health Information Management Association, records of minor patients may be destroyed when the patient reaches the age of majority.

    h. _____ In the family numbering system, records are best filed in alphabetical order.

    i. _____ Straight numeric filing is a system for filing records in the exact chronological order in which the patients were admitted.

    j. _____ The health information manager should develop a retention schedule for the transfer and destruction of medical records, registers, and indexes.

    k. _____ If a patient's name cannot be found in the master patient index, then the patient was never admitted in the facility.

    l. _____ A health maintenance organization is an entity that combines the provision of healthcare insurance and the delivery of healthcare services at predetermined payment rates.

    m. _____ A military hospital is a government-owned federal facility.

    n. _____ The chief financial officer is responsible for overseeing all accounting and financial affairs of the facility.

    o. _____ The attending physician has the major responsibility for assuring a complete and accurate medical record.

    p. _____ Nongovernmental for-profit proprietary hospitals provide the best overall quality health care.

    q. _____ The forms committee often provides the final approval of forms to be used in the medical record.

r. _____ To assure accurate communication, abbreviations should be avoided in the medical record.

s. _____ A certified coding specialist must have a least an associate's degree from an accredited college or university.

t. _____ The Commission on Accreditation of Rehabilitation Facilities accredits facilities that provide rehabilitative care.

u. _____ The terminal-digit filing system has 100 primary filing sections ranging from 00 to 99.

v. _____ Quantitative analysis and qualitative analysis accomplish the same results for medical record completion.

w. _____ Accreditation by The Joint Commission is a voluntary process.

x. _____ A final progress note can substitute for a discharge summary for patients who die within 48 hours of admission.

y. _____ If a physician dies, then his or her incomplete medical records may be filed as is, along with a written explanation.

z. _____ The primary focus of the screen format of computer-based patient records is the end user.

30. **Compare the following credentials:**
   a. RHIA

   b. RHIT

   c. CCS

   d. CHPS

TEST YOUR KNOWLEDGE

Select the best answer for the questions or incomplete statements.

1. The process by which an organization or agency performs an external review and grants recognition to the program of study or institution that meets certain predetermined standards is called:
   a. standardization.
   b. registration.
   c. formalization.
   d. accreditation.

2. In the following cancer registry accession register, what does the prefix of the patients' accession numbers represent?
   a. Date of accession
   b. Month of accession
   c. Year of accession
   d. Cancer stage

Cancer Registry Accession Register				
Account Number	Patient's Name	Primary	Site	Date of Diagnosis
09-0001/00	Cantu, Bobby	Liver	C22	01/08/2009
09-0002/02	Wilson, Joan	Colon	C18	01/08/2009
09-0245/02	Tyler, Kenneth	Lung	C34	01/08/2009
09-0004/01	Mason, Andre	Prostate	C61	01/08/2009
09-0004/02	Mason, Andre	Colon	C18	01/08/2009

3. Dr. Barbette is delinquent, with 10 of her 15 medical records needing to be completed. What is her delinquency rate?
   a. 5%
   b. 10%
   c. 33%
   d. 67%

4. Upon discharge analysis of a patient's record, the analyst does not see a discharge order written by the physician. What can the analyst assume?
   a. The patient died prior to discharge.
   b. The patient left against medical advice.
   c. The family members requested hospice care.
   d. The patient will continue treatment on an outpatient basis.

5. Which of the following is a secondary record for J. Pratt?
   a. ICD-9-CM code of 650 in the diagnostic index
   b. Emergency room record dated June 6
   c. Mental health record at Houston Honorary Adolescent Center
   d. Admitted and discharged same day with ICD-9-CM code of 650

6. How long should the master patient index be maintained?
   a. 5 years
   b. 10 years
   c. 20 years
   d. Indefinitely

7. The Hill-Burton Act of 1946:
 a. enacted legislation funding the construction of hospitals and other healthcare facilities.
 b. established the retrospective payment system.
 c. assured the provision of health care for the indigent.
 d. provided health care to Americans 65 years of age and older.

8. Dr. Thomas made an error in recording the progress notes in a patient's medical record. What is the first thing he should do to correct the error?
 a. Remove the page on which he made the error
 b. Tell the nursing staff to ignore the statement
 c. Draw a single line through the error
 d. Obliterate the error and enter correct entry

9. A patient is hospitalized for less than 48 hours. Which of the following is permissible in lieu of a discharge summary?
 a. Discharge order
 b. Final progress note
 c. Discharge diagnosis
 d. Final diagnosis

10. Who is responsible for developing bylaws governing physicians' completion of medical records?
 a. Governing board
 b. Chief of medicine
 c. Chief executive officer
 d. Medical staff

11. Which system avoids assigning a new number for each patient encounter?
 a. Straight numerical
 b. Serial numbering
 c. Unit numbering
 d. Serial-unit numbering

12. By signing a consent for treatment, the patient agrees to:
 a. allow the hospital to release information to his or her insurance company.
 b. treatments and procedures to be performed by healthcare providers.
 c. take all medications prescribed and dispensed by healthcare providers.
 d. allow hospital to dispose of property and values in the case of death.

13. Reviewing the record to assure the presence of a discharge summary is referred to as:
 a. legal analysis.
 b. qualitative analysis.
 c. documentation analysis.
 d. quantitative analysis.

14. A major advantage of the source-oriented medical record is the:
 a. speed at which individual sheets can be located.
 b. ease with which healthcare providers can follow the course of one problem.
 c. strict chronology that keeps episode of care clearly defined by date.
 d. forms are designed to support numbering and tracking of problems.

15. Which of the following would be most beneficial in locating a charged-out medical record?
 a. Outguide
 b. Transfer notice
 c. Requisition slip
 d. Master patient index

16. Which of the following filing systems would be most affected in the event of a divorce?
 a. Family
 b. Unit
 c. Serial
 d. Serial-unit

17. A patient had an appendectomy due to appendicitis. This operative report must be completed when?
a. Immediately after surgery
b. Within 24 hours of surgery
c. Within 48 hours of surgery
d. Within 15 days of discharge

18. A post-anesthesia note is required when?
a. Immediately after surgery
b. Within 24 hours of surgery
c. Within 48 hours of surgery
d. Within 15 days of discharge

19. A discharge summary:
a. may be completed in lieu of a clinical resume.
b. must be dictated and typed for ease of readability.
c. is not required for a stay of 48 hours or less.
d. is not required when death occurs within 48 hours or less.

20. Which of the following is an example of a government agency that has an interest in the standardization of records and data collection?
a. The Joint Commission
b. Department of Health and Human Services
c. American Medical Association
d. American Health Information Management Association

21. The health record may be used for personal and nonpersonal reasons. Which is an example of personal use of the health record?
a. Patient reviews record with provider for understanding of health status.
b. Health information professional assigns ICD-9-CM codes.
c. Accrediting agency reviews record to assure quality health care.
d. Employer reviews healthcare data to evaluate job injuries.

22. Place the following in terminal digit order: 01-34-54, 01-35-55, 02-05-49, 02-66-48
a. 01-34-54, 01-35-55, 02-05-49, 02-66-48
b. 02-05-49, 01-34-54, 01-35-55, 02-66-48
c. 02-66-48, 02-05-49, 01-35-55, 01-34-54
d. 02-66-48, 02-05-49, 01-34-54, 01-35-55

23. The condition that is primarily responsible for the patient's admission to the hospital is the _____ diagnosis.
a. primary
b. principal
c. preliminary
d. discharge

24. Which of the following is not a major hospital classification?
a. General
b. Special
c. Psychiatric
d. Cardiac

25. Which of the following would the physician include in the discharge summary?
a. Blood pressure and pulse
b. Review of systems
c. Do not resuscitate order
d. Instructions for future care

26. As the director of health information of a newly established acute-care facility, where would you expect to find directives concerning the minimum health record contents?
a. The Joint Commission
b. Credentials committee meeting minutes
c. Medical record committee meeting minutes
d. Benchmarks from area acute-care facilities

27. A health record analyst is reviewing the medical record for authentication of all entries. This process is commonly termed:
   a. qualitative analysis.
   b. quantitative analysis.
   c. closed record review.
   d. point-of-care review.

28. Information in a tumor registry is collected to:
   a. bill for treatment rendered.
   b. inform patients of their cancer status.
   c. improve patient care.
   d. determine the appropriate cancer stage.

29. LaToya wants to put her healthcare decisions in writing in the event she has an incurable or irreversible condition and is unable to communicate her wishes. What should she institute?
   a. Advance directive
   b. Executor of her estate
   c. Transfer on death
   d. Legal guardian

30. The automated record tracking system is a database that:
   a. locates misplaced health records.
   b. verifies the requested patient's name and health record number.
   c. stores current and past health record locations.
   d. records dissatisfaction of record requesters with service.

31. A health information technician wants to obtain a chronological list of all patients admitted to the facility during the third quarter with a diagnosis of appendicitis. Which database should the technician utilize?
   a. Accession register
   b. Master patient index
   c. Disease index
   d. Patient register

32. Which application is best suited for bar coding?
   a. Birth certificate registration
   b. Diagnostic and procedural coding
   c. Record tracking/location
   d. Misfiled records

33. During the month of December, there were 3489 discharges with 134 incomplete records. What was the incomplete record rate for the month?
   a. .384%
   b. 3.84%
   c. 26.03%
   d. 38.40%

34. Last month Houston Hospital discharged 517 patients. Each chart is approximately 1.8 inches thick. A shelving unit in the health information department has 7 shelves and each shelf is 36 inches. How many shelving units are needed to store 1 month of discharged records?
   a. 2.05
   b. 3.00
   c. 3.69
   d. 4.00

35. The arrangement that links healthcare financing and service delivery and allows payers to exercise significant economic control over how and what services are delivered is referred to as what?
   a. Medicare
   b. Medicaid
   c. Managed care
   d. Fee for service

36. Ellen, a 78-year-old end-stage renal cancer patient, is in need of palliative care. Which facility would best meet her needs?
   a. Skilled nursing facility
   b. Hospice
   c. Rehabilitation facility
   d. Home health care

37. At the close of World War II, the growth in the number of hospitals can be attributed to:
  a. Hill-Burton Act of 1946.
  b. Clinton Health Security Act of 1993.
  c. HIPAA of 1996.
  d. AARP, founded in 1958.

38. Which of the following agencies is concerned with communicable diseases, environmental health, and foreign quarantine activities?
  a. Centers for Medicare and Medicaid Services
  b. National Institutes of Health
  c. Health Resources and Services Administration
  d. Centers for Disease Control and Prevention

39. Which of the following organizations is responsible for developing standards and conducting investigations to determine compliance in matters related to occupational safety and health?
  a. DHHS
  b. CMS
  c. COBRA
  d. OSHA

40. Which act established the Patient Antidumping Law?
  a. HIPAA
  b. TEFRA
  c. COBRA
  d. OSHA

41. When this act was passed, it helped to improve the quality of health care, reduce cost, and enhance the effectiveness of health care.
  a. Health Information Portability and Accountability Act
  b. Tax Equity and Fiscal Responsibility Act
  c. Omnibus Budget Reconciliation Act
  d. Occupational Safety and Health Act

42. This hospital provides care to military personnel and their dependents. How is it classified?
  a. Voluntary
  b. Proprietary
  c. Government
  d. Not for profit

43. Manuel receives surgery in 1 day and is discharged to home. Where was he treated?
  a. Surgicenter
  b. Satellite clinic
  c. Ancillary department
  d. Observation unit

44. Hospital ownership is either:
  a. proprietary or government.
  b. charitable or government.
  c. stand-alone or with clinics.
  d. government or nongovernment.

45. According to TJC (formerly JCAHO) standards, a hospital is required to:
  a. provide charitable care to the indigent.
  b. promote performance improvement.
  c. employ an RHIA or RHIT.
  d. review and update policies yearly.

46. Warren, a 12-year-old Boy Scout, breaks his leg while hiking with the troop. Which type of facility might Bob's Boy Scout leader take him to for emergent treatment?
  a. Surgicenter
  b. Ambulatory care clinic
  c. Specialty hospital
  d. General hospital

47. Dr. Lewis is retired. Which medical staff membership might he be awarded?
  a. Courtesy
  b. Honorary
  c. Tributary
  d. Consulting

48. The governing board is responsible
for setting the overall direction of
the hospital. Other responsibilities
include all except which of the
following?
   a. Selecting TJC standards to uphold
   b. Selecting qualified administrative
   leadership
   c. Monitoring the quality of care
   d. Establishing bylaws in accordance
   with license

49. Which of the following is considered
a clinical support service?
   a. OB/GYN
   b. Cardiology
   c. Volunteer services
   d. Health information management
   department

50. Cecile, a 78-year-old female, needs
intermittent skilled nursing care.
Which facility would best meet her
needs?
   a. Skilled nursing facility
   b. Hospice
   c. Rehabilitation facility
   d. Home health care

© saicle/ShutterStock, Inc.

Healthcare Privacy, Confidentiality, Legal, and Ethical Issues

1. Introduction to the Legal System
   a. The legal system is the system of principles and processes by which people who live in a society deal with their disputes and problems, seeking to solve or settle them without resort to force. Laws govern the relationships among private individuals, organizations, and government. The legal system is a combination of private and public law.
      i. Private
         1. Also considered civil law
         2. Concerned with the recognition and enforcement of the rights and duties of private individuals and organizations (i.e., patient and healthcare facility)
         3. Legal issues between private parties are torts and contracts
            a. Tort
               i. An injury or wrong committed against an individual or his property
               ii. In tort action, one party asserts that wrongful conduct on the part of another caused harm and seeks compensation for the harm suffered.
            b. Contract
               i. Concerned with legally enforceable agreements between two or more individuals
               ii. In contract disputes, one party asserts that in failing to fulfill an obligation, the other party breached a contract, and the asserting party seeks either compensation or performance of the obligation as a remedy.
               iii. Court order: one party forces the breaching party to fulfill its alleged obligation.
      ii. Public
         1. Deals with the relationships between private parties and the government; consists of rules, criminal law, and government regulations
            a. Criminal
               i. Prohibits conduct considered injurious to society as a whole and provides for punishment of those found to have engaged in such conduct
               ii. Crime versus tort
                  1. Crime is an offense against a person or the public at large.
                  2. Tort is a civil wrong against an individual.

    b. Regulations

       i. Multiple government regulations require private individuals and organizations to follow specified courses of action in connection with their activities.

    c. Rule: a principle or regulation that governs an action, conduct, or procedure.

  iii. Sources of law. There are four main law affecting healthcare system.

    1. Constitution

      a. Supreme law of the land: supreme, highest law in the United States

      b. Establishes the general organization of the federal government, and grants certain powers to and places limits on the three branches of the federal government (executive, legislative, judicial)

      c. Each state has its own constitution.

        i. Express power: stated in Constitution (e.g., power to tax)

        ii. Implied power: not stated in Constitution. They are actions considered necessary and proper to permit Express power to be accomplished.

      d. Each city has its own charter.

      e. Constitution places limit on what state and federal government can do

        i. Constitutional right important to health care

          a. Due process (right to be fully heard)

          b. Right of privacy

          c. Right to be left alone

      f. Constitution overrides state and federal lower laws that are deemed unconstitutional

    2. Statutes

      a. Statutory or codified law refers to written laws or statutes enacted by such bodies as the United States Congress and state and local legislatures.

      b. Constitutional and federal law take precedence over conflicting state laws, and state laws take precedence over conflicting local government rules.

      c. Examples of federal laws affecting healthcare facilities

        i. American Recovery and Reinvestment Act

        ii. Safe Medical Devices Act

        iii. Americans with Disabilities Act

    3. Decisions of the court

      a. Common law or uncodified law derived from the common law of England applied to the courts of the United States

      b. Consist of principles that have evolved over time from court decisions resolving controversies

      c. When a case decision is considered to serve as an authority or example for subsequent similar or identical cases, the case is said to have set a legal precedent.

    4. Rules of administrative agencies

      a. Legislatures have delegated to administrative agencies the responsibility and power to implement various laws (e.g., DHHS).

b. The delegated powers include quasi-legislative power to adopt regulations and the quasi-judicial power to decide how the statutes and regulations apply to individual situations.
c. Legislatures delegate these powers because legislators do not have the time or expertise to address the complex issues involved in some areas that need to be regulated.
b. Branches of the Government (Federal and State)
  i. Executive (president or governor)
    1. Enforces and administers the law
    2. United States Constitution invests this power in the president, who is the administrative head of the executive branch.
    3. Oversees various agencies, including DHHS, which manages CMS
  ii. Legislative (Congress and state legislatures)
    1. Enacts laws
    2. Creates new legislation, amends or repeals existing legislation
    3. Federal and state levels (except Nebraska, which has only one house) consist of two houses, one composed of senators and the other representatives.
  iii. Judicial (U.S. Supreme Court, various state and federal courts)
    1. Responsible for interpreting the law through hearing and resolving disputes in accordance with the law
    2. Three sources of judicial power
      a. Federal courts
        i. Have jurisdiction over
          1. Cases involving questions of federal law
          2. Treaties
          3. Cases concerning maritime matters
          4. Cases that involve two or more states
        ii. Federal court system structure
          1. District courts (trial courts)
          2. Courts of appeal
          3. Supreme Court
      b. State courts
        i. Vary by state but can be divided into four general categories
          1. Trial courts of limited jurisdiction
          2. Trial courts of general jurisdiction
          3. Intermediate appellate courts
          4. Courts of last resort (supreme courts)
      c. Administrative agencies
        i. Empowered by law to make regulations with the force of the law, and can also conduct hearings and take measures to enforce these regulations (e.g., Food and Drug Administration, and Centers for Medicare and Medicaid services, and Internal Revenue Services)
    3. Each level of government (federal, state) has its own set of courts.
      a. Courts have different jurisdiction based upon geographical area, area of authority, and type of case.
      b. Trial and appellate courts
        i. Trial courts initially hear a case and pass judgment (original jurisdiction).
        ii. Litigants unsatisfied with trial court decisions may appeal their case to appellate courts (court of appeals).

Table 3-1	Federal and State Court Sequences of Appeals	
Level of Court	**Federal**	**State**
Highest appellate courts	U.S. Supreme Court (may consider appeals from state supreme courts on federal questions)	State supreme courts
Appellate courts	U.S. Court of Appeals	Circuit courts, district courts, and courts of common pleas
Special jurisdiction courts	U.S. Customs, Claims, and Tax	
Trial courts	U.S. District Courts	District, probate, family, criminal courts
Lower local courts (non-jury)		Traffic, police, small claims, Justice of Peace

1. Two types of review (see Table 3-1)
    a. Error correction monitors decisions of lower trial courts for proper application and interpretation of law; does not seek new evidence, but examines records of lower courts for errors.
    b. Sort cases for Supreme Court review
    c. Court interpret statutes and regulations, decide validity, follow precedent, or create common law (case law)
    d. When no statutes or regulation apply, courts adhere to principle of "let the decision stand" (stare decisis)
2. Health Record Requirements and Retention Guidelines
    a. Record Requirements
        i. Federal and state laws and regulations provide guidance as to patient record content, privacy, and security.
        ii. Some state laws and regulations specify that health records must be maintained by healthcare institutions and that the information must be kept confidential.
        iii. Most state law expressly allows a patient or authorized representative to inspect the health record (typically, a written request must be made and reasonable cost paid).
        iv. State licensing laws usually address at least the minimum content of a health record.
        v. In addition to federal, state, and local laws, numerous nongovernmental agencies specify standards for healthcare facilities (e.g., TJC).
        vi. TJC, American Osteopathic Association (AOA), Medicare/Medicaid Conditions of Participation (CoP), and other accrediting bodies provide standards for patient recordkeeping.

1. There should be one record per patient, with the following
   contents for an inpatient record:
   a. History and physical
   b. Documentation of infections and complications
   c. Consent forms
   d. Notes, reports, ancillary reports
   e. Discharge summary
   f. Final diagnosis
2. Outpatients:
   a. Encounter note
   b. Consent forms
   c. Diagnostic testing
   d. Presumptive diagnosis
   e. Medication reconciliation
   f. Allergies/Drug interraction

vii. CMS published meaningful use rules
   1. Meaningful use: set of standards defined by the Centers for
      Medicare and Medicaid Services (CMS) Incentive Programs that
      governs the use of electronic health records and allows eligible
      providers and hospitals to earn incentive payments by meeting
      specific criteria (Table 3-2).
   2. The goal of meaningful use is to promote the spread of
      electronic health records to improve health care in the United
      States.
      a. HITECH Act is a part of American Recovery and Reinvestment
         Act (ARRA)

Table 3-2 Meaningful Use Criteria

Stage 1: Meaningful use criteria focus on:	Stage 2: Meaningful use criteria focus on:	Stage 3: Meaningful use criteria focus on:
Electronically capturing health information in a standardized format	More rigorous health information exchange (HIE)	Improving quality, safety, and efficiency, leading to improved health outcomes
Using that information to track key clinical conditions	Increased requirements for e-prescribing and incorporating lab results	Decision support for national high-priority conditions
Communicating that information for care coordination processes	Electronic transmission of patient care summaries across multiple settings	Patient access to self-management tools
Initiating the reporting of clinical quality measures and public health information	More patient-controlled data	Access to comprehensive patient data through patient-centered HIE
Using information to engage patients and their families in their care		Improving population health

Reproduced from HealthIT.gov. EHR Incentives & Certification: Meaningful Use Definition & Objectives. http://www.healthit.gov/providers-professionals/meaningful-use-definition-objectives. Accessed March 4, 2014.

    b. Allocates $19 billion for health information technology incentive

    c. Incentives meant to reward hospital and eligible professionals who are meaningful users of certified electronic health records

    d. CMS published Proposed Rule for Meaningful Use Stage 1 on December 31, 2009

    e. CMS issued Final Rule on July 13, 2010

3. Benefits of the meaningful use of EHRs:

    a. Complete and accurate information

        i. With electronic health records, providers have the information they need to provide the best possible care.

        ii. Providers will know more about their patients and their health history before they walk into the examination room.

    b. Better access to information

        i. Electronic health records help providers access information needed to diagnose health problems earlier and improve the health outcomes of their patients.

        ii. Electronic health records allow information to be shared more easily among doctors' offices, hospitals, and across health systems, leading to better coordination of care.

    c. Patient empowerment

        i. Electronic health records empower patients to take a more active role in their health and in the health of their families.

        ii. Patients can receive electronic copies of their medical records and share their health information securely over the Internet with their families.

4. Stages of meaningful use

    a. To achieve meaningful use, eligible providers and eligible hospitals must adopt certified EHR technology and use it to achieve specific objectives.

    b. Meaningful use objectives and measures will evolve in three stages over the next 5 years:

        i. Stage 1 (2011–2012): data capture and sharing

        ii. Stage 2 (2014): advance clinical processes

        iii. Stage 3 (2016): improved outcomes

    c. Achieving meaningful use during stages requires meeting both core and menu objectives.

        i. All of the core objectives are required.

        ii. Eligible providers and hospitals may choose which objectives to meet from the menu set.

5. Eligible hospital objectives

    a. Improve quality, safety, efficiency, and reduce health disparities

        i. Clinical patient order entry

        ii. Drug–drug and drug–allergy checks

        iii. Drug–formulary checks

        iv. Problem list

        v. E-prescribing

        vi. Active medication list

        vii. Medication allergy list

        viii. Patient demographics

          ix. Vital, BIM, and growth chart
          x. Smoking status
          xi. Incorporate clinical lab test results
          xii. Generate lists of patient
          xiii. Report on quality measures
          xiv. Send reminders to patient
          xv. Clinical decision support
     b. Engage patients and families
          i. Electronic copy of health information
          ii. Electronic access for patients
          iii. After-visit summary
          iv. Patient education
     c. Improve care coordination
          i. Exchange key clinical information electronically
          ii. Medication reconciliation
          iii. Summary of care
     d. Improve population and public health
          i. Submit data to immunization registries
          ii. Send syndromic surveillance data to health agencies
     e. Ensure adequate privacy and security of protections for personal health information
          i. Protect electronic health information

b. Reporting Requirements
     i. In certain circumstances, federal and state law allows healthcare organizations to disclose confidential information without the patient's consent.
          1. Child abuse
          2. Abuse of adults and injuries to disabled persons
          3. Abortions
          4. Cancer
          5. Death or injury from use of a medical device
          6. Communicable diseases, including HIV/AIDS, tuberculosis, etc.
          7. Gunshot wounds
          8. Birth and death
     ii. Categories 1–8 do specify what can be reported without the consent of the patient due to state and federal law.
     iii. Except as otherwise permitted by law, anything outside of this cannot be disclosed unless the patient consented to the disclosure.

c. Retention Guidelines
     i. Forces influencing retention of health information are as follows:
          1. Healthcare providers' ability to
               a. Render continuing patient care
               b. Conduct education and research
               c. Defend a professional liability action
          2. Storage constraints
          3. Historical value
          4. Research and education
          5. Medium for storing records
          6. New technology
          7. Fiscal concerns
     ii. Retention schedule as recommended by AHIMA.

    d. Record Destruction
        i. Instances of health record destruction
            1. In ordinary course of business
            2. Provider's closure
        ii. Institution should have a policy addressing the controlling statute or regulation governing when a health record may be destroyed.
        iii. Records may be destroyed through shredding, burning, or some other means.
        iv. Some states require facility to maintain an abstract of patient data prior to destroying, or may require patient to be notified that his or her record will be destroyed.
        v. Facilities should maintain a permanent, dated, certified log of evidence of patient records that have been destroyed in the ordinary course of business.

3. Confidentiality, Consent, and Security of Health Records
    a. Creation of health record is the responsibility of healthcare facility and those who provide care to the patient.
    b. Ownership of Health Record
        i. Physical health record is the property of the healthcare provider, physician, or hospital that maintains it, because it is the healthcare provider's business record.
        ii. Patients have limited rights to access and control the disclosure of their information.
        iii. The patient and others have an interest in the information contained within the health record.
        iv. The patient and others as authorized have the right to access the information but do not have a right to possess the physical record.
    c. Confidentiality
        i. Privacy is the right of an individual to be left alone.
        ii. Information derived from a clinical relationship between patients and healthcare professionals is patient-specific health information.
            1. Healthcare providers should protect patient-specific health information from disclosure
        iii. Confidential communication is information given in the belief that it will not be disclosed to another party.
        iv. Confidentiality after death
            1. Patient's personal representative or the executor of the patient's estate may waive privilege.
    d. Privileged Communication
        i. Special relationship between patient and healthcare provider
        ii. Three elements of privileged communication
            1. Relationship between patient and provider
            2. Information must have been acquired through such a relationship.
            3. Information must have some connection with the provider's task of treating the patient.
    e. Types of Consent
        i. Do not resuscitate
            1. Tells medical professionals not to perform cardiopulmonary resuscitation (CPR) if the patient's breathing or heartbeat stops
            2. An adult patient may consent to DNR through a healthcare proxy or durable power of attorney.
        ii. Admission includes generalized consent that documents a patient's consent to receive medical treatment at the facility.

      iii. Release of information is consent for provider to release healthcare information for the purpose of reimbursement, continuity of care, or other reason, as authorized by the patient or patient's legal representative.

      iv. Informed consent (treatment and surgery)

         1. Process of advising a patient about treatment options and, depending on state laws, the provider may be obligated to disclose a patient's diagnosis, proposed treatment/surgery, reason for treatment/surgery, possible complications, likelihood of success, alternative treatment options, and risks if the patient does not undergo treatment/surgery

         2. Should include an explanation of the risks and benefits of treatment/surgery, alternatives, and evidence that the patient or appropriate legal representative understands and consents to the treatment/surgery

         3. TJC standards require that a patient consent to treatment and that the record contain evidence of consent.

         4. AOA requires a dated, timed, and signed informed consent for surgery on the patient's chart prior to surgery being performed.

         5. Medicare CoP state that all records must contain written patient consent for treatment and procedures specified by the medical staff, or by federal or state law

f. Advance Directive

    i. As part of the Omnibus Budget Reconciliation Act of 1990, the U.S. Congress passed the Patient Self-Determination Act. The act required providers participating in the Medicare and Medicaid programs to inform patients of their rights to express written preferences regarding healthcare decisions to be followed if the patient becomes unable to make or communicate decisions, such as a decision to withdraw life support systems.

    ii. Legal document in which patients provide instructions as to how they want to be treated in the event they become very ill and there is no reasonable hope for recovery

g. Durable Power of Attorney

    i. Legal document in which patients name someone close to them to make decisions about their health care in the event they become incapacitated

    ii. The durable power of attorney holder has the permission to request and receive information about the patient as detailed in the durable power of attorney.

    iii. Uniform Health Care Decisions Act (UHCDA): priority order list

        a. Spouse

        b. Adult child

        c. Living parents

        d. Adult sibling

        e. Not-related adult who has exhibited special care and concern for the individual

        f. Healthcare provider may see court appointment.

    iv. Also called a healthcare proxy

h. Security of Health Records

    i. Organizations must maintain the physical and electronic protection of the integrity, availability, and confidentiality of computer-based information and the resources used to enter, store, process, and communicate it.

      ii. Security of paper-based health records
         1. Maintain secure from unauthorized access
         2. Utilize a tracking system to locate records
         3. Educate personnel on confidentiality of patient information
      iii. Records must be protected from loss, theft, tampering, and destruction.

4. Laws and Regulations Regarding Health Records
   a. Statute of Limitations
      i. Legislatively imposed time constraints that restrict the period of time after the occurrence of an injury during which a legal action must be commenced
      ii. Should a cause of action be initiated later than the time prescribed, the case cannot proceed.
      iii. The statutory period begins when an injury occurs, although in some cases (usually involving foreign objects left in the body during surgery) the statutory period commences when the injured person discovers or should have discovered the injury.
      iv. The statute of limitation of health records varies by state. However AHIMA and the AMA offer guidelines for record retention. Adult health records should be retained for 10 years while minor health records until the age of majority plus the state statute of limitation. Immunization records, birth, death and surgical registers and the Master Patient Index should be maintained indefinitely. AMA states Medicare or Medicaid health records should be kept at least five years but AHIMA recommends the adult and minor health record retention guidelines regardless of payor. In order to preserve confidentiality when discarding records, all documents should be destroyed with the institution keeping a ledger of all records destroyed. The AMA suggests informing patients before discarding old records to give them the opportunity to claim their records or have them sent to another physician.

5. Release of Information and Subpoenas
   a. Release of Information
      i. Patient or legal representative may authorize disclosure of patient's healthcare information unless it would be in the patient's best interest not to have such information disclosed, such as psychiatric information.
      ii. The patient or legal representative controls access by all third parties except those to which the healthcare institution is required to report information of a medical nature or as otherwise provided by law.
   b. Subpoena
      i. Court order requiring someone to appear in court to give testimony
      ii. Disregarding a subpoena can result in contempt of court.
      iii. Common elements of valid subpoena
         1. Name of court where lawsuit is brought
         2. Names of parties to the lawsuit
         3. Docket number of the case
         4. Date, time, and place of the requested appearance
         5. Specific documents to be produced if a subpoena duces tecum is involved
            a. Subpoena duces is a written order commanding a person to appear, give testimony, and bring all documents (records) described in the subpoena to court.
         6. Name and telephone number of attorney who requested the subpoena

Table 3-3 Federal Laws and Regulations for Health Information	
Legislation	**Summary**
Drug Abuse and Treatment Act (1972)	Requires drug and alcohol abuse patient records to be kept confidential and not subject to disclosure except as provided by law.
Emergency Medical Treatment and Active Labor Act of the Consolidated Omnibus Budget Reconciliation Act (1985)	Hospitals and physicians who participate in the Medicare program must follow certain guidelines for the treatment and transfer of all patients, regardless of patient participation and eligibility for Medicare. Also referred to as antidumping law.
Federal Tort Claims Act (1946)	The U.S. government's immunity from tort liability was largely abolished and certain conditions for suits and claims against the U.S. government were established.
Freedom of Information Act (1966)	Individuals can seek access to information without the authorization of the person to whom the information applies when the information is held by a federal agency (except personal records such as medical records).
Health Care Quality Improvement Act (1986)	Established the National Practitioner Data Bank (NPDB), which contains information about practitioner's credentials, including previous medical malpractice payment and adverse action history.
Health Insurance Portability and Accountability Act (1996)	Mandated administrative simplification regulations that govern privacy, security, and electronic transactions standards for healthcare information.

      7. Signature, stamp, or seal of the official empowered to issue the subpoena

      8. Witness fees, where provided by law

   iv. Contempt of court

      1. Results when a person fails to obey a subpoena and is punishable by fine or imprisonment

   v. Subpoena ad testificandum

      1. Court order that requires a person to appear in court to testify

   vi. Subpoena duces tecum

      1. Court order that commands a person to come to court and produce whatever documents are named in the order

6. Healthcare Privacy

   a. The Standards for Privacy of Individually Identifiable Health Information ("Privacy Rule") established, for the first time, a set of national standards for the protection of certain health information.

Table 3-4 Federal and State Legislation Relevant to Health Care and Maintenance of Health Records

Legislation	Summary
Patient Self-Determination Act (1990)	Requires that all healthcare facilities notify patients age 18 and over that they have the right to have an advance directive placed in their medical record. Facilities must inform patients, in writing, of state laws and facility policies regarding implementation of advance directives. The patient record must document whether the patient has executed an advance directive. Allows a person to: 1. Make decision concerning medical care 2. Accept or refuse treatment 3. Present their request for treatment at time of admission (administrative directive or living will)
Privacy Act (1974)	Gives individuals some control over the information collected about them by the federal government; under this act, people have the right to: 1. Learn what information has been collected about them 2. View and have a copy of that information 3. Maintain limited control over the disclosure of that information to other persons or entities
Occupational Safety and Health Act (1970)	Created the Occupational Safety and Health Administration (OSHA), whose mission is to ensure safe and healthy workplaces.
Omnibus Budget Reconciliation Act (1987)	Created the Nursing Home Reform Act, which ensures residents of nursing homes receive quality care, requires provision of certain services, and establishes a residents' bill of rights.
Omnibus Budget Reconciliation Act (1990)	Requires reporting of adverse actions to the Centers of Medicare and Medicaid Services (CMS) and to state medical boards and licensing agencies.
Tax Equity and Fiscal Responsibility Act (1982)	TEFRA introduced the Peer Review Organization (PRO) program as a component of Medicare law to ensure the quality of care rendered to patients.
Uniform Business Records as Evidence Act (1936)	Stipulates that records can be admitted as evidence in a court of law if they were kept in the ordinary course of business. As of 1995, 46 of the 50 states had adopted it.
Uniform Healthcare Information Act (1985)	Serves as a model for state adoption and provides rules about health information management. As of 1996, only Montana and Washington had enacted this model legislation.

Table 3-5	Landmark Cases
Case	**Court Decision**
Behringer vs. Medical Center at Princeton (1991)	News of a physician on staff at the hospital where he was treated and diagnosed with AIDS was circulated among staff and patients. Physician sued the hospital for breach of duty to maintain confidentiality of his diagnosis. Court found hospital liable for failure to take reasonable precautions to ensure his information was held confidential.
Darling vs. Charleston Community Medical Hospital (1965)	Case dismantled doctrine of charitable immunity. Court held that the governing board has the duty to establish mechanisms for the medical staff to evaluate, counsel, and when necessary, take action against an unreasonable risk of harm to a patient arising from the patient's treatment by a personal physician. Court held that, based on the hospital's obligation to select high-quality physicians to be medical staff members, the hospital may be held liable for a patient's injury caused by a physician who does not meet those standards but was given medical staff membership and privileges.
Griswold vs. Connecticut (1965)	Court ruled that the right to privacy limits governmental authority to regulate contraception, abortion, and other decisions affecting reproduction.
Judge vs. Rockford Memorial Hospital (1958)	Director of nurses wrote a letter to a nurse's professional registry stating that the hospital wanted to discontinue a particular nurse's services because narcotics were disappearing whenever the nurse was on duty. Court found communication to be privileged, because the director of nurses had a legal duty to make the communication in the interests of society. Nurse's claims for damages were denied by the court.
Reisner vs. Regents of the University of California (1995)	Physician failed to warn his patient that she had contracted HIV through a blood transfusion. As a result, the hospital and physician were sued when the patient's sexual partner was exposed to the virus. The court held that the hospital was liable for the physician's failure to warn.

(continues)

Table 3-5 Landmark Cases (*continued*)	
Case	**Court Decision**
Tarasoff vs. Board of Regents (1976)	Determined that there was a duty to warn an individual against whom the patient has made a credible threat to harm.

   b. The U.S. Department of Health and Human Services (DHHS) issued the Privacy Rule to implement the requirement of the Health Insurance Portability and Accountability Act of 1996 (HIPAA).

   c. The Privacy Rule standards address the use and disclosure of individuals' health information ("protected health information") by organizations subject to the Privacy Rule ("covered entities"), as well as standards for individuals' privacy rights to understand and control how their health information is used.

   d. Within DHHS, the Office for Civil Rights (OCR) has responsibility for implementing and enforcing the Privacy Rule with respect to voluntary compliance activities and civil money penalties.

   e. See the Privacy Rule link in the references to view the entire rule.

   f. Goal of Privacy Rule
      i. A major goal of the Privacy Rule is to assure that individuals' health information is properly protected while allowing the flow of health information needed to provide and promote high-quality health care.
      ii. HIPAA rule is designed to be flexible and comprehensive to cover the variety of uses and disclosures that need to be addressed.

   g. Who is covered by the Privacy Rule
      i. The Privacy Rule, as well as all the Administrative Simplification rules, applies to health plans, healthcare clearinghouses, and any healthcare provider who transmits health information in electronic form in connection with transactions for which the Secretary of DHHS has adopted standards under HIPAA.
      ii. Health plans: individual and group plans that provide or pay the cost of medical care are covered entities.
         1. Health plans include health, dental, vision, and prescription drug insurers, health maintenance organizations (HMOs), Medicare, Medicaid, Medicare+Choice and Medicare supplement insurers, and long-term care insurers (excluding nursing home fixed-indemnity policies).
         2. Health plans also include employer-sponsored group health plans, government and church-sponsored health plans, and multi-employer health plans.
         3. Exceptions: a group health plan with fewer than 50 participants that is administered solely by the employer that established and maintains the plan is not a covered entity.
      iii. Healthcare providers: every healthcare provider, regardless of size, who electronically transmits health information in connection with certain transactions, is a covered entity.
      iv. Healthcare clearinghouses: entities that process nonstandard information they receive from another entity into a standard, including billing services, repricing companies, community health management information systems, and value-added networks and switches if these entities perform clearinghouse functions.

v. Business associate defined: in general, a business associate is a person or organization, other than a member of a covered entity's workforce, that performs certain functions or activities on behalf of, or provides certain services to, a covered entity that involve the use or disclosure of individually identifiable health information.

    1. Persons or organizations are not considered business associates if their functions or services do not involve the use or disclosure of protected health information, and where any access to protected health information by such persons would be incidental, if at all.

    2. A covered entity can be the business associate of another covered entity.

h. Which information is protected

    i. Protected health information (PHI): the Privacy Rule protects all "individually identifiable health information" held or transmitted by a covered entity or its business associate, in any form or media, whether electronic, paper, or oral.

    ii. "Individually identifiable health information" is information, including demographic data, that relates to:

        1. The individual's past, present, or future physical or mental health or condition

        2. The provision of health care to the individual

        3. The past, present, or future payment for the provision of health care to the individual, and that identifies the individual or for which there is a reasonable basis to believe it can be used to identify the individual

    iii. Individually identifiable health information includes many common identifiers (e.g., name, address, birth date, Social Security number).

    iv. The Privacy Rule excludes from protected health information employment records that a covered entity maintains in its capacity as an employer and education and certain other records subject to, or defined in, the Family Educational Rights and Privacy Act, 20 U.S.C. §1232g.

    v. De-identified health information. There are no restrictions on the use or disclosure of de-identified health information.

        1. De-identified health information neither identifies nor provides a reasonable basis to identify an individual.

        2. There are two ways to de-identify information:

            a. A formal determination by a qualified statistician

            b. Removal of specified identifiers of the individual and of the individual's relatives, household members, and employers is required, and is adequate only if the covered entity has no actual knowledge that the remaining information could be used to identify the individual.

7. Health Insurance Portability and Accountability Act (HIPAA) of 1996

  a. Goals of HIPAA (see Figure 3-1)

    i. Enacted to improve the portability and continuity of health insurance coverage in the group and individual markets, to combat waste, fraud, and abuse in health insurance and healthcare delivery, to promote the use of medical savings accounts, to improve access to long-term care services and coverage, to simplify the administration of health insurance, and for other purposes

    ii. Addresses issues related to the portability of health insurance after leaving employment

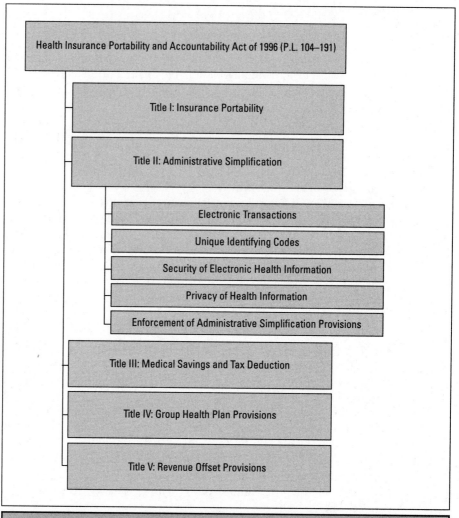

Figure 3-1   Five Portions of HIPAA

    iii. Created the Healthcare Integrity and Protection Data Bank (HIPDB), whose mission is to inform federal agencies about potential quality problems with clinicians, suppliers, and providers of healthcare services

    iv. Five portions of HIPAA

        1. Insurance portability

        2. Administrative simplification, including

            a. Standardization of electronic formats for transmission of 11 specific electronic transactions

            b. Unique identifying codes for healthcare providers, health plans, employers, and individuals

            c. Security of electronic health information

            d. Privacy of individually identifiable health information (Privacy Rule)

            e. Enforcement of the administrative simplification provisions

        3. Medical savings and tax deductions

        4. Group health plan provision

        5. Revenue offset provisions

b. Administration Simplifications
  i. CMS is responsible for implementing various provisions of HIPAA.
  ii. Requires DHHS (which manages CMS) to improve the Medicare program under Title XVIII of the Social Security Act (SSA), the Medicaid program under Title XIX of the SSA, and the efficiency and effectiveness of the healthcare system by encouraging the development of a health information system through the establishment of standards and requirements for the electronic transmission of certain health information
c. Privacy Rule (2002)
  i. HIPAA is first federal law that governs privacy of health information nationwide.
  ii. Prior to HIPAA Privacy Rule, there were no federal statutes or regulations of general application protecting the confidentiality of medical or personal information.
  iii. Ensures the protection of medical information shared with a covered entity, which are
    1. Healthcare providers
    2. Health plans
    3. Healthcare clearinghouses
  iv. Privacy Rule restricts use and disclosure of personal health information and gives patients greater access to and protection of their medical records.
  v. Protects a patient's fundamental right to privacy and confidentiality; patients can expect
    1. Privacy regarding their privileged communication
    2. Security standards to ensure facilities, equipment, and patient information are safe from damage, loss, tampering, theft, or unauthorized access
  vi. Protected health information (PHI)
    1. Personal health information given to a covered entity
    2. Includes any information that is oral or is recorded on paper or electronically about a person's physical or mental health, services rendered, or payment for those services, and that includes personal information connecting the patient to the record
    3. Examples of PHI
      a. Patient's name or address
      b. Social Security or other identification numbers
      c. Physician's personal notes
      d. Billing information
    4. Authorization is required for the disclosure of PHI for purposes other than
      a. Treatment
        i. Covered entities may communicate freely with patients about treatment options and health-related information
      b. Payment
      c. Healthcare operations
    5. Authorization is required to use PHI for
      a. Use or disclosure of psychotherapy notes
      b. Research purposes, unless a documented waiver is obtained from the institutional review board or privacy board
      c. Use and disclosure to third parties for marketing activities such as promoting services or selling lists of patients

     vii. The HIPAA Privacy Rule does not include medical record retention requirements.

        1. State laws generally govern how long medical records are to be retained.

        2. The HIPAA Privacy Rule requires that covered entities apply appropriate administrative, technical, and physical safeguards to protect the privacy of medical records and other PHI for whatever period such information is maintained by a covered entity, including through disposal. See 45 CFR 164.530(c).

d. Security

     i. Under the Security Rule, covered entities, regardless of their size, are required, under § 164.312(a)(2)(i), to "assign a unique name and/or number for identifying and tracking user identity."

        1. A "user" is defined in § 164.304 as a "person or entity with authorized access."

        2. Accordingly, the Security Rule requires covered entities to assign a unique name and/or number to each employee or workforce member who uses a system that maintains electronic protected health information (e-PHI), so that system access and activity can be identified and tracked by user.

        3. This pertains to workforce members within small or large healthcare provider offices, health plans, group health plans, and healthcare clearinghouses.

     ii. Encryption is a method of converting an original message of regular text into encoded text.

        1. The text is encrypted by means of an algorithm (type of formula).

        2. If information is encrypted, there is a low probability that anyone other than the receiving party who has the key to the code or access to another confidential process would be able to decrypt (translate) the text and convert it into plain, comprehensible text.

     iii. If covered entities allow employees to telecommute or work out of home-based offices and have access to e-PHI, they must implement appropriate safeguards to protect the organization's data.

        1. The automatic logoff implementation specification must be implemented if, after an assessment, the entity determines that the specification is a reasonable and appropriate safeguard in its environment.

     iv. Release of information form must include

        1. A description of the information to be used or disclosed, written in clear language

        2. Purpose of disclosure

        3. Who will receive the information

        4. Expiration date

        5. Revocation

        6. Statement that information released pursuant to authorization may be subject to redisclosure by the recipient and no longer protected

        7. Signature of patient or legal representative

            a. If legal representative, then a description of his or her authority to act must be included on authorization form

b. Consenting parties

   i. Minor: generally defined as an individual who is under the age of majority.

   1. Minors are unable to consent to their own care except in case of emancipated minor, medical emergencies, and certain identified health conditions.

   2. Minors usually exercise their rights through a parent or other legal guardian.

   ii. Emancipated minor: a minor who has been awarded the status of adult due to situational changes such as marriage, pregnancy and other qualified situations

   iii. Age of majority: the legal recognition that an individual is considered responsible for, and has control over, his or actions.

   1. The actions include consenting for health care, buying alcohol, getting married, enlisting in the armed forces, buying a house, and other actions.

   2. Legal age is 18 in most states.

   3. Age in Nebraska is 19, Mississippi is 21, and Nevada based age of majority upon graduating from high school.

   iv. Competent adult: an individual who is mentally capable and is above the age of majority.

   v. Incompetent adult: an individual who is no longer capable of controlling his or her action due to injury, illness, disability.

   1. Exercises his or her rights through an appointed agent or guardian

8. Disclosed medical record may contain sensitive information (e.g., HIV/AIDS, drug/alcohol use, mental illness)

v. PHI can be used or disclosed without authorization but with patient agreement to

1. Maintain a facility's patient directory

2. Inform family members or other identified persons involved in the patient's care or notify them on patient location, condition, or death

3. Inform appropriate agencies during disaster relief efforts

4. Public health activities related to disease prevention or control

5. Report victims of abuse, neglect, or domestic violence

6. Health oversight activities such as audits, legal investigations, licensure, or for certain law enforcement purposes or government functions

7. Coroners, medical examiners, funeral directors, or tissue/organ donations

8. Avert a serious threat to health and safety

9. In a bioterrorism threat or other public health emergency, HIPAA permits a covered entity to disclose PHI, without the patient's authorization, to public officials responding to the treat.

   a. The Privacy Rule recognizes that various agencies and public officials will need protected health information to deal effectively with a bioterrorism threat or emergency.

    b. To facilitate the communications that are essential to a quick and effective response to such events, the Privacy Rule permits a covered entity to disclose needed information to public officials in a variety of ways.

  10. Revocation of authorization

    a. The revocation must be in writing, and is not effective until the covered entity receives the written revocation.

    b. A written revocation is not effective with respect to actions a covered entity took in reliance on a valid authorization, or where the authorization was obtained as a condition of obtaining insurance coverage and other law provides the insurer with the right to contest a claim under the policy or the policy itself

vi. Minimum necessary disclosure of PHI

  1. Covered entities must develop policies and practices to make sure the least amount of health information is shared.

  2. Employees must identify who regularly accesses PHI along with the types of PHI needed and the conditions for access.

  3. Does not apply to use or disclosure of medical records for treatment

vii. Notice of privacy practices

  1. Patients have the right to adequate notice concerning the use or disclosure of their PHI on the first date of service delivery or as soon as possible after an emergency. New notices must be issued when the facility's privacy practices change.

  2. Notice of privacy practices must

    a. Contain patient's rights and covered entities' legal duties

    b. Be made available to patients in print

    c. Be displayed at the site of service and posted on a website whenever possible

  3. Once a patient has received notice of his or her rights, covered entities must make an effort to get written acknowledgment of receipt of notice of privacy practices from the patient, or document reasons why it was not obtained, and copies must be kept of all notices and acknowledgments.

viii. Privacy Rule grants patient rights over their PHI to include

  1. Receive notice of privacy practices at time of first delivery of service

  2. Request restricted use and disclosure, although the covered entity is not required to agree

  3. Have PHI communicated to them by alternate means and at alternate locations to protect confidentiality

  4. Inspect and amend PHI, and obtain copies, with some exceptions

  5. Request a history of disclosures for 6 years prior to the request

  6. Exceptions (disclosures for which an accounting is not required by covered entity) include disclosures

    a. Made for treatment, payment, healthcare operations, or with prior authorization

    b. To individuals of the PHI about themselves

    c. For use in the facility's directory or to persons involved in the individual's care or other notification purposes

    d. To meet national security or intelligence requirements

      e. To correctional institutions or law enforcement officials

      f. That occurred before the compliance date for the covered entity

    7. Contact designated persons regarding any privacy concern or breach of privacy within the facility or at DHHS

ix. Rights of minors

    1. Parents have the right to access and control the PHI of their minor children, except when state law overrides parental control such as

      a. HIV testing of minors without parental permission

      b. Cases of abuse

      c. When parents have agreed to give up control over their minor child

x. Responsibility of healthcare institution

    1. Allow patients to see and copy their PHI

    2. Designate a full- or part-time privacy official responsible for implementing the programs

    3. Designate a contact person or office responsible for receiving complaints

    4. Develop a Notice of Privacy Practices document

    5. Develop policies and safeguards to protect PHI and limit incidental use or disclosure

    6. Institute employee training programs so everyone knows about the privacy policies and procedures for safeguarding PHI

    7. Institute a complaint process, and file and resolve formal complaints

    8. Make sure contracts with business associates comply with the Privacy Rule

xi. HIPAA rules regarding psychotherapy notes

    1. Requires an authorization specifically allowing release of psychotherapy notes

    2. Defines psychotherapy notes as those taken by a mental health professional during a counseling session and kept separate from the rest of the medical record.

    3. Two key issues when determining which psychotherapy documentation is protected

      a. Type of documentation

      b. Where the records are kept

    4. Not all documentation by a mental health professional requires special protection—only the notes from a therapy session.

    5. Other documentation is handled in a similar manner to the rest of the medical record and includes prescriptions, medication monitoring, session start and stop times, modality and frequency of treatments, clinical test results, and summary items.

    6. When psychotherapy notes are maintained in another or with another record (e.g., medical record), they lose their special confidentiality protection

xii. Violation of Privacy Rule (civil and criminal penalties)

    1. Civil penalty of $100 up to a maximum of $25,000 per year for each standard violated

    2. Criminal penalty for knowingly disclosing PHI is up to $50,000 and 1 year in prison for obtaining or disclosing protected health information, up to $100,000 and up to 5 years in prison for obtaining or disclosing PHI under false pretenses, and up to

$250,000 and up to 10 years in prison for obtaining or disclosing PHI with the intent to sell, transfer, or use it for commercial advantage, personal gain, or malicious harm

8. Health Record Documentation

   a. The record can serve and protect only when caregivers make a personal commitment to good medical record documentation.

   b. The record should be complete, accurate, and legible to:

      i. Keep the healthcare team informed about patient progress

      ii. Enable caregivers to coordinate their efforts properly

      iii. Supply clinicians with data to evaluate and improve care

      iv. Ensure that timely decisions are made and communicated throughout the continuum of care

      v. Validate compliance with hundreds of requirements, including TJC accreditation standards and regulations established by federal, state, and local agencies

      vi. Furnish an objective basis for reimbursement by insurers

      vii. Provide a legal record of care rendered, thus defending against a malpractice claim

      viii. Furnish data to conduct research and clinical trials

   c. Patient record is used to:

      i. Establish duty

      ii. Determine if standards of care were met

      iii. Evaluate damages

      iv. Fix cause

   d. Departures from appropriate recordkeeping are used by the plaintiff's attorney to create the impression that care itself was negligent. These include:

      i. Alterations of entries without proper identification

      ii. Feuding among caregivers

      iii. Illegibility of written notes and orders

      iv. Late entries

      v. Missing data or test results

      vi. Omission of information

      vii. Time gaps

   e. Documentation Guidelines for Entries

      i. Entries should be complete, accurate, legible, timed, and signed by the author, using full name and credentials.

      ii. Entries should be made on or about the time of treatment.

      iii. Made on approved forms and filed by order of the chart

      iv. Made in the appropriate sequence in the record, avoiding gaps with previous entries and lapses in time

      v. Late entries should be clearly marked as such.

      vi. Entries by students, interns, and residents should be countersigned.

      vii. Only approved abbreviations and terminology should be used.

      viii. Corrections, addenda, and changes to entries should be done according to policy.

      ix. Adverse episodes and subsequent interventions should be written objectively.

9. Health Records in Court

   a. Definitions Relevant to Court Procedure

      i. Appeal: the process by which a decision of a lower court is brought for review to a court of higher jurisdiction, typically known as an appellate court

    ii. Court order: a written command or direction ordered by a court or judge

   iii. Cross examination: questioning of a witness by the opposing attorney

   iv. Defendant: the party against whom a complaint is brought

    v. Direct examination: initial questioning of a witness by the attorney who has requested the witness to testify

   vi. Jurisdiction: the power of authority which each court has to hear cases; a court's jurisdiction is determined by the subject matter of the case, the persons in the case, and by geographical area

  vii. Legal precedent: refers to a previous case decision that serves as an authority in identical or similar cases

 viii. Memorandum of law: a document prepared by an attorney, prior to trial, which outlines the case and notes past decisions that support the client's position; usually submitted to the court for reference

   ix. Motions: requests to the court made by plaintiff's or defendant's attorney

    x. Plaintiff: the party who brings a complaint against another

   xi. Pleadings: statements of complaint by plaintiff, answer from defendant, and possibly a counterclaim by defendant

  xii. Pretrial discovery: procedures whereby the attorneys for opposing sides in a case find out what information the opposing side possesses

 xiii. Re-cross examination: second series of questions directed to a witness by the opposing attorney; takes place following redirect examination

 xiv. Redirect examination: second series of questions directed to a witness by the attorney who had originally requested the witness to testify

  xv. Res gestae: "things done," which means that hearsay statements made during an incident are admissible as evidence

 xvi. Res ipsa loquitur: "The thing speaks for itself," which means that something is self-evident (e.g., erroneous surgical removal of healthy limb while leaving unhealthy limb)

 xvii. Res judicata: "The thing is decided," which means the final judgment of a competent court is conclusive

xviii. Respondeat superior: "Let the master answer," which means that an employer is responsible for the legal consequences of an employee's actions

 xix. Stare decisis: the doctrine that states that court decisions should be regarded as precedents for guidance in subsequent cases involving the same legal issues

  xx. Summation: statement made by an attorney at the closing of a trial, summarizing the client's case

 xxi. Summons: a court order notifying the defendant of a civil suit, and the date and place the defendant must appear to answer the complaint

 xxii. Tort: An injury of wrong committed against an individual or his or her property.

    1. Types of torts (intentional and unintentional)

      a. Malpractice

      b. Negligence

           c. Intentional torts (assault and battery)

           d. False imprisonment

           e. Defamation: oral (slander), written (libel)

           f. Invasion of privacy

           g. Fraud/intentional misrepresentation

           h. Inflicting of emotional or mental distress

      xxiii. Venue: the particular geographical area in which an action or prosecution may be brought to trial

      xxiv. Voir dire: a preliminary examination to determine the competency of a witness or juror

  b. Evidence

      i. Information that may be considered in the determination of a controversy taking place in a court of law

      ii. The means, sanctioned by law, of ascertaining the truth respecting a question of fact in a judicial proceeding

      iii. Best-evidence rule

         1. Original documents must be produced in a legal proceeding.

         2. Microfilm or other media reproductions are acceptable if the original record has been destroyed.

      iv. Types of evidence

         1. Direct: obtained from testimony of witnesses who possess actual knowledge of the facts of the case

           a. Whistleblower: raises concerns to external agency

         2. Indirect or circumstantial: facts that furnish reasonable ground for inferring the existence of some other connected facts

         3. Real or demonstrative: objects, documents, or anything that can be seen

         4. Hearsay

           a. Evidence based on someone else's knowledge and observations, not on that of the witness

           b. Health records are hearsay evidence.

           c. Even though health records are hearsay, they may be entered into court as evidence in exception to hearsay rules because they are business records, which are admissible into court as evidence.

      v. Admissibility

         1. Evidence that may be properly introduced in a legal proceeding

         2. The determination as to admissibility is based on legal rules of evidence and is made by the trial judge or a screening panel.

         3. For medical records to be admissible, they must meet the following criteria:

           a. Applicable to the business record rule

           b. The court must be confident that the information contained in the record is complete, accurate, and timely.

           c. The court must accept that the information was recorded as the result of treatment, not in anticipation of a legal proceeding.

         4. Discoverability

           a. Quality improvement, peer review, and incident reports are not discoverable in some states.

         5. Business record rule

           a. Records made and kept in the regular course of business may be entered into court as evidence.

           b. Medical records are business records.

6. Testifying about admissibility

  a. Typically, the health record custodian is called upon to authenticate records by providing testimony about the process or system that produced the records.

   i. An organization's recordkeeping program should consist of policies, procedures, and methods that support the creation and maintenance of reliable, accurate records.

   ii. If so, the records will be admissible into evidence.

  b. Electronic and imaged health records

   i. Case law and the Federal Rules of Evidence provide support to allow the output of an EHR system to be admissible in court.

   ii. "If data are stored in a computer or similar device, any printout or other output readable by sight, shown to reflect the data accurately, is an original."

vi. Legal proceedings

  1. Filing a civil suit

   a. Civil action is known by names of plaintiff and defendant, with plaintiff name listed first.

   b. Plaintiff's attorney pays fee and files a complaint or petition with clerk of the proper court to formally begin legal proceeding.

   c. Complaint states the facts on which the action is based, damages alleged, and the judgment or relief being sought.

  2. Civil pretrial procedure (see Table 3-6)

   a. Complaint

    i. Made by plaintiff

     1. Initial pleading in a lawsuit

     2. Plaintiff alleges a cause of action.

     3. Plaintiff request for wrong to be remedied by the court

   b. Answers to complaint by defendant

   c. Motions requesting court to make a variety of rulings

   d. Pretrial discovery

    i. Facilitates out-of-court settlements

    ii. Disclosure of facts and documents by one party at the request of the other

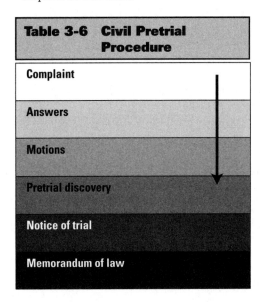

Table 3-6 Civil Pretrial Procedure

Complaint

Answers

Motions

Pretrial discovery

Notice of trial

Memorandum of law

           iii. Obtained through depositions and interrogatories that are used to prepare the case for trial

              1. Deposition

                  a. Sworn statement of fact

                  b. Made outside of court

                  c. May be admitted as evidence in court

              2. Interrogatories

                  a. Written questions presented to a party or witness

                  b. Designed to gather information to assist parties prepare for trial

        e. Notice of trial: a trial date is set.

        f. Memorandum of law: a case description may be written by attorneys for both sides.

      3. Civil trial process

        a. Jury selection

        b. Opening statements by plaintiff's and defendant's attorneys

        c. Presentation of the plaintiff's case

        d. Presentation of defendant's case

        e. Plaintiff's rebuttal

        f. Answer to plaintiff's rebuttal

        g. Closing arguments

        h. Instructions to jury by judge

        i. Verdict read

        j. Judgment and execution for remedy or damages to be assessed

        k. Appeal by disappointed party if judge refuses to grant a post-trial motion for a new trial

    c. Health Information Practitioner's Proper Conduct as a Witness

      i. Review record and deposition prior to testimony

      ii. Make a copy of the record and paginate prior to taking to court

      iii. Take original record and copy to court

      iv. Request to submit copy of record in lieu of original into court as evidence

      v. Witness may refer to health record to refresh recollection.

      vi. Dress conservatively

      vii. Be polite, sincere, courteous

      viii. Organize thoughts

      ix. Use simple and succinct terminology

      x. Pay attention to objections

      xi. Do not answer questions if not qualified to answer

      xii. Return original record to health care facility for proper storage

10. Negligence and Malpractice

  a. Principles of Liability

    i. Before an individual can bring a lawsuit to establish some form of liability (malpractice, negligence) against a healthcare provider, the individual must have established a relationship with that provider.

      1. Types of relationships

        a. Physician/patient

        b. Hospital/patient

        c. Hospital/physician

  b. Negligence

    i. Results when a person does not act the way a reasonably prudent person would act under the same circumstances

ii. Results from a person committing an act, or failure to act as a reasonably prudent person would act in the given circumstance

iii. When negligence results in patient injury, malpractice can be said to have occurred.

iv. Careless conduct that is outside the generally accepted standard of care

    1. Standard of care

        a. What an individual is expected to do or not do in a given situation

        b. Established by professional associations, statute or regulation, or by practice

        c. Considered to represent expected behavior unless a court finds differently

v. Negligence categorized

    1. Malfeasance: execution of an unlawful or improper act

    2. Misfeasance: improper performance of an act

    3. Malpractice

        a. Negligence or carelessness of a professional person such as a physician

        b. Patient injury or death due to negligence caused by a professional person such as a nurse, pharmacist, or physician

    4. Criminal negligence: reckless disregard for the safety or another; the willful indifference to an injury that could follow an act

vi. Four components must be present for plaintiff to recover damages caused by negligence.

    1. Duty: a treatment or service owed to a patient (e.g., duty to give the right medication to the right patient)

    2. Breach: failure to perform to the applicable standard of care (e.g., nurse gave patient wrong medication)

    3. Cause: breach of duty, causing the resulting injury (e.g., patient suffered hallucinations, resulting in her getting out of bed without help and falling)

    4. Damage: patient injured (e.g., when she fell, she broke her hip)

        a. Three types

            i. Nominal: awarded for the vindication of a right in which minimal injury can be proved

            ii. Actual: compensatory damages are awarded to "make the plaintiff whole."

            iii. Punitive: exemplary damages are awarded above and beyond actual damages when there is proof of outrageous, malicious, or intentional conduct.

Duty of Care + Breach of Duty of Care + Causation + Damages = ***Negligence***

---

vii. Statute of limitations: legislatively imposed time constraints that restrict the period of time after the occurrence of an injury during which a legal action must be commenced

viii. Tort: an action brought when party believes that another party caused harm through wrongful conduct and seeks compensation for that harm

   1. Three categories of tort liability
      a. Negligent
         i. When a person does not act the way a reasonably prudent person would act under the same circumstance
         ii. Care rendered is outside the generally accepted standard of care.
      b. Intentional
         i. The person committed an act knowing that harm would likely occur.
         ii. Assault and battery
            1. The individual does not give permission or authority for an act.
            2. Assault occurs when an individual is placed in reasonable anticipation of being touched in a way that is insulting, provoking, or will cause the individual physical harm.
            3. Battery consists of physical contact involving injury or offense.
         iii. Defamation of character
            1. A communication about someone to another person that tends to injure the former person's reputation
            2. Slander: spoken character defamation
            3. Libel: written character defamation
         iv. False imprisonment: a healthcare provider's effort to prevent a patient from leaving a hospital when the patient insists on leaving (does not include mental illness or persons with contagious diseases)
         v. Fraud: a willful and intended misrepresentation that could cause harm or loss to a person or property
         vi. Invasion of privacy: negligent disregard for patient right of privacy
         vii. Willful infliction of mental distress: includes mental suffering resulting from such things as despair, shame, grief, and public humiliation
      c. Liability without fault: property liability, wherein a manufacturer, seller, or supplier of equipment or supplies is liable to one with whom there is no contractual relationship and who suffers harm from the equipment or supplies
   ix. Assumption of risk
      1. A method used to limit liability either completely or in part
      2. A plaintiff who voluntarily exposes himself to a known and appreciated danger may not recover damages caused by incurring that risk.
   x. Breach of contract: involves express contracts and the failure to perform these contracts
   xi. Defamation
      1. Wrongful injuring of another person's reputation
      2. May expose the person to ridicule, contempt, or hatred and tends to diminish the esteem, respect, goodwill, or confidence in which the person is held
   xii. Failure to warn: also referred to as failure to protect; a negligence theory that applies to a psychiatrist's failure to take steps to protect an innocent third party from a dangerous patient

xiii. Good Samaritan statutes
  1. These statutes protect physicians and other rescuers from civil liability as a result of their acts or omissions in rendering emergency care.
  2. If, however, the rescuer acts in a willful, wanton, or reckless manner in providing emergency treatment, he or she cannot avail himself of the Good Samaritan statute as a defense.
xiv. Invasion of privacy: the dissemination of information about another person's private, personal matters
xv. Libel: defamation expressed in writing, pictures, or signs
xvi. Medical abandonment: unilateral severing, by the physician, of the physician–patient relationship without giving the patient reasonable notice, at a time when there is a necessity for continuing care
xvii. Repondeat superior
  1. "Let the superior respond" reflects the idea that the superior is responsible for the actions of the superior's employee or agent.
  2. Also referred to as vicarious liability
  3. Healthcare organization, such as hospital, is responsible for the negligent acts of its employees committed within the course and scope of their employment.
xviii. Res ipsa loquitur: "the thing speaks for itself"
  1. Injury would not ordinarily occur without someone's negligence.
  2. The medical professional had exclusive control and management over the instrument or cause of the accident.
  3. The injury could not have occurred as a result of any action by the patient.
xix. Slander: defamation expressed orally or with transitory gestures
xx. Statute of limitation: a law that sets forth a fixed time period in which a lawsuit must be brought

11. Computer-Based Health Records
  a. Computer-Based Records as Evidence
    i. Courts have developed standards for establishing the trustworthiness of computerized records.
  b. Security
    i. Procedures must be in place to protect information from sabotage, hackers, and viruses.
    ii. Use passwords and other authorization devices that are changed at regular intervals
    iii. Access control that can limit who is able to view, enter, edit data, or print various sections of the record
    iv. Controls that prevent tampering with, changing, or editing of existing entries
    v. Audit trails that can locate sources of attempts at unauthorized access
    vi. Limitations on printouts of record
    vii. Automatic log-off protocols when terminal is unused for a period of time
    viii. Limited access to patient records by employees on a need-to-know basis
    ix. Encryption codes that prevent stored or transmitted data from being intercepted by unauthorized individuals

12. Ethical Issues for Health Information Practitioners
   a. Ethics
      i. A process of reasoned discourse among decision makers
      ii. Decision makers must carefully consider the shared and competing values and ethical principles that are important to the decision to be made.
   b. Ethical decision making requires everyone to consider the perspectives of others.
   c. Ethical decision making demonstrates respect for others and recognizes the importance of doing good, respecting others, not harming others, and treating people fairly.
   d. Core Ethical Responsibilities of Health Information Practitioner
      i. Maintain an accurate and timely patient database
      ii. Be honest and respectful toward patients, peers, and public
      iii. Protect the privacy of all patients
      iv. Demonstrate compassion to patients and peers
      v. Design forms to ensure that patients understand what they are signing
      vi. Coding for research and reimbursement, and coding accurately, to avoid fraud and abuse violations
      vii. Designing and implementing the health information system to ensure completeness, accuracy, and timeliness of documentation
      viii. Releasing patient information with special attention to, and protections assigned for, genetic, adoption, drug and alcohol treatment, sexual and behavioral issues
      ix. Complying with regulations and standards from many sources, including the government, accreditation and licensure organizations, and the healthcare facility
      x. Reporting quality review outcomes honestly and accurately
      xi. Ensuring that research and decisions supporting activities are accurate and reliable
      xii. Releasing accurate information for public health purposes for patients with communicable diseases
      xiii. Supporting managers, by providing accurate reliable information about patients, providers, and patterns of care
      xiv. Ensuring that the patient record (paper-based and electronic formats) meets the standards of privacy and security
      xv. Participating in activities to ensure that the needs of the healthcare facility are met and not jeopardized
      xvi. Serve as an advocate for the patient, healthcare team, and community
      xvii. Work in the emerging e-health system to ensure that high-quality information is provided to patients and that patient privacy is protected
      xviii. Comply with all laws, regulations, and policies that govern health information management
      xix. Ensure the privacy, confidentiality, and security of patient information and report violators to the proper authorities
      xx. Uphold the AHIMA codes of ethical standards
   e. Obligations to Employer
      i. Demonstrate loyalty to the employer
      ii. Protect committee deliberations
      iii. Comply with all laws, regulations, and policies that govern the health information system
      iv. Recognize both authority and the power associated with the job responsibility

f. Obligations to Public

> **i.** Advocate change when patterns or system problems are not in the best interests of the patients
>
> **ii.** Refuse to participate in or conceal unethical practices
>
> **iii.** Report violations of practice standards to the proper authorities

13. Freedom of Information Act

a. Requires that records pertaining to the executive branch of the federal government be available to the public except for matters that fall within exempted areas

b. Exempted matter is considered to be unwarranted invasion of privacy

c. To meet the test of being an "unwarranted invasion of privacy," the following conditions must exist:

> **i.** The information must be contained in a medical, personnel, or a similar file.
>
> **ii.** Disclosure of the information must constitute an invasion of privacy.
>
> **iii.** The severity of such invasion must outweigh the public interest in disclosure.

14. Minimum Necessary Standard

a. Just because a person works in a healthcare facility, he or she does not have a blanket access to all patient information.

b. Only the minimum amount of information necessary to fulfill the purpose of the request should be shared with internal users and external requestors.

c. The minimum necessary standard does not apply in the following situations:

> **i.** Use or disclosure for treatment purpose
>
> **ii.** When patient has specifically authorized the release of more information
>
> **iii.** Disclosure pursuant to applicable law

15. Patient Protection and Affordable Care Act (PPACA)

a. PPACA, commonly called Obamacare or Affordable Care Act (ACA), is U.S. federal legislation signed into law by President Barack Obama on March 23, 2010. Together with the Health Care and Education Reconciliation Act, it represents the most significant government expansion and regulatory overhaul of the U.S. health system since the passage of Medicare and Medicaid in 1965.

b. ACA is aimed at increasing the affordability and rate of health insurance coverage for Americans and reducing the overall costs of health care (for individuals and the government). It provides a number of mechanisms—including mandates, subsidies, and tax credits—to employers and individuals to increase the coverage rate and health insurance affordability.

c. ACA requires insurance companies to cover all applicants within new minimum standards, and offer the same rate regardless of preexisting condition or sex. Additionally, these reforms are designed to improve healthcare outcomes and streamline the delivery of health care.

d. Congressional Budget Office projects that ACA will lower both future deficit and Medicare spending.

16. Amendment to HIPAA Privacy, Security, Breach Notification, and Enforcement Rules

a. On January 17, 2013, DHHS's Office for Civil Rights (OCR) issued the long-anticipated final omnibus amendments ("2013 Amendments") to the Privacy, Security, Breach Notification and Enforcement Rules

("HIPAA Rules"), as directed pursuant to the Health Information Technology for Economic and Clinical Health (HITECH) Act, enacted as part of the American Recovery and Reinvestment Act of 2009.

b. The 2013 Amendments were effective as of March 26, 2013, and compliance with applicable requirements generally must have been made within 180 days, by September 23, 2013 (with important exceptions for existing business associate arrangements).

c. Significant penalties apply for noncompliance.

Houston Honorary Hospital
Authorization for Release of Information

Name: _____   Medical Record #: _____

Address: _____   Phone: _____

Social Security #: _____   Date of Birth: _____

I authorize Houston Honorary Hospital to release my medical record information to the following person, facility, or agency:

Name: _____   Attention: _____   Phone: _____

Street: _____   City/Town: _____   State: ____   Zip: _____

The person filling out this form must provide details as to date(s) of requested information. Please note that a request for release of psychotherapy notes cannot be combined with any other type of request. Specify information to be released, e.g., Entire Record, Admission(s) Documentation, Discharge Summary(ies), Transfer Summary(ies), Evaluations, Assessments and Tests, Consultation(s) including names of consultant(s), Treatment Plan(s), ISP(s) & PSTP(s), Physical Exam & Lab Reports, Progress Note(s):

_____

_____

_____

_____

_____

_____

_____

Purpose for the authorization:
❑ **The subject of the information or Personal Representative initiated the authorization (specific purpose not required)**
or
❑ **Continuity of care**   ❑ **Facilitate billing**
❑ **Referral**   ❑ **Obtain insurance, financial or other benefits**
❑ **Other purpose (please specify):** _____

Figure 3-2   Sample Release of Information Form

Houston Honorary Hospital
Authorization for Release of Information (*continued*)

I understand that I have a right to revoke this authorization at any time. If I revoke this authorization, I must do so in writing and present it to the person at Houston Honorary Hospital. I understand that the revocation will not apply to information that has already been released pursuant to this authorization. This authorization will expire in 12 months unless otherwise specified (specify a date, time period or an event): _____
_____. I understand that once the above information is disclosed it may be redisclosed and no longer protected by federal or state privacy laws or regulations. I understand that authorizing the use or disclosure of the information identified above is voluntary. I need not sign this form to receive treatment or services from Houston Honorary Hospital. However, lack of ability to share or obtain information may prevent Houston Honorary Hospital, and/or other person, facility, or agency, from providing appropriate and necessary care.

_____   _____

Your signature or Personal Representative's signature   Date

_____

Print name of signer

THE FOLLOWING INFORMATION IS NEEDED IF SIGNED BY A PERSONAL REPRESENTATIVE

Type of authority (e.g., court appointed, custodial parent)

_____

Specially Authorized Releases of Information (please initial all that apply)

____ To the extent that my medical record contains information concerning alcohol or drug treatment that is protected by Federal Regulation 42 CFR, Part 2, I specifically authorize release of such information.

____ To the extent that my medical record contains information concerning HIV antibody and antigen testing that is protected by MGL c.111 §70F, or an HIV/AIDS diagnosis or treatment, I specifically authorize disclosure of such information.

_____
Your signature or Personal Representative's signature   Date

INSTRUCTIONS:
1. This form must be completed in full to be considered valid.
2. Distribution of copies: original to appropriate medical record; copy to individual or Personal Representative.

Houston Honorary Hospital Form Authorization for Release of Information
Page 2 of 2
HIPAA-F-7 (4/22/xx)

Figure 3-2   Sample Release of Information Form (*continued*)

§   THE STATE OF TEXAS   §   IN THE MATTER OF A

§   COUNTY OF COWBOYS   §   GRAND INVESTIGATION

TO THE SHERIFF OR ANY OTHER PEACE OFFICER

GREETINGS

WHEREAS the grand jury of Cowboys County is inquiring into certain offenses liable to indictment; and

WHEREAS Article 20.10 of the Texas Code of Criminal procedure provides that the attorney representing the state, in term time or in vacation may issue a summons or an attachment for any witness in the county, which summons or attachment may require the said witness to appear before the grand jury at a time fixed, or forthwith, without stating the matter under investigation; and

WHEREAS any Texas peace officer receiving this process shall execute the same forthwith by reading the same in the hearing of the said witness or by delivering a copy of this showing the time and manner of service, if served, and if not served, said officer shall show in his return the cause of his failure to serve it; and if the witness could not be found, he shall state the diligence he has used to find him, and what information he has as to the whereabouts of the witness;

NOW THEREFORE YOU ARE HEREBY COMMANDED to forthwith summon, the custodian of records, John Doe, Houston Honorary Hospital to appear before the 401st Judicial District Court Grand Jury for <u>August Term</u>, 20xx at 403 Tyson Street, 1st floor, Cowboy, Texas at 10 am on <u>September 20, 20xx</u>.

FURTHER, you are directed that the said witness shall bring with him the following writing or other thing desired as evidence in accordance with Article 24.02 of the Texas Code of Criminal procedure, and more specifically described as follows:

PRODUCE TRUE AND CORRECT COPIES OF MEDICAL RECORD ON JOHN DOE; DATE OF BIRTH December 25, 20xx.

Figure 3-3   Sample Subpoena Duces Tecum

§ **IN THE DISTRICT COURT OF**

§

§ **COWBOYS COUNTY, TEXAS**

§

§ **1051st JUDICIAL DISTRICT**

DIRECT QUESTIONS TO BE PROPOUNDED TO THE WITNESS, CUSTODIAN OF MEDICAL RECORDS FOR **Houston Honorary Hospital**

1. Please state your name and occupation.

2. Have you been served with a subpoena duces tecum for the production of medical records for John Doe?

3. Please state whether you have in your custody or subject to your control the records pertaining to John Doe.

4. Please hand the Notary Public propounding these questions a complete copy of all such records, reports, etc., described in the subpoena pertaining to Doe.

5. Are the records you have furnished the Notary Public in response to Question Number 4 a complete and accurate copy of the records described in the subpoena that you have on this individual?

6. Were records not produced that have been destroyed or purged?

7. Were these records kept in your regular course of business?

8. Is it in the regular course of your business, or of an employee in your office having personal knowledge of the acts recorded, to prepare the records or transmit the information included in the records of John Doe?

9. Were the records made at or near the time of the performance of the act recorded therein or reasonably soon thereafter?

10. Does the source of the information, and the method and circumstance of its preparation, establish the trustworthiness of the records, notes, and or reports?

_____

Signature of Custodian

BEFORE ME, THE UNDERSIGNED AUTHORITY on this day personally appeared _____, custodian of Medical Records for Houston Honorary Hospital known to me to be the person whose name is subscribed to the foregoing instrument in the capacity therein stated, and acknowledged to me that the answers to the foregoing questions are true as stated. I further certify that the records attached hereto are exact duplicates of the original records.

GIVEN UNDER MY HAND AND SEAL OF OFFICE, this the _____ day of _____ year of 20xx.

_____

Notary Public in and for the State of Texas

My commission expires _____

Figure 3-4 Sample Deposition

STATE OF TEXAS   §   IN THE _____

Vs.   §   COURT IN AND FOR

_____   §   COWBOYS COUNTY, TEXAS

AFFIDAVIT

Before me, the undersigned authority, personally appeared _____, who, being by me duly sworn, deposed as follows:

My name is _____, I am of sound mind, capable of making this affidavit, and personally acquainted with the facts herein stated:

I am the Custodian of the records of _____. Attached hereto are _____ pages of records from _____. These said _____ pages of records are kept by **Houston Honorary Hospital** in the regular course of business, at it was the regular course of business of **Houston Honorary Hospital**, for an employee or representative of **Houston Honorary Hospital**, with knowledge of the act, event, condition, opinion, or diagnosis, recorded to make the record or transmit information thereof to be included in such record; and the record was made at or near the time or reasonably soon thereafter. The records attached hereto are the original or exact duplicates of the original.

_____

Affiant

SWORN TO AND SUBSCRIBED before me the _____day of _____ of the _____ year.

_____

Notary Public
State of Texas

My commission expires _____

Figure 3-5   Sample Affidavit

This notice describes how medical information about you may be used and disclosed and how you can get access to this information. Please read it carefully.

Introduction to Privacy

We are required by law to maintain the privacy of your medical information. We are also required to give you this Notice about our privacy practices, our legal duties, and your rights concerning your medical information. We must follow the privacy practices that are described in this Notice while it is in effect. We reserve the right to change our privacy practices and the terms of this Notice at any time, provided such changes are permitted by law. We reserve the right to make the changes in our privacy practices and the new terms of our Notice effective for all medical information that we maintain, including medical information we created or received before we made the changes. If we make a significant change in our privacy practices, we will amend this Notice and make the new Notice available upon request.

You may request a copy of our Notice at any time. For more information about our privacy practices, or for additional copies of this Notice, please contact _____.

Joint Notice of Privacy

This Joint Notice applies to the privacy practices of **Houston Honorary Hospital** for the sole purpose of complying with the Health Insurance Portability and Accountability Act of 1996 (HIPAA), HIPAA Privacy Rules and with the Texas Medical Privacy Act, Texas Health & Safety Code § 181.

Uses and Disclosures of Medical Information

We use and disclose medical information about you for treatment, payment, and healthcare operations.

Treatment: We may use and disclose your medical information to a physician or other healthcare provider to provide treatment to you. This includes coordination of your care with other healthcare providers, and with health plans, consultation with other providers, and referral to other providers related to your care.

Payment: We may use and disclose your medical information to obtain payment for services we provide to you. Payment includes submitting claims to health plans and other insurers, justifying our charges for and demonstrating the medical necessity of the care we deliver to you, determining your eligibility for health plan benefits for the care we furnish to you, obtaining precertification or preauthorization for your treatment or referral to other healthcare providers, participating in utilization review of the services we provide to you and the like. We may disclose your medical information to another healthcare provider or entity subject to the federal Privacy Rules so they can obtain payment.

Healthcare Operations: We may use and disclose your medical information in connection with our healthcare operations. Healthcare operations include:
- Quality assessment and improvement activities
- Reviewing the competence or qualifications of healthcare professionals, evaluating practitioner and provider accreditation, certification, licensing or credentialing activities
- Medical review
- Legal services and auditing, including fraud and abuse detection and compliance
- Business planning and development

(*continues*)

Figure 3-6   Sample Notice of Privacy Practices

- Business management and general administrative activities, including management activities relating to privacy, customer service, resolution of internal grievances, and creating de-identified medical information or a limited data set

We may disclose your medical information to another provider or health plan that is subject to the Privacy Rules, as long as that provider or plan has a relationship with you and the medical information is for their healthcare quality assessment and improvement activities, competence and qualification evaluation and review activities, or fraud and abuse detection and prevention.

On Your Authorization: You may give us written authorization to use your medical information or to disclose it to anyone for any purpose. If you give us an authorization, you may revoke it in writing at any time. Unless you give us a written authorization, we cannot use or disclose your medical information for any reason except those described in this Notice.

To Your Family and Friends: We may disclose your medical information to a family member, friend, or other person to the extent necessary to help with your health care or with payment for your health care. We may use or disclose your name, hospital location, and general condition or death to notify, or assist in the notification of (including identifying or locating) a person involved in your care. We may also disclose your medical information to whomever you give us permission. Before we disclose your medical information to a person involved in your health care or payment for your health care, we will provide you with an opportunity to object to such uses or disclosures. If you are not present, or in the event of your incapacity or an emergency, we will disclose your medical information based on our professional judgment of whether the disclosure would be in your best interest. We will also use our professional judgment and our experience with common practice to allow a person to pick up filled prescriptions, medical supplies, or other similar forms of medical information.

Facility Directory: We may use your name, your location, your general medical condition, and your religious affiliation in our facility directories. We will disclose this information to members of the clergy and, except for religious affiliation, to other persons who ask for you by name. We will provide you with an opportunity to restrict or prohibit some or all disclosures for facility directories unless emergency circumstances prevent your opportunity to object.

Disaster Relief: We may use or disclose your medical information to a public or private entity authorized by law or by its charter to assist in disaster relief efforts.

Health-Related Services: We may use your medical information to contact you with information about health-related benefits and services or about treatment alternatives that may be of interest to you. We may disclose your medical information to a business associate to assist us in these activities.

Business Associate: We may disclose your medical information to a company or individual performing functions or activities to or on our behalf.

Marketing: We will not use your medical information for marketing purposes without your authorization. **Houston Honorary Hospital** uses commercially purchased lists. We must obtain your authorization for all marketing purposes except for face-to-face conversations about services and treatment alternatives. You may also receive information through a membership program that you have joined. If you have opted in or have joined a membership program and you no longer wish to receive further

Figure 3-6   Sample Notice of Privacy Practices (*continued*)

information, please indicate this in writing by completing a marketing opt-out form, which you may get by calling 777-777-7777.

Fundraising: We may use your demographic information and the dates of your health care to contact you for our fundraising purposes. We may disclose this information to a business associate or foundation to assist us in our fundraising activities. If you would like more information on the **Houston Honorary Hospital Foundation** or a description of how you may opt out of receiving future fundraising communications, please indicate this in writing by calling 777-777-7777 and requesting an opt-out form.

Public Benefit: We may use or disclose your medical information as authorized by law for the following purposes deemed to be in the public interest or benefit:
- Public health activities including disease and vital statistics reporting, child abuse reporting, adult protective services, and FDA oversight
- Employers, regarding work-related illness or injury
- Cancer registry
- Trauma registry
- Birth registry
- Health oversight agencies
- In response to court and administrative orders and other lawful processes
- To law enforcement officials pursuant to subpoenas and other lawful processes, concerning crime victims, suspicious deaths, crimes on our premises, reporting crimes in emergencies, and for purposes of identifying or locating a suspect or other person
- To coroners, medical examiners, and funeral directors
- To organ procurement organizations
- To avert a serious threat to health or safety
- In connection with certain research activities
- To correctional institutions regarding inmates
- As authorized by state worker's compensation laws
- To the military, to federal officials for lawful intelligence, counterintelligence, and national security activities, and to correctional institutions and law enforcement regarding persons in lawful custody

Individual Rights

You have the right to review or receive a copy of your medical information, with limited exceptions. You may request that we provide copies in a format other than photocopies. We will use the format you request unless we cannot practicably do so. You must make a request in writing to obtain access to your medical information. You may obtain a form to request access or a copy of your medical information from the Release of Information department located at the facility where you obtain your medical care. There is a charge for a copy of your medical information.

Accounting of Disclosures

You have the right to receive an accounting of all uses and disclosures of your health information that was not authorized by you and that was not used by **Houston Honorary Hospital** for the sole purposes of treatment, payment, and health care operations. You must request this accounting in writing. This accounting is maintained for a period of 6 years beginning on April 14, 20xx, the effective date of this Notice. You may obtain a form to request an accounting of disclosures from the Release of Information department located at the facility where you obtained your medical care. *(continues)*

Figure 3-6 Sample Notice of Privacy Practices (*continued*)

Restrictions: You have the right to request that we place additional restrictions on our use or disclosure of your medical information. We are not required to agree to these additional restrictions, but if we do, we will abide by our agreement (except in an emergency). You must make this request in writing.

Confidential Communications: You have the right to request that we communicate with you about your medical information by alternative means or to alternative locations. You must make your request in writing. We must accommodate your request if: it is reasonable; specifies the alternative means or location; and provides a satisfactory explanation of how payments will be handled under the alternative means or location you request.

Amendment: You have the right to request that we amend your medical information. Your request must be in writing, and it must explain why the information should be amended. We may deny your request if we did not create the information you want amended and the originator remains available or for certain other reasons. If we deny your request, we will provide you a written explanation. You may respond with a statement or disagreement to be appended to the information you want amended. If we accept your request to amend the information, we will make reasonable efforts to inform others (including people you name) of the amendment and to include the changes in any future disclosures of that information.

Electronic Notice: If you view this Notice on our website or by electronic mail (e-mail), you are entitled to receive a copy of this Notice in written form. Please contact us as directed below to obtain this Notice in written form.

Security of Your Information

Houston Honorary Hospital safeguards customer information using various tools such as firewalls, passwords, and data encryption. We continually strive to improve these tools to meet or exceed industry standards. We also limit access to your information to protect against its unauthorized use. The only **Houston Honorary Hospital** workforce members who have access to your information are those who need it as part of their job. These safeguards help us meet both federal and state requirements to protect your personal health information.

Questions or Concerns

If you would like more information about our privacy practices or have questions or concerns about this Notice, please contact the Privacy Office at the number listed below. If you believe your privacy rights have been violated, you may file a complaint, in writing, to the Houston Honorary Hospital Privacy Office located at
99999 Freeway, Suite 999
Houston, Texas 99999
or by calling 1-999-999-9999.

Or you may contact the U.S. Department of Health and Human Services (DHHS)
00000 Young Street, Suite 00000
Houston, Texas 99999
Voice Phone 000-000-0000
FAX 000-000-0000
TDD 000-000-0000

To e-mail the DHHS Secretary or other Department Officials, send your message to hhsmail@os.dhhs.gov.

Figure 3-6   Sample Notice of Privacy Practices (*continued*)

17. Right to Request a Restriction of Uses and Disclosures

  a. HIPAA Omnibus Rule affirms an individual's right to restrict the disclosure of his or her information to a health plan where

  i. The disclosure is for healthcare operations or payment and disclosure is not otherwise required by law

  ii. The PHI relates solely to a product or service for which the individual or a third party paid in full, out of pocket

  b. Upon such a request, covered entities must comply with such a restriction and must not disclose the restricted information to the individual's health plans.

  c. Business associates of a health plan are equally prohibited from receiving the restricted PHI.

  d. Omnibus Rule gives covered entities guidance on how to comply with this provision.

  i. Covered entities are not required to take the time to separate the restricted records, but DHHS does require them to flag or make notes to records to identify restricted PHI.

  ii. Covered entities should understand how this flag works within their own electronic health records.

  iii. Where covered entities cannot "unbundle" their services, they must explain this to the individual, and if there is no way to restrict the PHI for just one service or product, all services or products in the bundle must be restricted.

  iv. DHHS emphasizes that it is the mandatory duty of covered entities to unbundle and restrict the PHI where they can.

  v. As a protection for the covered entity, where a payment to the covered entity fails (e.g., bounced check), the covered entity can contact and disclose all relevant information to the health plan to secure payment, but only after it tries to remedy the situation with the individual, such as by a phone call seeking an alternative form of payment.

  vi. Covered entities are allowed to disregard the restriction where the provider needs to justify follow-up care that was not paid out of pocket.

18. Individuals' Right of Access to PHI

  a. Privacy Rule has always emphasized the importance of allowing individuals to have access to their own PHI.

  b. HIPAA Omnibus Rule requires that covered entities provide individuals with a copy of the PHI that is maintained in a designated record set in the form and format requested by the individual; if that is not possible, it must reach an agreement with the individual for the provision of that information electronically.

  c. The requested information must be provided within 30 days.

  d. Covered entities are allowed one 30-day extension if circumstances warrant a delay.

  e. Individuals may designate third parties to receive their information, and the covered entity is required by the HIPAA Omnibus Rule to send the information to that person upon a signed written request.

  f. Covered entities are not required to investigate each request to ensure the third party seeking the records is doing so honestly.

  g. Covered entities must have policies and procedures in place to verify the third party's identity when they request access to the PHI, as well as to protect the PHI as it is shared.

    h. Covered entities may charge fees for their efforts in response to a request for information, but the fee must be based on the actual costs incurred to provide the information.

    i. For paper records, the fee can include only the costs of supplies and labor, postage, and preparation of a summary of the contents.

    j. For electronic records, the fee can include labor costs, and, where requested by the individual, the costs for the electronic media on which the records are transferred (such as a CD or a USB drive), postage (where the electronic media is mailed), and a summary of the contents.

    k. The covered entity cannot allocate computer costs or data storage costs to the fee.

19. Fundraising

    a. These changes are both more permissive and more restrictive than the previous standards.

    b. Rule is more permissive: covered entities have significant flexibility in how they fundraise and how they offer individuals the opportunity to opt out.

    c. Rule is more restrictive: it prohibits a covered entity from sending fundraising communications once the individual has opted out of receiving such communications.

20. Marketing

    a. If the covered entity is receiving payment from a third party for making a "subsidized communication," then the covered entity must obtain authorizations; there are no longer any exceptions in this case.

    b. Because an authorization for each "subsidized communication" is now required, covered entities do not have to include information about these communications in their notices of privacy practices (NPPs).

    c. Covered entities do not have to include information in their NPPs about appointment reminders, treatment alternatives, and other services, which are for treatment and operations.

    d. The authorization is valid where it meets the general requirements for all HIPAA authorizations and tells the individual he or she may revoke the permission at any time.

    e. The authorization must notify the individual that a third party is paying the covered entity to make the communication. Such notice may be either general or situation- or product-specific, but must at least give the individual an idea of the intended purpose of the use or disclosure.

    f. HIPAA Omnibus Rule: exception for refill reminders, adherence reminders, and delivery system instructions. As long as the remuneration received by the covered entity is reasonably related to the cost of making the communication, and the covered entity does not make a profit, such reminders are not considered marketing communications.

21. Sale of PHI

    a. Pursuant to HITECH Act, a covered entity cannot "sell" an individual's PHI without the individual's authorization.

    b. HIPAA Omnibus Rule clarifies that "sale of PHI" includes a covered entity or business associate receiving, directly or indirectly, financial or nonfinancial remuneration in exchange for PHI.

    c. A change in ownership of the PHI is not required, and a lease, license, or even access might trigger the protections in this provision.

    d. Several exceptions protect many legitimate arrangements.

        i. For instance, the "sale of PHI" does not include disclosures for public health purposes, treatment, or operations.

       ii. Perhaps the largest exception is for disclosures by a covered entity or a business associate, in accordance with the Privacy Rule, for a reasonable, cost-based fee.

    e. If a covered entity or business associate will be receiving remuneration in exchange for PHI, it should evaluate the arrangement to ensure it meets an exception.

    f. If it does not, then the covered entity will have to secure the individual's authorization before proceeding.

22. **Decedents, 50-Year Release**

    a. The current HIPAA Privacy Rule requires covered entities to continue protecting the privacy of PHI indefinitely after an individual's death.

    b. This causes hardship for historians and other researchers who cannot access records due to HIPAA protections.

    c. HIPAA Omnibus Rule modifies the requirement so that the privacy protections apply for only 50 years after the date of death.

    d. DHHS emphasizes that this change does not displace stricter state or other laws, or the professional responsibility of medical providers.

    e. The change is not a mandate that entities keep their records for that long: HIPAA does not have record retention requirements.

23. **Decedents, Disclosures to a Family Member/Others Involved in Care**

    a. Changes to this section of the Privacy Rule arose from frustrations of family members of decedents who were unable to access information related to the death of their loved one.

    b. HIPAA Omnibus Rule allows covered entities to disclose the decedent's PHI to a family member or other person involved in the decedent's care or treatment, but only to the extent the PHI is relevant to the role the family member or other person played in the decedent's treatment.

    c. No release is permissible where the individual expressly stated before death that he or she preferred the PHI not be released.

    d. This is not a requirement, but rather a permission; if the covered entity doubts the identity or explanation of the person seeking the information, it may deny the request.

24. **Student Immunization in Schools**

    a. HIPAA Omnibus Rule allows covered entities in states that have compulsory vaccination laws to disclose immunization records to schools without obtaining formal parental authorization.

    b. A covered entity must simply obtain permission, which can be oral or written, and such permission documented in the covered entity's records.

    c. Does not change the fact that disclosures to immunization databases are considered public health disclosures, so no authorization is required.

    d. This part of the Omnibus Rule does not affect any state laws. If state law requires authorization for this type of disclosure, HIPAA does not preempt that state law.

25. **Expansion of Rule's Application: Definition of Business Associate**

    a. Inclusion of Subcontractors

       i. 2013 Amendments significantly expand the definition of a business associate to include subcontractors of business associates (and their subcontractors) that create, receive, maintain, or transmit PHI in performing a function, activity, or service delegated by the business associate to a subcontractor.

       ii. A covered entity must obtain satisfactory assurances in the form of a written contract or other arrangement from each business associate, and each business associate must do the same with regard to each subcontractor that handles PHI on its behalf, and so on—no matter how far "down the chain" the PHI flows.

   b. Inclusion of Health Information Organizations, Vendors of Personal Health Records, and Others That Facilitate Data Transmission
      i. Included in the definition of a business associate are entities that create, receive, maintain, or transmit PHI through electronic means, such as health information organizations (HIOs); vendors of personal health records; and others that facilitate data transmission.

   c. Compliance Deadlines for Business Associate Compliance
      i. Modified Breach Standard and Notification Rule
      ii. Breach: under current interim rule, defined as an inappropriate use or disclosure of PHI involving a significant risk of financial, reputational or other harm.
      iii. 2013 Amendments modify this definition by providing that an impermissible use or disclosure of PHI is presumed to be a breach, unless it can be demonstrated that there is a low probability that PHI has been compromised based upon a four-part risk assessment that considers:
         1. The nature and extent of the PHI involved in the breach
         2. The unauthorized person who used the PHI or to whom the disclosure was made
         3. Whether the PHI was actually acquired or viewed
         4. The extent to which the risk to PHI has been mitigated
      iv. If the risk assessment evaluation fails to demonstrate there is a low probability that any PHI has been compromised, breach notification is required.
      v. Certain exceptions to the definition of a breach continue to apply.

   d. Notification
      i. 2013 Amendments require covered entities to notify each affected individual whose unsecured PHI has been compromised.
      ii. Even if such breach is caused by a business associate, the covered entity is ultimately responsible for providing the notification (although the covered entity is free to delegate the breach response function to the business associate).
      iii. A business associate's, and the workforce member's, knowledge of a breach will be imputed onto a covered entity.
      iv. If the breach involves more than 500 persons, OCR must be notified in accordance with instructions posted on its website.
      v. The HIPAA-covered entity bears the ultimate burden of proof to demonstrate that all notifications were given or that the impermissible use or disclosure of PHI did not constitute a breach.
      vi. The covered entity must maintain supporting documentation, including documentation pertaining to the risk assessment.

26. Security Rule
   a. HIPAA Security Rule applies to electronic PHI (e-PHI) that is created, received, maintained, or transmitted by a covered entity.
   b. 2013 Amendments expand the application of the Security Rule to business associates (now defined to include subcontractors of business associates that handle PHI for or on behalf of business associates).
   c. Business associates must comply with all of the Security Rule's applicable administrative safeguards (e.g., security management procedures, training), physical safeguards (e.g., workstation security, device

and media controls), and technical safeguards (e.g., audit controls, transmission security).

    d. Business associates, including their subcontractors that handle PHI, must enter into agreements that require the business associates to comply with the Security Rule.

    e. A downstream business associate (or a business associate subcontractor) must notify the upstream entity of any security incident or breach under the breach notification rules.

27. Notice of Privacy Practices

    a. 2013 Amendments reflect modifications from the interim final rule that provide significant changes to covered entities' NPP regarding uses and disclosures that require authorization.

    b. While 2013 Amendments do not require the NPP to include all situations requiring authorization, the NPP must contain a statement indicating that most uses and disclosures of psychotherapy notes, marketing disclosures, and sale of PHI do require prior authorization, as well as the right of the individual to be notified in case of a breach of unsecured PHI.

28. Modifications to the HIPAA Privacy Rule Under GINA

    a. Genetic Information Nondiscrimination Act of 2008 (GINA) prohibits discrimination based on an individual's genetic information.

29. Legislation/Regulation Trends Impacting HIM

    a. Accountable care organization (ACO) changes:

        i. Requires new method for information exchange and need for quality data to ensure effective and coordinated patient care

        ii. Describes how data will be managed, shared, and protected

    b. Big Data: managing upcoming torrent of data from hospitals and other care settings; HIM professional plays a major role in evaluating and determining use

    c. Health information exchange (HIE): effective sharing of information across the continuum of care

    d. Longitudinal coordination of care: focus placed on long-term and post-acute-care settings to improve outcomes while decreasing hospital readmissions

    e. E-discovery: advanced technology and new regulations (such as HITECH Act) describe the process by which each party in a lawsuit will obtain and view electronically stored information

    f. Healthcare reform: ties reimbursement to quality of care

        i. Readmission rates, patient satisfaction scores, and other data-driven outcomes measures will play a major role in reimbursement

        ii. Increased quality monitoring and reporting

        iii. Expected to boost the need for highly trained HIM professionals

        iv. HIM professionals required to implement HIM-related policies mandated by the federal government

Table 3-7
Stage 1 versus Stage 2
Comparison Table for Eligible Hospitals and CAHs
Last Updated: August 2012

Core Objectives (16 total)

Stage 1 Objective	Stage 1 Measure	Stage 2 Objective	Stage 2 Measure
Use CPOE for medication orders directly entered by any licensed healthcare professional who can enter orders into the medical record per state, local, and professional guidelines	More than 30% of unique patients with at least one medication in their medication list admitted to the eligible hospital's or CAH's inpatient or emergency department (POS 21 or 23) have at least one medication order entered using CPOE	Use computerized provider order entry (CPOE) for medication, laboratory, and radiology orders directly entered by any licensed healthcare professional who can enter orders into the medical record per state, local, and professional guidelines	More than 60% of medication, 30% of laboratory, and 30% of radiology orders created by authorized providers of the eligible hospital's or CAH's inpatient or emergency department (POS 21 or 23) during the EHR reporting period are recorded using CPOE
Implement drug–drug and drug–allergy interaction checks	The eligible hospital/CAH has enabled this functionality for the entire EHR reporting period	*No longer a separate objective for Stage 2*	*This measure is incorporated into the Stage 2 Clinical Decision Support measure*
Record demographics • Preferred language • Gender • Race • Ethnicity • Date of birth • Date and preliminary cause of death in the event of mortality in the eligible hospital or CAH	More than 50% of all unique patients admitted to the eligible hospital's or CAH's inpatient or emergency department (POS 21 or 23) have demographics recorded as structured data	Record the following demographics • Preferred language • Gender • Race • Ethnicity • Date of birth • Date and preliminary cause of death in the event of mortality in the eligible hospital or CAH	More than 80% of all unique patients admitted to the eligible hospital's or CAH's inpatient or emergency department (POS 21 or 23) have demographics recorded as structured data

Table 3-7   Core Objectives (16 total) (*continued*)

Stage 1 Objective	Stage 1 Measure	Stage 2 Objective	Stage 2 Measure
Maintain an up-to-date problem list of current and active diagnoses	More than 80% of all unique patients admitted to the eligible hospital's or CAH's inpatient or emergency department (POS 21 or 23) have at least one entry or an indication that no problems are known for the patient recorded as structured data	*No longer a separate objective for Stage 2*	*This measure is incorporated into the Stage 2 measure of Summary of Care Document at Transitions of Care and Referrals*
Maintain active medication list	More than 80% of all unique patients admitted to the eligible hospital's or CAH's inpatient or emergency department (POS 21 or 23) have at least one entry (or an indication that the patient is not currently prescribed any medication) recorded as structured data	*No longer a separate objective for Stage 2*	*This measure is incorporated into the Stage 2 measure of Summary of Care Document at Transitions of Care and Referrals*
Maintain active medication allergy list	More than 80% of all unique patients admitted to the eligible hospital's or CAH's inpatient or emergency department (POS 21 or 23) have at least one entry (or an indication that the patient has no known medication allergies) recorded as structured data	*No longer a separate objective for Stage 2*	*This measure is incorporated into the Stage 2 measure of Summary of Care Document at Transitions of Care and Referrals*

(*continues*)

Table 3-7 Core Objectives (16 total) (*continued*)

Stage 1 Objective	Stage 1 Measure	Stage 2 Objective	Stage 2 Measure
Record and chart changes in vital signs: • Height • Weight • Blood pressure • Calculate and display BMI • Plot and display growth charts for children 2–20 years, including BMI	More than 50% of all unique patients age 2 and over admitted to eligible hospital's or CAH's inpatient or emergency department (POS 21 or 23), blood pressure, height, and weight are recorded as structured data	Record and chart changes in vital signs: • Height • Weight • Blood pressure (age 3 and over) • Calculate and display BMI • Plot and display growth charts for patients 0–20 years, including BMI	More than 80% of all unique patients admitted to the eligible hospital's or CAH's inpatient or emergency department (POS 21 or 23) have blood pressure (for patients age 3 and over only) and height and weight (for all ages) recorded as structured data
Record smoking status for patients 13 years old or older	More than 50% of all unique patients 13 years old or older admitted to the eligible hospital's or CAH's inpatient or emergency department (POS 21 or 23) have smoking status recorded as structured data	Record smoking status for patients 13 years old or older	More than 80% of all unique patients 13 years old or older admitted to the eligible hospital's or CAH's inpatient or emergency department (POS 21 or 23) have smoking status recorded as structured data
Implement one clinical decision support rule relevant to specialty or high clinical priority along with the ability to track compliance that rule	Implement one clinical decision support rule	Use clinical decision support to improve performance on high-priority health conditions	1. Implement five clinical decision support interventions related to four or more clinical quality measures, if applicable, at a relevant point in patient care for the entire EHR reporting period. 2. The eligible hospital or CAH has enabled the functionality for drug–drug and drug–allergy interaction checks for the entire EHR reporting period

Table 3-7 Core Objectives (16 total) (*continued*)

Stage 1 Objective	Stage 1 Measure	Stage 2 Objective	Stage 2 Measure
Report clinical quality measures (CQMs) to CMS or the States	For 2011, provide aggregate numerator, denominator, and exclusions through attestation or electronically through the Hospital Reporting Pilot	*No longer a separate objective for Stage 2, but providers must still submit CQMs to CMS or the States to achieve meaningful use*	*Starting in 2014, all CQMs will be submitted electronically to CMS.*
Provide patients with an electronic copy of their health information (including diagnostic test results, problem list, medication lists, medication allergies), upon request	More than 50% of all patients of the inpatient or emergency departments of the eligible hospital or CAH (POS 21 or 23) who request an electronic copy of their health information are provided it within 3 business days	Provide patients the ability to view online, download, and transmit their health information within 36 hours after discharge from the hospital	1. More than 50% of all unique patients discharged from the inpatient or emergency departments of the eligible hospital or CAH (POS 21 or 23) during the EHR reporting period are provided timely (available to the patient within 36 hours after discharge from the hospital) online access to their health information 2. More than 5% of all unique patients discharged from the inpatient or emergency departments of the eligible hospital or CAH (POS 21 or 23) during the EHR reporting period (or their authorized representatives) view, download, or transmit to a third party their health information

(*continues*)

Table 3-7 Core Objectives (16 total) (*continued*)

Stage 1 Objective	Stage 1 Measure	Stage 2 Objective	Stage 2 Measure
Provide patients with an electronic copy of their discharge instructions at time of discharge, upon request	More than 50% of all patients who are discharged from an eligible hospital or CAH's inpatient department or emergency department (POS 21 or 23) and who request an electronic copy of their discharge instructions are provided it	*This objective is eliminated from Stage 1 in 2014 and is no longer a separate objective for Stage 2*	*This measure has been incorporated into the View, Download, and Transmit objective for Stage 2*
Capability to exchange key clinical information (for example, problem list, medication list, medication allergies, diagnostic test results), among providers of care and patient authorized entities electronically	Performed at least one test of Certified EHR Technology's capacity to electronically exchange key clinical information	*This objective is eliminated from Stage 1 in 2013 and is no longer an objective for Stage 2*	*This measure is eliminated from Stage 1 in 2013 and is no longer a measure for Stage 2*
Protect electronic health information created or maintained by the Certified EHR Technology through the implementation of appropriate technical capabilities	Conduct or review a security risk analysis per 45 CFR 164.308 (a)(1) and implement security updates as necessary and correct identified security deficiencies as part of its risk management process	Protect electronic health information created or maintained by the Certified EHR Technology through the implementation of appropriate technical capabilities	Conduct or review a security risk analysis in accordance with the requirements under 45 CFR 164.308 (a)(1), including addressing the encryption/security of data at rest and implement security updates as necessary and correct identified security deficiencies as part of its risk management process

Table 3-7 Core Objectives (16 total) (continued)

Stage 1 Objective	Stage 1 Measure	Stage 2 Objective	Stage 2 Measure
Implement drug-formulary checks	The eligible hospital/CAH has enabled this functionality and has access to at least one internal or external drug formulary for the entire EHR reporting period	*No longer a separate objective for Stage 2*	*This measure is incorporated into the e-Prescribing measure for Stage 2*
Incorporate clinical lab test results into Certified EHR Technology as structured data	More than 40% of all clinical lab tests results ordered by an authorized provider of the eligible hospital or CAH for patients admitted to its inpatient or emergency department (POS 21 or 23) during the EHR reporting period whose results are either in a positive/negative or numerical format are incorporated in certified EHR technology as structured data	Incorporate clinical lab test results into Certified EHR Technology as structured data	More than 55% of all clinical lab tests results ordered by authorized providers of the eligible hospital or CAH for patients admitted to its inpatient or emergency department (POS 21 or 23) during the EHR reporting period whose results are either in a positive/negative or numerical format are incorporated in Certified EHR Technology as structured data
Generate lists of patients by specific conditions to use for quality improvement, reduction of disparities, research or outreach	Generate at least one report listing patients of the eligible hospital or CAH with a specific condition	Generate lists of patients by specific conditions to use for quality improvement, reduction of disparities, research, or outreach	Generate at least one report listing patients of the eligible hospital or CAH with a specific condition

(continues)

Table 3-7   Core Objectives (16 total) (*continued*)

Stage 1 Objective	Stage 1 Measure	Stage 2 Objective	Stage 2 Measure
Use Certified EHR Technology to identify patient-specific education resources and provide those resources to the patient if appropriate	More than 10% of all unique patients admitted to the eligible hospital's or CAH's inpatient or emergency department (POS 21 or 23) are provided patient-specific education resources	Use Certified EHR Technology to identify patient-specific education resources and provide those resources to the patient if appropriate	More than 10% of all unique patients admitted to the eligible hospital's or CAH's inpatient and emergency departments (POS 21 and 23) are provided patient-specific education resources identified by Certified EHR Technology
The eligible hospital or CAH that receives a patient from another setting of care or provider of care or believes an encounter is relevant should perform medication reconciliation	The eligible hospital or CAH performs medication reconciliation for more than 50% of transitions of care in which the patient is admitted to the eligible hospital's or CAH's inpatient or emergency department (POS 21 or 23)	The eligible hospital or CAH that receives a patient from another setting of care or provider of care or believes an encounter is relevant should perform medication reconciliation	The eligible hospital or CAH performs medication reconciliation for more than 50% of transitions of care in which the patient is admitted to the eligible hospital's or CAH's inpatient or emergency department (POS 21 or 23)
The eligible hospital or CAH that transitions its patient to another setting of care or provider of care or refers their patient to another provider of care should provide summary of care record for each transition of care or referral	The eligible hospital or CAH that transitions or refers its patient to another setting of care or provider of care provides a summary of care record for more than 50% of transitions of care and referrals	The eligible hospital or CAH that transitions its patient to another setting of care or provider of care or refers their patient to another provider of care should provide summary of care record for each transition of care or referral	1. The eligible hospital, or CAH that transitions or refers its patient to another setting of care or provider of care provides a summary of care record for more than 50% of transitions of care and referrals 2. The eligible hospital or CAH that transitions or refers its patient to another setting of care or provider of care provides a summary of care record either (a) electronically transmitted to a recipient using

Table 3-7	Core Objectives (16 total) (*continued*)		
Stage 1 Objective	**Stage 1 Measure**	**Stage 2 Objective**	**Stage 2 Measure**
			CEHRT or (b) where the recipient receives the summary of care record via exchange facilitated by an organization that is a NHIN Exchange participant or is validated through an ONC-established governance mechanism to facilitate exchange for 10% of transitions and referrals
			3. The eligible hospital or CAH that transitions or refers its patient to another setting of care or provider of care must either (a) conduct one or more successful electronic exchanges of a summary of care record with a recipient using technology that was designed by a different EHR developer than the sender's, or (b) conduct one or more successful tests with the CMS-designed test EHR during the EHR reporting period

(*continues*)

Table 3-7   Core Objectives (16 total) (*continued*)

Stage 1 Objective	Stage 1 Measure	Stage 2 Objective	Stage 2 Measure
Capability to submit electronic data to immunization registries or immunization information systems, and actual submission except where prohibited and in accordance with applicable law and practice	Performed at least one test of Certified EHR Technology's capacity to submit electronic data to immunization registries and follow-up submission if the test is successful (unless none of the immunization registries to which the eligible hospital or CAH submits such information has the capacity to receive the information electronically)	Capability to submit electronic data to immunization registries or immunization information systems, and actual submission except where prohibited and in accordance with applicable law and practice	Successful ongoing submission of electronic immunization data from Certified EHR Technology to an immunization registry or immunization information system for the entire EHR reporting period
Capability to submit electronic data on reportable (as required by state or local law) lab results to public health agencies, and actual submission except where prohibited and in accordance with applicable law and practice	Performed at least one test of Certified EHR Technology's capacity to provide electronic submission of reportable lab results to public health agencies and follow-up submission if the test is successful (unless none of the public health agencies to which eligible hospital or CAH submits such information has the capacity to receive the information electronically)	Capability to submit electronic data on reportable (as required by state or local law) lab results to public health agencies, and actual submission except where prohibited and in accordance with applicable law and practice	Successful ongoing submission of electronic reportable laboratory results from Certified EHR Technology to public health agencies for the entire EHR reporting period as authorized, and in accordance with applicable state law and practice

Table 3-7 Core Objectives (16 total) (*continued*)

Stage 1 Objective	Stage 1 Measure	Stage 2 Objective	Stage 2 Measure
Capability to submit electronic syndromic surveillance data to public health agencies, and actual submission except where prohibited and in accordance with applicable law and practice	Performed at least one test of Certified EHR Technology's capacity to provide electronic syndromic surveillance data to public health agencies and follow-up submission if the test is successful (unless none of the public health agencies to which an eligible hospital or CAH submits such information has the capacity to receive the information electronically)	Capability to submit electronic syndromic surveillance data to public health agencies, and actual submission except where prohibited and in accordance with applicable law and practice	Successful ongoing submission of electronic syndromic surveillance data from Certified EHR Technology to a public health agency for the entire EHR reporting period
NEW	**NEW**	Automatically track medications from order to administration using assistive technologies in conjunction with an electronic medication administration record (eMAR)	More than 10% of medication orders created by authorized providers of the eligible hospital's or CAH's inpatient or emergency department (POS 21 or 23) during the EHR reporting period for which all doses are tracked are tracked using eMAR

(*continues*)

Table 3-7   Menu Objectives (Eligible hospitals and CAHs must report on 3 of 6 menu objectives)

Stage 1 Objective	Stage 1 Measure	Stage 2 Objective	Stage 2 Measure
Record advance directives for patients 65 years old or older	More than 50% of all unique patients 65 years old or older admitted to the eligible hospital's or CAH's inpatient department (POS 21) have an indication of an advance directive status recorded	Record whether a patient 65 years old or older has an advance directive	More than 50% of all unique patients 65 years old or older admitted to the eligible hospital's or CAH's inpatient department (POS 21) during the EHR reporting period have an indication of an advance directive status recorded as structured data
NEW	NEW	Record electronic notes in patient records	Enter at least one electronic progress note created, edited, and signed by an eligible provider for more than 30% of unique patients admitted to the eligible hospital or CAH's inpatient or emergency department during the EHR reporting period
NEW	NEW	Imaging results consisting of the image itself and any explanation or other accompanying information are accessible through CEHRT	More than 10% of all scans and tests whose result is an image ordered by an authorized provider of the eligible hospital or CAH for patients admitted to its inpatient or emergency department (POS 21 and 23) during the EHR reporting period are incorporated into or accessible through Certified EHR Technology

Table 3-7   Menu Objectives (*continued*)

Stage 1 Objective	Stage 1 Measure	Stage 2 Objective	Stage 2 Measure
NEW	NEW	Record patient family health history as structured data	More than 20% of all unique patients admitted to the eligible hospital or CAH's inpatient or emergency department (POS 21 or 23) during the EHR reporting period have a structured data entry for one or more first-degree relatives or an indication that family health history has been reviewed
NEW	NEW	Generate and transmit permissible discharge prescriptions electronically (eRx)	More than 10% of hospital discharge medication orders for permissible prescriptions (for new or changed prescriptions) are compared to at least one drug formulary and transmitted electronically using Certified EHR Technology
NEW	NEW	Provide structured electronic lab results to ambulatory providers	Hospital labs send structured electronic clinical lab results to the ordering provider for more than 20% of electronic lab orders received

Reproduced from the Centers for Medicaid and Medicare Services (2012). Stage 1 vs. Stage 2 Comparison Table for Eligible Hospitals and CAHs. https://www.cms.gov/Regulations-and-Guidance/Legislation/EHRIncentivePrograms/Downloads/stage1vsStage2CompTablesforHospitals.pdf. Last Updated: August 2012. Accessed March 4, 2014.

PRACTICAL APPLICATION OF YOUR KNOWLEDGE

1. Answer the following questions on the organization of the legal system:
   a. What are the three levels of the government and the sources or documents that outline their power?
      1.

      2.

      3.

   b. What are the three branches of federal and state government and their duties?
      1.

      2.

      3.

   c. Distinguish between public and private law. Which usually deals with disputes between patients and healthcare providers?

   d. Discuss the rules of administrative agencies and give an example of an administrative agency that affects healthcare legislation.

2. Health Record Requirements and Retention Guidelines
   a. List the contents that should be included in an inpatient health record according to TJC.

   b. As manager of the health information department, you are constructing a retention schedule. Using AHIMA guidelines, state the length of time the following documents should be maintained:

Document	Retention Guideline
Adult patient health record	
Minor patient health record	
Diagnostic images (e.g., X-rays)	
Disease index	
Fetal heart monitor record	
Master patient index	
Operative index	
Physician index	
Register of births	
Register of deaths	
Register of surgical procedures	

3. Confidentiality, Consent, and Security of Health Records

    a. What is confidential information?

    b. Who is the owner of the health record?

    c. Who has the authority to release information from the health record?

    d. When is authorization not required to release PHI?

    e. What are the three elements of a privileged communication?

    f. State three types of consent.

    g. What is informed consent? What should be included in an informed consent?

    h. From what threats to the security of records must a health information practitioner protect those records?

4. Laws and Regulations Regarding Health Records

    a. Summarize the following federal legislation:

Legislation	Summary
Freedom of Information Act (1966)	
Drug Abuse and Treatment Act (1972)	
Privacy Act (1974)	
Natural Death Act (1989)	
Health Insurance Portability and Accountability Act (1996)	

5. Release of Information and Subpoenas
  a. To meet HIPAA requirements, a Release of Information form must collect what information?

  b. Subpoenas
    1. Match the term to its description or definition
        a. Subpoena duces tecum
        b. Subpoena ad testificandum
        c. Contempt of court
      1. _____ Results when a person fails to obey a subpoena and is punishable by fine or imprisonment
      2. _____ Court order that commands a person to come to court and produce whatever documents are named in the order
      3. _____ Court order that requires a person to appear in court to testify
  c. List eight common elements of a valid subpoena.
    1.

    2.

    3.

    4.

    5.

    6.

    7.

    8.

6. Health Insurance Portability and Accountability Act

    a. Discuss the administration simplification provisions.

    b. Discuss the Privacy Rule.

    c. What is PHI?

    d. Mark these statements concerning the HIPAA Privacy Rule as True or False.

        1. _____ The HIPAA Privacy Rule protects a patient's fundamental right to privacy and confidentiality.

        2. _____ A covered entity is a healthcare provider, health plan, or healthcare clearinghouse that transmits health information in electronic form.

        3. _____ PHI is anything that connects a patient to his or her health information.

        4. _____ After signing an authorization, the patient can decide to revoke it.

        5. _____ An authorization must contain an expiration date.

        6. _____ PHI includes all health information that is used or disclosed except PHI in oral form.

        7. _____ The healthcare facility must obtain patient agreement to use or disclose PHI for public health activities related to disease prevention.

        8. _____ In general, disclosure of PHI must be limited to the least amount needed to get the job done correctly.

        9. _____ The Privacy Rule gives patients the right to take action if their privacy is violated.

        10. _____ The Privacy Rule gives patients the right to request a history of routine disclosures.

7. Health Record Documentation

    a. List 10 guidelines for documentation in the health record.

        1.

        2.

        3.

        4.

        5.

        6.

        7.

        8.

        9.

        10.

    b. A physician charts the information of a patient in the wrong health record. Describe how the documentation can be corrected in each patient's record.

8. Health Records in Court

    a. Describe the following steps:

Step	Description
Complaint	
Answers	
Motions	
Pretrial discovery	
Notice of trial	
Memorandum of law	

    b. Describe the steps of the civil pretrial procedure.

    c. A patient sues your facility for malpractice. Describe the steps in a legal proceeding by which this case may be decided from its beginning to its conclusion.

9. Malpractice and Negligence
   a. Describe the four components that must be present for a plaintiff to recover damages caused by negligence.

       1.

       2.

       3.

       4.

10. Compruter-Based Health Records
   a. List five methods to secure computer-based health records from unauthorized access.

       1.

       2.

       3.

       4.

       5.

11. Ethical Issues for Health Information Practitioners

    a. List 10 ethical obligations of the health information practitioner.

        1.

        2.

        3.

        4.

        5.

        6.

        7.

        8.

        9.

        10.

12. Define the Following Terms:
   a. Admissibility

   b. Advance directive

   c. Assault and battery

   d. Business record rule

   e. Evidence

   f. Defamation

   g. Defendant

   h. Deposition

   i. Hearsay

   j. Interrogatory

   k. Law

   l. Libel

m. Malpractice

n. Negligence

o. Plaintiff

p. Res gestae

q. Res ipsa loquitur

r. Res judicata

s. Respondeat superior

t. Stare decisis

u. Statute of limitations

v. Tort

w. Venue

TEST YOUR KNOWLEDGE

Select the best answer for the questions or incomplete statements.

1. A nurse employed by your hospital gossiped about a discharged inpatient, which resulted in the patient's good reputation being questioned by his neighbor. This is known as what?
   a. Libel
   b. Slander
   c. Perjury
   d. Defamation

2. A third-party payer has requested copies of a patient's records. The patient has been diagnosed as having AIDS. The hospital's policy for release of information in this instance should ensure that the:
   a. record is sent by overnight express.
   b. physician gives consent for a copy of the record to be released.
   c. a subpoena duces tecum is received from the third-party payer.
   d. patient has signed a consent specifically authorizing release of this diagnosis.

3. A properly completed and signed authorization is required for release of all health information, except when a(n):
   a. patient has died.
   b. patient presents to the hospital with a highly contagious disease that must be reported to the state health department.
   c. patient's spouse suspects the patient has AIDS and is afraid of contracting the disease.
   d. insurance company request copies of the patient's previous hospitalization record.

4. Which of the following is an example of respondeat superior?
   a. The hospital is held responsible for a pharmacist medication error.
   b. A physician with honorary staff status is sued by a current inpatient for malpractice.
   c. The director of nurses gives instructions to a staff nurse.
   d. The attending physician testifies against the surgeon in a malpractice case.

5. You are the supervisor of release of information and have been subpoenaed to bring records to court. With what document may you have been served?
   a. Subpoena duces tecum
   b. Subpoena ad testificandum
   c. Subpoena gestae
   d. Subpoena respondeat

6. Refusing to honor a subpoena may result in:
   a. the case being postponed.
   b. arrest of the attending physician.
   c. being held in contempt of court.
   d. receiving a court order.

7. According to the American Health Information Management Association, the suggested retention schedule for the master patient index is how long?
   a. 5 years
   b. 10 years
   c. 25 years
   d. Permanently

8. The statute of limitation sets:
   a. the maximum dollar amount that can be collected from a malpractice case.
   b. standards for the maintenance of pharmaceuticals.
   c. a minimum amount of time after an event occurs for a suit to be taken in court.
   d. a time period for the completion of medical records.

9. As supervisor of release of information you have been subpoenaed to court. You are qualified to testify in response to a subpoena duces tecum as to:
   a. the quality of care rendered by the medical staff to the patient.
   b. how the health records are maintained in the facility's regular course of business.
   c. the accuracy of a respiratory therapist's documentation.
   d. whether the confidentiality of the health information has been violated.

10. In a nonemergent situation, protected health information may be released to another hospital with the:
    a. written authorization of the patient.
    b. permission of the attending physician.
    c. death of the patient.
    d. receipt of a phone call from the patient's spouse.

11. Which of the following demonstrates the doctrine of res ipsa loquitur?
    a. A surgeon places a pacemaker in a patient.
    b. A surgeon erroneously leaves an instrument in a patient.
    c. A radiology technician takes an X-ray of the wrong leg of a patient.
    d. A nurse neglects to give a patient her prescribed medication.

12. A patient has a primary diagnosis of alcohol abuse and dependence. What information may be released without express authorization of the patient?
    a. Admission and discharge dates only
    b. The patient's physical health status
    c. The patient's attending physician's name
    d. No information at all

13. TJC requests to view a patient's health record, which contains a diagnosis of AIDS. The director of health information should:
    a. call the facility's attorney.
    b. deny access to TJC.
    c. obtain written authorization from the patient or legal representative.
    d. allow access to the record upon request of TJC.

14. Which rule requires covered entities to assign a unique name and/or number for identifying and tracking user identity?
    a. Privacy Rule
    b. Security Rule
    c. Administrative Rule
    d. None of the above

15. Which of the following is required to be present in an informed consent?
    a. Explanation of risks and benefits of treatment and or surgery
    b. List of referral physicians to obtain another expert opinion
    c. Alternative facilities that may treat the patient
    d. Cost of treatment and surgery

16. A school representative brings a minor to the facility with a broken arm, which requires surgery. Who may consent to the treatment of the patient?
    a. The school representative
    b. The minor patient
    c. The person with legal custody of the minor patient
    d. No consent is necessary in the emergent situation.

17. In a physician-owned clinic, the health record is the property of the:
    a. patient.
    b. admitting physician.
    c. physician-owned clinic.
    d. hospital to which the physician has admitting privileges.

18. A hospital fails to obtain informed consent prior to surgery on a patient. Which of the following may the hospital have performed?
- **a.** Slander and tort
- **b.** Defamation and liability
- **c.** Libel and tort
- **d.** Assault and battery

19. Tort claims have to do with what?
- **a.** Wrongful conduct that has caused harm in public law
- **b.** Unauthorized treatment
- **c.** Public and criminal wrongs
- **d.** Breach of contract

20. Health records may be admitted into court as evidence due to the:
- **a.** hearsay rule.
- **b.** business records rule.
- **c.** Privacy Act.
- **d.** HIPAA.

21. The powers of the three branches of the federal government are documented in the:
- **a.** United States Constitution.
- **b.** Act of Congress.
- **c.** administrative law.
- **d.** Articles of the Republic.

22. Bob brings a lawsuit against Houston Hospital for damages done to his knee during surgery. What term best describes Bob?
- **a.** Defendant
- **b.** Bailiff
- **c.** Plaintiff
- **d.** Attorney

23. Susan brings a lawsuit against Houston Hospital for wrongfully damaging her knee during surgery. What is this wrongful act called?
- **a.** Tort
- **b.** Slander
- **c.** Libel
- **d.** Assault

24. Austin Hospital is closed and sold to Houston Hospital. Which of the following entities owns the physical hospital health record?
- **a.** The patients
- **b.** Houston Hospital
- **c.** Austin Hospital
- **d.** The physicians who treated the patients

25. HIPAA Privacy Rules:
- **a.** take precedence over all other federal and state laws.
- **b.** are not relevant to children's hospitals.
- **c.** provide a federal foundation for privacy requirements of health information.
- **d.** are not subject to state laws.

26. PHI refers to _____ health information.
- **a.** private
- **b.** protected
- **c.** previous
- **d.** preliminary

27. Authorizations are always required for the use or disclosure of psychotherapy notes except in which of the following situations:
- **a.** health insurance carrier
- **b.** carry out payment, treatment, and operations
- **c.** employee- and employment-related activities
- **d.** media-related activities

28. Steve has submitted a written authorization to request a copy of his medical chart. However, Steve's psychiatrist has determined that access to his PHI might endanger his life or safety. What should the covered entity do concerning the request?
- **a.** Provide an appeals process to Steve for the denial
- **b.** Confirm the psychiatrist decision and deny the request
- **c.** Release requested information to Steve's legal guardian
- **d.** Release requested information to Steve

29. In regard to a patient's request for his PHI, which of the following statements is true?
    a. A cost-based fee may be charged to view the PHI.
    b. No fee may be charged for PHI.
    c. A cost-based fee may be charged for personnel expenses.
    d. A cost-based fee may be charged for making a copy of the PHI.

30. Steve submits a written request to Houston Hospital for a copy of his PHI on August 19. By what date must the covered entity comply?
    a. August 29
    b. September 3
    c. September 8
    d. September 18

31. Nurse Cecile makes an error in a patient's medical chart. What should she do?
    a. Remove the page with the error
    b. Obliterate the error
    c. Line through the error, then add her correction, stating "correction" or "error"
    d. Remove the page with error and add page with correction

32. Jennifer submits a written request to Houston Hospital for a copy of her PHI on August 19. The information is stored offsite. By what date must the covered entity comply?
    a. August 29
    b. September 19
    c. September 30
    d. October 18

33. Where can patients find a complete description of how PHI is used in a healthcare facility?
    a. Notice of privacy practice
    b. Medical staff rules and regulations
    c. Governing board bylaws
    d. HIM policies and procedures

34. The notice of privacy practice:
    a. provides patients with a fee scale of private rooms.
    b. must be provided to every individual at the first time of contact or service with the covered entity.
    c. gives the covered entity permission to release information to private insurance companies.
    d. explains to patients that the facility is a private institution and provides services on a fee-for-service basis.

35. The directory of patients maintained by a covered entity:
    a. requires patients to maintain their name and room number in the directory.
    b. allows patients to restrict information maintained on them in the directory.
    c. may not be released.
    d. must be maintained for 5 years.

36. Sworn testimony usually collected before a trial is a(n):
    a. subpoena.
    b. tort.
    c. deposition.
    d. complaint.

37. Bob brings a lawsuit against Houston Hospital for damages done to his knee during surgery. What term best describes Houston Hospital?
    a. Defendant
    b. Bailiff
    c. Plaintiff
    d. Complaintee

38. The MPI (master patient index) serves which of the following purposes?
    a. Links to the patient record and facilitates patient identification that is critical to the quality and safety of patient care
    b. Influences retention of patient medical records
    c. Means of identifying off-site storage and retrieval methods
    d. Maintains a longitudinal patient record from birth to death

39. With proper written authorization from a patient, Houston Hospital obtains a copy of the patient's health record from Austin Hospital. Houston Hospital then releases the information from Austin Hospital to Dallas Hospital. What is this practice called?
   a. Redisclosure
   b. Release of information
   c. Voir dire
   d. Ad testificandum

40. With proper written authorization from a patient, Houston Hospital obtains a copy of the patient's health record from Austin Hospital. Houston Hospital then releases the information from Austin Hospital to Dallas Hospital. This practice is:
   a. never appropriate, because medical information should not be redisclosed.
   b. mandated by HIPAA to ensure continuity of patient care.
   c. regularly practiced due to the threat of medical lawsuits.
   d. noncompliant with HIPAA, but compliant with FIOA.

41. Which of the following subpoenas will require the director of medical records to personally appear in court and produce documents and other records?
   a. Subpoena ad testificandum
   b. Subpoena duces in tecum
   c. Subpoena to quash
   d. None of the above

42. As a witness for Houston Hospital, the health information manager should:
   a. refuse to turn over copies of medical records to the court that demonstrate negligence on the part of the hospital.
   b. never tell the court that medical records were not able to be retrieved or were lost.
   c. give copies of medical records to constable upon request.
   d. refuse to turn over copies of medical records to the court without a subpoena duces tecum or court order.

43. Public health laws mandate reporting of certain diseases, which do not require the patient's consent for release of this information. These include:
   a. deaths and herpes.
   b. births and viral meningitis.
   c. births and cancer cases.
   d. deaths and viral meningitis.

44. An incompetent adult is an individual who is no longer capable of controlling his or her action due to all EXCEPT which of the following?
   a. Injury
   b. Illness
   c. Disability
   d. All of the above

45. Manuel was in a severe car accident and unable to grant permission for treatment. Therefore, his wife:
   a. must obtain legal guardianship to speak for patient.
   b. has no right to consent to or deny treatment for Manuel.
   c. must obtain legal counsel to represent Manuel.
   d. may give consent for his treatment.

46. Nipa was admitted to a Houston Community Hospital for gallbladder removal. Which of the following information about her is considered confidential?
   a. Previous history and treatment of a concussion
   b. Date of birth
   c. Address upon admission
   d. All information is considered confidential

47. Jim is 15 years old when treated for appendicitis with subsequent appendectomy. At what age will Jim be when his records may be destroyed, if the state's age of majority is 18 years of age?
   a. 18
   b. 25
   c. 28
   d. 30

48. LaToya, a 16-year-old student, is hospitalized for pneumonia. She was ambulatory and mentally competent upon admission. LaToya is a married mother of two. Her mother is contacted to be informed of her daughter's status. Who may authorize treatment for LaToya?
  a. LaToya
  b. LaToya's mom
  c. LaToya's husband
  d. No consent is required in an emergent situation.

49. Bob, a 93-year-old male, was admitted and treated for a myocardial infarction. Due to his history of Alzheimer's disease, his daughter is his legal guardian. Bob lives with his son. Upon discharge from the hospital, his primary physician requests copies of his medical record. Who is required to sign an authorization for release of the medical record information to the physician?
  a. Bob
  b. Bob's daughter
  c. Bob's son
  d. Due to continuity of care, an authorization is not mandatory.

50. Of the following, which requestor is NOT required to submit the patient's written authorization to obtain copies of the patient's medical record from the hospital?
  a. The patient
  b. The patient's attorney
  c. The patient's physician
  d. The hospital's attorney

Healthcare Statistics, Research, and Epidemiology

1. Statistics
   a. Definition of Statistics
      i. The overall science of extracting information from a set of data and using the information to make inferences about that larger set of data
      ii. The study of variation
      iii. Descriptive statistics: statistical data concerning the attributes of a population
      iv. Inferential statistics: statistical data collected from a sample to make inferences about the population from which the sample is extracted
   b. Purposes of healthcare statistics; may be collected concurrently or retrospectively
      i. Strategic planning: determine changes to current structure of organization (e.g., equipment, staffing, facilities)
      ii. Compare past with current performance indicators
         1. Determine trends of medical staff
         2. Research and education
         3. Determine performance of ancillary units
         4. Quality improvement, credentialing, and utilization review
      iii. For accreditation compliance
         1. The Joint Commission (TJC, formerly the Joint Commission on Accreditation of Healthcare Organizations, JCAHO)
         2. Department of Health and Human Services (DHHS)
         3. Centers for Medicare and Medicaid Services (CMS)
         4. American College of Surgeons (ACS)
         5. American Osteopathic Association (AOA)
         6. Other organizations that have set standards and for which statistics can verify adherence to criteria
      iv. Healthcare agencies
         1. World Health Organization (WHO): the International Classification of Diseases (ICD) systems were developed under WHO.
         2. National Vital Statistics System (NVSS): responsible for the official vital statistics of the United States

3. National Center for Health Statistics (NCHS): federal government's principal vital and health statistics agency, which provides statistical information that will guide actions and policies to improve the health of the American public

4. Centers for Disease Control and Prevention (CDC): promotes health and quality of life by preventing and controlling disease, injury, and disability

5. State public health departments

c. Facilities That Maintain Healthcare Statistics
   i. Acute care
   ii. Long-term care
   iii. Home health care
   iv. Ambulatory care
   v. Veterinary care
   vi. Hospice
   vii. Psychiatric institutions
   viii. Insurance companies
   ix. Other facilities that provide health care

d. Standardized Data Sets for Healthcare Statistics
   i. Uniform Hospital Discharge Data Set (UHDDS): minimum common core of data on Medicare and Medicaid hospital discharges
   ii. Uniform Ambulatory Care Data Set (UACDS): minimum common core of data on ambulatory visits
   iii. Minimum Data Set for Long-Term Care: federally mandated standard assessment form used to collect demographic and clinical data on nursing home residents, which are used to develop a resident assessment protocol (RAP) summary for each resident
   iv. National Committee on Vital and Health Statistics: revised the UHDDS and approved UACDS
   v. Data Elements for Emergency Department System (DEEDS): uniform collection of data in hospital based emergency departments
   vi. Healthcare Effectiveness Data and Information Set (also known as 'The Health Plan Employer Data Information Set', HEDIS): sponsored by the National Committee for Quality Assurance (NCQA); a set of standard performance measures designed to provide purchasers and consumers of health care with the information they need to compare the performance of managed healthcare plans

e. Health Information Practitioner's Role
   i. Decide if health information collected meets statistical needs of healthcare facility
   ii. Be aware of sources of data within the facility
   iii. Be prepared to merge other data with data from the health record
   iv. Collect quality health data
   v. Organize data into databases
   vi. Statistically analyze collected data
   vii. Develop, generate, and interpret healthcare statistical reports

2. Vital Statistics
   a. Crucial events in life such as births, deaths, adoptions, marriages, and divorces
   b. NCHS recommends standard forms, which most states adopt to develop birth, death, and fetal death certificates.
   c. States have responsibility for the preparation of birth, death, and fetal death certificates; local registrar maintains and forwards certificates to state registrar; and states share this information with the NCHS.

d. Certificates (birth, fetal death, death)
  i. Certificate of live birth is used for registration purposes and is composed of two parts. The first part contains information related to the child and parents, and the second part is used to collect data on the mother's pregnancy.
  ii. The fetal death certificate is completed when a pregnancy results in a stillbirth. It contains information about the parents (including occupational data), the history of the pregnancy, the cause and date of the fetal death, and significant conditions of the fetus or mother.
  iii. Data from death certificates are used to compile causes of death. Death certificates contain information on the decedent, place of death, medical certification, and disposition of the body.

3. Analysis of Hospital Services
  a. Basic Healthcare Terms
    i. Hospital inpatient: a patient who is provided with room, board, and continuous general nursing services in an area of the hospital where patients generally stay at least overnight
    ii. Hospital newborn inpatient: a patient who is born in the hospital at the beginning of the current inpatient hospitalization. Newborns are usually counted separately in calculating some hospital performance indicators (e.g., average daily census, occupancy rate).
    iii. Inpatient hospitalization: a period in a person's life during which he or she is an inpatient in a single hospital without interruption, except by possible intervening leaves of absence
    iv. Inpatient discharge: the termination of a period of inpatient hospitalization through the formal release of the inpatient by the hospital; the term is used for patients who are discharged alive, against medical advice (AMA), or who died while hospitalized.
    v. Hospital outpatient: a hospital patient who receives services in one or more of the outpatient facilities when he or she is not currently an inpatient or home care patient
    vi. Census: number of patients present at any given time; see Table 4-1 as an example
    vii. Daily inpatient census: number of patients present at the official census-taking time (usually 12 midnight) each day, plus the number of patients admitted and discharged the same day
    viii. Inpatient service day: unit of measure denoting the services received by one inpatient in one 24-hour period
    ix. Total inpatient service days: sum of all inpatient service days for each of the days in the period under consideration; see Table 4-2

Table 4-1 Census

Patients in MICU on May 3, 20xx, at 11:30 AM
John Howard
Shirlyn Thomas
Carla Tyson
Census = 3

Table 4-2   Houston Hospital Total Inpatient Service Days

Patient Name	Inpatient Service Days for MICU
John Howard	6
Shirlyn Thomas	9
Carla Tyson	13
Total	**28**

   x. Length of stay: the number of calendar days from admission to discharge; for example, discharged May 9, admitted May 3 = 6 days

     1. Patients admitted and discharged the same day are assigned one inpatient service day.

     2. Patients admitted on one day and discharged the very next day are assigned one inpatient service day.

  xi. Total length of stay: the sum of days' stay of any group of inpatients discharged during a specific period of time; see Table 4-3

  xii. Inpatient bed count: the number of available facility inpatient beds both occupied and vacant on a given day

 xiii. Inpatient bed count day: the unit of measure denoting the presence of one inpatient bed, either occupied or vacant, set up and staffed for use in one 24-hour period

  xiv. Hospital inpatient autopsy: the postmortem examination performed in a hospital facility (performed by a pathologist or other responsible physician) on the body of a patient who died during inpatient hospitalization

  xv. Hospital autopsy: postmortem examination of the body of an individual who at some time in the past was a previous patient but who was not an inpatient at the time of death; this is performed by a pathologist or an assigned physician on staff

 xvi. Nosocomial infection: infections acquired during hospitalization

b. Inpatient Discharge Analysis

   i. Health record information is reviewed to determine types of services provided, length of stay, discharge status, and other data to assist in calculating hospital performance indicators.

Table 4-3   Total Length of Stay

Patient Name	Admitted	Discharged	Length of Stay (LOS)
John Howard	January 3	January 9	6
Shirlyn Thomas	January 18	January 27	9
Carla Tyson	January 14	January 27	13
Total			**28**

Table 4-4 Gains and Losses

Gains	Losses
Admissions to hospital (does not include DOAs)	Discharges (including deaths) from hospital
Transfers into hospital service or unit from another hospital service or unit	Transfers out of hospital service or unit to another hospital service or unit

c. Gains and Losses (see Table 4-4)
d. Assigning a Patient to a Service or Unit
    i. Medical staff organized into services or units
    ii. Describes the professional activities of existing medical staff units or specialty clinical education programs
e. Common Services Rendered by a Hospital
    i. Internal medicine
    ii. Surgery
    iii. Obstetrics and gynecology
    iv. Neonatal medicine
    v. Anesthesiology
    vi. Pediatric medicine
    vii. Radiology
    viii. Diagnostic imaging
    ix. Neurology
    x. Psychiatry
    xi. Pathology
f. Reports from Discharge Data (may be calculated by service or unit or on a daily, weekly, monthly, or annual basis)
    i. Hospital performance indicators
        1. Number of admissions and discharges
        2. Average daily census
        3. Average length of stay
        4. Occupancy rate
        5. Mortality rates
        6. Autopsy rate
        7. Infection rates
        8. Consultation rate
        9. Other indicators of hospital performance
    ii. Information on patient demographics
    iii. Case mix (grouping of patients based on a set of characteristics)
    iv. Expected sources of payment
    v. Other relevant information
g. Hospital Performance Indicator Formulas for Commonly Computed Healthcare Rates and Percentages

$$\text{Average Daily Census} = \frac{\text{Total service days for the unit for the period}}{\text{Total number of days in the period}}$$

$$\text{Average Length of Stay} = \frac{\text{Total length of stay (discharge days)}}{\text{Total discharges (includes deaths)}}$$

$$\text{Percentage of Occupancy} = \frac{\text{Total service days for a period}}{\text{Total bed count days in the period}} \times 100$$

$$\text{Hospital Death Rate (Gross)} = \frac{\text{Number of deaths of inpatients in period}}{\text{Number of discharges (including deaths)}} \times 100$$

$$\text{Hospital Death Rate (Net)} = \frac{\text{Number of deaths of inpatients in period} - \text{Inpatient deaths} < 48 \text{ hours}}{\text{Number of discharges (including deaths)} - \text{Inpatient deaths} < 48 \text{ hours}} \times 100$$

$$\text{Gross Autopsy Rate} = \frac{\text{Total inpatient autopsies for a given period}}{\text{Total inpatient deaths for the period}} \times 100$$

$$\text{Net Autopsy Rate} = \frac{\text{Total number of autopsies or inpatient deaths}}{\text{Total inpatient deaths minus unautopsied coroners' or medical examiners' cases}} \times 100$$

$$\text{Hospital Autopsy Rate (Adjusted)} = \frac{\text{Total hospital autopsies}}{\text{Number of deaths of hospital patients whose bodies are available for hospital autopsy}} \times 100$$

$$\text{Fetal Death Rate} = \frac{\text{Total number of intermediate and/or late fetal deaths for a period}}{\text{Total number of live births} + \text{intermediate and late fetal deaths for the period}} \times 100$$

$$\text{Neonatal Mortality Rate (Death Rate)} = \frac{\text{Total number of newborn deaths for a period}}{\text{Total number of newborn infant discharges (including deaths) for the period}} \times 100$$

$$\text{Maternal Mortality Rate (Death Rate)} = \frac{\text{Total number of obstetric maternal deaths for a period}}{\text{Total number of obstetric discharges (including deaths) for the period}} \times 100$$

$$\text{Cesarean Section Rate} = \frac{\text{Total number of cesarean sections performed in a period}}{\text{Total number of deliveries in the period (including cesarean sections)}} \times 100$$

4. Presentation of Data
   a. Data should be presented in a manner that catches the reader's attention, encourages interest, and makes data easy to interpret and use.
   b. Tables
      i. Columns of figures, each labeled to identify contents
      ii. Include title, date, and person who prepared table
      iii. Include narrative explanation of what table depicts (see Figure 4-1)

Houston Hospital January, 20xx Statistics of code 250.00			
Gender	Age	LOS	Discharges
Male	25.6	8.3	85
Female	24.0	4.2	43

Figure 4-1 Example of a Table

c. Frequency Distribution
    i. Groups data into classes
        1. Rules for classes
            a. 5 to 15 classes
            b. Smallest and largest figures represented
            c. Each item fits into one class only
            d. Classes should cover equal ranges of values
            e. A histogram is an example
d. Graphs
    i. Horizontal axis (independent variable)
    ii. Vertical axis (dependent variable)
    iii. Types of graphs
        1. Bar: used to report count values of categorical data (see Figure 4-2)
        2. Histogram: graphic representations of frequency distributions (see Figure 4-3)
        3. Line graph: used to provide a simple visual method of monitoring trends over time (see Figure 4-4)
        4. Pie chart: displays frequencies in each category (see Figure 4-5)
        5. Cause and effect diagrams: used to place factors that are expected to affect a problem, condition, or project in causal order; also called fishbone diagram (see Figure 4-6)

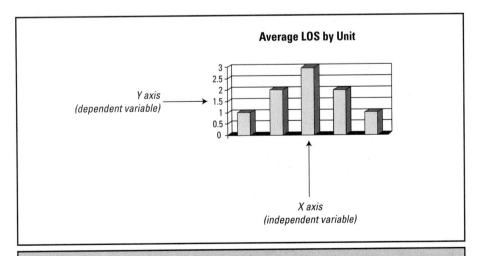

Figure 4-2 Example of a Bar Graph

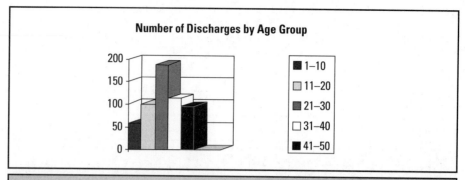

Figure 4-3   Example of a Histogram

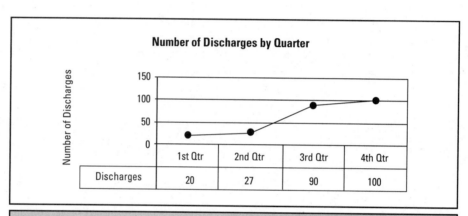

Figure 4-4   Example of a Line Graph

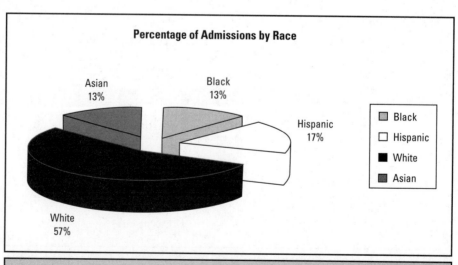

Figure 4-5   Example of a Pie Chart

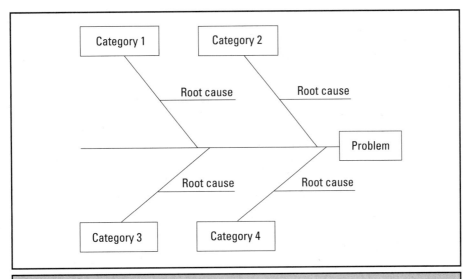

Figure 4-6   Example of a Cause and Effect Diagram

6. Pareto chart: similar to a bar chart or histogram; occurrences on chart are ordered from the most frequently occurring or most important category to the least frequent or least important (see Figure 4-7)
7. Scatter diagram: used to plot the points for two variables that may be related to each other (see Figure 4-8)
8. Frequency polygon graph: similar to a histogram; graph of a frequency distribution in line form rather than a bar graph (see Figure 4-9)

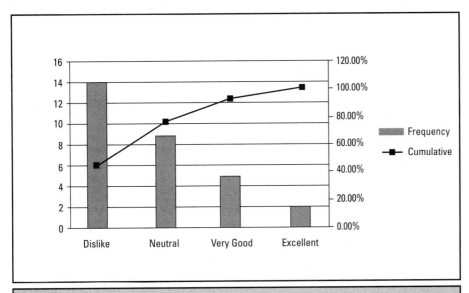

Figure 4-7   Example of a Pareto Chart

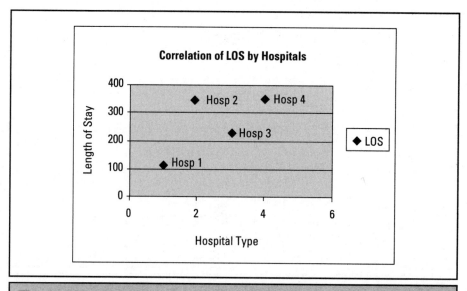

Figure 4-8   Example of a Scatter Diagram

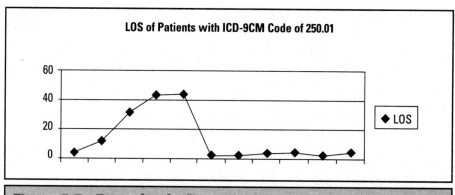

Figure 4-9   Example of a Frequency Polygon

5. Common Healthcare Statistical Measures and Tests
  a. Terms and Definitions
    i. Population
      1. Any defined aggregate of objects, persons, or events (sum total) subject to statistical study
    ii. Parameter: statistic calculated on a population value
    iii. Sample
      1. Any sub-aggregate drawn from the population
      2. A small group drawn from the population to make inferences about that population
    iv. Estimate: any statistic calculated on a sample of observations
    v. Types of samples
      1. Random sample: sample in which every member of the population has an equal probability of being included (e.g., 15 names placed in a hat and 10 drawn out)

  2. Cluster sample: random selection of a number of subjects from naturally occurring groups or clusters; the unit chosen is not an individual but a group of individuals who are grouped together (e.g., persons living in a ZIP code)

  3. Stratified sample: samples of a population that consists of a number of subgroups or strata that may differ in characteristics being studied (e.g., ethnic groups)

  4. Systematic sample: a sample drawn by taking every nth item from a list of the population (e.g., from a list of 100 names, select every 10th name on list)

  5. Sampling error: the principle that the characteristics of a sample are not identical to the characteristics of the population from which the sample is drawn

b. Ratios, Proportions, and Rates

  i. These measures indicate the number of times something happened relative to the number of times it could have happened.

  ii. The general formula for calculating ratios, proportions, and rates is $x/y = z$, where x is a sample, y is the population, and z is the ratio, proportion, or rate.

  iii. Ratios: the quantities being compared may be expressed so that x and y are completely independent of each other, or x may be included in y

  iv. Proportions: a type of ratio in which x is a subset or sample of y and the numerator is always included in the denominator

  v. Rates: used to measure events over a period of time

c. Measures of Central Tendency

  i. Typical values tend to lie centrally within a set of data arranged according to magnitude

  1. Mean: average calculated by adding the values of all observations and dividing the total by the number of observations

  2. Median: middle-most value when values are ranked in numeric order

  3. Mode: value that occurs most frequently

  a. When no value repeats more than once, there is no mode

  b. When several values repeat with the same frequency, each is the mode

d. Measures of Variability (also called measures of variation or measures of dispersion)

  i. The amount of variability of the measurement around the mean or median

  ii. The degree to which numerical data tend to be spread about an average value

  1. Range: the difference between the highest and lowest values

  2. Variance: how values are spread or dispersed around the mean; computed by squaring each deviation from the mean, summing them, and then dividing their sum by the degrees of freedom ($n - 1$)

  a. Degrees of freedom: any of the statistically independent values of a sample that are used to determine the property of the sample, as the mean or variance

  3. Standard deviation

  a. How values are spread or dispersed around the mean

  b. The most common measure of variation

    c. The square root of the variance

    d. Small standard deviation implies data are close to mean and large standard deviation implies data are more spread out from the mean.

    e. Example: December discharges for Houston Hospital had a mean of 6 days and a standard deviation of 2. Therefore, if a patient stayed in the hospital 1 standard deviation above the mean, he had a length of stay of 8 days (6 + 2 = 8). If a patient had a length of stay of 2 days, then he was in the hospital 2 standard deviations below the mean (6 − 2 − 2 = 2).

e. Normal Distribution

    i. Measures of central tendency and variation are interpreted as they relate to the normal distribution.

    ii. Theoretical family of distributions that may have any mean or any standard deviation

    iii. A bell-shaped curve (also referred to as normal curve) that is symmetrical about the mean

        1. 50% of observations fall above the mean and 50% fall below the mean.

        2. Each side of the mean extends to a tail.

        a. When the research hypothesis is directed to only one end of the curve, it is considered a one-tailed test. An alternative hypothesis (hypothesis that states there is an association between the independent and dependent variables) in which the researcher makes a prediction in one direction results in outcomes at one end of the curve.

        b. If the researcher makes no prediction about the direction of the results (more or less), the alternative hypothesis is two-tailed. Thus, the outcomes may fall at both ends of the curve.

        3. In Figure 4-10, the mean, median, and mode are all at 0.

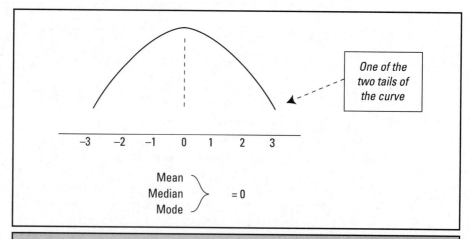

Figure 4-10   Example of a Bell-Shaped Curve

4. The standard deviation indicates how many observations fall within a certain range of the mean.
5. Values range from minus infinity to plus infinity, and
    a. 68.26% of all values fall within 1 standard deviation of the mean in each direction.
    b. 95.44% of all values fall within 2 standard deviations of the mean in each direction.
    c. 99.74% of all values fall within 3 standard deviations of the mean in each direction.
    d. Values that are more than 3 standard deviations from the mean in either direction are called outliers.

f. Test of Significance
  i. Purpose is to determine whether observed differences between groups, or relationships between variables in the sample being studied, are likely to be due to sampling error or are likely to reflect true differences or relationships in the population of interest.
  ii. The method utilized to test the null and alternative hypotheses
    1. Hypothesis
        a. Identifies the goal of the research and poses a tentative assumption to be tested
        b. Indicates the nature of the difference or relationship that is being tested
    2. Null hypothesis (symbolized as H_0) states there is no difference or relationship in the population under study.
    3. Alternative hypothesis states there is a difference or relationship in the population under study.
  iii. Commonly used methods to test the null hypothesis include T-test, chi-square, Pearson correlation coefficient, regression analysis, and analysis of variance (ANOVA).
    1. T-test determines if there is a significant difference between two groups with respect to the independent and dependent variables. (See Figure 4-11.)
        a. Independent variable is the variable to be manipulated; also called the experimental or treatment variable.
        b. Dependent variable is the variable that is measured to determine the effects of the experimental treatment; also referred to as the control.
    2. Chi-square determines if there is a significant difference between observed and expected frequencies; used for nominal data.
    3. Pearson correlation coefficient (see Figure 4-12)
        a. Expressed as r
        b. Ranges from 0 to ± 1
        c. Used to assess the direction and degree of relationship between two variables
        d. As r approaches 0, there tends to be less correlation between the variables; as r approaches 1, there tends to be more correlation.
        e. Coefficient of determination
            i. r-squared (or r^2)
            ii. Tells how much of the variation in y is accounted for by the x variable

Houston Hospital Length of Stay of Patients on Unit A and Unit B

Unit A	Unit B
1	2
3	2
4	4
5	4
7	6
7	7
8	7
9	7

T-Test: Paired Two Sample for Mean

	Unit A	Unit B
Mean	5.5	4.875
Variance	7.428571429	4.696428571
Observations	8	8
Pearson correlation	0.955350077	
Hypothesized mean difference	0	
df	7	
t-stat	1.929612462	
P(T<=t) one-tail	0.047488246	
t Critical one-tail	1.894577508	
P(T<=t) two-tail	0.094976492	
t Critical two-tail	2.36462256	

If t-stat > critical value, then reject H_0; if t-stat < critical value, accept H_0

Figure 4-11   Sample T-Test

Houston Hospital Length of Stay of Patients on Unit A, Unit B, and Unit C

Unit A	Unit B	Unit C
1	2	5
3	2	6
4	4	6
5	4	7
7	6	8
7	7	9
8	7	10
9	7	10

	Unit A	Unit B	Unit C
Unit A	1		
Unit B	0.955350077	1	
Unit C	0.96780197	0.95	1

Unit B with C

Unit A with C

Figure 4-12 Sample Correlation Coefficient

    iii. If $r = .80$, then $r^2 = .64$, and 64% of variation in y is accounted for by the x variable.
4. Regression analysis determines the extent to which one or more explanatory variables can predict an outcome variable (see Figure 4-13).
  a. Coefficient of determination (r^2)
    i. Ranges from 0 to 1
    ii. Represents the squared correlation between the explanatory variable(s) and the outcome variable
    iii. The value of r^2 indicates the proportion of variability in the outcome that is explained by the predictor variable(s).
    iv. The closer r^2 is to one, the stronger the prediction.
    v. P-value associated with r^2 indicates the probability that the observed value of r^2 could occur through sampling error alone.
5. ANOVA determines if there is a significant difference between two or more groups (see Figure 4-14).
iv. The computed result of the test of significance is called the test statistic or t-stat. The absolute value of the t-stat is compared to the critical value. If the t-stat is greater than the critical value, then the researcher will reject the null hypothesis.

Houston Hospital Length of Stay of Patients on Unit A and Unit B

Unit A	Unit B
1	2
3	2
4	4
5	4
7	6
7	7
8	7
9	7

Summary Output

Regression statistics

Multiple r	0.955350077
r square	0.91269377
Adjusted r square	0.898142732
Standard error	0.869858605
Observations	8

r^2 means 91% of variation in unit B can be accounted to unit A

ANOVA

	df	SS	MS	F	Significance F
Regression	1	47.46007605	47.46007605	62.72361809	0.000215151
Residual	6	4.539923954	0.756653992		
Total	7	52			

	Coefficients	Standard Error	t-stat	p-value	Lower 95%
Intercept	−0.357414449	0.800982857	−0.446219848	0.671090496	−2.317350327
Unit B	1.201520913	0.15171055	7.919824372	0.000215151	0.830298298

Figure 4-13 Sample Regression Analysis

1. Measures the size of the difference or relationship observed in the sample
2. The probability that the observed value of the test statistic could occur in the event that the null hypothesis is true is called the p-value, which ranges from 0 to 1.
   a. p-value answers the question: how likely is it that the observed difference or relationship is due to chance or due to sampling error?
   b. As the p-value approaches 0, the smaller the probability that the observed difference or relationship is due to chance or sampling error.

Houston Hospital Length of Stay of Patients on Unit A, Unit B, and Unit C

Unit A	Unit B	Unit C
1	2	5
3	2	5
4	4	6
5	4	7
7	6	7
7	7	8
8	7	9
9	7	10

ANOVA: Single Factor
Summary

Groups	Count	Sum	Average	Variance
Unit A	8	44	5.5	7.428571429
Unit B	8	39	4.875	4.696428571
Unit C	8	57	7.125	3.267857143

ANOVA

Source of variation	SS	df	MS	F	p-value	F crit
Between groups	21.58333333	2	10.79166667	2.10324826	0.147035257	3.466794851
Within groups	107.75	21	5.130952381			
Total	129.3333333	23				

If t-stat > critical value, then reject H_0; if t-stat < critical value, accept H_0

Figure 4-14   Sample ANOVA

v. Level of significance (see Figure 4-15)
1. Also referred to as alpha level and symbolized by the Greek letter α
2. p-value is compared to level of significance to determine whether to accept or reject the null hypothesis; if p-value is less than the alpha level, then the researcher will reject the null hypothesis.
3. Common levels of significance are .05 and .01.
   a. At .05, the probability is smaller than 5 in 100 that the observed difference or relationship is due to sampling error or chance.
   b. At .01, the probability is smaller than 1 in 100 that the observed difference or relationship is due to sampling error or chance.
vi. Type I error: rejecting the null hypothesis when it is true
vii. Type II error: accepting the null hypothesis when it is false

Test of Significance		
T-Test: Paired Two Sample for Mean .05 Level of Significance		
	Unit A	**Unit B**
Mean	15.5	14.875
Variance	7.428571429	4.696428571
Observations	8	8
Pearson correlation	0.955350077	
Hypothesized mean difference	0	
df	7	
t-stat	1.929612462	
P(T<=t) one-tail	0.047488246	
t Critical one-tail	1.894577508	
P(T<=t) two-tail	0.094976492	
t Critical two-tail	2.36462256	

p-value of a one- or two-tailed test at .05 level of significance; reject H_0

Figure 4-15   Sample Level of Significance Test

6. Research
   a. Scientific inquiry or question to increase the body of knowledge; may be applied or basic
      i. Applied research is directed toward improvement of actual practice.
      ii. Basic research is directed toward general explanations.
   b. Common Terms in Research
      i. Independent variable
         1. The variable to be manipulated
         2. Also called the experimental or treatment variable
      ii. Dependent variable
         1. The variable that is measured to determine the effects of the experimental treatment
         2. Also referred to as the control
      iii. Reliability: accuracy of the data in the sense of its reproducibility; the likelihood that the experiment will yield the same results on repeated trials
      iv. Validity
         1. Degree to which an instrument measures what it should measure
         2. Assesses relevance, completeness, accuracy (the result of an active effort to comprehend and verify; shows careful conformity to the fact or truth), and correctness (free from errors, mistakes, or faults)
   c. Scientific Method for Performing Research
      i. Define the problem (statement of the problem); determine population under study
      ii. Review the literature addressing previous or related investigations

       iii. Formulate a hypothesis

           1. Define the null and alternative hypotheses

           2. State the independent and dependent variables

       iv. Select a research method or design, including tools to be used

           1. Experimental

           2. Observational study

           3. Surveys and questionnaires

           4. Interviews

           5. Historical-prospective

           6. Participant observation

           7. Cross-sectional or prevalence study

           8. Cohort study

           9. Case control

       v. Collect the data from sample abstracted from population

       vi. Analyze the results

           1. Test of significance (T-test, chi-square, ANOVA, etc.)

           2. Compare computed result of p-value to alpha level or compare test statistic to critical value

           3. Accept or reject null hypothesis

       vii. Draw conclusions

7. Epidemiology

  a. Definition

       i. The study of disease and the determinants of disease in populations

       ii. The study of clinical and healthcare trends or patterns and the ability to recognize trends or patterns within large amounts of data

       iii. The study of the distribution and determinants of diseases and injuries in human populations

  b. Common Epidemiological Terms

       i. Health: state of complete physical, mental, and social well-being, and not merely the absence of disease

       ii. Levels of prevention

           1. Primary: prevention by reducing exposure

           2. Secondary: early detection and treatment

           3. Tertiary: alleviation of disability resulting from disease

       iii. Rehabilitation: attempt to restore an affected individual to a useful, satisfying, and self-sufficient role in society

       iv. Risk factor: associated with an increased likelihood that the disease will develop at a later time

       v. Cohort: a group under study for a period of time

       vi. Epidemic: the occurrence in a community or region of a group of illnesses of similar nature, clearly in excess of normal expectancy

       vii. Endemic: the habitual presence of a disease or infectious agent within a geographical area or the usual prevalence of a given disease within such area

       viii. Prevalence rate (PR): the number of existing cases of a disease in a specified time period, divided by the population at that time; describes the magnitude of an epidemic

$$PR = \frac{\text{All new and preexising cases of a specific disease during a given time period} \times 10^{10}}{\text{Total population during the same time period}}$$

1. Example:

$$\frac{\text{Number of children 12 years and under with bacterial meningitis in Houston, Texas} \times 10^{10}}{\text{Number of children 12 years and under in Houston, Texas}}$$

ix. Incident rate (IR): the number of newly reported cases of a disease in a specified time period, divided by the population at that time; used to compare the frequency of disease in populations

$$\text{IR} = \frac{\text{Total number of new cases of a specific disease during a given period of time} \times 10^{10}}{\text{Total population at risk during the same time period}}$$

1. Example:

$$\frac{\text{New Texas cases of children 12 years and under with bacterial meningitis in July 20xx} \times 10^{10}}{\text{Number of Texas children 12 years and under in July 20xx}}$$

x. Relative risk (RR): used to determine which groups have a greater risk of developing the disease under study

$$\text{RR} = \frac{\text{Incidence rate exposed } (I_r e)}{\text{Incidence rate unexposed } (I_r o)}$$

xi. Epidemiological research
  1. Descriptive cross-sectional prevalence study
    a. Concurrently describes or examines the distribution of disease or characteristics and health outcomes at one specific point or period in time
    b. Used when little is known about the disease or characteristic under study
    c. Used to generate hypotheses, not to test them
  2. Case-control or retrospective
    a. Analytical study design in which a disease or health condition is examined to determine possible causes
    b. Researcher collects data on disease and controls by looking back in time.
  3. Prospective: determines whether the characteristics or suspected risk factors preceded the disease or health condition
  4. Cohort: prospective study in which subjects are separated into two groups based upon their exposures or health characteristics and then followed forward to determine whether they develop the disease
  5. Historical prospective: past records are used to collect information regarding the exposure characteristics or risk factors under study
  6. Experimental studies for clinical and community trials: modify the health characteristics that are found to cause the disease by using healthcare interventions that control progression of the disease or prevent the disease from occurring

PRACTICAL APPLICATION OF YOUR KNOWLEDGE

1. Healthcare Statistics

    a. Define statistics.

    b. Explain the importance of maintaining healthcare statistics.

    c. What is the health information manager's role in healthcare statistics?

    d. Write the formulas for the following hospital performance indicators:
        i. Average daily census

        ii. Average length of stay

        iii. Occupancy rate

        iv. Death rate (gross versus net)

        v. Gross autopsy rate

        vi. Net autopsy rate

        vii. Hospital-adjusted autopsy rate

    e. The Oncology Department Committee has established a quality monitor to report and review all cancer cases with the diagnosis of carcinoma of the lung, right upper lobe, and a frozen-section pathology report indicating normal lung tissue. What would be the correct formula to accurately calculate the percentage of cases that meet these criteria?

2. Vital Statistics
   a. Describe vital record information collected in healthcare institutions.

3. Statistical Measures
   a. Discuss the measures of central tendency.

   b. Describe the measures of dispersion.

   c. What does the standard deviation tell the researcher about the distribution?

   d. Explain the relationship of the confidence interval to the p-value.

   e. Explain the following terms:
   i. Test of significance

   ii. Level of significance

   iii. Test statistic

   iv. p-value

   v. Critical value

   vi. Confidence interval

   vii. T-test

viii. ANOVA

ix. Chi-square

x. Pearson r correlation coefficient

xi. Coefficient of determination

f. Describe a normal distribution.

g. Write the general formula for calculating ratios, proportions, and rates.

4. Research
   a. Define research.

   b. Describe various research methods.

   c. What test of significance would be used to determine the significant difference in frequencies between the two groups under study?

   d. List the steps in the scientific method of performing research.

   e. Define hypothesis, alternative hypothesis, and null hypothesis.

   f. Which hypothesis is tested utilizing the scientific method?

g. Considering a two-tailed test and given the data and T-test results in the table, decide if the researcher should accept or reject the following null hypothesis at the .05 level of significance:

H_0: There is no significant difference at the .05 level of significance in the monthly average length of stay of inpatients admitted in Texas and California acute-care hospitals for the past year.

Average Length of Stay in Texas and California Acute-Care Hospitals by Month

Month	Texas	California
Jan	5	11
Feb	7	12
Mar	6	12
Apr	10	13
May	7	9
Jun	7	9
Jul	7	7
Aug	8	13
Sep	9	19
Oct	12	19
Nov	4	5
Dec	5	7

T-Test: Paired two sample for means

	Texas	California
Mean	7.25	11.33333333
Variance	5.113636364	19.33333333
Observations	12	12
Pearson correlation	0.804584565	
Hypothesized mean difference	0	
df	11	
t-stat	−4.866928756	
P(T<=t) one-tail	0.000248569	
t Critical one-tail	1.795883691	
P(T<=t) two-tail	0.000497139	
t Critical two-tail	2.200986273	

5. Epidemiology
  a. Discuss the importance of gathering epidemiology statistics in relation to an outbreak of a highly infectious disease.

  b. Prevalence rate
    i. Define.

    ii. Write the formula.

    iii. Give an example.

  c. Incidence rate
    i. Define.

    ii. Write the formula.

    iii. Give an example.

6. Computation of Hospital Performance Indicators

For questions a–c, utilize the following annual hospital report to calculate the requested hospital performance indicators.

Annual Statistics for General Hospital (non-leap year)

Admissions		Bed Count	
Adults and children	15,450	Adults and children	450
Newborns	680	Bassinets	60
Inpatient Service Days		Total Length of Stay	
Adults and children	125,031	Adults and children	89,231
Newborns	7090	Newborns	986
Discharges (including deaths)		Surgery Statistics	
Adults and children	15,684	Number of patients operated on	899
Newborns	623	Surgical procedures performed	926

Inpatient Deaths			Miscellaneous	
Total adults and children			Cesarean sections	95
Less than 48 hr	20		Deliveries	669
More than 48 hr	321		Obstetric discharges	
Total newborns			(including deaths)	780
Less than 48 hr	10		Hospital infections	68
More than 48 hr	1		Post-op infections	18
Anesthesia deaths	2		Consultations	5800
Fetal deaths				
(Intermediate and late)	4			
Maternal deaths	1			
Post-op deaths	68			

Inpatient Autopsies			Other Autopsies	
Adults and children	18		Coroner's cases	2
Newborn	1		(Unavailable for autopsy)	
			Hospital outpatients	6

a. Calculate the average length of stay.

b. Calculate the death rate.

c. Calculate the gross autopsy rate.

d. If General Hospital had 1000 inpatient service days for March, what was the average daily census?

7. You are the newly employed statistician at Memorial Hospital. The management information system is currently being redesigned. To assure that the statistics are being calculated correctly, you manually calculate the statistics to assure accuracy. The following statistics are given for the month of July:

Memorial Hospital Occupancy Rate	
Category	**Number**
Admissions	929
Discharges	909
Discharge days	4988
Census days	5022
Beds	250
Patients remaining last day of month	184

What was the occupancy rate? Round off to one place behind the decimal.

TEST YOUR KNOWLEDGE

Select the best answer for the questions or incomplete statements.
Use the following table for questions 1–4.

Month	Total Admissions	Total Discharges	Inpatient Service Days	Length of Stay	Bed Count
January	945	910	6750	6615	250
February	901	889	7130	6082	250
March	872	894	7470	5668	300

1. Calculate the average daily census for the month of January. Round off to a whole number.
   a. 213
   b. 216
   c. 218
   d. 237

2. Calculate the average daily census for the quarter. Round off to a whole number.
   a. 201
   b. 204
   c. 234
   d. 237

3. Calculate the average length of stay for the quarter. Round off to one place behind the decimal.
   a. 6.7
   b. 6.8
   c. 7.8
   d. 7.9

4. Calculate the occupancy rate for the quarter. Round off to one place behind the decimal.
   a. 75.4%
   b. 76.4%
   c. 88.8%
   d. 89.2%

5. The standard deviation (SD) describes the range of dispersion from the average or mean. The smaller the SD, the more the values in the distribution are:
   a. skewed around the mean.
   b. scattered out from the mean.
   c. varied from the mean of the population.
   d. closer to the mean.

6. A patient who is admitted into the hospital at 9:01 AM and dies at 11:58 PM the same day would be:
   a. counted as one inpatient service day.
   b. subtracted from the daily inpatient census count for the date of admission.
   c. reported based on number of hours of care rendered instead of inpatient service days.
   d. subtracted from the daily inpatient census count for the next day following his or her death.

Use the following information for questions 7–11.

In the month of July, 7 adults, 1 child, and 1 newborn died at Houston Hospital. A total of 256 admissions and 237 discharges for adults and children were reported for the same month. Live births for July were 114 with 5 fetal deaths recorded (3 early, 1 intermediate, and 1 late). Autopsies were performed on 3 adults, the child, the newborn, and 1 late fetal death case. One of the adult bodies was released to the coroner for examination. Additionally, 1 patient died in the emergency room and was autopsied. Three home care patients died and were brought to the hospital for autopsy.

7. What was the death rate (gross) for the month? Round off to two places behind the decimal.
   a. 2.95%
   b. 3.38%
   c. 3.52%
   d. 3.79%

8. What was the gross autopsy rate for the month? Round off to two places behind the decimal.
   a. 42.86%
   b. 55.56%
   c. 66.67%
   d. 77.78%

9. Calculate the net autopsy rate for the month. Round off to two places behind the decimal.
   a. 50.00%
   b. 55.56%
   c. 62.50%
   d. 66.67%

10. Calculate the fetal death rate for the month. Round off to two places behind the decimal.
    a. 1.72%
    b. 1.75%
    c. 4.20%
    d. 4.39%

11. What was the hospital adjusted autopsy rate for the month? Round off to two places behind the decimal.
    a. 41.67%
    b. 62.50%
    c. 69.23%
    d. 75.00%

12. If the researcher wants to set the p-value at .05, what would the alpha level be?
    a. .001
    b. .01
    c. .05
    d. .95

13. Calculate the mode for the following distribution: 2, 4, 5, 5, 6, 7, 10, 5
    a. 5.0
    b. 5.5
    c. 6.0
    d. 7.0

14. A researcher wants to test the following null hypothesis: There is no significant difference in the number of deaths at for-profit and not-for-profit hospitals. Which test of significance should the researcher use?
    a. T-test
    b. Pearson product moment correlation coefficient
    c. Regression analysis
    d. Chi-square

15. Woman's Hospital had a total of 225 live births, 5 intermediate and late fetal deaths, and 4 early fetal deaths during the month of March. There were 235 newborn discharges for the month. Compute the fetal death rate for March.
    a. 1.77
    b. 1.78
    c. 2.17
    d. 4.00

16. In a normal distribution, a researcher calculated a mean of 15 and a standard deviation of 5. What is the value of 3 standard deviations below the mean?
    a. 0
    b. 8
    c. 10
    d. 12

17. The surgical department of Houston Hospital conducted a study on post-surgical deaths and age of patients. The researcher hypothesized, "there is a relationship between post-surgical deaths and the age of the patients." This statement is generally called what?
    a. Statement of the problem
    b. Hypothesis
    c. Independent variable
    d. Dependent variable

18. Mr. and Mrs. Howard are making plans to choose a community hospital that renders quality health care. They have narrowed the hospitals to four in the Houston area. They will make their final decision based on the local hospitals' post-op death rates. Based on the following data, which hospital will Mr. and Mrs. Howard decide to utilize?

Community Hospital				
Community Hospital	Patients Operated On	Surgical Operations	Post-op Deaths	Deaths
Get Well General	132	204	3	9
Stay Healthy Wellness Center	154	189	4	8
Houston Honorary	148	199	4	9
Tyson Memorial	163	213	3	7

    a. Get Well General
    b. Stay Healthy Wellness Center
    c. Houston Honorary
    d. Tyson Memorial

19. Based upon the following statistics during the month of December, what was the fetal death rate for Houston Hospital?

Fetal Deaths	
Fetal Deaths	**Number**
Early	240
Intermediate	40
Late	32
Births	980
Deliveries	994
Newborn discharges	1008

a. 6.84%
b. 7.31%
c. 7.43%
d. 31.85%

20. Calculate the gross autopsy rate for Houston Hospital given the following data.

Gross Autopsy Rate	
Category	**Value**
Discharges (including deaths)	1000
Death	
Total deaths	56
Inpatient deaths (including two coroner cases)	52
Outpatient deaths	2
Home care deaths	2
Autopsies	
Total autopsies	13
Inpatient autopsies	10
Outpatient autopsies	1
Home care autopsies	2

a. 17.86%
b. 19.23%
c. 23.21%
d. 25.00%

21. Houston Hospital has 520 beds and 70 bassinets, and discharged 1454 adult and child inpatients and 332 newborns during the month of September. A total of 9202 discharge days were recorded at the time of discharge for these adults and children and 1554 discharge days for newborns. Census days for adults was 9901, 331 for children, and 905 for newborns. What was the average daily census for adults and children?
    a. 341
    b. 347
    c. 358
    d. 359

22. A normal distribution has a mean of 87 days and a standard deviation of 13. How many days are 3 standard deviations below the mean?
    a. 48
    b. 84
    c. 100
    d. 126

23. As Director of Health Information at Mercy Hospital, MiMi Goodstudy is responsible for assuring that the hospital statistics are recorded correctly. She reports that 14 patients were discharged from the medical service from June 1 through June 15. The length of stay for each patient was 17, 3, 4, 25, 8, 7, 13, 10, 5, 11, 9, 21, 3, and 1. What was the median stay for these patients?
    a. 8.0
    b. 8.5
    c. 9.0
    d. 9.5

24. As Director of Health Information at Mercy Hospital, Linda is responsible for assuring that the hospital statistics are recorded correctly. She reports that 14 patients were discharged from the medical service from June 1 to June 15. The length of stay for each patient was 17, 3, 4, 25, 8, 7, 13, 10, 5, 11, 9, 21, 3, and 1. What was the average length of stay for the first 15 days of June?
    a. 8.0
    b. 8.5
    c. 9.8
    d. 11.1

25. As Director of Health Information at Mercy Hospital, Tella is responsible for assuring that the hospital statistics are recorded correctly. She reports that 15 patients were discharged from MICU from October 1 to October 31. The length of stay for each patient was 20, 3, 17, 3, 4, 25, 8, 7, 13, 10, 5, 11, 9, 21, and 1. What was the average length of stay for these patients?
    a. 8.9
    b. 9.8
    c. 10.5
    d. 11.1

Use the following statistics of Houston Hospital for questions 26–27.

Houston Hospital January Statistics	
Category	**Value**
Beds	509
Admissions	1145
Census days	10,225
Discharges	1244
Deaths	20
Autopsies	13
Medical examiner cases	1

26. What was the net autopsy rate?
   a. 63.82%
   b. 65.01%
   c. 68.42%
   d. 100%

27. What was the death (gross) rate?
   a. 1.59%
   b. 1.61%
   c. 1.67%
   d. 1.71%

28. Calculate the average daily census for June.
   Admissions: 610
   Discharges: 673
   Patients remaining last day of month: 198
   Discharge days: 1055
   Beds: 301
   Inpatient service days: 1113
   a. 34
   b. 35
   c. 36
   d. 37

29. During March, 19 patients were discharged with a total of 209 discharge days. Which of the following may be calculated from the aforementioned data?
   a. Average daily census
   b. Average length of stay
   c. Average daily discharges
   d. Average monthly discharges

30. During the previous year, a large county in Texas reported 28 homicides to the Health Department. There were 35% from gunshot wounds, 25% from stabbings, 3% due to domestic violence, and 2% from road rage. Given the preceding data, what would be the best graphical presentation?
   a. One-variable bar graph
   b. Line graph
   c. Table
   d. Pie chart

31. During the month of April, several patients had the exact same length of stay. The following reports number of patients with the same length of stay. What was the average length of stay?

Average Length of Stay	
Number of Patients	**Length of Stay**
1	105
209	3
311	2

a. 17.6
b. 12.3
c. 4.8
d. 2.6

32. The surgical department of Houston Hospital conducted a study on post-surgical deaths and age of patients. The researcher hypothesized, "There is no relationship between post-surgical deaths and the age of the patients." This statement is generally called the:
a. research hypothesis.
b. statement of the problem.
c. review of literature.
d. null hypothesis.

Use the following table for questions 33–39 about Houston Hospital.

Annual Patient Data for Houston Hospital		
Number	January–May	June–December
Beds	500	512
Bassinets	50	48
Admissions		
Adults	604	652
Children	201	198
Newborn live births	183	189
Discharges		
Adults	500	600
Children	150	205
Newborns	173	199
Deaths		
Adults	3	4
Children	0	2
Newborns	1	2
Inpatient Service Days		
Adults	4001	4500
Children	235	268
Newborn	498	606
Discharge Days		
Adults	4355	3998
Children	202	300
Newborn	500	599
Fetal Deaths		
Early	5	7
Intermediate	3	5
Late	1	3

33. Calculate the average daily census for newborns for the year.
    a. 2
    b. 3
    c. 4
    d. 5

34. Calculate the average length of stay for adults and children.
    a. 5.9
    b. 6.0
    c. 6.1
    d. 6.8

35. Calculate the average daily inpatient census (adults and children) for the year.
    a. 22
    b. 23
    c. 24
    d. 25

36. Calculate the newborn death rate.
    a. 0.81%
    b. 1.34%
    c. 4.03%
    d. 7.26%

37. Calculate the occupancy rate (adults and children) for the year.
    a. 2.44%
    b. 4.87%
    c. 5.46%
    d. 87%

38. Based on the occupancy rate, how would you describe the financial solvency of the hospital?
    a. Excellent
    b. Very good
    c. Good
    d. Poor

39. Calculate the fetal death rate.
    a. 2.18%
    b. 3.13%
    c. 3.23%
    d. 6.45%

40. Based on the following statistics for the month of December, what was the fetal death rate for Houston Hospital?

Fetal Death Rate for Houston Hospital	
Category	Value
Live births	980
Deliveries	994
Newborn discharges	1008
Fetal deaths (early)	240
Fetal deaths (intermediate)	40
Fetal deaths (late)	32

    a. 6.84%
    b. 7.31%
    c. 7.43%
    d. 31.85%

Use the following information for questions 41–44.

Patient Jones was admitted to Houston Honorary Hospital on June 28 for tachycardia. The physician discharged Ms. Jones on July 8 with a discharge diagnosis of "rule out stress."

41. How many discharge days were rendered to Ms. Jones upon discharge?
   a. 7
   b. 9
   c. 10
   d. 11

42. How many inpatient service days were rendered to Ms. Jones during June?
   a. 0
   b. 2
   c. 3
   d. 10

43. How may discharge days were rendered to Ms. Jones during June?
   a. 0
   b. 1
   c. 2
   d. 10

44. How many inpatient service days were rendered to Ms. Jones during July?
   a. 0
   b. 7
   c. 8
   d. 10

45. What was the average daily census in a 500-bed hospital that had 14,942 inpatient service days and 15,001 discharge days during the month of October?
   a. 482
   b. 483
   c. 484
   d. 498

46. Last year, Houston Hospital averaged 98 births a month with a standard deviation of 6. There were 107 births in January. How does the number of births in January compare to the average?
   a. It is 1 standard deviation above the mean.
   b. It is 1.5 standard deviations above the mean.
   c. It is 1 standard deviation below the mean.
   d. It is 1.5 standard deviations below the mean.

47. Given the Pearson r calculations in the following table, calculate the coefficient of determination of the patients' lengths of stays in July and August.

Patient Length of Stay (LOS) for July and August		
Patient	**July**	**August**
Jones	15	16
Tyson	12	15
Thomas	11	12
Howard	10	10
Johnson	9	5
Williams	2	2
	July	**August**
Pearson r July	1	
Pearson r August	0.918506	1

 a. .081
 b. .843
 c. 1.00
 d. 1.91

48. A researcher tested to determine if there is a significant difference in the number of male and female HIM students at the .05 level of significance. In the study, the researcher observed a total of 16 students, 2 male and 14 female. Given the chi-square contingency table, how many male students should the researcher have postulated or expected?

Chi-Square Contingency Table		
	Male	**Female**
Expected	x	y
Observed	2	14

 a. 0
 b. 2
 c. 8
 d. 14

49. A physician's clinic was visited by 10 adolescent patients. Their weights were 79, 82, 78, 81, 87, 92, 99, 79, 80, and 84. What was the mean weight of the patients?
 a. 79.0
 b. 81.5
 c. 83.0
 d. 84.1

50. Given the following data and ANOVA results, decide if the researcher should accept or reject the following null hypothesis (H_0): There is no significant difference at the .05 level of significance in the number of inpatient autopsies performed at East, West, and North Hospitals for the past year.

Annual Autopsy Report for East, West, and North Hospitals

Month	East	West	North
January	4	2	12
February	4	1	12
March	4	1	34
April	5	1	5
May	7	1	43
June	1	2	23
July	0	2	20
August	0	4	19
September	6	1	16
October	7	5	23
November	4	3	17
December	5	2	12

ANOVA: Single factor

Summary

Groups	Count	Sum	Average	Variance
East	12	47	3.916666667	5.901515152
West	12	25	2.083333333	1.71969697
North	12	236	19.66666667	107.6969697

ANOVA

Source of Variation	SS	df	MS	F	p-value	F crit
Between groups	2242.388889	2	1121.194444	29.16784917	5.06887E-08	3.284924333
Within groups	1268.5	33	38.43939394			
Total	3510.888889	35				

a. Accept null hypothesis
b. Reject null hypothesis
c. Resulted in a Type I error
d. Not enough information to calculate

FORMULAS FOR COMMONLY COMPUTED HEALTHCARE RATES AND PERCENTAGES

$$\text{Average Daily Census} = \frac{\text{Total service days for the unit for the period}}{\text{Total number of days in the period}}$$

$$\text{Average Length of Stay} = \frac{\text{Total length of stay (discharge days)}}{\text{Total discharges (includes deaths)}}$$

$$\text{Percentage of Occupancy} = \frac{\text{Total service days for a period}}{\text{Total bed count days in the period}} \times 100$$

$$\text{Hospital Death Rate (Gross)} = \frac{\text{Number of deaths of inpatients in period}}{\text{Number of discharges (including deaths)}} \times 100$$

$$\text{Hospital Death Rate (Net)} = \frac{\text{Number of deaths of inpatients in period} - \text{Inpatient deaths} < 48 \text{ hours}}{\text{Number of discharges (including deaths)} - \text{Inpatient deaths} < 48 \text{ hours}} \times 100$$

$$\text{Gross Autopsy Rate} = \frac{\text{Total inpatient autopsies for a given period}}{\text{Total inpatient deaths for the period}} \times 100$$

$$\text{Net Autopsy Rate} = \frac{\text{Total inpatients for a given period}}{\text{Total inpatient deaths minus unautopsied coroners' or medical examiners' cases}} \times 100$$

$$\text{Hospital Autopsy Rate (Adjusted)} = \frac{\text{Total hospital autopsies}}{\text{Number of deaths of hospital patients whose bodies are available for hospital autopsy}} \times 100$$

$$\text{Postoperative Death Rate} = \frac{\text{Postoperative deaths}}{\text{Number of who die within 10 days of surgery}} \times 100$$

$$\text{Fetal Death Rate} = \frac{\text{Total number of intermediate and/or late fetal deaths for a period}}{\text{Total number of live births} + \text{intermediate and late fetal deaths for the period}} \times 100$$

$$\text{Neonatal Mortality Rate (Death Rate)} = \frac{\text{Total number of newborn deaths for a period}}{\text{Total number of newborn infant discharges (including deaths) for the period}} \times 100$$

$$\text{Maternal Mortality Rate (Death Rate)} = \frac{\text{Total number of obstetric maternal deaths for a period}}{\text{Total number of obstetric discharges (including deaths) for the period}} \times 100$$

$$\text{Cesarean Section Rate} = \frac{\text{Total number of cesarean sections performed in a period}}{\text{Total number of deliveries in the period (including cesarean sections)}} \times 100$$

$$\text{Infection Rate} = \frac{\text{Number of infection occurrences in a period}}{\text{Number of discharges in the period}} \times 100$$

$$\text{Postoperative Infection Rate} = \frac{\text{Number of infections in clean surgical cases in a period}}{\text{Number of surgical operations in the period}} \times 100$$

Quality Management and Performance Improvement

1. **Clinical Quality Assessment**
   a. Definitions of Terms
      i. Adverse event: the result of medical intervention in which the outcome was unforeseen and unexpected.
      ii. Benchmarking: performance comparison of one organization with that of a similar organization in that area
      iii. Compliance: process of meeting a prescribed set of standards or regulations to maintain active accreditation, licensure, or certification status
         1. Compulsory or voluntary
         2. Accreditation, licensure, certification
            a. Accreditation: the act of granting approval to a healthcare organization
            b. Licensure: the act of granting a healthcare organization or an individual healthcare practitioner permission to provide services of a defined scope in a limited geographical area
            c. Certification: approval for a healthcare organization to provide services to a specific group of beneficiaries
      iv. Error: an unintended act, either of omission or commission, or an act that does not achieve its intended outcome
      v. Indicator
         1. A quantifiable measurement or standard to distinguish acceptable from unacceptable performance.
         2. Performance measure that enables healthcare organizations to monitor a process to determine whether the organization is meeting process requirements
         3. May be established and implemented internally, externally, or generically
         4. May be written as ratio, such as number of admissions meeting criteria × 100 / number of admissions
      vi. Performance improvement: set of activities designed to increase the existing level of effectiveness or efficiency of existing performance
      vii. Quality: degree of excellence; superior in kind

   viii. Quality assurance: group of activities designed to measure the quality of a service, product, or process, with the intention to maintain a desired standard

   ix. Quality assessment: process of measuring and evaluating service activities to determine the current level of quality

   x. Quality control: a group of activities designed to detect and recognize positive and negative variances with the existing performance and to ensure predictable outcome

   xi. Quality improvements: methods or activities designated for the purpose of increasing the quality of a service or product

   xii. Quality management: the process of coordinating all quality activities as necessary towards the accomplishment of desirable performance outcome

   xiii. Sentinel event: an unexpected occurrence involving death or serious physical or psychological injury to a patient

   xiv. Root cause analysis: process for identifying the basic or causative factor that underlines variation in performance

   xv. Safety: all healthcare facilities are required to report all suspected and identified patient safety occurrences related to care or lack of care, that resulted, or could have resulted, to a patient.

   xvi. Total quality management: a mentality or philosophy based upon continuous quality improvement in the complete process of providing care

   xvii. Pay for performance (P4P): financially reward providers who achieve specific quality goals or patient safety goals.

   xviii. "Never event": hospital-acquired conditions considered by CMS to be preventable, high cost, and resulting in additional cost or high volume

   xix. Accountable care organization (ACO): a legal entity that is recognized and authorized under applicable state, federal, or tribal law as identified by a taxpayer identification number (TIN), and formed by one or more ACO participants that work together to coordinate and manage care for Medicare fee-for-service beneficiaries

   1. The ACO must be accountable for the quality, cost, and overall care of the beneficiaries assigned to the ACO.

   xx. The quality of healthcare services is regulated by the conditions of participation and by state health department regulations.

b. Historical Perspectives

   i. Through the law, regulations, standards, and required review processes, the federal, state, and local government and other stakeholders have influence in the quality management of healthcare facilities and their services.

   1. The 1700s

   a. In the mid-1700s, Pennsylvania Hospital becomes the model for the organization and development of hospitals.

   b. In 1760, New York State begins the practice of medical licensure.

   c. In 1765, first physician training school was funded.

   d. In 1771, New Jersey begins the practice of medical licensure.

   2. The 1800s

   a. In 1837, Massachusetts General Hospital sets limitations on clinical practice in the first granting of clinical privileges.

b. In 1847, American Medical Association was formed by a group of physicians for the purpose of establishing and supporting code of ethics for physicians in their duties to their patients and the profession.

c. In 1851, Massachusetts General Hospital establishes the first disease/procedure index by classifying patient disposition.

d. In 1854, Florence Nightingale introduced new protocols for nurses during the Crimean War, that included Row nurses interacting with their patients and the ventilation and sanitation systems.

e. In 1872, New England Hospital for Women and Children organizes a general training school for nurses.

f. In 1874, American Medical Association encourages the creation of independent state licensing boards.

g. In 1898, American Hospital Association was funded to promote the public welfare by providing better health care in hospitals.

h. In the 19th century, as the population grew, so did medical schools (to nearly 400).

3. The 1900s

  a. In 1910, Flexner Report indicates unacceptable variation in medical school curricula.

  b. American College of Surgeons (ACS; founded in 1913) seeks to establish standards.

    i. When ACS began collecting data from health records, it was realized that the health record documentation was inadequate.

    ii. In 1917, ACS establishes the Hospital Standardization Program (minimum standard of care).

    iii. In 1919, ACS adopted minimum standards essential to proper care and treatment of hospital patients.

  c. In 1920, most medical colleges meet rigorous academic standards and are approved by the American Association of Medical Colleges.

  d. 1935, Social Security Act passed; it provides assistance and benefits to dependent children, maternal and child welfare, unemployment compensation, and benefits to the elderly.

  e. From 1935 until the end of World War II in 1945, hospital admissions increase.

  f. Shortly after the war, the economy grows, and technological advances continue in the medical field.

  g. In 1946, Hill-Burton Act establishes funding to build new hospitals.

  h. In 1952, the Joint Commission on Accreditation of Hospitals (JCAH) was formed.

  i. In 1953, JCAH published its first set of standards for hospitals.

  j. In 1953, Department of Health, Education, and Welfare (HEW) is formed to address healthcare-related issues in the United States; it is reorganized into Department of Health and Human Services (DHHS) in 1980.

  k. In 1965, Congress passed the Social Security Amendment, which establishes Medicare and Medicaid coverage for citizens 65 years of age or older (PL 89-97).

l. In 1970, Occupational Safety and Health Act is passed, mandating employers to provide a safe and healthy working environment.

m. In 1972, as a result of PL 92-603, professional standard review organizations (PSROs) are formed; they are now referred to as quality improvement organizations (QIOs).

n. In 1976, condition of participation was developed.

o. In 1980, the JCAH introduced accreditation standards.

p. In 1982, the Tax Equity and Fiscal Responsibility Act (TEFRA) changed the reimbursement structure from retrospective-determined cost-based payment to prospectively established fixed price determined by patients' final principal diagnosis, thus creating the prospective payment system (PPS).

q. In 1982, Peer Review Organizations (PRO) were created, now referred to as Quality Improvement Organizations (QIOs).

r. In 1982, state and regional peer review organizations contract with the Health Care Financing Administration (HCFA).

s. In 1983, prospective payment for Medicare was established (PL 98-21).

t. In 1983, HCPCS codes were developed and used to report healthcare services provided to Medicare and Medicaid (1986) patients treated in ambulatory care setting.

u. In 1985, JCAH revisited and revised its QA standards for monitoring and evaluating healthcare administrative and business operations.

v. In 1985, Consolidated Omnibus Budget Reconciliation Act (COBRA) establishes Emergency Medical Treatment and Active Labor Act (EMTALA) ("patient antidumping law").

w. In 1985, Health Care Quality Improvement Act (HCQIA; PL 99-660) established the National Practitioner Data Bank (NPDB), a clearinghouse to collect and release information to eligible parties for the purpose of identifying problematic or incompetent healthcare practitioners.

x. In 1985, JCAH developed a 10-step model for monitoring and evaluating effectiveness of QA efforts.

y. In 1986, condition of participation was expanded.

z. In 1986, JCAH developed the project called Agenda for Change.

aa. In 1987, JCAH changed its name to the Joint Commission on Accreditation of Healthcare Organizations (JCAHO).

bb. In 1989, Agency for Healthcare Research and Quality (AHRQ) promotes information that improves quality, reduces cost, and enhances the effectiveness of health care.

cc. In 1989, Agency for Health Care Policy and Research was created (PL 101-239).

dd. In the 1990s, JCAH became the Joint Commission on Accreditation of Healthcare Organizations (JCAHO).

ee. In the 1990s, JCAHO evaluation and monitoring standards expanded to include ambulatory care.

ff. In 1991, the National Committee for Quality Assurance (NCQA) accredits managed care organizations (MCOs) using method similar to JCAHO.

      gg. In 1990, JCAHO monitoring and evaluation process expands to include medical staff review activities.

      hh. In 1990, PRO is required to inform licensing boards of physician sanctions (PL 101-508).

      ii. In 1992, Computer-Based Patient Record Institute is created.

      jj. In 1992, accreditation manual transitions from quality assurance to quality improvement.

      kk. In 1994, JCAHO launches the Orion Project.

      ll. In 1996, the Health Insurance Portability and Accountability Act (HIPAA) passed (PL 104-191).

      mm. In 1997, the ORYX initiative incorporates outcome measures and monitoring into healthcare accreditation processes.

      nn. In 1990, Deming's total quality management philosophy begins to spread in U.S. health care.

      oo. In 1990, JCAHO integrates quality improvement into the accreditation process.

      pp. In 1993, Health Care Quality Improvement Program redirects PROs' focus toward improving quality.

    4. The 2000s to present

      a. In 2001, ambulatory payment classification system is initiated.

      b. In 2002, HCFA becomes Centers for Medicare and Medicaid Services (CMS).

      c. In 2002, peer review organizations (PROs) are renamed quality improvement organizations (QIOs).

      d. On April 14, 2001, the standard for privacy of individually identified health information (the privacy rule) takes effect.

      e. By April 14, 2003, covered entity must comply.

      f. In January 2004, JCAHO begins unannounced tracer methodology for healthcare accreditation review process.

      g. On January 1, 2007, JCAHO launches its new, shortened name—The Joint Commission (TJC)—and its new logo.

      h. During 2000s, TJC places emphasis on patient safety.

      i. 2010 healthcare reform

c. The definition of quality can be complex and controversial because of the different views of stakeholders.

    i. Quality assurance (QA): a common term for many years

      1. Was known to be reactive, retrospective, policing, and in many ways punitive

      2. Often involved determining who was at fault after something went wrong

      3. Term is less likely to be used in today's healthcare industries

    ii. Quality assessment: review of patient record to determine whether an item of required documentation is present or absent

      1. Chart analysis

      2. Chart deficiency tracking and reporting

    iii. Quality improvement (QI): newer term that involves both prospective and retrospective reviews

      1. Aimed at improvement, measuring where you are, and figuring out ways to make things better

      2. Specifically attempts to avoid placing blame

      3. Attempts to create systems to prevent errors from happening

    iv. Main difference between QI and QA is QI's focus on improvement, which influences how people respond to a quality project

  d. Pioneers of Quality Improvement (see Table 5-1)
   i. Avedis Donabedian
    1. Developed the three classes of quality assessment in health care
     a. Structure: looks at the organization's complete make-up and resources to support the delivery of care.
      i. Indirectly assess care by looking at certain provider characteristics and the physical and organizational resources available to support delivery of care
      ii. Capability for providing care
      iii. Example: policies and procedures
     b. Process: looks at what was done during the delivery of care
      i. Interactions between patient and providers
      ii. Examines healthcare professional's decision-making processes as he or she directs a patient's course of treatment, or, at organizational level, investigates the procedures that guide operational decisions
      iii. Example: peer review of medical records
     c. Outcome: looks at the end result of the patient
      i. Reviews end results or product of the patient's encounter with the system
      ii. Example: mortality rate
   ii. Kaoru-Kaoru Ishikawa
    1. Early collaborator with Deming and Juran during their visits to Japan (1950s)
    2. Developed cause-and-effect diagram or fishbone
   iii. Phillip Crosby
   iv. W. Edwards Deming
   v. Brian Joiner
   vi. Joseph M. Juran
  e. Quality Assessment Models
   i. Deming's 14 principles
    1. Create consistency toward purpose of the product or service
    2. Adopt new philosophy
    3. Focus on quality process flow of the product rather than mass inspection
    4. Price tag does not always indicate quality; end practice of rewarding based on price tag; embrace long-term relationship, trust, loyalty, and honesty
    5. Constantly assess and improve all processes
    6. Institute on-the-job training, job orientation, continued education, equipment training, etc.
    7. Institute leadership, remove workmanship barriers, be realistic, understand all staff cannot be above average
    8. Drive out fear (no one performs best under fear)
    9. Break down barriers within the organization by improving communication
    10. Eliminate numerical quotas; quota causes loss, chaos, dissatisfaction, burnout, boredom, turnover, etc.
    11. Eliminate quick-fix solution
    12. Eliminate inconsistent slogans and exhortation
    13. Create an open atmosphere of creativity; identify and uplift talented staff

Table 5-1 Synopsis of Crosby, Deming, Joiner, and Juran's Philosophy of Quality Improvement

Crosby	Deming	Joiner	Juran
1. Quality means complete conformance to standards 2. Quality should mean zero defects 3. Advocated goal setting 4. Advocated merit pay 5. Advocated development of educational activities 6. Valued team decision making	1. Developed 14 principles and 7 deadly diseases 2. Emphasized quality processes 3. Believed workers are naturally committed to excellent performance but managers desire directions 4. Disagreed with merit pay for performance 5. Disagreed with continuous performance evaluation 6. Advocated continuous education for workers 7. Advocated team building and group process	1. Developed the Joiner Triangle 2. Believed quality must start at the top of the organization 3. Believed in ensuring customer and staff loyalty and satisfaction 4. Advocated scientific approach to identifying cause of problem and developing solution plan 5. Believed in teamwork, involvement, side-by-side management, and open door management	1. Developed Trilogy process 2. Emphasized both quality process and quality outcomes 3. Believed in performance evaluation 4. Advocated merit pay for performance 5. Advocated corrective action plan 6. Advocated team building and group process 7. Believed in developing quality standards to monitor performance

Data from Abdelhak, M., Grostick, S., Hanken, & M. A., (2012). *Health information: Management of a strategic resource.* St. Louis: Saunders Elsevier.

14. Involve everybody within the organization in working toward the transformation or improvement of the organization
15. Six dimensions of healthcare quality as defined by the Institute of Medicine
    a. Safe: avoid injury to patient from the care intended to help them
    b. Patient centered: provide care that is respectful and responsive to individual patients
    c. Effective: avoid over- and under-utilization
    d. Equity: provide quality care to all individuals regardless of personal characteristics such as geographical location, gender, ethnicity, and socioeconomic status
    e. Timely: reduce wait times and delays
    f. Efficient: avoid waste

      ii. Deming's seven deadly diseases in quality management

          1. Lack of vision, mission, plan, and purpose of the product or service

          2. Emphasizing short-time profits

          3. Inconsistent, unfair, and unmeasurable evaluation, and merit rating

          4. Employee job dissatisfaction

          5. Customer, vendor, and community dissatisfaction

          6. Excessive medical cost

          7. Excessive cost of liability

      iii. Juran's principles

          1. Product or service must meet customer's need

          2. Product or service must be free from deficiencies

f. Quality Improvement

      i. Definition: characterized by the recipient of the service or product. Therefore, it is essential that quality is built into all services, processes, and products in healthcare delivery systems.

      ii. Quality improvement activities: related activities geared toward improving current status

          1. QI activities can be very helpful in improving how things work.

          2. Trying to find where the "defect" in the system is, and figuring out new ways to do things can be challenging and fun.

          3. It's a great opportunity to "think outside the box."

      iii. Methodologies and models for performing, assessing, and building quality into healthcare services

          1. Internal

              a. Vision

              b. Mission

              c. Goals

          2. External

              a. The Joint Commission (TJC)

              b. Commission on Accreditation of Rehabilitation Facilties (CARF)

              c. QIOs (formerly PROs)

              d. Quality improvement organizations (formerly peer review organizations, or PROs)

                 i. Peer review organizations

              e. CMS

                 i. Centers for Medicaid and Medicare Services, previously known as Health Care Financing Administration (HCFA)

              f. Health Insurance Portability and Accountability Act (HIPAA)

      iv. Development and refinement of TJC standards relating to quality improvement (see Table 5-2)

      v. In each of the cases in Table 5-3, the court ruled that the hospital and medical staff have the right and obligation to oversee quality of professional services rendered by the medical staff.

      vi. Healthcare accrediting and licensing agencies (see Table 5-4)

g. Methods to Improve Quality

      i. Department of Health and Human Services (HHS)

          1. In November 2001, announced the quality initiative to assure quality health care for all Americans through accountability and public disclosure

Table 5-2   Development and Refinement of TJC Standards Relating to Quality Improvement

Year	Responsibility
1952	Expanded standard of care
	Established structured set of standards
1972	Established a standard for medical audits
1975	Required hospitals to demonstrate consistency in care
1979	Required coordination and integration of all quality-of-care activities into hospital-wide program
1985	Ten-step model for quality evaluation introduced
	Hospital required to monitor the following: medical record, surgical cases, blood usage, drug usage, pharmacy, and therapeutics
1986	Launched *Agenda for Change*
1994	Accreditation manual for hospitals changes from departmental standards to functions critical to patient care
2004	Changed from scheduled and announced site visit to unscheduled and unannounced site visit with tracer methodology site review

      2. Hospital Compare: a tool that provides information on 20 hospital quality measures that assess how well hospitals in a geographical area care for all their adult patients with particular medical conditions (see Table 5-5)

  ii. Clinical practice guidelines

      1. Systematically developed statements used to assist provider and patient decisions about appropriate health care for specific clinical circumstances

      2. Developed with the goal of standardizing clinical decision making

      3. Meant to be flexible and do not necessarily apply in every case

      4. Example: American Diabetes Association recommends statins be considered for people with diabetes over the age of 40 who have a total cholesterol level $\geq$ 135 and that there be a blood pressure goal of < 130/80 mmHg for people with diabetes.

 iii. Clinical protocols

      1. Treatment recommendations often based on guidelines

      2. The step-by-step description of an accepted procedure recommended by an authoritative body

      3. Example: If the blood sugar is > 150, give ____ units of a specific type of insulin. (It would also state how often the therapy could be given, and what tests or evaluations are to be performed and when, to determine the effectiveness of therapy, and when the physician must be contacted because something is not working.)

Table 5-3 Relevant Court Cases

Year	Case	Decision
1965	*Darling vs. Charleston Community Hospital*	The court ruled that the hospital must assume certain responsibilities for care of the patient. The court ruled that a hospital was negligent for permitting a general practitioner to perform orthopedic surgery. The court ruled that the hospital had a duty to apply reasonable standards to the practice of its physicians because it was responsible for the privileging of physicians on its staff.
1973	*Gonzales vs. Nork and Mercy Hospital*	The court found the hospital negligent if it knew, had reason to know, or should have known of the surgeon's incompetence.
1981	*John vs. Misericordia Hospital*	The court found that the hospital owes a duty to its patients in selecting medical staff members and granting privileges.

Table 5-4 Healthcare Accrediting and Licensing Agencies

Abbreviation	Agency	Areas of Responsibility
AAAHC	Accreditation Association for Ambulatory Health Care	Specializes in assisting ambulatory healthcare organizations to improve quality of their services
ACS	American College of Surgeons	Initiated standard review in healthcare practices
CARF	Commission on Accreditation of Rehabilitation Facilities	Responsible for evaluating quality of care in organizations providing rehabilitative treatment
HEDIS	Health Plan Employer Data and Information Set	Responsible for collecting data on managed care plans
TJC (formerly JCAHO)	The Joint Commission (formerly Joint Commission on Accreditation of Healthcare Organizations)	Refined ACS standards and assumed responsibility for accreditation
NCQA	National Committee for Quality Assurance	Certifies qualified healthcare professionals in quality assurance
NAHQ	National Association of Healthcare Quality	Certifies qualified healthcare professionals in promoting continuous QI efforts

Table 5-5   Hospital Quality Measures

Condition	Measure
Acute myocardial infarction (AMI)/heart attack	Aspirin at arrival
	Aspirin at discharge
	Beta blocker at arrival
	Beta blocker at discharge
	ACE inhibitor or angiotensin receptor blocker (ARB) for left ventricular systolic dysfunction
	Smoking cessation
	Thrombolytic agent received within 30 minutes of hospital arrival
	Percutaneous coronary intervention (PCI) received within 120 minutes of hospital arrival
Heart failure	Left ventricular function assessment
	ACE inhibitor or angiotensin receptor blocker (ARB) for left ventricular systolic dysfunction
	Comprehensive discharge instructions
	Smoking cessation
Pneumonia	Initial antibiotic received within 4 hours of hospital arrival
	Pneumococcal vaccination status
	Blood culture performed before first antibiotic received
	Smoking cessation
	Oxygenation assessment
	Appropriate initial antibiotic selection
Surgical infection prevention	Prophylactic antibiotic received within 1 hour prior to surgical incision
	Prophylactic antibiotics discontinued within 24 hours after surgery end time

Reproduced from the Centers for Medicaid and Medicare Services (2013). Hospital Quality Initiative, Overview Summary. http://www.cms.gov/Medicare/Quality-Initiatives-Patient-Assessment-Instruments/HospitalQualityInits/index.html

4. Protocols frequently take the form of branching grids, with yes and no answers, leading to directions based on the answers. (For example: Is blood sugar > 200? If yes, give [dose]; if no, is it < 100?)
5. Sources for clinical practice guidelines and protocols
   a. Agency for Healthcare Research and Quality (AHRQ)
   b. National Guideline Clearinghouse: a public resource for evidence-based clinical practice guidelines
iv. Tools for implementing clinical guidelines and protocols
   1. Critical paths: display goals for patients and provide the corresponding ideal sequence and timing of staff actions to achieve those goals with optimal efficiency
   2. Clinical pathways: structured plans of care
   3. Care maps: multidisciplinary standards that outline the processes of care and expected outcomes within predetermined time frames
v. TJC recommends an evaluation and monitoring model to advance the transition from a quality assessment approach to a concept of improving quality. TJC developed a 10-step process to achieve the goals and objectives of a monitoring and evaluation program.
   1. Assign responsibility
   2. Delineate scope of care
   3. Identify important aspects of care
   4. Identify indicators
   5. Establish thresholds
   6. Collect and organize data
   7. Initiate evaluation
   8. Take actions to improve care and services
   9. Assess the effectiveness of actions and maintain the gain
   10. Communicate results to affected individuals and groups
vi. Avedis Donabedian developed a sound model for assessing quality in the healthcare arena. Donabedian's model is based on the structure, process, and outcome models for assessing measurement approach to quality.
   1. Structure: measures the ability of the organization to coordinate all its resources such as physical, human resources, facility, technology, policies and procedures, financial, and other characteristics as needed to successfully support the delivery of healthcare services
   2. Process: measures the ability of the organization to foster and focus on positive interactions between the receiver of healthcare service and the provider of service throughout the course of the care
   3. Outcome: measures and focuses on the end result of the care provided and the overall satisfaction level of the patient with the care received
vii. The plan, do, check, act (PDCA) system was developed by Walter Shewhart and W. Edwards Deming and became popular beginning in Japan. It has become one of the most commonly used models in quality improvement.
   1. Planning phase: data collection and analysis to propose a solution for an identified problem
   2. Do (or implementation) phase: tests the proposed solutions

        3. Checking phase: investigates the effectiveness of solutions over a period of time

        4. Act phase: formalizes the changes that have proved effective in the do and check stages

    viii. Brian Joiner, a supporter of W. Edwards Deming's philosophy, developed a seven-step method to assess quality.

        1. Define the project

        2. Study the current situation

        3. Analyze the potential causes

        4. Implement a solution

        5. Check the results

        6. Standardize the improvement

        7. Establish future plans

    ix. Re RN and Krousel-Wood M developed a six-step method.

        1. Record adverse or other outcomes of interest

        2. Use statistical techniques to determine variation

        3. Seek suggestions on a trial basis

        4. Monitor results

        5. If improvement occurs, implement suggestions and standardize

        6. Seek further suggestions for improvement

h. Data Quality Monitoring

    i. Qualitative analysis: check various aspect of the medical record to ensure applicable and required documentation are present

        1. Check presence of all necessary authorizations; consents present and signed by the patient or appropriate legal representative

        2. Correct and consistent patient's identification on every paper or electronic document

        3. Primary and secondary diagnosis documented and authenticated, including present on admission

        4. History and physical exam, discharge summary, consultation report, and applicable progress notes documented within the timeframe specified by applicable regulations

        5. Orders present for all consultations, diagnostic tests, and procedures results in the patient medical record and authenticated.

    ii. Qualitative: perform a detailed review the documentation to ensure consistency

        1. Review record to ensure consistency of documentation written by various healthcare providers

        2. Determine medication ordered is consistent with medication administration

        3. Analyze medical record to ensure consistency of diagnosis, reports, care plan, orders, and discharge summary

        4. Received medical record from other health care reviewed and acknowledged

        5. Instructions and education to patient and family members documented

        6. Abnormal findings addressed with the patient or legal representative

    iii. Legal analysis: review the medical record to ensure it adequately represents the business record for the organization

        1. Entries recorded on legally recognized/approved forms, legible, timely, no unexplained gap within documentation

2. Entries consistent with organization policy, and applicable standards and regulations
3. Medical record entry errors corrected in a legal manner
4. Entries authenticated by the person with the knowledge of the act
5. All documentation within the record belong to same patient
i. Project Management
  i. Rooted in engineering and oriented toward quantitative application methods
  ii. Initiation
    1. Occurs when participants observe there is a gap between organization performance and expected outcomes
    2. Project teams take on multiple tasks.
      a. Identify improvement opportunity
      b. Research and define performance expectations
      c. Implement process education
      d. Measure performance
      e. Document and communicate findings
      f. Analyze and compare internal and external data
  iii. Planning
    1. Identifies expected impact on organization
    2. Design
      a. Development of alternative solutions
      b. Gantt charts
        i. Project management tool used to schedule important activities
        ii. Charts divide a horizontal scale into days, weeks, or months and a vertical scale into project activities or tasks
      c. PERT charts
  iv. Execution
    1. Once plan is completed, execution begins
    2. Installation of equipment or construction begins
    3. Training
    4. Measure performance
  v. Closure
    1. Evaluation and control
j. Role of HIM Staff in QI
  i. Participate in QI planning
  ii. Identify deviations from norm
  iii. Identify areas needing improvement
  iv. Provide chart/information
  v. Collect data
  vi. Analyze data
  vii. Benchmark collected data
  viii. Interpret data
  ix. Display data
  x. Present data
  xi. Implement required changes
  xii. Monitor and evaluate changes
  xiii. Communicate
  xiv. Update/revise/or create supportive policy

k. Internal Customers of HIM: quality improvement is fostered by identifying customers and their needs and tailoring services to meet customers' needs
    i. Other HIM staff within HIM department
    ii. Receptionists
    iii. Physicians
    iv. Laboratory technicians
    v. Nurses and other medical assistants
    vi. Business services
    vii. Radiology technicians
    viii. Pharmacists and pharmacy staff
    ix. Janitorial staff
    x. Physical therapists, respiratory therapists
    xi. Social workers and social service staff
    xii. Patient advocates, volunteers
    xiii. Eligibility counselor
    xiv. Risk management staff
    xv. Utilization review staff
    xvi. Quality assurance staff
    xvii. Business associates
    xviii. Students and researchers
    xix. Office of patient financial service
    xx. Billing office
    xxi. Other departments

l. External Customer to HIM Department: some external customers can also be internal customers at a given time, based on the role-reversal functions
    i. Patient
    ii. Vendor
    iii. Physician
    iv. Licensing agencies
    v. Accreditation agencies
    vi. Law enforcement agencies with needs to know
    vii. Medical examiners
    viii. Patient advocates
    ix. Patient's identified personal representatives
    x. Local, state, and federal agencies with needs to know

m. Competencies in e-HIM
    i. Establishing and guiding national, local, and state health information policy development and implementation
    ii. Establishing and implementing policies, practices, and procedures governing all aspects of HIM
    iii. Establishing and implementing standards for privacy, security, and confidential of health information
    iv. Establishing and implementing policies and standards for monitoring of data integrity, accuracy, validity, and authenticity, and version control
    v. Developing health information format and content standards to ensure the collection of accurate, timely, and complete health information
    vi. Facilitating communication of health information across organizational healthcare teams and among different entities

       vii. Facilitating the concurrent use of health information for multiple purposes (e.g., direct patient care, outcomes measurement and evaluation, wellness and prevention, research, public health and policy development)

    viii. Managing compliance, regulatory, accreditation, licensure, and recertification programs and activities

       ix. Analyzing and synthesizing qualitative and quantitative health information for various and diverse needs and audiences

        x. Developing, designing, and implementing clinical vocabularies

       xi. Helping consumers to access and obtain diverse and often complex health information

     xii. Informing and educating consumers about health information issues

    xiii. Providing the context to understand, analyze, and interpret health information

    xiv. Helping providers understand data flow and reporting requirements within the context of dynamic rules, regulations, and guidelines

     xv. Leading business process redesign efforts

n. Data Collection

        i. The primary source of clinical data in the healthcare industry is the medical record, because it contains subjective and objective information related to the episode of care. Other data such as insurance, registry, reimbursement, and census data are considered to be secondary data sources, because data were taken from the medical record and entered into the subcategory of health-related records. Primary data are further classified into identifiable data or patient-specific data, and secondary data are further classified into aggregate or non-patient-specific data.

       ii. Methods for collecting data

          1. Questionnaire

          2. Survey

          3. Face-to-face interview

          4. Mail

          5. Phone

          6. Primary

          7. Secondary

o. Service and Products

        i. HIM management must establish a service delivery and expectation standard for all services and products provided. It is important that HIM staff know the deadlines for the specific services or products the department has to offer.

       ii. See Table 5-6 for an example of service and product delivery.

p. Services and Products Offered by HIM Department

        i. Chart retrieval

       ii. Coding

      iii. Abstracting

      iv. Chart analysis

        v. Release of information

      vi. Disclosure tracking

     vii. Record processing

    viii. Filing

       ix. Chart maintenance

        x. Record imaging and indexing

       xi. Transcription

Table 5-6	Example of Service and Product Delivery	
Service	**Receivers of Service(s) (with a need to know)**	**Time Frame**
Release of information	1. Business services within your facility	With the exception of stat request, all other requests are processed within 5 working days from the date received.
	2. Risk management staff	
	3. Utilization review staff	
	4. Quality assurance staff	
	5. Business associates	
	6. Researchers	
	7. Office of patient financial service	
	8. Billing office	
	9. Patient	
	10. Healthcare providers	
	11. Licensing agencies	
	12. Accreditation agencies	
	13. Law enforcement agencies	
	14. Medical examiners	
	15. Patient advocates	
	16. Patient's identified personal representatives	
	17. Local, state, and federal agencies	
	18. Others	

     xii. Hard copy and electronic storage
   xiii. Research processing
   xiv. Loose sheet processing
    xv. Chart tracking
q. Tools for Collecting and Displaying Data
   i. Data analysis: determine what type of data are available, then determine how to display those data.
  ii. Types of data
    1. Nominal: category of data that can be named. It is sometimes called categorical data. Gender and ethnicity are examples of nominal data. Nominal data are best displayed using bar graphs or pie charts.
    2. Ordinal: category of data that can be ranked or ordered. It is sometimes called ranked data. This type of data allows the researcher to determine how respondents feel about a particular issue—for example, by using a Likert scale (1 = strongly disagree, 2 = disagree, 3 = neutral, 4 = agree, and 5 = strongly agree). The data are best displayed using bar graphs and pie charts.

3. Discrete: category of data that represent a distinct and separate value. Number of children in the family, number of suspended claims, and number of coding errors are examples of discrete data.

4. Continuous: category of data that has infinite number as a possible value. Measurements that have decimal points or values such as vital signs are examples of continuous data. They are best displayed using histograms or run charts.

iii. Critical elements of data collection

1. Understanding what to observe and collect
2. Consistency of data collection
3. Timeliness
4. Design of data collection tools
5. Design of users' guide or instruction sheet
6. Orientation
7. Criteria for data selection
8. Data display and presentation

iv. Data analysis and presentation

1. Bar graphs
   a. Simple: can be used to measure different types of data that cannot be broken into subcategories (e.g., John has 5 misfiles; Susan has 20 coding errors; Paula processed 500 medical record disclosures in January).
   b. Clustered: gives a breakdown of simple bar graphs (e.g., John misfiled 2 OB charts and 3 ER charts; Susan has 5 codes that were missing fifth digits, 11 codes that were missing fourth digits, and 4 codes that were not appropriate for outpatient services; Paula processed 175 legal requests, 50 subpoena requests, 200 disability requests, and 75 insurance requests in the month of January).
   c. Stratified: allows display of total and subtotal at the same time

2. Pareto chart: type of bar graph that displays categories of data in descending order of frequency or significance

3. Pie chart: illustrates how an individual component of chart relates to the whole

4. Radar chart: displays before and after data. It is used to identify the strengths and weaknesses of an activity. It also identifies opportunities for improvement.

5. Run chart: line graph that displays the progress and variations of data over time. Also known as a time plot. It is used to identify existing processes needing improvement and to show whether the improvement was successful. Its trend and pattern can be identified easily by its movement away from the midpoint (average).

6. Scatter diagram: indicates a relationship between two variables

7. Storyboards: a graphic and/or text display tool used to communicate details of principal investigator's activities on a poster

v. Idea-generating techniques

1. Brainstorming
   a. Used to generate ideas to encourage creativity and a free flow of ideas; example of a brainstorming topic can be customer-satisfaction form design

        b. Tips for conducting brainstorming session
           i. Allow each person to generate as many ideas as possible
           ii. Do not label any idea as good or bad
           iii. Provide a comfortable, free, and informal environment
           iv. Limit group to no fewer than 5 and no more than 13 people
           v. Limit discussion to 1 hour or less
     2. Nominal group technique
        a. Comparable to brainstorming
        b. The group members generate the ideas; however, after ideas are generated, they are objectively ranked or rated in the order of priority.
        c. Technique that allows group to narrow the focus of discussion or make decision without extended circular discussion
  vi. Data organization
     1. Cause and effect diagrams (also called fishbone diagram); utilized to separate root causes for an effect or problem
     2. Check sheet: indicates how often an event occurs (check sheets contribute to data for the creation of histograms, run charts, etc.)
     3. Decision matrix: grid design to rank ideas and proposals. It allows for scoring of each alternative and helps prioritize objectives.
     4. Flow chart
        a. Pictorial illustration of sequenced steps to complete a process
        b. Utilize multiple shapes (oval, rectangle, diamond), lines, and arrows to create a flow chart
        c. Determine the starting point, the middle point, and the ending point of the process
        d. All activities from end to finish arranged in sequential order
        e. Oval at the top indicates the starting point; oval at the bottom indicates the ending point
        f. Rectangles in the middle indicate the activities that must be performed during the process
        g. Diamond shapes indicate areas of the decision-making process
        h. Benefits of flow chart usage (see Figure 5-1)
           i. Identifies unnecessary delay in process
           ii. Identifies work redundancy, misunderstanding, and inefficiency
  vii. Survey or questionnaire
     1. Gathers feedback from a large group of people
     2. Examples of auditing forms are in Table 5-7 and Table 5-8
r. Performance Improvement Plan
  i. Purpose of performance improvement
     1. All performance improvement plans must define the purpose of the plan. The plan also must be established in accordance with the organization's vision statement in mind. The plan will include the goals and objectives. For example, the purpose of a performance improvement plan for HIM release of information can be to provide a framework to ensure all disclosures are disclosed efficiently in support of patient confidentiality and privacy.
  ii. Elements of performance improvement plan
     1. Statement of mission
     2. Statement of vision

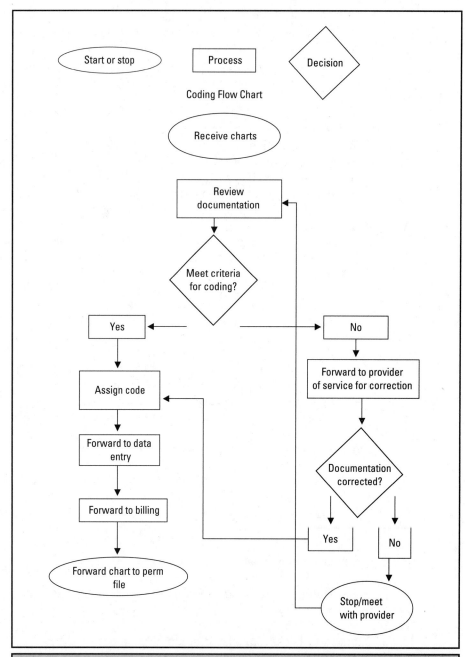

Figure 5-1   Example of a Flow Chart

3. Objectives
4. Organizational values and culture
5. Leadership
6. Organizational structure
7. Performance measure objectives
8. Methodology for improvement
9. Annual review plan
10. Communication models

Table 5-7 Example of an Auditing Form

#	General Medical Records Auditing Form for Improving Medical Record Documentation		
	Criteria	**Yes**	**No**
1	Does documentation in the medical record conform to the organization's policies?		
2	Are the documentations in the medical record legible?		
3	Are all entries dated?		
4	Is patient's identifying demographic information documented?		
5	Is there an evidence of consent for treatment?		
6	Does the medical record chart contain patient identification data?		
7	As appropriate, is there evidence of informed consent?		
8	Was the information documented in a timely manner?		
9	Was the documentation pattern uniform or consistent?		
10	Was there an evidence of provider authentication?		
11	Were the errors corrected appropriately?		
12	Was there evidence on known allergy documentation?		
13	Were all forms used in the chart approved by the organization?		
14	Did all forms in the chart belong to the same patient?		
15	Was there a documentation of history and physical?		
16	Was there evidence that a provider has reviewed consultation reports?		
17	Was documentation of reason for visit present?		
18	Was there documentation of present medical illness?		
19	Was there documentation of past medical histories?		
20	Was there documentation of clinical assessment?		
21	Were vital signs documented?		
22	Was there documentation of special studies ordered?		
23	Was there documentation of treatment plan?		
24	Was there documentation of medical findings or diagnosis?		
25	Was there documentation of referral?		

Table 5-8   Example of an Auditing Form

Specific Medical Records Auditing Form for Assessment of Patient Care			
#	**Criteria**	**Yes**	**No**
1	Was patient assessed for pain?		
2	Is patient currently having pain?		
3	Was the location of the pain documented?		
4	Was the intensity of the pain documented?		
5	Was the duration of the pain documented?		
6	Was the quality of the pain documented?		
7	Was the associated contributing factor documented?		
8	Was current or previous intervention documented?		
9	Was the outcome of the intervention documented?		
10	Does patient assessment include physical assessment?		
11	Does patient assessment include social assessment?		
12	Does patient assessment include psychological assessment?		
13	Does patient assessment include spiritual assessment?		
14	Does patient assessment include cultural assessment?		
15	Was pain management or care plan documented?		
16	Was treatment or medication documented?		
17	Was the patient and/or patient's family educated regarding pain?		
18	Was the critical point regarding patient education documented?		
19	As appropriate, was the patient reassessed?		
20	Was patient care coordinated among other appropriate professionals?		

iii. Scope of activities
 1. Includes an overall assessment of the function to be performed, with special focus on continual process improvement for all related activities
 2. Example: The scope of HIM ROI performance improvement plan can include but is not limited to the following:
  a. Form design (authorization for uses and disclosures)
  b. Forms management and control
  c. Satisfaction of patients, providers, staff
  d. Validity of authorizations
  e. Disclosure logs
  f. Tracking of disclosure

s. Retention of Performance Improvement Data and Reports

    i. All performance improvement (PI) data and reports are kept according to the facilities policies and procedures relating to PI data retention. However, TJC recommends that PI data are kept for a minimum of 3 years, from one accreditation to another re-accreditation, and until any recommendations have been addressed fully.

    ii. Confidentiality statement

        1. All performance improvement information must be maintained in a locked file cabinet within the designated quality management service department or administrative offices as appropriate.

        2. The performance improvement data, reports, and minutes shall be accessible only to those participating in the program.

        3. Performance improvement information, records, proceedings, and communication submitted to performance improvement committees or their agents are protected from disclosure under state codes such as the Texas Health and Safety Code Ann. Section 161.031 and 161.032, Texas Medical Practice Act, Tex. Occ. Code Ann. Section 151.022(2), (8) and 160.007.

        4. Privileged information is not admissible at trial unless the holder waives the privilege.

t. Continuous Quality Improvement (CQI)

    i. CQI is a never-ending cycle. It is a concept that came out of industry. Rather than creating a culture of blame if things do not go well, the focus is on a team approach to improvement that rewards the group when things get better.

    ii. Benefits of CQI

        1. A continuously learning organization

        2. Improvement projects that are strategically aligned to give knowledge to key customers, providers, and suppliers at every level of the hospital

        3. An integrated, customer-focused business plan for all organization functions

        4. Improved satisfaction among patients, physician, employees, and payers

        5. Reduced expenses as a result of removing waste, needless complexity, and rework

        6. Assistance with meeting accreditation standards

    iii. FOCUS

        1. Find a process to improve

        2. Organize to improve a process

        3. Clarify what is known

        4. Understand variation

        5. Select a process improvement

    iv. Process improvement plan model (see Figure 5-2)

        1. Plan

            a. Most complex part of the process; unrealistic planning will result in unachievable outcome

            b. Identify the specific service to improve

            c. Define the target population(s)

            d. Define the unique needs and characteristics of the target population(s)

            e. Define and acknowledge the deviation from standard

    f. Develop service to meet the needs of the target population(s)

    g. Determine data needed to monitor the improvement

    h. Create a timeline of resources, activities, training, and target dates

    i. Develop a data collection plan, the tools for measuring outcomes, and thresholds for determining when targets have been met

2. Do

    a. Directly correlated with the effectiveness of the plan phase

    b. Educate all staff as appropriate

    c. Develop continued or ongoing staff education plan

    d. Develop or revise policies and procedures

    e. Implement interventions

    f. Collect data to ensure validity and reliability of conformance to standard.

3. Check

    a. These are the assessments of the plan and do phases; used to validate effectiveness.

    b. Analyze collected data

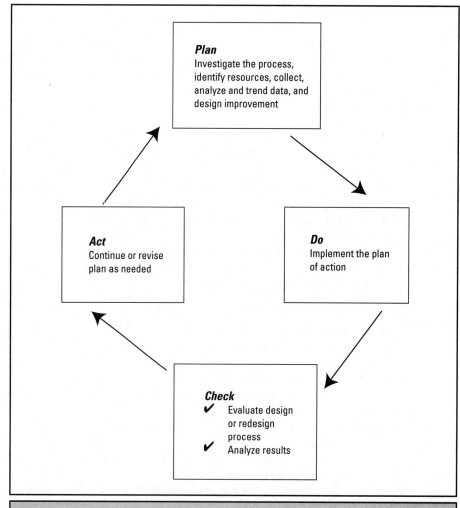

Figure 5-2   The PDCA Cycle

        c. Study the results of data and evaluate reasons for variation

        d. Modify the plan as necessary

        e. Ask key questions

           i. What specifically is being assessed?

           ii. Does the tool capture the desired data?

           iii. What does the finding indicate about the process?

           iv. Were the desired outcomes achieved?

    4. Act

        a. This is a determination phase.

        b. Act on what is learned and determine the next steps.

        c. A determination is made to continue with the plan as implemented or to revise the whole or certain steps of the plan due to findings.

        d. If the intervention is successful, work to make it part of standard operating procedure.

        e. If it is not successful, analyze sources of failure, design new solutions, and repeat the PDCA cycle.

  u. Understanding TJC

    i. Accreditation process: to earn and maintain accreditation, a facility must undergo an on-site survey by a TJC survey team at least every 3 years. The objective of the survey is to evaluate the facility and provide educational guidance that will help the staff continue to improve the facility's performance.

    ii. Survey team: the survey team may spend several days at the facility observing activities, interviewing patients and staff, and reviewing documents. The team spends a significant amount of time observing staff provide care. The team may track a patient in person and or through medical records to find out how the systems and processes work in supporting patient care. The surveyors do not judge directly whether the care given to a specific patient is good or bad, right or wrong. Rather, they determine what activities are carried out, how well they are performed.

    iii. Evaluation: different members of the survey team may look at specific areas of the facility according to their expertise, but they work together closely at every step, integrating their findings to reach conclusions. At the end of the survey, the team scores the facility on how well it meets the standards.

    iv. Figure 5-3 provides a mock survey form; Figure 5-4 provides a variance tracking record; and Figure 5-5 provides sample daily key notes.

2. Utilization Management

  a. Defined

    i. Utilization management or utilization review is a method of controlling healthcare costs and quality of care by reviewing the appropriateness and necessity of care provided to patients. Utilization management or utilization review is embedded in a hospital quality program. The goal of a utilization management department is to review the facility's efficiency in the provision of services and determine whether staff are using resources in the most cost-effective manner. Good utilization management prevents underutilization and overutilization of services, resources, and facilities are outcomes.

The following is a sample of a site visit survey to record the time, date, attendees, surveyed areas, survey methodology, findings, impressions, and recommended solutions.

Blank Form	Sample Completed Form
Date:	**April 4, 20xx**
Start: **End:**	**Start:** 10:30 AM **End:** 12:30 PM
Staff/Dept in Attendance:	**Staff/Dept in Attendance:**
	Jane: Nursing Department
	Debra: HIM Department
	Paul: Pharmacy Department
	Carol: Social Services Department
Area Surveyed:	**Area Surveyed:**
	Examination room
	Intake area
	Medical record
	Restroom
	Educational and instructional area
Method of Survey:	**Method of Survey:**
	Medical record review
	Environmental review
	Patient tracing
Findings:	**Findings:**
	1. Closed medical record review revealed 8 out of 25 charts reviewed have no documentation of H&P on surgical patients
Recommendation:	**Recommendation:**
	1. Conduct immediate focus audit
	2. Educate providers of service and support staff
	3. Educate HIM staff
	4. Conduct mock daily, weekly, or monthly reviews
Overall Impression:	**Overall Impression:**

Figure 5-3   Example of Blank and Completed TJC Survey Form

Completed by: _____

Instructions:
- ➤ Record the area surveyed (e.g., lab)
- ➤ Record the date the area was surveyed (some site visits may last for several days or weeks)
- ➤ Record the findings (activities rated below expected standards)
- ➤ Record the corrective action plan(s) needed to correct the deficiency
- ➤ Record the person responsible for the corrective action plan
- ➤ Record the status of the correction, with the date it was monitored or resolved
- ➤ Monitor and document until the problem is resolved within the established target date
- ➤ Communicate standard compliance status as appropriate

Area Surveyed	Date	Findings	Action	Contact Person	Progress/ Comment
					[ ] Resolved Date_____ [ ] Pending
					[ ] Resolved Date_____ [ ] Pending
					[ ] Resolved Date_____ [ ] Pending
					[ ] Resolved Date_____ [ ] Pending
					[ ] Resolved Date_____ [ ] Pending

Figure 5-4   Example of TJC Variance Tracking Record

1. Post site visit announcements
2. Always monitor and be aware of surroundings
3. Update, review, revise, and create policies and procedures as appropriate
4. Review all manuals and get clarification when needed
5. Assure that all posted signs are posted correctly
6. Organize your environment for positive impression
7. Correct any previously identified problems
8. Mentally and physically prepare yourself for the day
9. Be ready to discuss what you do
10. Be prepared to lead a tour of your facility
11. Think about how to educate the visitors about your service
12. Clear any obstructions in your area or hallway
13. Know the continuum process flow of your site
14. Have all keys available
15. Remember patient's rights, privacy, and confidentiality
16. Remember to wear comfortable, professional working clothes with name badge
17. Be ready to demonstrate that you are prepared in case of emergency
18. Know how to alert staff and patients during emergencies
19. Remember the types of safety in-services you have attended in the last year (fire, emergency preparedness, injury prevention, etc.)
20. Know the escape route
21. Know where, why, how, and when to use different types of fire extinguisher
22. You may have to explain your role during an internal or external disaster
23. Know emergency contact numbers (emergency, fire, etc.)
24. Check the environment for hazardous materials
25. Be familiar with abuse, neglect, exploitation, and advance directives
26. Check refrigerators, drawers, cabinets, and under the sink
27. Remember that it is not allowed in the premises if it is not listed on the MSDS list
28. Think about infection control at all times
29. Remember to always address the surveyor by name (Mr., Ms., Dr., etc.)
30. Know the mission, vision, and values statement
31. Always focus attention on patient
32. Be ready to explain or show how you trace patients through the continuum of care
33. Be ready to explain your role when a critical lab value is identified
34. Think about your processes from the beginning of patient referral to the end
35. Remember it did not happen unless it was documented
36. Remember to document appropriately and completely
37. Log off on computers when you are done using them
38. Remember, do not place patient identifying information in the trash can—always shred
39. Remember HIPAA and patient confidentiality during disclosure of information
40. Be ready to discuss your organizational procedures during internal and external data abstractions for research and other legally mandated reporting

Figure 5-5   Example of TJC Daily Key Notes for Site Accreditation Visit

    ii. Public Law 92-603 of 1972 established professional standards review organizations (PSROs). These organizations comprise licensed physicians whose goal is to determine if services provided were medically necessary and cost effective.

    iii. TEFRA (1982) replaced PSROs with PROs. Fifty-three PROs, now known as quality improvement organizations (QIOs), are responsible for each state, territory, and the District of Columbia. These nongovernmental agencies are empowered to evaluate performance relative to quality and appropriateness of service and can recommend punitive action to CMS.

    iv. CMS and TJC require UM (utilization management) programs by law.

    v. NCQA state managed care plans must monitor medical care delivered to detect possible over- or underutilization of services. Managed care plans must have a written UM plan and an appeals process.

b. Some Medical Services Requiring Utilization Management

    i. Inpatient confinement

        1. Surgical and nonsurgical confinements

        2. Skilled nursing facility

        3. Rehabilitation facility

        4. Inpatient hospice

        5. Maternity confinement

    ii. Reconstructive procedures and procedures that may be considered cosmetic

    iii. Selected durable medical equipment

    iv. Medical injectables

    v. Surgical procedures

    vi. Elective (nonemergent) transportation by ambulance or medical van and all transfers via air ambulance

    vii. All home healthcare services

    viii. Requests for in-network level of benefits for nonparticipating physicians and providers for nonemergent services

    ix. Dental implants and oral appliances

    x. Services that may be considered investigational or experimental

    xi. Special programs

        1. Mental health, substance abuse, or behavioral health services

        2. Maternity management programs, including genetic testing, antenatal testing, prenatal consultations and counseling

        3. Infertility programs

        4. Pharmacy precertification for certain pharmaceuticals

        5. Major organ transplant evaluations and transplants, including but not limited to kidney, liver, heart, lung, and pancreas, and bone marrow replacement or stem cell transfer after high-dose chemotherapy

        6. Outpatient imaging precertification for CT (computed tomography scan), MRI (magnetic resonance imaging), nuclear cardiology, PET (positron emission tomography) scans

c. Case Management

    i. Defined as coordination, development, and provision of patient care plans for the patients with complicated cases. The goal is to provide patient care plan in a cost-effective manner to patients with complicated cases.

    ii. Peer review

       1. Crucial component of Medicare reimbursement process

       2. Individual hospitals submit claims for payment of covered services to fiscal intermediary by way of a standardized billing form.

       3. For Medicare claims, fiscal intermediary transmits duplicate of all claims for a review period to PRO to determine:

         a. Whether services are reasonable and medically necessary

         b. Whether services could be furnished effectively on an outpatient basis as opposed to inpatient admission

         c. Medical necessity, reasonableness, and appropriate inpatient services

         d. Inappropriate medical or other practices resulting in inappropriate admission or fraudulent billing for reimbursement

         e. Validity of diagnostic and procedural information submitted to request reimbursement

         f. Completeness and adequacy of care provided

         g. Whether the quality of services meets professionally recognized standards of care

       4. The goal of the peer review is for the PRO physician reviewer to identify three primary issues.

         a. Utilization concerns

         b. Quality concerns

         c. Diagnosis related groups' concerns

  d. Four Phases of Project Management

    i. Initiation: acknowledging a deficiency in current performance and expected outcome. Leadership commits to improving the deficiency and achieving a better outcome.

       1. Project must have a sponsor

       2. Must have a clear stable mission to accomplish

       3. Must have vision

       4. Must have applicable resources, skills, diverse expertise, commitment

    ii. Planning: establishing a standard to measure the success of the project

       1. Generate alternative solutions; design a step-by-step approach

       2. Identify task, cost, time, and responsible parties

         a. Gantt chart is an effective tool for planning and tracking implementation of a project

         b. PERT chart is an effective tool to use if a more quantitative approach is required because it can identify the critical activities that must be completed on time for the entire project to meet its final deadline

           i. Also called critical path method (CPM)

         c. Both PERT and Gantt charts require planner to identify critical tasks, duration of each task, and expected completion date.

    iii. Execution: finalization of the initiating and planning phase. Installing applicable equipment; developing policies and procedures; defining process, product, and outcome; testing; training staff; standardized weekly or monthly communication to entire organization. Make the project calendar available to all. Measure success weekly or monthly and adjust accordingly.

       iv. Closure: phase at which the project becomes an integral part of the organization's operations

          1. Organizational culture and structure are critical to the success of project management

   e. Utilization Review Process: goal of utilization management—to maintain or increase quality of care and to improve access to timely and quality care through efficient provision and utilization of service.

       i. Preadmission review (prospective review)

          1. Review prior to admission that determines if the procedure and reason for potential admission is appropriate and necessary

          2. Consists of comparing patient's medical condition with standard criteria that specify clinical indications for admission; criteria are intensity of service/severity of illness criteria (IS/SI)

       ii. Admission review: review at time of admission to determine medical necessity and appropriateness

       iii. Concurrent review: review of medical necessity for tests and procedures ordered during an inpatient hospitalization

       iv. Discharge review: review at time of discharge that determines if the patient meets specific discharge screen criteria. The discharge review may involve arranging appropriate home healthcare services for the discharged patient.

       v. Retrospective review: review conducted by the PRO for evaluation of quality issues, cost and outliers issues, and issues of utilization management and appropriateness of care

   f. Centers for Medicare and Medicaid Services (CMS)

       i. Scope of work

          1. Under the authority of the Health Care Financing Administration (now CMS), PSROs (now QIOs) began to be phased out in 1982. Upon its closure, the peer review organization was enacted to ensure services provided for Medicare beneficiaries are

             a. Reasonable and medically necessary

             b. Of a quality that meets professionally recognized standards in health care

             c. Provided in the most effective and economic setting

          2. CMS current scope of work focused on

             a. Clinical quality outcomes

             b. Payment error prevention

3. Risk Management

   a. Definitions

       i. Risk management is the management of any event or situation that could potentially result in an injury to an individual or financial loss to the healthcare institution.

       ii. Consists of policies, procedures, and practices that reduce risk and liabilities for injuries that may occur

       iii. Objectives

          1. To create and maintain a safe, healthy, environment and enhance quality care

          2. To minimize risk of medical or accidental injuries and losses

          3. Provide cost-effective techniques to insure against financial loss

b. Risk Management Program
   i. Elements
      1. Risk identification: identifying areas of existing or potential loss. The essential tool used to identify risk is the incident report.
      2. Risk control: prevention and control of risks and minimizing number of occurrences for which the facility may be held liable
      3. Risk financing: plan to financially cover losses; funds may include self insurance, insurance pools, and commercial insurance
   ii. Components
      1. Loss prevention and reduction
      2. Claims management
      3. Safety and security
      4. Employee programs
      5. Patient relations
   iii. Methodology
      1. Occurrence screening
         a. Adverse patient occurrences
         b. Potential compensable events
      2. Incident report
         a. Reportable incidents are written and investigated.
         b. Root cause analysis is done to determine underlying factors of a sentinel event.
      3. Patient advocacy
   iv. Near miss: an occurrence that does not necessarily affect an outcome because the error was caught in time, but that carries a significant chance of being a serious adverse event if it is not caught
      1. Near misses are not reviewed by The Joint Commission under the current sentinel event policy
      2. Near misses are good tools in developing policy and procedure
      3. Valuable tools to use for evaluation of processes and staff education
      4. Monitor reports more carefully to reduce any associated potential risk
      5. Good tools to use in monitoring high-risk and high-volume areas of concern
   v. Incident and occurrence report: a performance improvement system set up to collect and track all different types of incidents
      1. A valuable tool used to provide ongoing education to all employees
      2. Aids in developing policies and procedures and structuring of patient-related care
   vi. Sentinel event: an unexpected occurrence involving death or serious physical or psychological injury
      1. Any event that signals a need for immediate investigation and response (e.g., loss of limb or loss of function)
         a. Unanticipated death of a full-term infant
         b. Abduction of any patient receiving care, treatment, or service
         c. Discharge of an infant to the wrong family
         d. Surgery on a wrong body part or on a wrong patient
         e. Rape of anyone in the healthcare facility (e.g., patient, staff member, provider, vendor)

      f. Unintended foreign object left in a patient during a procedure

      g. Suicide of any patient receiving care, treatment, and service in a staffed round-the-clock care setting, or within 72 hours of discharge

   vii. Use of risk management information

      1. Improve system processes

      2. Increase patient and employee satisfaction

      3. Improve clinical outcomes

      4. Decrease risk factors

c. Reportable Events

   i. Adverse related events

      1. Unauthorized medication

      2. Omission

      3. IV infiltration

      4. Wrong dose

      5. Wrong patient

      6. Wrong medication

      7. Wrong site

      8. Wrong route

      9. Wrong dosage

      10. Wrong time

      11. Wrong technique

      12. Wrong drug preparation

      13. Wrong rate

      14. Drug interaction

      15. Drug allergy

      16. Food and drug interaction

      17. Deteriorated drug

   ii. Other types of reportable events

      1. Patient abuse

      2. Patient neglect

      3. Medically unstable at discharge

      4. Returning to intensive care unit within 24 hours of being transferred out

      5. Unplanned return to surgery for same condition

      6. Patient fall

      7. Missed diagnosis

      8. Delayed diagnosis

      9. Blood transfusion error

      10. Complication with anesthesia

      11. Unanticipated death

      12. Suicide/unsuccessful suicide attempt

      13. Prenatal death

      14. Inappropriate use of restraints

      15. Operative injury or complications

      16. Unexpected admission, readmission, or return to emergency center following inpatient or outpatient care for same condition

      17. Equipment failure

      18. Infant abduction

      19. Blood transfusion reaction

      20. Unauthorized inpatient departure

      21. Patient injury while in restraints

      iii. Role of a risk manager
- **1.** Carefully review organization's policies and procedures and staff's ability to execute them
- **2.** Maintain open channel of communication with any person injured in the facility until satisfactory resolution of the claim or lawsuit has been reached
- **3.** Provide information to the organization's insurer and represent the organization at all formal meetings and legal proceedings related to injury claims

      iv. Sentinel events (unexpected occurrence involving death or serious physical or psychological injury)
- **1.** Surgery on wrong patient
- **2.** Infant discharged to wrong family
- **3.** Rape
- **4.** Blood transfusion related to blood group incompatibilities
- **5.** Surgery on wrong body part
- **6.** Unanticipated death
- **7.** Infant abduction
- **8.** Suicide
- **9.** Permanent loss of major function associated with medication or surgical error

      v. Medication reconciliation: a National Patient Safety Goal aimed at addressing a major cause of medication-related sentinel events and reducing medication errors

4. Credentialing

  a. Defined

      i. The reviewing, verifying, validating, and evaluating of the key factors that determine an individual practitioner's ability to carry out certain patient care activities and granting of professional privileges

      ii. According to TJC, credentialing is the "authorization granted by the governing board to a practitioner to provide specific patient care services in the hospital within defined limits, based on an individual practitioner's license, education, training, experience, competence, health status, and judgment."

      iii. Crucial role in maintaining high-quality professional care to the patients. Many legal and ethical landmarks have made it clear that the hospital has the obligation to select its staff carefully and to grant them privileges as appropriate to ensure the staff are highly educated, trained, experienced, qualified, and competent to deliver needed services.

      iv. The medical staff consists of individual practitioners who are permitted by law to provide patient care services within their scope of practice, without direct supervision.
- **1.** Examples: physicians, dentists, clinic psychologists, podiatrists
- **2.** Most independent practitioners seek to remain independent by joining hospital medical staff rather than being traditional employees of the hospital
- **3.** Process of ensuring qualifications for medical staff members is unique because of its peer review process

      v. Source of verifying credentialing: "primary source" is the original source of a specific credential that can verify the accuracy of a qualification reported by an applicant. Examples: medical school, graduate medical education program, and state medical board.

b. Purpose

 i. To ensure that medical staff members only perform procedures and services that they are qualified and competent to perform through training and experience

 ii. Key aspects

  1. Initial appointments to the medical staff

  2. Initial delineation and granting of clinical privileges

  3. Periodic reappointment to the medical staff

  4. Periodic renewal or revision of clinical privileges

c. Medical Staff

 i. Functions of medical staff

  1. Adopt medical staff bylaws

  2. Provide patient care and carry out other professional responsibilities

  3. Actively participate in and exercise professional leadership in measuring, assessing, and improving the performance of the organizations within which they practice

  4. Continually improve the quality of healthcare services delivered

  5. Provide patient care within their professional competence

  6. Provide patient care as reflected in the scope of their clinical privileges

  7. Participate in ongoing measurement, assessment, and improvement of both clinical and nonclinical processes

 ii. Characteristics of medical staff

  1. Each medical staff member and all others with delineated clinical privileges are subject to medical staff and departmental bylaws, rules and regulations, and policies and are subject to review as part of the organization's performance improvement activities.

  2. Each medical staff member is fully licensed.

  3. Each medical staff member is permitted by law and by the hospital to provide patient care services independently in the hospital.

  4. Each medical staff member has delineated clinical privileges that define the scope of patient care services he or she may provide independently in the hospital.

 iii. Medical staff record maintenance

  1. A separate record is maintained for each individual requesting medical staff membership or clinical privileges.

  2. Complete applications are acted on within a reasonable period of time, as specified in the medical staff bylaws.

  3. Each file is consistent with applicant's consents for inspection of records and documents pertinent to his or her licensure, specific training, experience, current competence, and ability to perform the privileges requested, and, if requested, applicant appears for an interview.

  4. The bylaws, rules and regulations, and policies of the medical staff indicate that the applicant for reappointment or renewal of clinical privileges is required to submit any reasonable evidence of current ability to perform privileges that may be requested.

5. Each applicant pledges to provide for continuous care for his or her patients.
6. Signed acknowledgment for release and immunity from civil liability

iv. Required TJC medical staff bylaws

1. The method of selecting officers
2. The qualifications required for the medical staff position
3. The responsibilities and functions required for the position
4. The tenures of officers
5. The conditions and mechanisms for removing officers from their positions
6. Requirements for frequency of meetings and for attendance
7. Effective communication among the medical staff, hospital administration, and governing body
8. Mechanisms for corrective action, including indications and procedures for automatic and summary suspension of an individual's medical staff membership or clinical privileges
9. A description of the medical staff's organization, including categories of medical staff membership, when such exist
10. A description of appropriate officer positions, with the stipulation that each officer is a medical staff member
11. When necessary, the medical staff bylaws and rules and regulations are revised to reflect the hospital's current practices with respect to medical staff organization and functions.
12. The medical staff bylaws, rules and regulations, and policies and the governing body's bylaws do not conflict.
13. If significant changes are made in the medical staff bylaws, rules and regulations, or policies, medical staff members and other individuals who have delineated clinical privileges are provided with revised texts of the written materials.
14. Neither body may unilaterally amend the medical staff bylaws or rules and regulations.
15. Medical staff bylaws and rules and regulations create a framework within which medical staff members can act with a reasonable degree of freedom and confidence.
16. The medical staff implement a process to identify and manage matters of individual physician health that are separate from the medical staff disciplinary function.
17. There is an executive committee of the medical staff.
18. The executive committee's function, size, and composition and the method of selecting its members are defined in the medical staff bylaws.
19. The chief executive officer of the hospital or his or her designee attends each executive committee meeting on an ex-officio basis, with or without vote.
20. Participation of the medical staff in organization performance improvement activities
21. Mechanism by which medical staff membership may be terminated
22. Mechanisms, including a fair hearing and appeal process, for addressing adverse decisions for existing medical staff members and other individuals holding clinical privileges for renewal, revocation, or revision of clinical privileges

d. Types of Membership Privileges

    i. Appointment or reappointment of qualified applicants to an existing medical unit is designated by category, which describes the degree to which members use the facility, length of time of appointment, or some other factor specific to institution.

        1. Active

        2. Honorary

        3. Courtesy

        4. Faculty

        5. Associate or provisional

        6. Consulting

        7. Disaster

        8. House staff

        9. Temporary

e. Purpose of Clinical Privileges

    i. Delineates the types of procedures that can be performed by each provider of care

    ii. Delineates the types of care and treatment that can be carried out by each provider of care

    iii. Delineates the types of patients to whom the healthcare provider will be allowed to have access

f. Credentialing Application Process

    i. Practitioner applies for membership and requests clinical privileges.

        1. The medical staff bylaws and the medical staff rules and regulations delineate what needs to be collected and reviewed during the credentialing phase. They also delineate the processes and responsibilities for approval and denial of medical staff clinical privileges and membership.

        2. Categories of applicants

            a. Type one

                i. Physician

                ii. Dentist

                iii. Podiatrist

            b. Type two

                i. Physician assistant

                ii. Advanced nurse practitioner

                iii. Allied health providers

                iv. All other licensed and certified staff

        3. Applicant information

            a. Demographic and identifying information

            b. Education

            c. State licensure number

            d. State licensure expiration date

            e. Previous employers

            f. Prior malpractice claims

            g. Denial of medical privileges with other institutions

            h. Narcotics number

            i. Third-party payment program involvements

            j. Name of references/letter

            k. Acknowledgment of Medicare/Medicaid fraud regulations

            l. Revocation of medical privileges with other institution

            m. Suspension of medical privileges with other institution

        n. Voluntary relinquishment of licensure

        o. Involuntary relinquishment of licensure

  ii. Credential verification

      1. Education

      2. Liability insurance coverage

      3. Current licensure

      4. Clinical competence

      5. Satisfactory health status

 iii. Privilege delineation

      1. Process to determine specific procedures and services a practitioner is permitted to perform under jurisdiction of institution

      2. Applicant's documented experience

      3. The results of healthcare treatment and outcomes

      4. The conclusions drawn from performance-improvement activities as appropriate

      5. Benchmarking of staff activities is considered when delineating clinical privileges.

      6. Documentation of basis for granting privileges

      7. Classification or categorization of privileges is well defined, and the standards to be met by the applicant are stated clearly for each category.

      8. When medical staff clinical departments exist, all licensed independent practitioners are assigned to at least one clinical department and are granted clinical privileges that are relevant to the care provided in that department.

      9. There is a satisfactory method to coordinate appraisal for granting or renewal or revision of clinical privileges when an individual currently holding clinical privileges or applying for clinical privileges requests privileges that are relevant to the care provided in more than one department or clinical specialty area.

     10. The exercise of clinical privileges within any department is subject to the rules and regulations of that department and to the authority of the department head.

     11. When there are no medical staff clinical departments, all individuals with clinical privileges have their privileges recommended and the quality of their care reviewed through designated medical staff mechanisms, described in the medical staff or governing body bylaws and rules and regulations.

     12. Practitioners who diagnose or treat patients via telemedicine link are subject to the credentialing and privileging processes of the organization that receives the telemedicine service.

     13. The medical staff recommends the clinical services to be provided by telemedicine.

     14. Appraisal for reappointment to the medical staff or renewal or revision of clinical privileges is based on ongoing monitoring of information concerning the individual's professional performance, judgment, and clinical or technical skills.

     15. The chief executive officer or his or her designee may grant temporary clinical privileges, when appropriate.

     16. Disaster privileges may be granted when the emergency management plan has been activated and the organization is unable to handle the immediate patient needs.

17. Whatever mechanism for granting and renewal or revision of clinical privileges is used, evidence indicates that the clinical privileges are hospital-specific and based on the individual's demonstrated current competence.

18. Appointment or reappointment to the medical staff and the granting, renewal, or revision of clinical privileges is made for a period of no more than 2 years.

   iv. Credentialing department chair

      1. Responsible for coordinating, reviewing, evaluating, and validating timeliness and appropriateness of submitted application

      2. Upon satisfactory review, the departmental chair requests privilege verification

      3. Maintains documentation

      4. Forwards the application and the request for clinical privileges to credentialing committee for further review

   v. Credentialing committee

      1. Functions in advisory capacity and is not empowered to make appointment

      2. Conducts peer review of applicant

      3. Makes recommendation for appointment and privileges to executive committee

      4. Aspects of role of credentialing committee

         a. Receives the reviewed application from departmental chair

         b. Reviews the application and the request for clinical privileges

         c. Forwards its recommendation, membership application, and the request for clinical privileges to the executive credentialing review committee

         d. Can recommend approval with condition, approval with no restriction, or denial

   vi. Executive committee

      1. Recommendation to governing board based upon

         a. The medical staff's structure

         b. The mechanism used to review credentials and to delineate individual clinical privileges

         c. Recommendations of individuals for medical staff membership

         d. Recommendations for delineated clinical privileges for each eligible individual

      2. Role of executive committee

         a. Gathers accurate, thorough, sufficient, and reliable information to ascertain that the professional staff applicants who were recommended for employment or contract are qualified and competent to be granted privileges for the appropriate task and services

         b. Forwards recommendations for appointment, reappointment, or denial of clinical privileges to the governing body

         c. Has governance responsibilities, delegated by the medical staff, within the organization

         d. Has the primary authority over activities related to the functions of the medical staff and over activities related to the quality of care, and functions of performance improvement of the professional services provided by individuals with clinical privileges

    e. Receives and acts on reports and recommendations from medical staff committees, clinical departments, and assigned activity groups

    f. Empowered to act on behalf of the medical staffs in the related medical staff meetings

vii. Governing board approves or denies membership and privileges.

    1. The governing body is ultimately responsible and accountable for the quality of services provided in its facility. Therefore, the final approval or denial of privileges remains the responsibility of the governing body. The credentialing and recredentialing are carried out according to the established and adopted bylaws, medical staff rules and regulations, and policies and procedures of the facility.

    2. The governing board depends on the reports and professional recommendation from its credentialing professional review committee. The governing board relies on its credentialing professional review committee to gather accurate, thorough, sufficient, reliable information to ascertain that the professional staff applicant who was recommended for employment or contract is qualified and competent to be granted privileges for the appropriate tasks and services.

    3. Role of governing board

        a. Approves medical staff bylaws

        b. Addresses and acknowledges its legal accountabilities and responsibilities to the patient population that it serves

        c. Establishes a quality-focused, criteria-based process for selecting a qualified and competent medical staff

        d. Declares the final action for approval or denial of privileges

        e. Enhances collaboration and participation of assigned medical staff and other assigned leaders in developing, reviewing, and revising applicable policies and procedures to support credentialing process

        f. Depends on the reports and professional recommendation from its executive committee

viii. Reappointment

    1. Practitioner profile

        a. Mechanism to integrate information compiled from quality management activities into credentialing process to determine reappointment

        b. Reappointment criteria may be different from initial appoint criteria

g. Continuing Education

    i. All individuals with clinical privileges participate in ongoing continuing education activities related to their granted privilege.

    ii. Continuing education must be documented, must be made available, and must become part of an indicator regarding qualifications for reappointment or renewal or revision of individual clinical privileges.

    iii. The educational activities must be related to the type of care performed by the particular medical staff and, in part, care offered by the hospital.

h. Credentialing Staff
- **i.** Functions
  - **1.** Able to organize and prioritize work
  - **2.** Able to follow instruction precisely
  - **3.** Able to develop and/or implement policies and procedures
  - **4.** Able to maintain confidentiality of information
  - **5.** Able to coordinate heavy correspondence
  - **6.** Able to secure hard-to-get but necessary information
  - **7.** Has good handwriting and oral communication skills
  - **8.** Knows credentialing and recredentialing requirements
  - **9.** Knows proper terminology

i. Examples of Credentialing Process Guidelines and Credentialing Data Collection Form (Figure 5-6, Figure 5-7, and Figure 5-8)

j. Conditions of Participation
- **i.** Quality assessment and performance improvement (QAPI): the hospital must develop, implement, and maintain an effective, ongoing, hospital-wide, data-driven QAPI program.
- **ii.** The hospital's governing body must ensure that the QAPI program reflects the complexity of the hospital's organization and services; involves all hospital departments and services (including those services furnished under contract or arrangement); and focuses on indicators related to improved health outcomes and the prevention and reduction of medical errors.
- **iii.** The hospital must maintain and demonstrate evidence of its QAPI program for review by CMS.
  - **1.** Standard: program scope
    - **a.** The program must include, but not be limited to, an ongoing program that shows measurable improvement in indicators for which there is evidence that it will improve health outcomes and identify and reduce medical errors.
    - **b.** The hospital must measure, analyze, and track quality indicators, including adverse patient events, and other aspects of performance that assess processes of care, hospital service, and operations.
  - **2.** Standard: program data
    - **a.** The program must incorporate quality indicator data including patient care data, and other relevant data (e.g., information submitted to, or received from, the hospital's quality improvement organization)
    - **b.** The hospital must use the data collected to:
      - **i.** Monitor the effectiveness and safety of services and quality of care
      - **ii.** Identify opportunities for improvement and changes that will lead to improvement
    - **c.** The frequency and detail of data collection must be specified by the hospital's governing body.
  - **3.** Standard: program activities
    - **a.** The hospital must set priorities for its performance improvement activities that:
      - **i.** Focus on high-risk, high-volume, or problem-prone areas
      - **ii.** Consider the incidence, prevalence, and severity of problems in those areas
      - **iii.** Affect health outcomes, patient safety, and quality of care

1. Credentialing, like an employment or contracting process, must be performed in a manner consistent with applicable local, state, and federal laws.
2. All staff participating in the credentialing process must be familiar with the local, state, and federal credentialing requirements.
3. The facility must ensure compliance with all applicable credentialing standards.
4. The applicant must sign an authorization for disclosure of information from requested third-party agents such as previous schools, employers, etc.
5. The facility must develop or adopt credentialing data collection tools.
6. The faculty must maintain adequate filing for general correspondence, confidential correspondence, and medical correspondence.
7. The faculty must maintain a tickler file for requested items.
8. Medical bylaws must include time frame for completing credentialing application process.
9. Applicant is responsible for providing all information the institution requests.
10. The applicant must conduct all requests for information at the direction, approval, and authority of the credentialing professional review committee.
11. Received information is treated as confidential and only shared as necessary within the credentialing review staff.
12. Sanctions and disciplinary action for rediscosure of information to other external agencies are addressed in the bylaws and the policies and procedures.
13. Credentialing information is requested promptly.
14. A checklist is used to identify what information is lacking in the application process.
15. The application for credentialing privilege is not complete until all required information has been received from all requested parties.
16. Decision to grant or deny privilege must be based on patterns of professional practice rather than a single occurrence, unless the single occurrence is considered to be a violation of the standard.
17. The governing board must communicate decision regarding the granting or denial of privileges to the applicant in writing.
18. Copies must be sent to the applicant's credentialing file, applicant, and performance improvement/risk management file.
19. The bylaws must provide appeal procedures for those who may wish to appeal adverse decisions.
20. With the exception of legal cases, all files regarding denials of privileges must be kept for a minimum of 1 year from the date decision was made.

Figure 5-6 Example of Credentialing Process Guidelines

Data from the NCQA. Accreditation Programs. http://www.ncqa.org/Programs/Accreditation.aspx. Accessed March 4, 2014.

b. Performance improvement activities must track medical errors and adverse patient events, analyze their causes, and implement preventive actions and mechanisms that include feedback and learning throughout the hospital.

c. The hospital must take actions aimed at performance improvement and, after implementing those actions, must measure its success, and track performance to ensure that improvements are sustained.

4. Standard: performance improvement projects. As part of its quality assessment and performance improvement program, the hospital must conduct performance improvement projects.

a. The number and scope of distinct improvement projects conducted annually must be proportional to the scope and complexity of the hospital's services and operations.

b. A hospital may, as one of its projects, develop and implement an information technology system explicitly designed to improve patient safety and quality of care. This project, in its

Instructions: List all required items. Place a check mark in the box to indicate the item's completion.

	Items	Yes	No	Comment
1.	Application completed			
2.	Requested privileges specified			
3.	Attestation to correctness and completeness of information submitted			
4.	Authorization to request, disclose, and/or share information is signed			
5.	Special consent is signed as needed			
6.	Copy of state license is attached			
7.	Copy of board certificate or eligibility letter is attached			
8.	Proof of professional liability is attached			
9.	Names of three professional recommendations submitted			

Figure 5-7 Example Data Collection Tool for Completion of Credentialing Application

initial stage of development, does not need to demonstrate measurable improvement in indicators related to health outcomes.

c. The hospital must document which quality improvement projects are being conducted, the reasons for conducting these projects, and the measurable progress achieved on these projects.

d. A hospital is not required to participate in a QIO cooperative project, but its own projects are required to be of comparable effort.

5. Standard: executive responsibilities. The hospital's governing body (or organized group or individual who assumes full legal authority and responsibility for operations of the hospital), medical staff, and administrative officials are responsible and accountable for ensuring the following:

a. An ongoing program for quality improvement and patient safety, including the reduction of medical errors, is defined, implemented, and maintained.

b. The hospital-wide QAPI efforts address priorities for improved quality of care and patient safety, and all improvement actions are evaluated.

c. Clear expectations for safety are established.

d. Adequate resources are allocated for measuring, assessing, improving, and sustaining the hospital's performance and reducing risk to patients.

e. The determination of the number of distinct improvement projects is conducted annually.

iv. Compliance with federal, state, and local laws

1. The hospital must be in compliance with applicable federal laws related to the health and safety of patients.

Instructions: As applicable, write the date each item was sent out to the other third-party agent for verification, and the date each item was received, in the appropriate column.

	Items	Received Date	Pending	Sent Date	Contact Person
1.	Proof of professional liability verification				
2.	Three professional recommendations				
3.	Verification of past and/or pending professional disciplinary actions				
4.	Verification of voluntary and involuntary limitations, loss of clinical privileges, or reduction of privileges				
5.	Confirmation from national practitioner data bank (NPDB)				
6.	Confirmation from American Medical Association (AMA)				
7.	Confirmation from Drug Enforcement Agency (DEA)				
8.	Verification of educational background				
9.	Verification of training				
10.	Verification of employment history				
11.	Verification of prior membership termination				
12.	Verification and approval by credentialing committee				
13.	Recommendation for appointment forwarded to administrative staff				
14.	Appointment for recommendation by medical staff administration forwarded to governing board				
15.	Notification of approval, approval with conditions, or denial				
16.	Confirmation of physical and mental fitness to perform requested privilege				
17.	Conflict of interest statement signed				
18.	Signed statement of medical staff bylaws				
19.	Signed statement agreeing to report any malpractice and changes in related health status				

Figure 5-8   Example of Status Check Sheet for Credentialing Data Collection Process

    2. The hospital must be:
        a. Licensed or
        b. Approved as meeting standards for licensing established by the agency of the state or locality responsible for licensing hospitals
    3. The hospital must assure that personnel are licensed or meet other applicable standards that are required by state or local laws.

k. Patient rights: a hospital must protect and promote each patient's rights.
    i. A hospital must inform each patient, or when appropriate, the patient's representative (as allowed under state law), of the patient's rights, in advance of furnishing or discontinuing patient care whenever possible.

l. Medical Staff
    i. The hospital must have an organized medical staff that operates under bylaws approved by the governing body and is responsible for the quality of medical care provided to patients by the hospital.

m. Governing Body
    i. The hospital must have an effective governing body legally responsible for the conduct of the hospital as an institution.
    ii. If a hospital does not have an organized governing body, the persons legally responsible for the conduct of the hospital must carry out the functions specified in this part that pertain to the governing body.

n. Medical Record
    i. The hospital must have a medical record service that has administrative responsibility for medical records.
    ii. A medical record must be maintained for every individual evaluated or treated in the hospital.
        1. Standard: organization and staffing
            a. The organization of the medical record service must be appropriate to the scope and complexity of the services performed.
            b. The hospital must employ adequate personnel to ensure prompt completion, filing, and retrieval of records.
        2. Standard: form and retention of record
            a. The hospital must maintain a medical record for each inpatient and outpatient.
            b. Medical records must be accurately written, promptly completed, properly filed and retained, and accessible.
            c. The hospital must use a system of author identification and record maintenance that ensures the integrity of the authentication and protects the security of all record entries.
                i. Medical records must be retained in their original or legally reproduced form for a period of at least 5 years.
                ii. The hospital must have a system of coding and indexing medical records. The system must allow for timely retrieval by diagnosis and procedure, to support medical care evaluation studies.
                iii. The hospital must have a procedure for ensuring the confidentiality of patient records. Information from or copies of records may be released only to authorized individuals, and the hospital must ensure that unauthorized individuals cannot gain access to or alter patient records.

Original medical records must be released by the hospital only in accordance with federal or state laws, court orders, or subpoenas.

3. Standard: content of record
   a. The medical record must contain information to justify admission and continued hospitalization, support the diagnosis, and describe the patient's progress and response to medications and services.
      i. All entries must be legible and complete, and must be authenticated and dated promptly by the person (identified by name and discipline) who is responsible for ordering, providing, or evaluating the service furnished.
         1. The author of each entry must be identified and must authenticate his or her entry.
         2. Authentication may include signatures, written initials or computer entry.
      ii. All records must document the following, as appropriate:
         1. Evidence of a physical examination, including a health history, performed no more than 7 days prior to admission or within 48 hours after admission
         2. Admitting diagnosis
         3. Results of all consultative evaluations of the patient and appropriate findings by clinical and other staff involved in the care of the patient
         4. Documentation of complications, hospital-acquired infections, and unfavorable reactions to drugs and anesthesia
         5. Properly executed informed consent forms for procedures and treatments specified by the medical staff, or by federal or state law if applicable, to require written patient consent
         6. All practitioners' orders, nursing notes, reports of treatment, medication records, radiology, and laboratory reports, and vital signs and other information necessary to monitor the patient's condition
         7. Discharge summary with outcome of hospitalization, disposition of case, and provisions for follow-up care
         8. Final diagnosis with completion of medical records within 30 days following discharge

5. **Accreditation: act of granting approval to a healthcare organization**
   a. The approval is based on whether the organization has met a set of voluntary standards developed by accreditation agency.
   b. The Joint Commission: example of a voluntary accreditation agency
   c. Accreditation confirms the quality of a services provided by the organization.
   d. The "stamp of approval" by the accrediting agency lets consumers of services know the organization is committed to meeting higher standards.

6. **Joint Commission Accreditation Status**
   a. Accredited: organization demonstrated full compliance with TJC standards
   b. Accreditation with follow-up survey: organization did not fully comply with TJC accreditation standard at the time of the on-site survey and requires a follow-up within 30 days to 6 months

    i. Organization must address and resolve the identified problem area within the time specified to bring itself to compliance with standards

  c. Contingency accreditation: organization did not meet all TJC standards at the time of the on-site survey

    i. Organization that receives contingency accreditation may appeal

  d. Preliminary denial of accreditation: organization is significantly noncompliant with TJC standards in multiple performance areas

    i. Organization that receives contingency accreditation may appeal

    ii. Organization may present additional information

  e. Denial of accreditation: all applicable denial procedures have been exhausted, and organization has been denied accreditation

7. **Licensure: act of granting a healthcare organization a permission to provide services of defined scope in a limited geographical area**

  a. State governments issue licenses based on regulations specific to the healthcare practice.

  b. States issue licenses to individual hospitals, physicians, and nurses.

  c. It is illegal for healthcare organizations or healthcare professionals to provide service without a license.

8. **Certification: granting approval for a healthcare organization to provide services to a specific group of beneficiaries**

  a. Healthcare organization must meet the Conditions of Participation to receive funding through the Medicare and Medicaid programs.

  b. The programs are administered through the Centers for Medicare and Medicaid Services.

9. **Compliance: process of meeting a prescribed set of standards or regulations to maintain active accreditation, licensure, or certification status**

  a. Review Process

    i. Some review processes are compulsory; others are voluntary.

    ii. Each review agency develops written standards or regulations that serve as a basis for its review process.

    iii. Healthcare facilities must continue to monitor any review changes and updates policies as appropriate.

    iv. Keep current sets of agency review standards on hand at all times to help maintain compliance

      1. Compulsory: review performed to fulfill legal or licensure requirements.

      2. Voluntary: review conducted at the request of the healthcare facility seeking accreditation or certification

10. **National Patient Safety Goals: an initiative established to proactively reduce errors in all healthcare settings**

  a. Improve Communication

    i. Create list of "do not use" abbreviations and symbols that are not to be used

    ii. Read back a spoken order to the person who gave the order

  b. Use Medicine Safely

    i. Create a list of medicines with names that look alike or sound alike; update the list yearly

    ii. Label all medicines

  c. Prevent Infection

    i. Use the hand-washing guideline from World Health Organization (WHO) or Centers for Disease Control and Prevention (CDC)

    ii. Use approved guideline to prevent infections

    d. Check Patient Medicines
        i. Reconcile all medications that a patient is currently taking
        ii. Give a list of the patient's medications to the next caregiver
        iii. Give a list of the patient's medications to the patient/family member/legal representative
    e. Prevent Falls
    f. Prevent Bedsores
    g. Identify Patient Safety Risk
        i. Identify suicidal patients
    h. Identify Patients Correctly
        i. Use at least two ways to identify patient (e.g., name and date of birth)

11. Environment of Care
    a. Successful Improvement Activities
        i. Staff and human resources management
        ii. Medical equipment management
        iii. Safety management
        iv. Hazardous materials management
        v. Security management
        vi. Waste management
        vii. Disaster and incident management
        viii. Building and utility management
        ix. Workplace violence

12. **Legal Implications of Performance Improvement: Performance improvement activities are affected by numerous standards, laws, rules, and regulations.**
    a. Avoidance of Risk: in pursuit of quality care, healthcare organizations constantly looking for ways to avoid negative consequences.
        i. Failure to meet expected standard creates risk.
        ii. The higher the risk, the higher the unsatisfied patient, the higher the loss of market share, the higher the exposure to legal actions.
        iii. Since 1970, technology has improved, healthcare costs have increased, the number of lawyers has grown, and various lawsuits have shown that continuous quality assessment and performance improvement is a key to ensuring high-quality outcomes and reduction of risk.
    b. Tort Law: Civil Action
        i. Provide the basis for private parties to resolve disputes in a civil courts
        ii. Private party: individual, group, business, corporation, nongovernmental organization
        iii. Most notable tort in health care: negligence (malpractice)
        iv. In malpractice, generally the hospital or provider, or both, are sued for being careless and thereby causing injury or harm to the patient.
        v. One party usually seeks monetary payment for harm or damages caused by another party.
            1. Criminal actions are prosecuted by the government against the private party (individuals) accused of committing a crime.
            2. In criminal cases, the government generally seeks a jail sentence.
    c. Elements of Negligence or Malpractice: four elements must be present for a successful negligence/malpractice action.
        i. Duty to use due care: acting as a reasonably prudent person would act under a given set of circumstances

      ii. Breach of duty: whether due care was exercised

      iii. Damages: must show the actual harm or damage occurred

      iv. Causation: must be a connection that the breach of duty cause the damage or harm

d. Differentiating Quality Improvement Activities from Research Activities: Both quality improvement and research are aimed at improving some element of care. Each falls under different regulations and different requirements, so incorrect classification may have significant implications.

      i. Quality improvement activity focuses on confidential data—data collection and data analysis activities to improve service

        1. Quality improvement activities and their outcomes are applied only to organization at which they were conducted.

      ii. Research is a systematic investigation that revolves around testing, and or evaluation designed to develop or contributed to generalized knowledge.

        1. The result of research activities may be applied to the general population being studied.

        2. Results of research activities are generally published in a scientific or professional journal.

      iii. Research must be approved by the institutional review board (IRB) before it can be conducted.

e. Peer Review Protection: records/minutes relating to medical staff committees' discussions, deliberations, and proceedings are kept confidential

      i. Cannot be disclosed outside of the medical staff processes

      ii. Oral and written information related to peer review activities excluded from discoverability

      iii. Is shielded and cannot be introduced at trial to support a patient's malpractice action against a physician or hospital.

f. Immunity from Liability: Health Care Quality Improvement Act of 1986 was designed to make the peer review process more effective

      i. Eliminates the fear of legal liability on the part of the participant

g. Disclosing Adverse Events to a Patient or the Patient's Family

      i. As hard as it may be, ethical standards require that adverse events (negative outcomes) be disclosed to the patient or family.

      ii. The treating physician is responsible for disclosing the adverse event to the patient or family.

      iii. Documentation in patient health record

        1. Factual description of the adverse event

        2. Evidence that the adverse event was discussed with the patient or family member, including date, time, and parties present

        3. Evidence of follow-up discussion with patient and family member

      iv. Communication of adverse event to patient or family member

        1. Factual explanation of the circumstances of the adverse event

        2. Explanation of its impact to patient

        3. Corrective action plan

        4. Assurance that the physician/designated individual/patient care team will remain available to discuss any concerns the patient or family may have

      v. Adverse event report: a tool utilized to report, track, and mitigate occurrences. It *must* not be incorporated as part of the patient's health record.

PRACTICAL APPLICATION OF YOUR KNOWLEDGE

1. Quality Assessment and Performance Improvement
    a. Define the following terms:
        i. Quality

        ii. Quality improvement

        iii. Quality assessment

        iv. Total quality management

        v. Quality indicators

        vi. Benchmarking

        vii. Quality management

    b. Methods to Improve Quality
        i. List the TJC 10-step process to achieving the goals and objectives of a monitoring and evaluation program.

        ii. List and describe the Avedis Donabedian model for assessing quality in the healthcare arena.

        iii. What method was developed by Walter Shewhart and made popular by W. Edwards Deming? Define each of the four phases.

iv. What is the seven-step model that was developed by Brian Joiner to assess quality improvement?

v. List the six steps in the model developed by Re RN and Krousel-Wood M.

vi. Describe the accomplishments of Crosby, Deming, Joiner, and Juran.

Crosby	Deming	Joiner	Juran

vii. Describe the philosophy of Crosby, Deming, Joiner, and Juran.

Crosby	Deming	Joiner	Juran

viii. List Deming's 14 principles.

ix. List Deming's seven deadly diseases in quality management.

c. Court Cases
i. Fill in the following blanks regarding the effects of court decisions on quality of healthcare services.

Court Cases		
Year	**Case**	**Decision**
	Darling vs. Charleston Community Hospital	The court ruled that the hospital must assume certain responsibilities for care of the patient. The court ruled that a hospital was negligent for permitting a general practitioner to perform orthopedic surgery. The court ruled that the hospital had a duty to apply reasonable standards to the practice of its physicians because it was responsible for the privileging of physicians on its staff.
1973	*Gonzales vs. Nork and Mercy Hospital*	
1981		The court found that the hospital owed a duty to its patients in selecting medical staff members and granting privileges.

d. Spell out the following acronyms of external agencies influencing quality of health care.
i. TJC (formerly JCAHO)

ii. CARF

iii. QIO (formerly PRO)

iv. CMS

          v. HCFA

          vi. HIPAA

          vii. TPR

e. Performance Improvement
        i. What is the purpose of performance improvement?

        ii. List the 10 core elements to be included in a performance improvement plan.
           1.

           2.

           3.

           4.

           5.

           6.

           7.

           8.

9.

10.

f. List some of the benefits of continuous quality improvement.
   i.

   ii.

   iii.

   iv.

   v.

g. List some of the internal customers of the HIM department.

h. List some of the external customers of the HIM department.

i. List ways to identify the needs of your customers.

j. List some of the services or products your department has to offer.

k. Draw the PDCA cycle and describe the activities of each step in the cycle.

l. Define CQI and its purpose.

m. Write out definitions for the acronym FOCUS.

F:_____

O:_____

C:_____

U:_____

S:_____

n. Describe data collection methods for performance improvement.

o. Is information collected during the CQI process confidential? Explain your answer.

2. Utilization Review

    a. List the three main goals of the QIO (formerly PRO) physician reviewers.

        i.

        ii.

        iii.

    b. Define the following segments of utilization review process:

        i. Preadmission review

        ii. Admission review

        iii. Concurrent review

        iv. Discharge review

        v. Retrospective review

3. Risk Management

    a. List three objectives of risk management.

        i.

        ii.

        iii.

    b. What are the three main elements of risk management?
        i.

        ii.

        iii.

4. Credentialing
    a. Define credentialing.

    b. What is the purpose of credentialing?

    c. List 10 elements of the information that is required for the applicant's credentialing file.
        i.

        ii.

        iii.

        iv.

        v.

        vi.

        vii.

viii.

ix.

x.

d. Identify the type of credentialing for which the professional practitioners in the following table can apply by placing a check mark under the appropriate category type.

Credentialing of Professional Health Practitioners		
	Category	
Practitioner	**Type One**	**Type Two**
Physician assistant		
Advanced nurse practitioner		
Physician		
Allied health provider		
Dentist		
Podiatrist		
Other licensed and certified providers		

e. List five types of membership privileges.
   i.

   ii.

   iii.

   iv.

   v.

    f. List five functions of the credentialing staff.
       i.

       ii.

       iii.

       iv.

       v.

5. Tools for Collecting and Displaying Data
    a. What is the primary source of healthcare data?

    b. What is the difference between primary and secondary sources of healthcare data?

    c. Give an example of both primary and secondary healthcare data.

    d. Define the following types of data and give examples of each.
       i. Nominal

       ii. Ordinal

iii. Discrete

iv. Continuous

e. List six critical elements of data collection.
   i.

   ii.

   iii.

   iv.

   v.

   vi.

f. Define the following data collection and data display tools:
   i. Bar graph

   ii. Pie chart

   iii. Radar chart

   iv. Run chart

   v. Scatter diagram

   vi. Storyboard

g. Use the following table to answer questions i–iv.

Requests for Medical Records vs. Number of Invalid Disclosures			
	Number of Requests	**Invalid**	**Percentage of Invalid Disclosures**
January	592	7	1.18
February	560	10	1.78
March	452	48	10.61
Jan–Mar Quarter			
April	780	54	6.92
May	485	73	15.05
June	652	19	
Apr–Jun Quarter			
July	543	21	3.86
August	651	11	1.68
September	702	10	1.42
Jul–Sep Quarter			
October	486	41	8.43
November	385	45	12.93
December	620	9	1.45
Oct–Dec Quarter			
Total			

i. Calculate the percentage of invalid disclosures for the month of June.

ii. Calculate the totals for each quarter and the year.

iii. Which of the quarters has the greatest number of invalid disclosures?

iv. Which quarter demonstrates an improvement in proper medical record disclosure?

h. Matrix of performance improvement tools

    i. In the following table, place a check mark (✔) in the space next to the tool that will be most useful in collecting or displaying data during the following phases: *problem identification, data analysis, planning solution,* and *program evaluation.*

Problem Solving Activities and Tools

Tools	Problem Identification	Data Analysis	Planning Solution	Evaluating
Brainstorming				
Cause and effect diagram				
Checklist				
Check sheet				
Control chart				
Flow chart				
Histogram				
Pareto chart				
Run chart				
Scatter diagram				

TEST YOUR KNOWLEDGE

1. Which of the following functions became mandatory under Title XVIII of the Social Security Act?
   a. Quality improvement
   b. Risk management
   c. Utilization review
   d. Quality assessment

2. The manager of the utilization review department wants to identify patients who are not suitable for inpatient admission and then redirect them to an appropriate healthcare setting to obtain healthcare services. When would the manager need to collect data?
   a. Prospectively
   b. Concurrently
   c. Retrospectively
   d. During long-term care review

3. Which of the following utilization review activities is being performed when a patient's record is reviewed at regular intervals to determine the appropriateness of care rendered and bed utilization?
   a. Preadmission
   b. Admission
   c. Concurrent stay
   d. Retrospective

4. At most, TJC accreditation is granted for ___ months.
   a. 12
   b. 18
   c. 36
   d. 48

5. Which of the following processes is not mandatory for healthcare facilities?
   a. Accreditation
   b. Certification
   c. Licensure
   d. AHA registration

6. To receive reimbursement for treating Medicare and Medicaid patients, healthcare organizations must:
   a. be contracted with PPS reimbursement.
   b. be contracted to HMO.
   c. meet the federal Conditions of Participation.
   d. accept major credit cards.

7. What action(s) would assist the manager of the health information management department in improving customer perception of the quality of services provided by the department?
   a. Establish 1-week turnaround time for all dictated reports
   b. Refuse to fax patient information to protect patient confidentiality
   c. Refuse to let other departments into medical records department
   d. Identify specific customer needs to improve customer satisfaction with services

8. As related to quality patient care, physicians who are members of the ambulatory care clinics meet monthly to review documentation of treatment plan and patient outcomes. This type of review, in which a physician's healthcare documentation is reviewed by his/her professional colleagues, is known as what?
   a. Concurrent review
   b. Focused audit review
   c. Retrospective review
   d. Peer review

9. In a healthcare facility, who is responsible for the appropriateness and assurance of quality care?
   a. Chief executive officer
   b. Medical staff
   c. Governing board
   d. Hospital attorney

10. During a quality improvement audit, it was noted that a medical record coder was consistently up-coding certain diagnoses. The facility is conducting investigations to determine how much money to reimburse its third-party payers for overpayment. All of the following departments would receive data about the investigation *except* the _____ department.
    a. compliance
    b. billing
    c. health information management
    d. social services

11. The purposes of PROs include determining all of the following *except* whether:
    a. services provided were medically necessary.
    b. the quality of services provided met professionally recognized standards of health care.
    c. the care was provided in the most economical setting consistent with the patient's healthcare needs.
    d. the healthcare facility had met accreditation and licensing standards.

12. Jola is a 13-year-old patient of Dr. Welch at Houston Hospital. Houston Hospital has implemented electronic health records. At Jola's discharge, due to downtime, a manual medication script was generated and filled at the hospital, along with a discharge summary and patient instructions that were given to the patient's family member by the discharging nurse. The patient's condition got worse and she returned to the hospital within 48 hours of discharge. Investigation revealed that the patient was discharged home with the wrong medication. Which of the following might potentially be responsible?
    a. Physician
    b. Hospital
    c. Pharmacist
    d. All of the above

13. The purpose of _____ was to establish a continuous, data-driven accreditation process that uses performance measures and data focused on core measures.
    a. Agenda for Change
    b. ORYX initiative
    c. ORION project
    d. data aggregation

14. Which of the following is not the role of a HIM professional in a quality improvement process?
    a. Collect data
    b. Organize data
    c. Trend data
    d. Validate clinical data

15. The utilization manager reviews the record to determine which healthcare setting will be appropriate for the identified procedure. Which of the following functions is the manager performing?
    a. Retrospective
    b. Continued stay
    c. Preadmission
    d. Focused

16. The Joint Commission specifies that all of the following aspects of performance standard must be routinely evaluated, except:
    a. blood usage.
    b. medical record.
    c. drug usage.
    d. form usage.

17. Which of the following organizations was a forerunner for the evaluation of quality medical care in healthcare organizations?
    a. The Joint Commission (TJC, formerly JCAHO)
    b. Quality Improvement Organization (QIO, formerly PRO)
    c. Professional Standard Review Organization (PSRO)
    d. Centers for Medicare and Medicaid (CMS)

18. The members of which group are responsible for recommending clinical privileges to the governing body?
    a. Executive committee
    b. Medical staff
    c. Credentialing coordinator
    d. Credentialing staff

19. Which of the following is not a research related framework?
    a. Intended to create generalized knowledge
    b. Designed to test new methods
    c. Does not require subject's consent
    d. Desire to be published or presented

20. During the credentialing process, the applicant was granted active membership. The applicant can utilize the clinical privilege for a maximum period of how long?
    a. More than 3 years
    b. Fewer than 5 years
    c. 2 years or fewer
    d. More than 10 years

21. Which of the following is not a type of idea-generation technique?
    a. Brainstorming
    b. Affinity diagrams
    c. Nominal group technique
    d. Benchmarking

22. Which of the following data organization methods is a tool that can be used to organize, categorize, and reduce information to a more usable form?
    a. Nominal group technique
    b. Decision matrix
    c. Bar graph
    d. Control chart

23. Which of the following is a sequential representation of steps in a decision-making process?
    a. Bar graph
    b. Run chart
    c. Flow chart
    d. Line graph

24. What type of data collection tool will be useful in collecting the number of charts reviewed for coding accuracy, the type of errors, and the number of errors made by each coder?
    a. Interview
    b. Check sheet
    c. Tally sheet
    d. Histogram

25. What will be the most effective data presentation tool to use in comparing staff productivity?
    a. Run chart
    b. Pareto chart
    c. Bar chart
    d. Cause and effect

26. Physician members of the psychiatry committee meet to review psychology cases that are referred for quality issues and that deviate from the Houston, Texas, area standards of care. This type of review, in which a physician's record is reviewed by his or her professional colleagues, is known as what?
    a. Concurrent review
    b. Clinical pertinence review
    c. Peer review
    d. A physician reviewer

27. What does affinity grouping do?
    a. Organizes similar ideas into logical groupings
    b. Generates a large number of creative ideas from a group
    c. Plots the points for two variables to determine whether they are related to each other
    d. Displays frequencies of responses

28. In 1965, which of the following established legal liability for hospitals?
    a. P.L. 92-603
    b. CMS
    c. JCAHO
    d. *Darling vs. Charleston Community Memorial Hospital*

29. What does brainstorming do?
    a. Organizes similar ideas into logical groupings
    b. Generates a large number of creative ideas from a group
    c. Plots the points for two variables to determine whether they are related to each other
    d. Displays frequencies of responses

30. Congress passed which of the following programs to mandate medicare cost control?
    a. TJC
    b. TEFRA
    c. HEDIS
    d. CMS

31. Which of the following can be used to show the frequency for each interval or category of nominal, ordinal, and discrete date?
    a. Frequency polygon
    b. Bar graph
    c. Scatter diagram
    d. Pareto diagram

32. Which of the following terms refers to the process of planning for change?
    a. Change management
    b. TQM
    c. Change agent
    d. Benchmarking

33. Nurse Bob wants a multidisciplinary approach to outline individualized patient goals and an appropriate time frame for expected optimal efficiency patient care. Which should he use?
    a. Critical pathways
    b. Clinical protocols
    c. Critical guidelines
    d. Clinical pathways

34. To assure that patient care problems can be remedied immediately, Nurse Bob should perform which type of quality data collection?
    a. Preadmission screening
    b. Prospective
    c. Concurrent
    d. Retrospective

35. Nurse Bob wants to use the screening criteria for utilization review that most healthcare facilities utilize to determine the need for inpatient services and justification for continued stay. Which of the following should he use?
    a. Tracer methodology
    b. Clinical protocols
    c. Critical pathways
    d. Severity of illness

36. Bob, who is the manager of the utilization review department, wants to monitor and evaluate the prevention of inappropriate admissions. When should Bob collect data?
    a. Prospectively
    b. Concurrently
    c. Retrospectively
    d. Continued stay

37. Risk management is the:
    a. activities directed at reducing a potential liability.
    b. group of processes used to measure how efficiently health care is managed.
    c. process of determining whether healthcare services meet predetermined criteria.
    d. mechanism to monitor and ensure customer satisfaction.

38. An attorney subpoenas the quality improvement committee meeting minutes of Houston Community Hospital. Should the minutes be released?
    a. Yes, or the hospital will risk being in contempt of court
    b. Yes, because all subpoenas must be honored
    c. No, the attorney needs a court order because a subpoena is not adequate
    d. No, because quality improvement committee meeting minutes are protected from subpoenas

39. Utilization management is the:
   a. group of activities used to ensure that facilities and resources are used appropriately to meet the healthcare and patient care needs.
   b. group of processes used to measure how efficiently health care is managed.
   c. process of determining whether healthcare services meet predetermined criteria.
   d. mechanism to monitor and ensure customer satisfaction.

40. The National Guideline Clearinghouse (NGC) provides:
   a. data concerning the competence of healthcare providers.
   b. clinical guidelines that may be used voluntarily.
   c. clinical guidelines that are mandated by the federal government.
   d. a mechanism to monitor and ensure customer satisfaction.

41. The clinician failed to obtain a signed consent form from Bob prior to surgery. His attorney may argue that Bob is a victim of:
   a. failed consent.
   b. improper consent.
   c. negligence.
   d. assault and battery.

42. To ensure the patient will leave the hospital as scheduled, effective discharge planning begins at which of the following?
   a. Preadmission
   b. Preauthorization
   c. Admission
   d. Discharge

43. TEFRA caused the reimbursement structure to change from a:
   a. manual to an electronic billing system.
   b. cost-based program to a retrospective payment.
   c. retrospective to a prospective payment system.
   d. retrospective to a concurrent utilization review system.

44. Which of the following systems can the hospital query to identify quality of care of a prospective applicant?
   a. Fraud and Abuse Data Bank
   b. Healthcare Integrity and Protection Data Bank
   c. National Practitioner Data Bank
   d. Privacy Integrity Information Breach Data Bank

45. The goal of clinical practice guidelines is to:
   a. describe the outcomes of healthcare-related services.
   b. standardize clinical decision making.
   c. standardize the content of clinical pathways.
   d. regulate accreditation standards.

46. Which department will most likely be responsible for taking corrective action regarding the following quality indicator? "Ninety-five percent (95%) of physician appointments/reappointments will be completed within 90 days of receipt of all required application materials."
   a. Risk management
   b. Quality improvement
   c. Utilization management
   d. Credentialing

47. Who is responsible for *Healthy People 2020*?
   a. ODPHP within DHHS
   b. National Committee for Quality Assurance
   c. The Joint Commission
   d. Office of the Inspector General

48. You are assisting the nursing department in writing indicators to determine appropriate ratios and formulas and to determine data collection time frames. One important aspect of care is the documentation of patients' education. More specifically, the nursing department would like to assess its documentation of education on colostomy care for patients with new colostomies. Concerning the preceding scenario, what would be the most effective time frame for collecting the requested data?
  a. Prospectively
  b. Concurrently
  c. Retrospectively
  d. Ongoing

49. The utilization review coordinator reviews inpatient records at regular intervals to justify necessity and appropriateness of care to warrant further hospitalization. The utilization review activities being performed constitute a:
  a. preadmission review.
  b. continued stay review.
  c. retrospective review.
  d. discharge review.

50. Public disclosure:
  a. was developed to publicly report valid information about the quality of care delivered in the nation's hospitals.
  b. established retrospective utilization management guidelines.
  c. grants accreditation to charitable healthcare organizations.
  d. provides statistical analysis of hospital quality indicators.

Information Technology and Systems

1. Timeline for the Evolution of Health Information Systems (Figure 6-1)
2. Information Technology
    a. Hardware
        i. Physical equipment of computers and computer systems
        ii. Consists of both electronic and mechanical equipment
    b. Software
        i. Set of instructions required to operate computers and their applications
        ii. Operating system software: sets of instructions that direct actual computer functions
        iii. Application software: set of instructions used to accomplish various types of processes
    c. Categories of Computers
        i. Supercomputers
            1. Fastest and highest-capacity machines built today
            2. Can cost millions of dollars and are used in large-scale activities such as weather forecasting and mathematical research
        ii. Mainframe systems
            1. Only computers available until 1960s
            2. Can perform millions of instructions per second and hundreds of users can be connected at the same time
        iii. Midrange systems
            1. Minicomputers
                a. Introduced in 1960s
                b. Can support up to 4000 connected users at the same time via terminals consisting of a keyboard and a video screen
                c. Cheaper than mainframes
            2. Workstations
                a. Introduced in 1980s
                b. Very powerful desktop computers
                c. Comparable to midsize mainframe but sits on a desktop
                d. Used as servers to microcomputers connected through a network

1960s–1970s	1980s	1990s	2000s	2010s
Financial Focus • Few clinical systems • In-house development • Shared systems • Turnkey systems • Transaction processing	**Continuing Financial Focus** • More clinical development • Standalone systems • Distributed systems • Management information systems (MIS)	**Focus on Clinical Systems** • Integration of systems • Executive information systems • Decision support systems • Enterprise-wide systems • Office automation • Virtual systems	**Standards** • E-health • Internet • Intranets • Extranets • Clinical repositories • Data warehouses • Data mining	• Electronic health records (EHRs) • ICD-10 • HITECH

Figure 6-1   The Evolution of Health Information Systems

       iv. Microcomputers
         1. Also called personal computers (PCs)
         2. Introduced in 1970s
         3. Variety of sizes, including desktop, laptop, palmtop, personal digital assistant, and penbased
       v. Web appliances
         1. Used in conjunction with Internet to navigate the Web
         2. One device sits on top of a television and allows user to surf the Internet using a remote control device
         3. Do not have processing units or storage devices
     d. Computer Peripherals
       i. Peripherals are usually described in terms of input, processing and memory, output, storage, and communication
         1. Input devices: keyboard, microphone, scanner, pointing device such as a mouse, trackball, light pen, intelligent tablet, sensors for biometrics (e.g., fingerprints, handprints, and iris scans)
         2. Processing and memory: central processing unit (CPU) and capacity to hold the data being processed
         3. Output devices: printers, monitors, and speakers
         4. Storage devices: floppy disk drive, hard disk drive, magnetic tape, compact disk, zip disk, optical disk drive
         5. Communication devices: used to assist communications among computers (e.g., a modem)
   3. Information System
     a. Definition
       i. A collection of related components that interact to perform a task to accomplish a goal
       ii. The integration of several elements of a business process to affect a specific outcome
       iii. A process that refines raw facts into meaningful information
       iv. Provides opportunities to improve internal operations, create competitive advantage in the marketplace, improve patient care delivery, enhance research, and provide better service

b. System Characteristics
  i. A group of components that interact to accomplish a goal or an objective
  ii. Components interact with each other through defined relationships
  iii. Self-adapt and respond to environmental changes
  iv. Composed of
    1. People
    2. Data
    3. Work processes
    4. Information technologies
  v. Elements
    1. Inputs
    2. Processing mechanisms
    3. Outputs

4. Design and Development of Health Information System (HIS)
  a. Six Components of an HIS
    i. Patient scheduling, admission, discharge, and transfer; system provides central notification about patients
    ii. Business and financial systems such as patient accounting and billing
    iii. Communication and networking applications transmit and manage messages among departments
    iv. Departmental systems such as radiology and pharmacy
    v. Documentation systems used to collect, store, and retrieve patient data
    vi. Reminder and advice functions assist healthcare providers in planning patient care activities
  b. System Software
    i. System
      1. Set of instructions that direct actual computer operation functions
      2. Acts as a conductor for all the hardware components and application software
    ii. Application: set of instructions used to accomplish various types of business processes
    iii. Three main types of system software
      1. Operating system: master program that manages the basic operations of the computer (OSX, Windows, Linux, UNIX)
      2. Utility programs: used to support, enhance, or expand existing programs (backup processes, virus protection, data recovery)
      3. Language translator: translates a program written by a programmer into machine language; includes graphical user interfaces (GUI) such as icons, forms
  c. Application Software
    i. Productivity: word processing, accounting, database management, graphic presentations, scheduling, e-mail, time management
    ii. Specialty software: programs specific for a particular industry (Encoders)
    iii. Education and reference: encyclopedias, anatomy atlases, library search engines
    iv. Entertainment: games, audio, video

    d. Programming Languages

        i. Machine language

            1. Binary representation

                a. 0,1

                b. 1 kilobyte = 1024 bytes

                c. Typewritten page ≈ 2 kilobytes

                d. Quantities of bytes

Name	Value in Bytes
Kilobyte (KB)	1024^1 or (1.024×10^3)
Megabyte (MB)	1024^2 or (1.049×10^6)
Gigabyte (GB)	1024^3 or (1.074×10^9)
Terabyte (TB)	1024^4 or (1.100×10^{12})

        ii. Assembly language

        iii. High-level languages

            1. BASIC

            2. COBOL

            3. FORTRAN

            4. Pascal

            5. MUMPS

            6. Java

            7. HTML

            8. XML

        iv. Very high-level languages: structured query language (SQL)

        v. Natural languages: artificial intelligence (technologies used in developing machines that imitate human qualities such as learning and reasoning)

e. Strategic Information System Planning

        i. Process of identifying and assigning priorities to the various upgrades and changes that might be made in an organization's information system

        ii. Ensures all changes contribute to the achievement of the organization's strategic goals and objectives

        iii. Establishes enterprise-wide priorities for information systems

        iv. Serves as a guide to make decisions of resource allocations

        v. Sets stage for system-development life cycle

        vi. Lead by the chief information officer

f. System Development Life Cycle (SDLC)

        i. Information engineering: a collection of processes used for the planning, analysis, design, and development of information systems on an enterprise-wide basis

        ii. After the chief information officer has led the development and establishment of a strategic plan for information systems, the organization will follow a structured process for selecting and implementing new computer-based systems.

        iii. There are many versions of the SDLC, but all include 4 major phases and 12 steps:

            1. System analysis

                a. Identify business issue or problem that needs to be solved

                b. Assess feasibility of the system and define the scope of project

    c. Assess information needs of users and define the functional
requirements of system

    d. Provide a system that meets user and/or department needs and
that also supports the strategic objectives of the organization

    e. Tools for system analysis

        i. Data dictionary

            1. Detailed road map of the database

            2. Defines each data field or column according to the
following

                a. Name of computer

                b. Type of data field

                c. Length of data field

                d. Edits place on the data field

                e. Values allowed to be placed in the data field

                f. A clear definition of each value

            3. Data modeling technique that is a repository for all
primitive-level data structures and data elements within
a system

Project:	Master Patient Index
Label:	Sex
Entry Type:	Data Element
Description:	Patient Gender
Alias:	None
Values:	M = Male F = Female

                a. Figure 6-2 provides a graphic representation of the
flow of data through a system. Can be a logical or
physical data flow.

Data Flow Name	Data Flow Symbol
External entity: receiving or sending data	
Process: changes inputs to outputs	
Data store: location of data storage	
Data flow	

Figure 6-2　Data Flow Diagram

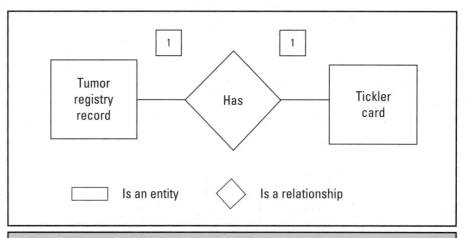

Figure 6-3   Entity Relationship Diagram (ERD)

    ii. Decomposition diagram: breaks down problems into smaller levels of detail; usually depicted in a hierarchy chart

    iii. Entity relationship diagram: data modeling technique that depicts the logical design of a database schema (see Figure 6-3)

        1. Entities are objects such as people, places, things, or events that make up the data of a database

        2. Relations are links or ties that exist between or among entities

        3. Attributes describe both entities and relationships

2. System design

    a. Specify details of new system (logical and physical design)

    b. Decide how system will be designed or selected

        i. Built in-house

        ii. Turnkey (vendor selection, request for proposal)

    c. Data modeling

        i. Used as a plan for building complex organizational databases

        ii. Based on strategic plan for development of organizational information system

        iii. Provides graphical picture of the business data needs

        iv. Helpful in developing the general information systems master plan and identifying business data and how they relate to one another

        v. Steps in data modeling process

            1. Formation of data modeling team

            2. Selection of data modeling tools (e.g., computer-aided software engineering)

            3. Studying user requirements and defining these through the use of data modeling diagrams

                a. Identify scope of project

                b. Collect data about process to be automated

            4. Development of database design

    vi. Three levels of data models
        1. Conceptual
            a. Business data model
            b. One conceptual data model maintained for the enterprise that represents the information needs of the organization
            c. Defines the database requirements of the enterprise in a single description
            d. Used to develop external and internal models
            e. Input received from end users
            f. Contents consist of
                i. Diagrams (picture of data needs of enterprise)
                ii. Glossary (data dictionary)
                iii. Narratives (explain what diagram and glossary mean)
                iv. Access patterns (what data are accessed, how often, in what order to determine transaction times)
        2. External
            a. Also called logical data model
            b. View data by a specific group of users of a specific processing application
            c. Input received from end users
        3. Internal
            a. Also called physical data model
            b. Depicts how data are physically represented in the database
            c. Concerned with data structures, file organization, and mechanisms and techniques to most efficiently store data and make use of the database system
            d. IS develops without interaction of users
  vii. Computer-aided software engineering (CASE) tools
        1. Computerized development tools to improve the efficiency, accuracy, and completeness of the system development process
        2. Used in data modeling activity
        3. Create entity relationship diagrams
        4. Assist in the electronic development of diagrams such as data models, data flow diagrams, and program structure charts, and data dictionaries
 viii. Rapid application development (RAD)
        1. Accelerated approach to information system analysis and design
        2. Assist with prototyping the system
        3. Initiated by conducting a joint application design session
   ix. Joint application design (JAD)
        1. Provides opportunity for substantial end-user input and speeds the development process
        2. Group of end users, analysts, and technical development professionals meet over a period of days to analyze the current system, identify goals and objectives for the new system, and identify the new system functions

   3. System implementation
  - **a.** Select project manager
  - **b.** Make system operational
  - **c.** Test system
  - **d.** Train users
  - **e.** Prepare site
  - **f.** Install hardware and software
  - **g.** Manage organization change and system impact
  - **h.** Development of backup and recovery procedures
  - **i.** Convert to new system

   4. System evaluation
  - **a.** Evaluate system against established criteria
  - **b.** Technical staff oversee
    - **i.** System backups
    - **ii.** Software upgrades
    - **iii.** Equipment maintenance and replacement
    - **iv.** Ongoing user training and assistance
    - **v.** Disaster recovery

  iv. Twelve steps in system development life cycle
  - **1.** Request for development
  - **2.** Requirements and system analysis
  - **3.** System design
  - **4.** Specification of functions
  - **5.** Coding of computer programs
  - **6.** Testing of systems
  - **7.** Development of system documentation
  - **8.** User training
  - **9.** User conversion
  - **10.** Operating of the system
  - **11.** System maintenance
  - **12.** System changes and upgrades

  v. Nolan's six-stage theory
  - **1.** An institution is at a certain maturity level in information technology at any given time
    - **a.** Initiation: initiation of automation
    - **b.** Expansion: growth of automation
    - **c.** Control: management of information technology growth
    - **d.** Integration: integrates systems through policies and procedures
    - **e.** Data administration: databases developed and information is critical
    - **f.** Maturity: growth of application is the focus on strategic importance of organization

5. Classification of Healthcare Information Systems
  - **a.** Various information system applications are currently utilized in the healthcare environment. Table 6-1 provides an overview of these applications.

6. Database Management System
  - **a.** Database Management System (DBMS)
    - **i.** An integrated set of programs that manages access to the database
    - **ii.** Software that supports the operation of the database
    - **iii.** Personal DBMS: used for small projects (e.g., personal address book)

iv. Server-based DBMS: runs on a server computer and is separate application from a personal system (e.g., employee information—Oracle allows you to link multiple tables and also maintain consistency between them)

Table 6-1	Classification of Healthcare Information Systems		
Functional Areas	**Structure or Work Processes**	**Span Across the Healthcare Enterprise**	**Purpose**
Administrative 1. Admissions, discharges, transfers (ADT) 2. Human resources 3. Materials management 4. Facilities management	**Access to Information** For example: Results reporting system	**Individual** For example: Word processing (Microsoft Word) Spreadsheets (Microsoft Excel) Presentation (Microsoft PowerPoint) Statistical (SPSS)	**Transaction Processing System (TPS)** Collects and stores data about transactions Manages the different kinds of transactions that occur in a healthcare facility For example: Patient admissions, employee time cards, supply purchases
Financial 1. Budgeting 2. Billing 3. Payments	**Access to Information Tools** For example: Results reporting system	**Workgroup** For example: E-mail	**Management Information System (MIS)** Supported by transaction processing systems Provides routine information to managers for decision making
			Enterprise-wide System Automates information at the point of service, supports patient care, analyzes clinical practices (*continues*)

Table 6-1	Classification of Healthcare Information Systems (continued)		
Functional Areas	**Structure or Work Processes**	**Span Across the Healthcare Enterprise**	**Purpose**
Clinical 1. Electronic medical record (EMR) 2. Results reporting 3. Patient care management 4. Order entry 5. Point-of-care documenta-tion 6. Nursing services 7. Laboratory 8. Pharmacy 9. Clinical decision support 10. Research, QI, peer review	**Enforcement of Rules** For example: Automated system for application or practice guidelines and critical paths Automation of most or all work such as a computerized hospital information kiosk	**Organization** For example: Internet	**Decision Support System (DSS)** Using databases, it is an interactive system that helps managers solve problems and make decisions For example: Clinical DSS that alerts physician when lab results are outside normal range
Outpatient 1. Appointment scheduling 2. Patient billing 3. Electronic insurance payment 4. Automatic payment posting 5. Patient collection and mail-merge 6. Medical record data capture and retrieval 7. Prescription writing 8. Report generation		**Outside the Organization**	**Executive Information System** Interactive system that allows top managers to answer "what if" queries and project trends Several databases are attached to type of system including external and internal operations and special management

Table 6-1   Classification of Healthcare Information Systems (*continued*)

Functional Areas	Structure or Work Processes	Span Across the Healthcare Enterprise	Purpose
Research 1. Data mart 　Data subset extracted from larger database 2. Data mining 　Broad view of data			**Expert System** Generates advice or suggests a decision A knowledge system built from a set of rules applied to specific problems
			Office Automation Day-to-day processing and communication tasks (word processing, spreadsheets, databases, e-mail)

   b. Database
- **i.** A collection of stored data, typically organized into fields, records, and files
- **ii.** A structured computer file for data storage designed to enable editing the data, query and retrieval, and computer processing efficiency

   c. Characteristics
- **i.** Building blocks of information
- **ii.** Organized integrated collection of data
- **iii.** Data stored as a set of logical files that are accessed in a manner meaningful to the user
- **iv.** Reduces redundant information
- **v.** Consistency of information
- **vi.** Standardization and flexibility of the information

   d. Four Levels of Data Organization
- **i.** Item: data entity describes attribute of an object
- **ii.** Record
  - **1.** Items that relate to an object or entity are combined into a record
  - **2.** Each data item for a record occupies a field on the physical storage medium
  - **3.** Size is measured by bytes or characters
- **iii.** File: collection of related records
- **iv.** Database: structured computer file for data storage

e. Five Major Database Models

   i. Relational: data stored in predefined tables that contain rows and columns similar to a spreadsheet

      1. Column or field is a basic fact (e.g., LAST_NAME, FIRST_NAME, DOB, RACE)

      2. Row or record is a set of columns or a collection of related data items. (e.g., Tyson, Carla, 9/20/1959, African American)

      3. Key field uniquely identifies each row in a table; two types of keys:

         a. Primary key: ensures each row in a table is unique and does not change value; may be counter or randomly generated number

         b. Foreign key: column of one table that corresponds to a primary key in another table; together they allow two tables to be joined together

      4. All data stored in tables with relationships between the tables

      5. Relation created by sharing a common data element

      6. Stores currency, real numbers, integers

   ii. Hierarchical

      1. Supports treelike structure that consists of parent (root) and child segments; many-to-many relationships difficult to represent

      2. Each parent has a child or more; each child has only one parent

      3. User queries database; search seeks answer from parent to child

   iii. Network

      1. Similar to hierarchical, except that a child can have more than one parent

      2. Parent referred to as owner; child as member

      3. Supports many-to-many relationship

   iv. Object-oriented

      1. Stores objects of data

      2. Can model relational data or data types, such as graphics, movies, and audio

   v. Object-relational

      1. Combines best of relational and object-oriented

      2. Uses both traditional data types (currency, integers, and strings) and advanced data types (graphics, movies, and audio)

f. Types of Organizational Databases

   i. Transactional database

      1. Also called operational or production database

      2. Stores and manages all the detailed data needed to support the operation of the entire healthcare facility

      3. Supports all daily transactions of an organization (ADT, lab, accounting, inventory)

   ii. Analytical database

      1. Stores extracted pieces of data from selected transactional databases

      2. Designed to support high-level managers in making strategic and tactical decisions

      3. Used to analyze complex relationships, discover trends, perform "what if" explorations

iii. Distributed database
  1. Logically interrelated collection of stored data and a description of these data that are physically distributed over a computer network
  2. Database is split into a number of fragments; each fragment stored on one or more computers under the control of a separate DBMS
  3. Database fragments serve specific local applications and are stored locally on a server; can also access other global databases and applications throughout the network
iv. External database
  1. Organizations obtain information from sources outside of the organization
  2. May access information from a commercial source via the Internet
v. Data warehouse
  1. Provides organization the ability to access data from multiple databases and to combine the results into a single question and reporting interface
  2. Sets up large stores of data for strategic decision support analysis
  3. Selected data are extracted from multiple sources in the organization's information system
  4. Subject-oriented, integrated, time-variant, and nonvolatile collection of data in support of management's decision-making process
  5. Integrates organization-wide data into a single repository from which managers can pose ad hoc queries, run reports, and perform a variety of analyses
  6. Analytical databases designed to support strategic and tactical decision making
  7. Organization uses historical data and integrates them with a variety of analytical techniques to help solve problems
  8. For the value of the data warehouse to be realized, techniques such as data mining must be applied
vi. Data mart
  1. Subset of a data warehouse that supports the requirements of a particular department or business function
  2. Focuses on the data needs for a specific department or business function, as opposed to a warehouse that stores data for the entire organization
  3. Tailored to meet needs of department
  4. Amount of historical data and level or granularity (detail) can be specific to needs of department
vii. Data mining
  1. Encourages a broad view of all data for a set of patients to explore relationships among the data that might not be readily apparent during the initial hypothesis
  2. The extraction of data from large databases to uncover previously unknown information to help managers make decisions
  3. Helps uncover previously unknown and hidden information trends

Table 6-2 Information Security (Definition of Terms)

Privacy	The right of an individual to limit access by others to some aspects of their person
Confidentiality	Based on a special doctor–patient relationship and refers to the expectation that the information collected will be used for the purpose for which it was gathered; limiting disclosure of private matters
Security	Means to control access and protect information from accidental or intentional disclosure to unauthorized persons and from alteration, destruction, or loss
Informational Privacy	The right of individuals to keep information about themselves from being disclosed to anyone
Cybersecurity	The state of being protected against the criminal or unauthorized use of electronic data, or the measures taken to achieve this

    4. Identifies patterns and relationships among variables using predictive modeling, database segmentation, link analysis, and deviation detection

    5. Must have a data warehouse to perform data mining

7. Information Security (see Table 6-2)

  a. Legislation Regarding Patient Privacy

    i. Privacy Act of 1974: safeguards privacy of health records in federal institutions

    ii. Health Insurance Portability and Accountability Act (HIPAA) of 1996: implemented security and privacy rules for health information

  b. Security Fundamentals for Health Information

    i. Protect privacy of patient-related data from intrusion

      1. Unauthorized use activity by authorized users

      2. Hackers

      3. Downloaded files

      4. Trojan horses

    ii. Ensure integrity of information

      1. Protect data and programs from accidental or unauthorized intentional change

      2. Ensure data entered into system are protected from unauthorized modification or deletion

    iii. Ensure availability of information to authorized users in a timely fashion

      1. Denial of user access may result from system intrusion such as a worm

      2. Unavailability may result from natural disaster or human error

  c. Security Program

    i. Establish a security organization (chief security officer, privacy officer)

    ii. Implement an employee awareness program

    iii. Conduct risk analysis and assessment

iv. Establish access control (tracking system)

v. Implement physical and management controls (passwords, lock doors, limit access)

vi. Develop a disaster recovery and business community plan (disaster plan)

vii. Implement network controls (viruses)

d. Prevention and Control

   i. Personnel

      1. Employees should have access to information on a need-to-know basis

      2. Should sign confidentiality agreements and be made aware of privacy and security policies and procedures

      3. Terminate or revise information access upon employee leaving or moving within the organization

   ii. Physical: equipment and information should be secure from threats and unauthorized access

   iii. Hardware

      1. Should be secured from extreme temperatures, power outages, and other environmental threats

      2. Should be installed according to manufacturer instructions

   iv. Software

      1. System in place for system development life cycle

      2. Access to specific applications should be limited

         a. Integrity controls (file record counts, hash totals, block counts, check sums)

         b. System should automatically log all transactions

         c. Audit trails

   v. External

      1. Firewalls

         a. System to prevent access to a private network from the outside or limit access to the outside from within

         b. Types

            i. Proxy server

            ii. Packet filter

            iii. Application gateway

      2. Encryption: changes readable text into a set of different characters and numbers based on a mathematical algorithm

      3. Internet security: Secure Sockets Layer (SSL) protocol; web servers that support an SSL session have an address that begins with *https* instead of *http*

   vi. Communication

      1. Authentication

         a. System knows user is authorized

            i. Passwords: use should include password aging and should allow only one log-in per user identification at a time

            ii. Tokens or cards: card generates a unique sequence of numbers, and, through an algorithm, assigns the user access privileges for an application

            iii. Biometric devices: unique trait of a human that can be used for automatic recognition, such as fingerprints, retinal eye patterns, or speech

            iv. Access controls: granted by role of user and the permitted roles for specific information access

8. Emerging Technologies
- **a.** Videoconferencing
  - **i.** Provides video, audio, computer, and imaging system connectivity
  - **ii.** Allows several physicians to collaborate
  - **iii.** Information from computerized patient record (CPR) can be viewed on the same screen with a physician's image and diagnostic imagery
- **b.** Groupware: combines different document types with the corresponding work process into a tightly integrated work flow
- **c.** Information kiosk: computer station to which patients and others have access for information on a variety of subjects
- **d.** Speech recognition: technology that permits interaction with system using voice
- **e.** Telephone Interface Systems
  - **i.** Private branch exchanges (PBX)
  - **ii.** Circuit-switching technology
  - **iii.** Packet-switching technology
  - **iv.** Computer-telephone integration
- **f.** Computer Telephone Applications and Caller Assistance: call control, caller identification, collection of call event data, and caller interaction
- **g.** Internet Protocol (IP) Telephony: allows real-time calls to be initiated through the Internet instead of public telephone system
- **h.** Web Centers: telephone support for the facility's website
- **i.** Fax on Demand: user selects from a list of available fax sources by keying in the corresponding number of a fax title or from multiple fax messages via the telephone
- **j.** Telemedicine
  - **i.** Exchange of medical information between sites via electronic communications for the health and education of the patient or healthcare provider and for improving patient care
  - **ii.** Uses bandwidth to transmit various forms of information (bandwidth is a measure of how much information can be transmitted simultaneously through a communication channel and is measured in bits per second, or bps)
  - **iii.** Types include facsimile (fax), audio, still images, and full-motion video
- **k.** Three-Dimensional Imaging: contains all three spatial dimensions and is easier to understand when viewed
- **l.** Personal digital assistants (PDAs): allow for portable computing and rapid access to information sources
- **m.** Wireless Networking: provides network connectivity without ethernet or other wires
- **n.** Smart Cards
  - **i.** Credit-card–size cards that contain integrated circuit technology
  - **ii.** Integrated circuit contains a processor and memory subsystem.
  - **iii.** A portable and secure way to carry information
- **o.** Virtual private network: creates the illusion of a fast, secure network, but shares a public network such as the Internet or other IP network
- **p.** Smart Phones
  - **i.** Apps

9. Internet Technologies
- **a.** Network Architecture
  - **i.** The way a computer network is set up; its basic design or architecture

   ii. Two main types of network architectures
- **1.** Local area network (LAN)
  - **a.** Connects computers in a relatively small area (room, building)
  - **b.** Client–server network
  - **c.** Peer-to-peer network
  - **d.** Hybrid network (mixture of client–server and peer-to-peer)
- **2.** Wide area network (WAN)
  - **a.** Connects devices across a large geographical area (state or world), such as the Internet
  - **b.** Consists of two or more connected LANs

b. Internet
- **i.** Consists of thousands of loosely connected networks (LANs, WANs) and no single group is responsible for it; each network on the Internet is independent, but each network communicates with the Internet using the same networking language.
- **ii.** Protocols
  - **1.** Relies on software called browsers
  - **2.** TCP/IP protocol for transmission of data
  - **3.** IP refers to unique network address that is assigned to each computer on the Internet.
  - **4.** The specific algorithm assigned to the transfer of data through web browsers is the Hypertext Transfer Protocol (HTTP).
  - **5.** HTTP determines how information is formatted and transmitted and what action browsers take in response to commands (HTTPS is secure mode).
- **iii.** Tools for preparing documents to be viewed through browser
  - **1.** HTML: Hypertext Markup Language
  - **2.** SGML: Standard Generalized Markup Language
  - **3.** XML: eXtensible Markup Language
- **iv.** Java
  - **1.** Programming language
  - **2.** Allows construction of stand-alone applications that can be transferred across the Web and run independently on a client computer
  - **3.** Applets
    - **a.** Small programs (applications) at the top of HTML page that run on client side
    - **b.** Available through the user's web browser
    - **c.** Temporarily downloaded to the user's machine and performs calculations in real time
  - **4.** Servlet: functions like an applet but resides on server side, not client side
- **v.** Security tools
  - **1.** Provide encryption for Internet connections
  - **2.** Organizations should use SSL
  - **3.** CMS requires all Internet transmissions containing patient data to be sent using SSL to protect patient confidentiality
  - **4.** Allows browser and server of the web transmission to authenticate identities and encrypt the data transfer

    c. Intranet

        i. Special form of a LAN

        ii. Networking capability within one organization that uses Internet technologies, software that uses HTML, and web browser software to accomplish computer communications within the organization

        iii. Servers are located inside a firewall or security barrier and can be accessible only to authenticated users on a specific network

    d. Extranets

        i. Similar to intranet

        ii. Provides network connectivity between suppliers to allow direct connection between networks

    e. E-commerce: the marketing, buying, selling, and support of products and services over the Internet, intranets, and extranets

        i. Allows consumers to learn about medicines they are taking, buy medicines, learn about diseases and disease prevention, and other activities

        ii. Involves electronic data interchange (EDI) and electronic funds transfer (EFT) payment systems

        iii. Multiple uses

            1. Physician referral services

            2. Lists of healthcare classes and seminars

            3. Information on clinical trials

            4. Uses Internet to create bulletin boards, electronic surveys, newsletters, and e-mail information on diagnoses and treatment of diseases

            5. External links to federal agencies and other organizations that provide health care

            6. Builds strategic alliance with customers, suppliers, consultants, and competitors

    f. E-health: provision of health information and services through Internet technologies

        i. Storing personal health data

        ii. Reference information on a variety of health issues

        iii. Manage healthcare superstores

10. Electronic Health Records

    a. Definitions

        i. Healthcare information: all information, oral or recorded in any form, related to any care, service, or procedure to diagnose, treat, or maintain the physical or mental condition of an individual identified patient. It is obtained in the course of a patient's health care from a healthcare provider, from the patient, from a member of the patient's family or an individual with whom the patient has a close personal relationship, or from the patient's legal representative.

        ii. Patient medical record: primary repository for information concerning a patient's health care, uniquely representing patients and serving as a dynamic resource for the healthcare industry

        iii. Health informatics: science that deals with health information, its structure, acquisition, and uses

        iv. Computer-based patient record: an electronic patient record that resides in a system specially designed to support users by providing accessibility to complete and accurate data, alerts, reminders, clinical decision support systems, links to medical knowledge, and other aids

v. Electronic health record (EHR)

1. Any information relating to the past, present, or future physical or mental health or condition of an individual; resides in electronic systems used to capture, transmit, receive, store, retrieve, link, and manipulate multimedia data for the primary purpose of providing health care and health-related services

2. Form of computer-based health record in which information is stored by whole files instead of by individual data elements

3. EHR should do the following

   a. Have a positive impact on workflow operations

   b. Improve administrative process

   c. Include uniform core data elements and standardized coding

   d. Use common data dictionary

   e. Perform searches

   f. Provide 24-hour access with rapid retrieval

   g. Link to other information systems

   h. Provide real-time alerts and possible remedies

4. EHR building blocks

   a. Data: raw material of information system

   b. Information: collection of data that contains meaning when processed

   c. Knowledge: formalization of the relationships among elements of information and data

   d. Infrastructure: technology architecture required to maintain EHR

   e. Registration: admission, discharge, transfer

   f. Data interface standards

      i. Health Level 7 and vocabulary dictionaries and interface engines used to transfer data, sometimes translating or reformatting as required

      ii. May be transferred to repositories for future use

      iii. Designed to deliver the individual patient's information to the care team via the clinical workstation, where the content and presentation capability take over

5. EHR vocabularies

   a. Used to represent and communicate concepts, including symptoms, diagnoses, procedures, and health status

   b. Text processing: computer processing of natural language

   c. Natural language processing: all terms and expressions used by a discipline in its models

   d. Script-based system: combines keywords and scripts; may be a predesigned expression that represents information about consequences of care processes

6. Legislation

   a. American Recovery and Reinvestment Act (ARRA; Stimulus Act)

      i. February 2009, President Barack Obama signed into law the Health Information Technology for Economic and Clinical Health Act (HITECH) as part of ARRA

         1. $147 billion to rescue and reform healthcare industry

         2. Provides funding for hospitals and physicians for the adoption of health information technology to drive electronic health record (EHR) adoption

   3. Required government to develop standards by 2010 that allow for nationwide electronic exchange and use of health information to improve quality and coordination of care

   4. Invested $19.2 billion in reimbursement incentives to for eligible professionals and hospitals to take steps to become meaningful users of certified EHRs

    a. Meaningful use

     i. Set of standards defined by the Centers for Medicare and Medicaid Services incentive programs that governs the use of electronic health records and allows eligible providers and hospitals to earn incentive payments by meeting specific criteria

      1. Stage 1: data capture and sharing

      2. Stage 2: advance clinical processes

      3. Stage 3: improved outcomes

     ii. Cybersecurity

      1. Federal breach law

      2. US-CERT's Control Systems Security Program (CSSP)

      3. Federal Risk and Authorization Management Program (FedRAMP) on cloud computing security assessment

  b. Health Evaluation Through Logical Processing (HELP)

   i. Comprehensive hospital information system that combines clinically based modules with a financial database

   ii. Integrates information from admitting, radiology, pharmacy, pathology, nursing, respiratory therapy, and clinical laboratories

   iii. Creates an EHR

   iv. Designed to

    1. Accommodate research subsystems to facilitate clinical research, including cost and quality components

    2. Combine communications and clinical alert features through time-drive and data-drive rules

  c. Health Level 7 (HL7)

   i. Electronic interchange of clinical, financial, and administrative information among disparate health information systems

   ii. Allows for the transmission of data from one computer to another

   iii. Used for intrainstitution transmission of orders; clinical observations and clinical data, including test results; admission, transfer, and discharge records; and charge and billing information

  d. Institute of Medicine established to do the following

   i. Examine current state of medical record systems

   ii. Identify impediments to development and use of improved record systems

   iii. Identify ways to overcome impediments

   iv. Develop a research agenda to advance medical record systems

   v. Develop a plan for improved medical record systems, including means for updating systems

   vi. Recommend policies and other strategy to achieve improvements

11. Information Resources Management (IRM)

  a. Encompasses all the management concepts concerned with the creation, usage, storage, and disposal of information in a business setting

b. Provides the plan to integrate all information processes, computer and manual, and all information technologies associated with computers, telecommunications, office automation, distributed processing, and selection and implementation of computer systems

c. Assumes that information is a valuable resource that must be managed, no matter what form it takes or in what medium it is stored

d. Chief information officer (CIO) is the senior-level executive manager of IRM and is responsible for leading the strategic information system planning process, helping the leadership team use information systems in support of strategic planning and management, and overseeing the organization's IRM functions

12. Role of Health Information Manager in Information Systems

   a. Information broker: intermediary between a client and an information product or group of services

   b. Advocate for effective system development or selection by assuming prominent role in the system development life cycle

   c. Custodian of patient health information, regardless of media on which it is maintained

   d. Establishes policies, procedures, systems, and safeguards to ensure patient health information is documented, maintained, and disclosed in accordance with all health information laws, regulations, and standards

   e. Ensures the functionality of electronic health record systems with respect to the practice of health information management and its support of other business functions of the organization

   f. Under the Information Engineering Domain

     i. Strategic planning: identification of goals and the critical success factors of the enterprise

     ii. Data modeling: development of a detailed logical database design

     iii. Process modeling: analyzing the processes of an organization, usually on a departmental basis

     iv. Data administration: administrative rather than technical functions associated with data and database management

     v. Interface design: content or layout of screens and reports; may use CASE tools such as screen painters, report generators, or prototyping software

   g. Information Retrieval and Analysis, and Policy Development

13. Fundamentals of Health Workflow Process Analysis and Redesign

   a. As part of the ARRA of 2009, the HITECH Act established the implementation of a national infrastructure for an electronic health record (EHR). Administered by the Department of Health and Human Services (HHS) through the Office of the National Coordinator for Health Information Technology (ONC); incentives for eligible professionals and hospitals administered by the Centers for Medicare and Medicaid Services.

   b. Goal of HITECH is to improve individual health, health care, and public health.

   c. Implementing health information systems across an organization requires a magnitude of change.

     i. Change management is a structured approach to transition of individuals, teams, and organizations from a current state to a desired future state.

        1. Human–technology interaction during the change process

            a. Who will lead the process of change management?

            b. What will be the components of the change management program?

            c. When will the program be implemented—beginning of the process, implementation, and assessment?

            d. Where and in which ways will the discussion about change take place?

            e. Why it is necessary to develop a change management program?

            f. How will the program become operational?

      ii. Helps employees to cope with and adapt to the changes the industry faces

      iii. Change initiatives fail because they do not take human, political and symbolic elements into consideration.

      iv. Four principles of change management

          1. Elicit support from people within the system

          2. Understand the current state of the organization

          3. Understand where you want to be and what the measures will be

          4. Communicate, involve, enable, and facilitate involvement from people early, openly, and as completely as possible

d. Tools Used to Bring About Change: process modeling and organization-wide change management

e. Life Cycle of Information Technology Implementation and Organizational Change

    i. Phases of health IT life cycle

        1. Planning

          a. Project conception, initiation, project tracking

        2. Implementation

          a. Go-live and activation of software

        3. Stabilization

          a. Gaps found between previous workflows and new workflows

        4. Optimization

          a. New normal levels of patient care

          b. Clinicians and support staff identified most of the work-arounds or best practices to continue operations

        5. Transformation

          a. Organization begins to understand how to manage the system

          b. Change is embraced

f. Process Hierarchy for Workflow Analysis and Design for Planning and Implementing Ongoing Change

    i. Level 1: enterprise to enterprise

        1. Referrals, full service, and community care among multiple locations for a population of patients

    ii. Level 2: venue to venue

        1. Care of a service line in a given setting

    iii. Level 3: roles to patient

        1. Interactions of providers with patients and with each other

    iv. Level 4: task to task

        1. Detailed steps for a procedure of care

    v. Level 5: application function

        1. Use of data or information within an EHR, decision support or exchange application

g. Methodologies for Understanding Processes
  i. Observation of current daily workflow
  ii. Modeling workflow based on the formal scope of professional practice standards
  iii. Simulation of the proposed workflow steps
  iv. Quality-based deployment strategies (e.g., Lean, Six Sigma)
    1. Goal is to eliminate waste or redundancies in practices while providing the best possible patient outcomes
  v. Continuous workflow improvement with functional technology advances

h. Workflow Mapping Tools and Their Depiction
  i. Oval: shows where the workflow begins and ends
  ii. Rectangles: represent a process activity, task, or analysis
  iii. Diamonds: show a decision-making process
  iv. Circles: signify connectors from one activity to another

i. Value Stream Mapping
  i. A recognized Six Sigma methodology
  ii. Type of process mapping or flow charting of the value stream that includes all the steps in producing and delivering a service
  iii. Shows workflow from a system perspective and can help determine how to measure and improve the system or process
  iv. Typically done from the perspective of the patient, where the goal is to optimize the patient's journey through the system

j. Steps for Creating a Process Map or Workflow
  i. Assemble a stakeholder planning team
  ii. Determine the level of detail desired, the methodology to employ, and the participants needed
  iii. Schedule the mapping event, venue, and supplies
  iv. Give the team sufficient background on the approach to use
  v. Complete the mapping event
  vi. Create a mapping chart using standard symbols
  vii. Create a picture and check for accuracy
  viii. Identify problem areas and gaps between the current state and the future state
  ix. Prioritize projects that will address the gaps

14. Migrating to an Electronic Health Record
  a. When beginning the migration to an EHR, develop a strategic plan that outlines the process.
  b. Three Basic Steps in the Development of a Strategic Plan
    i. Review the mission and vision of the organization and ensure that they are current. Mission describes who you serve; vision provides a view of the future that can be communicated throughout the organization.
    ii. If the mission and vision are not current, make modifications that will help move the organization toward a quality EHR that will improve patient care.
    iii. Develop goals that are reasonable, measurable, and tactical.
  c. Electronic Health Record Life Cycle
    i. Description of planned migration to EHR
      1. Include a needs assessment phase, establish a migration steering committee, and ensure there is understanding that this is an ongoing process
        a. Process of identifying the system technology and software needed to advance to an EHR

  b. Each constituent unit in the organization determines its needs for an EHR

  2. Develop a timeline for choosing and implementing an electronic health record

  3. Verify availability of the financial and human resources required to plan, select, implement, and maintain an EHR

  ii. Prototype development

  1. Determine type of technology and software needed

  2. Organizations with no electronic systems will need to start at ground zero in migration to an EHR.

  3. Some organizations may have legacy systems—computerized systems that were developed by the organization's staff over a period of years or that were purchased from a vendor.

  4. Some organizations have legacy systems with some vendor solutions—that is, systems that have added components to the legacy systems without or with some interoperability.

  5. Some organizations have contracted with one vendor for many integrated systems. In this case, a primary vendor system was used to develop computerized or electronic systems.

  iii. Selection of a system

  1. Develop a project team to make decisions for the organization with careful selection of team members and strong leadership, management, and health IT skills.

  a. Team should include change agents, clinical, and ancillary representatives.

  b. Team responsibilities

  i. Conduct needs assessment that will determine which type of system is required to fulfill the needs of the users of the EHR.

  ii. Develop or support efforts for development of a request for information (RFI; a tool to ask vendors about their products) and request for proposals (RFP; an open request to vendors for specific answers to the needs of an organization)

  iii. Assist with the development of an organizational culture for readiness to "go live"

15. **Configuring Electronic Health Records**

  a. Meaningful Use (MU)

  i. The use of certified EHR systems is a central construct in achieving meaningful use along with the constructs of health information exchange (HIE) and the use of clinical quality measures to achieve meaningful use goals at each stage of implementation. Certification of an EHR will be tightly linked to the metrics developed for meaningful use. Some MU metrics, such as the ones identified in the security and data collection areas, can be viewed almost as system specifications.

  ii. Established by the ARRA passed in 2009, which intended that providers and hospitals not only implement certified electronic health records, but also make meaningful use of those systems and the data contained in them. Incentive payments through the CMS were used to ensure this occurs. MU will assist with the use of computerized physician order entry (CPOE) for medication orders directly entered by any licensed healthcare professional who can enter orders into the medical record per state, local, and professional guidelines. EHRs and health information technology are expected to be implemented in a manner such that achievement of goals that support the five underlying principles can be directly measured and demonstrated.

   iii. Five underlying principles that drive meaningful use of patients' health information
     1. Improving quality, safety, and efficiency of health care
     2. Engaging patients in their care
     3. Increasing coordination of care
     4. Improving the health status of the population
     5. Ensuring privacy and security of health information

   iv. Requirements for meaningful use of the EHR implemented in three stages
     1. Stage 1: Eligible providers (EPs) and eligible hospitals (EHs) collect and share patient data.
     2. Stage 2
       a. MU requirements include expectations for health information exchange, more demanding requirements for e-prescribing and incorporating structured laboratory results, and the expectation that providers will electronically transmit patient care summaries to support transitions in care across unaffiliated providers, settings, and EHR systems.
       b. Increasingly robust expectations for health information exchange in stages 2 and 3 support and make real the goal that information follows the patient.
     3. Stage 3: Focus on promoting improvements in quality, safety, and efficiency leading to improved health outcomes, focusing on decision support for national high-priority conditions, patient access to self-management tools, access to comprehensive patient data through robust, patient-centered health information exchange, and improving population health.

b. EHR Certification
   i. Certification assures purchasers and other users that an EHR system offers the necessary technological capability, functionality, and security to help them meet MU criteria and realize the benefits of improved patient care.
   ii. A certified EHR meets the minimum data set requirements and has the potential to satisfy the requirements used to measure meaningful use now and in the future.
   iii. Criteria for a certified EHR are directly tied to the meaningful use criteria.
   iv. Certification can be for an entire EHR system or for individual modules. If the entire system is certified, each module in the EHR is also considered certified.
   v. In July 2004, Certificate Commission for Health Information Technology (CCHIT) was started as a private sector–led initiative to certify health information technology (IT) products.
     1. It began certifying EHRs in 2006 and claimed to have established the first comprehensive, practical definition of which capabilities were needed in these systems.

    2. The certification criteria were developed through a voluntary, consensus-based process engaging diverse stakeholders, and the Certification Commission was officially recognized by the federal government as a certifying body.

    3. CCHIT claimed to have certified 75% of EHR systems on the market by 2009 and has announced its intention to become an ONC Authorized Testing and Certification Body.

  vi. ONC offers other organizations the option to become an ONC Authorized Testing and Certification Body (ONC-ATCB). At the beginning of 2011, six organizations were authorized to certify EHRs: CCHIT, Surescripts, ICSA Labs, SLI Global Solutions, InfoGard Laboratories, and Drummond Group.

  vii. The Health Information Technology for Economic and Clinical Health (HITECH) Act ties the standards, implementation specifications, and certification criteria adopted in the ONC ruling to the incentives under the Medicare and Medicaid EHR incentive programs by requiring the meaningful use of certified EHR technology. The ONC ruling creates specific standards, beginning in 2011, in four areas.

    1. Vocabulary standards: standardized nomenclatures and code sets used to describe clinical problems and procedures, medications, and allergies

    2. Content exchange standards: used to share clinical information such as clinical summaries, prescriptions, and structured electronic documents

    3. Transport standards: used to establish a common, predictable, secure communication protocol between systems

    4. Privacy and security standards: authentication, access control, transmission security; privacy and security standards relate to, and span across, all of the other types of standards

  viii. Certified EHR technology will be tested and certified as being capable of complying with adopted standards.

c. Health Information Exchange (HIE)

  i. Represents the mobilization of healthcare information electronically. Supports the flow of information within organizations, between organizations, between different modules of an EHR, between different EHRs, across regions, between regions or states, and ultimately across the nation. Supports the flow of information to the person and place where it is needed at the time it is required and in a manner that is secure and preserves patient privacy. The information arrives in a form that is usable by the person needing it.

  ii. Interoperability: the ability of diverse systems and organizations to work together (interoperate). HIE and the interoperability of health information systems are virtually synonymous concepts. HIE provides interoperability between disparate health information systems, delivering patient information when and where it is needed.

  iii. Functionality can be viewed as either unidirectional or bidirectional. When HIE requires information to be sent in only one direction, such as when updating registries, it is referred to as pushing the data out to the other application or user. Unidirectional information flow can also occur when a system has the ability to query a database and pull down the required information. This can be automated, as in automated updates to formulary information. Most HIEs require bidirectional communications where the user needs to enter/update information as well as query that same information.

    iv. HIE improves safety, quality, and efficiency and engages patients in their own health care.

    v. HIE supports coordination of care by facilitating scheduling of consultations, diagnostic tests, or other procedures and allowing multiple caregivers to view the same information simultaneously.

    vi. HIE improves population health by managing secondary data sources such as immunization reporting systems that can aggregate patient data for nationwide comparisons.

    vii. HIE ensures patient information privacy and security through secure encrypted transmission of information.

    viii. HIE provides electronic backup of patient data.

d. Clinical Quality Measures

    i. HITECH requires that HHS give preference to clinical quality measures that have been endorsed by the organization that HHS contracts with. Medicare Improvement for Patients and Providers Act (MIPPA) of 2008 added this requirement as well, requiring that preference is given to measures that have been selected for the Reporting Hospital Quality Data for Annual Payment Update program.

    ii. HHS contracted with the National Quality Forum (NQF) for quality measures.

    iii. It is the responsibility of the eligible professionals and the eligible hospitals to understand compliance issues regarding clinical quality measures.

    iv. Quality measures include other areas such as pediatrics, long-term care, obstetrics, dental care/oral health, mental health, and substance abuse.

    v. In 2014, all providers, regardless of whether they are in Stage 1 or Stage 2 of meaningful use, will be required to report on the 2014 clinical quality measures (CQMs) for eligible professionals and 2014 clinical quality measures (CQMs) for eligible hospitals finalized in the Stage 2 rule. This means eligible professionals will need to report 9 measures, and eligible hospitals will need to report 16. CQMs may be reported electronically, or via attestation.

    vi. National Quality Strategy Domains

    There is also a new requirement in 2014 that the quality measures selected must cover at least 3 of the 6 available National Quality Strategy (NQS) domains, which represent the Department of Health and Human Services' NQS priorities for healthcare quality improvement.

    The 6 NQS domains are:

    1. Patient and Family Engagement

    2. Patient Safety

    3. Care Coordination

    4. Population/Public Health

    5. Efficient Use of Healthcare Resources

    6. Clinical Process/Effectiveness

        i. http://www.cms.gov/Regulations-and-Guidance/Legislation/EHRIncentivePrograms/2014_ClinicalQualityMeasures.html

     e. Clinical Decision Support (CDS)
- **i.** An application that contains rules to support and advise care providers about treatment alternatives
- **ii.** Provides clinicians, staff, patients, or other individuals with knowledge and person-specific information, intelligently filtered or presented at appropriate times to enhance health and health care
- **iii.** Supports patient safety; approximately 98,000 Americans die each year due to medical errors, mostly due to medication errors
- **iv.** May be used to aid with diagnosing and treating patients

     f. Expert Systems
- **i.** Clinical algorithm
  1. Forerunners of modern practice guidelines; follows a flow chart until a decision is reached
  2. Benefits: makes knowledge easy to encode
  3. Limitations
     - **a.** Clinicians can deviate from the path with the algorithm.
     - **b.** New etiologies or causes of disease or new treatments may not be pursued because they are not part of the algorithm.
- **ii.** Bayes' Theorem and usage of Bayesian statistics
  1. The probability of a disease is calculated based on prior knowledge and then updated as new information changes the probability.
  2. Limitation of Bayes' Theorem: when multiple findings are important in a diagnosis and multiple diagnoses are possible, it requires high computational complexity quickly. For that reason, large-scale use of Bayesian statistics has not really occurred in any kind of diagnostic computer system.
  3. Production rules: if/then rules that are used quite extensively in many therapeutic decision support applications. The system combines evidence from different rules to arrive at a diagnosis. Two types of rule-based expert systems exist: backward-chaining systems (where the system constantly pursues a goal and then asks questions to try to get to that goal state) and forward-chaining systems (where the system follows a prescribed path, in essence similar to clinical algorithms' attempt to reach the answer). The generic rule is "If test X shows result Y, then conclude Z, where Z may be some sort of diagnosis"; oftentimes there is a certainty factor.
     - **a.** MYCIN: the first rule-based expert system in medicine, which attempted to diagnose two infectious diseases, meningitis and bacteremia. It used the backward-chaining approach and asked questions sometimes seemingly relentlessly in its attempt to reach a diagnosis.
     - **b.** MYCIN was not used everywhere because the rule bases were large and difficult to maintain.

     g. Creation and Use of Data Entry Templates
- **i.** Methods of data capture
  1. Hard documents scanned into the system
  2. Information downloaded directly from other computer information systems, depending on the compatibility of the two systems. HIE standards will play a critical role. A variation of this form of data capture is the interfacing or feeding of data directly from other data-capture devices, such as blood pressure monitors or electrocardiographs.

3. Data entry templates

    i. Templates are important tools for collecting data entered into the system manually; they help ensure the quality of the data and provide data-capture efficiencies through effective design and use.

        1. Support collection of quality data and improve efficiency of data capture

        2. Provide a structure format for the user that is familiar and easy to use

        3. Can speed data entry by providing suggested default values

        4. Can be built to limit the data type (yes/no, male/female)

            a. Built-in ranges to avoid erroneous entries. Example: requiring blood pressure or other physiological measurements to be within a realistic range of values.

            b. Pick lists, which restrict users to making a selection from a list of values such as available lab tests. Data are entered consistently and accurately, leaving no room for misinterpretation.

            c. Data entry templates can require that certain fields be completed for the form to be submitted, minimizing the omission of critical information.

h. Computerized Provider Order Entry (CPOE)

    i. A powerful tool to support implementation of standard care plans, reduce errors, and guide clinicians to utilize best practices in their care planning sessions.

    ii. Order sets

        1. A tool to translate evidence-based clinical knowledge into actions at the point of care; supports error reduction, quality improvement, and reduced healthcare process variability. Predefined care plans, detailing the essential steps in the treatment of patients with well-defined clinical problems, are designed to translate published guidelines into local workflow.

        2. Quick orders and order sets for frequently ordered items can significantly speed up the ordering process for clinicians. Several quick orders can be combined in an order set; order sets enable a group of quick orders to be executed in sequence without having to select each quick order individually.

        3. It is time consuming to create, manage, update, and distribute a large collection of predefined orders and order sets.

        4. Order sets require clinical expertise and must incorporate the most current research to ensure best practices are in place.

        5. Authoring order sets is often a local process requiring custom development and programming that involves the time, and expert knowledge and skills, of a number of people. Typically, an EHR will provide specific tools for authoring and displaying order sets created for local use to ease the development burden and improve turnaround time.

        6. Nationally developed order sets for common disease states or procedures also exist.

i. Architecture

    i. Provides a framework for hardware and software configuration. The data infrastructure focuses on the data needs to operate a healthcare organization. Operational and clinical needs of meaningful use of data must be supported.

      ii. Using uniform definitions, data elements must be determined for the required data sets.

        1. Uniform Hospital Discharge Data Set (UHDDS): long-standing data set begun in the 1960s to provide information at a national level

        2. Uniform Ambulatory Care Data Set (UACDS)

        3. Minimum Data Set for Long-Term Care

        4. Data Elements for Emergency Department Systems (DEEDS)

        5. Health Plan Employer Data and Information Set (HEDIS)

      iii. Structured and unstructured data

        1. Structured and discrete data are readable by a computer and capture data by individual fields to provide structure.

          a. When decision support systems are built, structured data can be used to provide information for clinical and administrative decision making.

          b. Includes CPOE system, or information collected into a registration database.

        2. Unstructured data are not readable by a computer.

          a. Include handwritten or transcribed narrative notes that are scanned into a system

          b. Notes: readable but not usable for clinical decision support system

          c. Includes document image data, transcribed reports, video data (e.g., ultrasound images), audio data (e.g., voice notations), vector graphic data (e.g., fetal monitor or electrocardiogram reports), and diagnostic image data (e.g., magnetic resonance image)

      iv. Collection and storage

        1. Data need to be stored for longevity and safety.

          a. Data repository: an open-structure database that is not dedicated to the software of any particular vendor or data supplier, in which data from diverse sources are stored so that an integrated, multidisciplinary view of the data can be achieved; also called a central data repository or, when related specifically to healthcare data, a clinical data repository

          b. Data warehouse: a database that makes it possible to access data from multiple databases and combine the results into a single query and reporting interface

          c. Clinical data repository: a frequently updated database that provides users with direct access to detailed patient-level data as well as the ability to drill down into historical views of administrative, clinical, and financial data

          d. Picture archiving and communication system (PACS): stores radiology images; reduces the need for film storage and allows for digital storage of images. Because of the size of digital images, storage area networks (SANs) may be required. PACS also allows for the remote reading of radiology images when needed.

    j. Other Systems

      i. Patient-flow management systems

        1. Help identify the location of the patient at all times and ensure that staff are at the proper locations

        2. Can alert staff when a patient is ready for surgery and can link the patient location to the orders entered

ii. Supply chain

    1. Includes the requisitioning, inventory, and tracking of supply usage.

    2. Supplies and labor: the two largest components of a hospital's operating budget; linking supply chain management systems to the EHR helps ensure contract compliance and usage tracking

    3. Helps reduce surgery delays and supports device registries so patients can be identified if a device recall occurs (e.g., pacemaker)

PRACTICAL APPLICATION OF YOUR KNOWLEDGE

1. Discuss the evolution of information systems in health care.

2. List and describe the various categories of computer systems.

3. List five programming languages.

4. Define an information system and give an example.

5. Distinguish between system and application software.

6. Describe the following five types of information systems.
   a. Transaction processing system (TPS)

   b. Management information system (MIS)

   c. Executive information system (EIS)

   d. Expert system (ES)

   e. Decision support system (DSS)

7. Match the type of information system with the scenario in which it would be best used (TPS, MIS, EIS, ES, DSS).

 a. _____ The CEO of Houston Ambulatory Care Clinic is performing strategic planning. She needs to ask "what if" questions to assist with the process.

 b. _____ The admissions, discharge, and transfer system.

 c. _____ Dr. Johnson queries the system with a patient's symptoms to obtain possible diagnoses.

 d. _____ Dr. Thomas obtains an alert stating that his patient's lab values are higher than the norm.

 e. _____ Odell Tyson, RN, is charge nurse for the medicine unit. She queries the system to obtain the census.

8. Considering the four levels of data organization, use the relational database table to label the item, record, and file.

Relational Database Table

ID	Last Name	First Name	Address	Date of Birth	Dx Code	Pr Code	Amount Owed
1.	Tyson	Carla	1458 Spruce	9/20/1959	250.00		$50
2.	Thomas	Shirlyn	889 Oh	2/6/1972	141.03	74.1	$10
3.	Johnson	Casandra	394 Pleasant	3/27/1970	852.02	01.24	$30
4.	Rodriquez	Marilyn	789 Gerind	5/9/1980	864.15	50.61	$65
5.	Stariha	Carolyn	225 Needville	4/16/1972	403.91	39.95	$87
6.	Rodriguez	Irma	745 Valley	12/5/1984	414.00	36.06	$34

 a. If a researcher wanted to obtain all patients from a database with the last name of "Rodriquez," what method would he or she use to extract the data?

 b. With the method you identified in the previous question, list at least three types of reports that can be obtained from the above file.

 c. Select the phrase that best describes each term.

1. _____ record	**a.** smallest storage unit for data	
2. _____ field	**b.** list of information describing the field	
3. _____ database	**c.** question asked by user, answer to which is in database	
4. _____ query		
5. _____ data dictionary	**d.** columns (fields) and rows of related information in a database	
6. _____ table		
7. _____ entity	**e.** collection of related data items treated as a unit	
	f. persons, locations, things, or concepts that can be collected or stored as data	
	g. a collection of stored data, typically organized into fields, records, and files	

9. Compute the following:
   a. A discharge summary is one typewritten page. Approximately how many kilobytes is the discharge summary?

   b. An operative report is 3072 bytes in length. How many kilobytes is the report?

   c. A transcription company types approximately 5000 reports a month. The average report is 4.5 kilobytes in length. How many megabytes are needed to store the transcribed documents?

10. The ambulatory care clinic is planning to implement an electronic health record system. The health information director needs to make a graphical representation of the proposed flow of the information in the electronic medical record. What tool for system analysis will assist with this graphic representation?

11. Discuss the administrative, financial, clinical, outpatient, and research information systems and give an example of each.

12. Define the functions of a database management system.

13. Discuss the five major database models.

14. Describe the relational database and how data are arranged and manipulated.

15. Distinguish among data warehouse, data mart, and data mining.

16. List and explain the four major phases of the system development life cycle.

17. Discuss methods to assure the security and protection of health information.

18. Explain authentication tools used by information systems.

19. Discuss how intranets and extranets utilize Internet technologies.

20. Identify network protocols used with the Internet.

21. Explain functional requirements and expectations for the electronic health record.

22. Discuss the role of the health information professional with regard to information systems.

23. Why is a firewall needed in an information system?

24. You have just been hired for the position of chief information officer at Houston Memorial Hospital. Discuss what your duties include.

25. What are e-commerce and e-health?

26. What is the relationship between the American Reinvestment and Recovery Act (ARRA) of 2009 and health information technology?

27. How did the Health Information Technology for Economic and Clinical Health (HITECH) Act affect the implementation of a national infrastructure for an electronic health record?

28. Describe the Office of the National Coordinator for Health Information Technology and its connection to the Department of Health and Human Services.

29. List four principles of change management.

30. Describe the phases of the health IT life cycle.

31. Discuss a process hierarchy for workflow analysis and design for planning and implementation.

32 Describe the workflow mapping of the following symbols:
   a. Oval

   b. Rectangle

   c. Diamond

   d. Circle

33. What are the steps for creating a process workflow?

34. Discuss meaningful use.

35. Explain how a health information exchange works.

36. Discuss computerized physician order entry in relation to meaningful use.

37. How does clinical decision support enhance patient safety?

38. Explain data capture.

39. How do templates affect data entry?

40. What is the relationship between computer architecture and data sets?

41. Differentiate between structured data and unstructured data.

42. Compare and contrast a data repository, a data warehouse, and a clinical data repository.

TEST YOUR KNOWLEDGE

1. Which of the following is an example of a clinical information system?
   a. Executive information system
   b. Results reporting
   c. ADT
   d. Master patient index

2. Which job title is most appropriate to manage the information resource management in a healthcare institution?
   a. Chief information officer
   b. Health information manager
   c. System analyst
   d. Data administrator

3. The physicians of the pediatric clinic need a system to assist with diagnosing patients. Which of the following systems will be most advantageous?
   a. Executive information system
   b. Extranet
   c. Management information system
   d. Decision support system

4. To make the electronic medical record documentation more efficient for the surgery nursing service, which of the following systems should be employed?
   a. Point of care
   b. Decision support system
   c. Admission, discharge, and transfer system
   d. Data mart

5. The CEO needs a system to assist with strategic planning and making "what if" decisions. What is the information system that will best meet her needs?
   a. Executive information system
   b. Expert system
   c. Decision support system
   d. Data warehouse

6. The pharmacy department requests a focused information system that will allow it to research its historical data in great detail. Which system should the pharmacy use?
   a. Data warehouse
   b. Data mining
   c. Data mart
   d. Expert system

7. In an electronic health record system, how are sonograms processed?
   a. Video
   b. HTML
   c. Images
   d. Audio

8. The Houston Hospital information system requires a mechanism for recording access and transactions of its users. What authentication tool can be implemented?
   a. Ethernet
   b. Token ring
   c. Turnaround document
   d. Token card

9. In the system analysis phase of the system development life cycle, which tool is used to break down problems into smaller levels of details?
   a. Entity relationship diagram
   b. Hierarchy chart
   c. Data dictionary
   d. Flow chart

10. The health information department is going to store 2500 discharge summaries on optical disk. Each discharge summary is approximately 3072 bytes in length. How many kilobytes of space are needed to store the data?
    a. 3 KB
    b. 30.72 KB
    c. 7500 KB
    d. 7,680,000 KB

11. Health Level 7 (HL7) allows for the:
    a. communication and clinical alerts through time drive and data drive.
    b. electronic interchange of clinical, financial, and administrative information among disparate health information systems.
    c. creation of an electronic health record to accommodate research subsystems that facilitate clinical research.
    d. integration of information from admitting, radiology, pharmacy, pathology, nursing, respiratory therapy, and clinical laboratories.

12. GUI is an acronym for _____, which provides an environment using icons, tool bars of pull-down menus, and click, point, and drag with the mouse.
    a. assembly level language
    b. graphical user interface
    c. binary system
    d. COBOL

13. Houston Hospital has been collecting data on physician credentialing for 4 years. The credentials specialist wants to retrieve all the physicians in the database who are pediatricians. Which tool should be used to run the report?
    a. XML
    b. HTML
    c. HTTP
    d. SQL

14. You want to depict the movement of patient information from the time of admittance to the point of discharge. Which of the following tools is most appropriate?
    a. Data modeling
    b. Decomposition diagram
    c. Hierarchy chart
    d. Data flow diagram

15. You are developing a web page for the health information department. Which software would you most probably use?
    a. COBOL
    b. Pascal
    c. HTML
    d. Java
    e. Both c and d

16. As HIM director, you are involved in a project to assist the systems analyst in creating a central repository of all data elements utilized in the master patient index database. An example of this documentation includes: Length: 1 character, Type: alphanumeric, Value: M = Male and F = Female. This resource is known as what?
    a. Data flow diagram
    b. Decision table
    c. Entity relationship diagram
    d. Data dictionary

17. Bob has been hired to implement an information system for the radiology department. Which of the following will provide him with the ability to determine the best staffing pattern for efficient patient care?
    a. Executive information system
    b. Decision support system
    c. Knowledge management system
    d. Expert system

18. Bob, as director of nursing, suggests a point-of-care system, which should include a(n):
    a. clinical decision support system.
    b. executive decision support system.
    c. knowledge management system.
    d. robotics component for assessing vitals.

19. Which of the following is supported by a tactical database?
    a. Executive information system
    b. Results reporting
    c. ADT
    d. Staff scheduling

20. Houston Hospital requires a transaction-oriented information system. Which of the following might they purchase?
    a. R-ADT system
    b. Medical decision support
    c. Executive information system
    d. Electronic mail

21. Bob is programming the management information system for the entry of discharge summaries. Which data type should he use to code the discharge summary?
    a. Image
    b. Numeric
    c. Text
    d. Audio

22. Barbette plans to query the database to determine the number of female discharges, age 20–25, with an ICD-9-CM diagnostic code of 250.01, during December of last year. Which of the following might she use?
    a. Rich text language
    b. Integrated text language
    c. Knowledge-based language
    d. Structured query language

23. The CEO of Houston Hospital wants an information system that combines data with analysis tools to facilitate "what if" questions for posing future optional scenarios. Which should she purchase?
    a. Expert system
    b. Executive information system
    c. Decision support system
    d. Both executive information system and decision support system

24. ICD-9-CM codes are which type of data?
    a. Text
    b. Numeric
    c. Alphanumeric
    d. Alpha

25. During system analysis, Bob uses a tool that shows relations between data. What is he using?
    a. Data dictionary
    b. Entity relationship diagram
    c. Data flow chart
    d. Relational flex chart

26. Java compilers are usually found in:
    a. web browsers.
    b. spreadsheets.
    c. databases.
    d. word processors.

27. Which of the following is an attribute for an MPI entry?
    a. Admission date
    b. Physician order entry
    c. Medical record
    d. Financial record

28. The CIO of Houston Hospital suggests a system designed to provide diagnostic and other expert advice to clinicians from various resources. Which should she purchase?
    a. Clinical information system
    b. Picture archiving and communication system
    c. Clinical decision support system
    d. Executive information system

29. An order entry system is a component of a(n):
    a. clinical decision support system.
    b. clinical information system.
    c. executive information system.
    d. database management system.

30. Benefits of an electronic medical record over a paper-based system include no lost charts and:
    a. improved hands-on patient care.
    b. better clinician bedside manners.
    c. decreased allergic drug reactions.
    d. better data collection.

31. An application of a clinical information system would be in _____ management.
    a. quality improvement
    b. financial
    c. human resources
    d. materials

32. Which of the following health information applications lends itself well to automation?
    a. Patient communication
    b. Follow-up with clinicians
    c. Indexing
    d. Employee counseling

33. Master programs that manage the basic operations of the computer are called:
    a. utility programs.
    b. language translators.
    c. operating systems.
    d. user interfaces.

34. The process of sorting through the organization's data to identify unusual patterns is called:
    a. data mining.
    b. language translation.
    c. operating systems.
    d. user interfaces.

35. A type of database where data are stored in predefined tables that contain rows and columns similar to a spreadsheet is called a(n) _____ database.
    a. executive
    b. objective
    c. subjective
    d. relational

Use the following table to answer questions 36–37. Choose the best answer.

Sample Relational Database

Name	Gender	Age	City
Washington	Female	24	Houston
Applegate	Male	44	Houston
Matthews	Female	12	Sugar Land

36. The preceding is a relational database table. What is an alternative name for each row?
    a. File
    b. Record
    c. Field
    d. Relation

37. The preceding is a relational database table. What is an alternative name for each column?
    a. File
    b. Record
    c. Field
    d. Relation

38. Barbette is reading her email and the following window pops up:

> Medical Record Committee
> meeting today, 3 PM

This is an example of a(n):
a. reminder.
b. alert.
c. Java.
d. GUI.

39. Dr. Bob ordered Zithromax for his newborn patient. A window pop-up read the following:

> Patient 2 days old. Do you want to continue with this medication order?

This is an example of a(n):
a. reminder.
b. alert.
c. Java.
d. GUI.

40. The pharmacy department wants to set up a database to research and study adverse reactions to Coumadin. Which of the following should be established?
a. External data model
b. Conceptual data model
c. Internal data model
d. Data mart

41. Dr. Bob queries the EHR to determine the best medication for his 2-day-old newborn. Which system would be most beneficial?
a. Executive decision support
b. Clinical decision support
c. Tactical decision support
d. Operational decision support

42. Houston Hospital utilizes wireless laptops for documenting in the EHR. Which security protocol system provides the strongest security?
a. WEP
b. WiFi
c. WPA
d. TCP/IP

43. An interface engine:
a. serves as a bridge between applications.
b. allows for point-to-point connection.
c. is a type of hardware.
d. is a type of software.

44. Within an e-mail there is an embedded object that enables direct access to another related web page. What type of link is the embedded object?
a. Hyperspace
b. Hypertext
c. GUI
d. Java

45. Based upon the following table, calculate the payback period in years for the purchase of a scanner.

Cost Chart				
	Year 1	Year 2	Year 3	Year 4
Current system cost	$3000	$3000	$3000	$3000
New system cost	$5300	$1100	$1100	$1100
Yearly difference in cost	$2300	$1900	$1900	$1900
Cumulative difference in cost	($2300)	($400)	$1500	$3400

a. 1
b. 2
c. 3
d. 4

46. Barbette, director of HIM, writes a proposal for an electronic chart tracking system. She states that the purchase of the $30,000 system will save approximately $9000 per year in personnel time. She has conducted a:
    a. cost-benefit analysis.
    b. break-even analysis.
    c. cost-effectiveness analysis.
    d. payback period.

47. To improve patient safety, Dr. Bob encourages administration to purchase an EHR with medication alerts. Which of the following has he conducted?
    a. Cost-benefit analysis
    b. Break-even analysis
    c. Cost-effectiveness analysis
    d. Payback period

48. The manager of record retrieval requires a system to assist with making day-to-day decisions. Which system would be most effective?
    a. Tactical decision support system
    b. Executive decision support
    c. Clinical decision support
    d. Operational decision support

49. The HIM department has set up and installed the new scanner, trained users, and performed testing. It is in the _____ phase of system implementation.
    a. system conversion
    b. system development
    c. system performance
    d. system start-up

50. Which individual is mostly likely to use a tactical decision support system?
    a. CEO
    b. Director of HIM
    c. Coding supervisor
    d. Physician

Biomedical Sciences

The following is a common list of drugs, the conditions they treat, and the tests used to determine the diagnosis.

Common Drug References

Drug	Conditions Treated	Diagnostic Tests
acetaminophen (Tylenol)	Fever and pain Simple headaches and muscle aches The minor aches and pains of the common cold and flu Backache Toothache Minor pain of arthritis Menstrual cramps Pain due to teething, immunizations, tonsillectomy, and childhood illnesses	Physical examination Temperature monitoring
albuterol (Proventil)	Bronchial spasms (including asthma and bronchial spasm due to exercise)	Allergy testing Bronchoscopy Chest radiography Chest ultrasonograph Chest X-ray Pulmonary function test Pulmonary ventilation scan
alprazolam (Xanax) [Tranquilizer]	Symptoms of anxiety Anxiety disorders	Psychological examination Physical examination

(*continues*)

Common Drug References (*continued*)

Drug	Conditions Treated	Diagnostic Tests
amitriptyline (Elavil) [Tricyclic antidepressant]	Mental depression May be prescribed for bulimia (an eating disorder), chronic pain, the prevention of migraine headaches, and the pathological weeping and laughing syndrome associated with multiple sclerosis	Psychological examination Physical examination
amlodipine (Norvasc)	High blood pressure (hypertension) Angina pectoris	Stress test EKG Blood pressure monitoring CAT scan
amoxicillin (Amoxil) [Antibiotic for bacterial infections]	Gonorrhea Middle ear infections Skin infections Upper and lower respiratory tract infections Infections of the genital and urinary tract	Physical examination Culture Urine test Blood test if needed
amoxicillin clavulante (Augmentin)	Lower respiratory, middle ear, sinus, skin, and urinary tract infections caused by specific bacteria that produce a chemical enzyme called beta lactamase that makes some infections particularly difficult to treat	Physical examination Culture Urine test Blood test if needed
atovastatin calcium (Lipitor) [Cholesterol-lowering drug]	Elevated cholesterol levels	HDL and LDL blood tests

azithromycin (Zithromax) [Antibiotic related to erythromycin]	Mild to moderate skin infections
	Upper and lower respiratory tract infections, including pharyngitis (strep throat), tonsillitis, sinus infections, worsening of chronic obstructive pulmonary disease, and pneumonia
	Sexually transmitted infections of the cervix or urinary tract
	Genital ulcer disease in men
	In children:
	  Middle ear infection
	  Pneumonia
	  Tonsillitis
	  Strep throat
		UGI
		Physical examination
		Culture
		Urine test
		Blood test if needed

cephalexin (Keflex, Keftab) [Cephalosporin antibiotic]	Bacterial infections of the respiratory tract, middle ear, bones, skin, and reproductive and urinary systems	Physical examination Culture Urine test Blood test if needed

Common Drug References (*continued*)

Drug	Conditions Treated	Diagnostic Tests
cimetidine (Tagamet) [Histamine blocker]	Heartburn Acid indigestion Sour stomach	UGI
cisplatin (Platinol)	Various types of cancers, including sarcomas, some carcinomas (e.g., small cell lung cancer and ovarian cancer), lymphomas, and germ cell tumors	Biopsy
codeine	Pain	Physical examination
cyclobenzaprine HCl (Flexeril) [Muscle relaxant that, when combined with rest and physical therapy, provides relief of muscular stiffness and pain]	Muscle spasms resulting from injuries such as sprains, strains, or pulls	Physical examination
cyclosporine (Sandimmune Neoral)	Organ transplant surgery to help prevent rejection of organs (kidney, heart, or liver) by suppressing the body's immune system and to avoid long-term rejection in people previously treated with other immunosuppressant drugs	Bleeding time Platelet aggregation test Clot retraction test Blood count (WBC, RBC)
dexamethasone (Decadron)	Inflammation and symptoms from a variety of disorders, including rheumatoid arthritis and severe cases of asthma Primary or secondary adrenal cortex insufficiency (lack of sufficient adrenal hormone) Severe allergic conditions, such as drug-induced allergies Blood disorders, such as various anemias Certain cancers (along with other drugs) Skin diseases, such as severe psoriasis Collagen (connective tissue) diseases, such as systemic lupus erythematosus Digestive tract disease such as ulcerative colitis High serum levels of calcium associated with cancer Fluid retention due to nephrotic syndrome (a condition in which damage to the kidneys causes the body to lose protein in the urine) Eye diseases such as allergic conjunctivitis With other drugs, lung diseases such as tuberculosis	Blood count (WBC, RBC)

(*continues*)

Common Drug References (*continued*)

Drug	Conditions Treated	Diagnostic Tests
diazepam (Valium) [Benzodiazepine]	Anxiety disorders, including short-term relief of the symptoms of anxiety Symptoms of acute alcohol withdrawal Relax muscles Relieve the uncontrolled muscle movements caused by cerebral palsy and paralysis of the lower body and limbs Involuntary movement of the hands (athetosis) Tight, aching muscles With other medications, convulsive disorders such as epilepsy	Psychological examination Physical examination
digoxin (Lanoxin) [Improves the strength and efficiency of the heart, which leads to better circulation of blood and reduction of the uncomfortable swelling that is common in people with congestive heart failure]	Congestive heart failure Certain types of irregular heartbeat Other heart problems	Stress test EKG Blood pressure monitoring CAT scan
diltiazem HCl (Cardizem)	Angina pectoris (chest pain usually caused by lack of oxygen to the heart due to clogged arteries)	Stress test EKG Blood pressure monitoring CAT scan
ferrous sulfate (Feosol) [Form of the mineral iron, which is important for many functions in the body, especially for the transport of oxygen in the blood]	Dietary supplement Iron deficiencies and iron-deficiency anemia	Blood count (RBC) Blood screen
fluoxetine (Prozac) [Selective serotonin reuptake inhibitor (SSRI)]	Depression Obsessive-compulsive disorder (OCD) Panic disorders	Psychological examination Physical examination

Common Drug References (*continued*)

Drug	Conditions Treated	Diagnostic Tests
haloperidel (Haldol)	Mental disorders such as schizophrenia Tics (uncontrolled muscle contractions of face, arms, or shoulders) and the unintended utterances that mark Tourette's syndrome Short-term treatment of children with severe behavior problems, including hyperactivity and combativeness Severe nausea and vomiting caused by cancer drugs Drug problems, such as LSD flashback and PCP intoxication Symptoms of hemiballismus (a condition that causes involuntary writhing of one side of the body)	Psychological examination Drug screen Complete blood count
heparin [Anticoagulant, a blood thinner]	Prevents the formation of blood clots	Bleeding time Platelet aggregation test Clot retraction test
herazasin HCl (Hytrin)	High blood pressure (hypertension) Symptoms of benign prostatic hyperplasia (BPH)	Stress test EKG Blood pressure monitoring CAT scan
hydrocodone bitatrate (Vicodin) [Narcotic analgesic (painkiller) and cough reliever with a non-narcotic analgesic]	Moderate to moderately severe pain Cough	Physical examination
levothyroxine sodium (Levoxyl synthroid) [Synthetic thyroid hormone]	Thyroid gland not making enough hormone Enlarged thyroid (a goiter) or at risk for developing a goiter Cancers of the thyroid Thyroid production low due to surgery, radiation, certain drugs, or disease of the pituitary gland or hypothalamus in the brain	T_3 T_4 TSH

(*continues*)

Common Drug References (*continued*)

Drug	Conditions Treated	Diagnostic Tests
lisinopril (Prinivil)	High blood pressure (hypertension)	Stress test EKG Blood pressure monitoring CAT scan
loratadine (Claritin) [Antihistamine]	Sneezing, runny nose, stuffiness, itching, and tearing eyes caused by hay fever or other upper respiratory allergies Swollen, red, itchy patches of skin caused by hives	Bronchoscopy Chest radiography Chest ultrasonograph Chest X-ray Pulmonary ventilation scan
lorazepan (Ativan) [Benzodiazepine]	Anxiety disorders Relief of the symptoms of anxiety	Psychological examination Physical examination
meperidine (Demerol) [Narcotic analgesic]	Moderate to severe pain	Physical examination
metformin HCl (Glucophage) [Oral antidiabetic medication]	Type 2 (non-insulin-dependent) diabetes	FBS, PPBS, GTT, c-peptide, glucagon Blood urea nitrogen (BUN) and plasma creatinine test to detect kidney function
methyldopa (Aldomet)	High blood pressure (hypertension)	Stress test EKG Blood pressure monitoring CAT scan
metoclopramide HCl (Reglan) [Increases the contractions of the stomach and small intestine to help the passage of food]	Symptoms of diabetic gastroparesis	UGI LGI
metoprolol tartrate (Lopressor) [Beta blocker]	High blood pressure (hypertension) Angina pectoris (chest pain usually caused by lack of oxygen to the heart due to clogged arteries) Myocardial infarction (heart attack)	Stress test EKG Blood pressure monitoring CAT scan

Common Drug References (*continued*)

Drug	Conditions Treated	Diagnostic Tests
nabumetone (Relafen) [Nonsteroidal anti-inflammatory drug]	Inflammation, swelling, stiffness, and joint pain associated with rheumatoid arthritis and osteoarthritis	Physical examination
nadolol (Corgard)	Angina pectoris (chest pain, usually caused by lack of oxygen to the heart due to clogged arteries) High blood pressure (hypertension)	Stress test EKG Blood pressure monitoring CAT scan
naproxen (Anaprox, Aleve) [Nonsteroidal anti-inflammatory drug]	Mild to moderate pain and menstrual cramps Inflammation, swelling, stiffness, and joint pain associated with rheumatoid arthritis and osteoarthritis (the most common form of arthritis), and for ankylosing spondylitis (spinal arthritis), tendinitis, bursitis, acute gout, and other conditions May be prescribed for juvenile arthritis	Physical examination
nifedipine (Procardia XL) [Calcium-channel blocker]	High blood pressure (hypertension)	Stress test EKG Blood pressure monitoring CAT scan
nitroglycerin (Nitro-dur, NitroQuick, Nitrogard)	Angina pectoris	Stress test EKG Blood pressure monitoring CAT scan
oxybutynin HCl (Ditropan) [Relaxes bladder muscles]	Incontinence	Physical examination
oxytocin (Pitocin)	Induce labor Increase the strength or duration of labor contractions	Fetal monitor Labor and delivery assessment

(continues)

Common Drug References (*continued*)

Drug	Conditions Treated	Diagnostic Tests
paroxetine HCl (Paxil) [Selective serotonin reuptake inhibitor (SSRI)]	Serious, continuing depression that interferes with patient's ability to function Obsessive-compulsive disorder Panic disorder Generalized anxiety disorder Social anxiety disorder Post-traumatic stress disorder Major depression	Psychological examination Physical examination
phenobarbital sodium (Bellatal, Luminal) [Barbiturate that depresses the activity of the brain and nervous system]	Induce sleep Insomnia (for up to 2 weeks) Prevent and treat seizures	CAT scan Complete blood work-up EKG EEG
potassium (K-Dur)	Low potassium levels in people who may face potassium loss caused by digitalis, non-potassium-sparing diuretics, and certain diseases	Potassium (K^+)
prednisone (Deltasone) [Steroid drug]	Inflammation Symptoms in rheumatoid arthritis and severe cases of asthma Abnormal adrenal gland development Allergic conditions (severe) Blood disorders Certain cancers (along with other drugs) Diseases of the connective tissue including systemic lupus erythematosus Eye diseases of various kinds Flare-ups of multiple sclerosis Fluid retention due to nephrotic syndrome Lung diseases, including tuberculosis Meningitis (inflamed membranes around the brain) Prevention of organ rejection Rheumatoid arthritis and related disorders Severe flare-ups of ulcerative colitis or enteritis (inflammation of the intestines) Skin diseases Thyroid gland inflammation Trichinosis (with complications)	Bronchoscopy Chest radiography Chest ultrasonograph Chest X-ray Pulmonary ventilation scan

Common Drug References (*continued*)

Drug	Conditions Treated	Diagnostic Tests
promethazine HCl (Phenergan) [Antihistamine]	Nasal stuffiness and inflammation and red, inflamed eyes caused by hay fever and other allergies Itching, swelling, and redness from hives and other rashes Allergic reactions to blood transfusions With other medications, anaphylactic shock (severe allergic reaction) Sedative and sleep aid for both children and adults Prevent and control nausea and vomiting before and after surgery Prevent and treat motion sickness With other medications, for pain after surgery	Physical examination Culture Urine test Blood test if needed
propoxyphene (Darvon, Darvocet-N, Propoxy)	Pain	Physical examination
propranolol HCl (Inderal) [Beta blocker]	High blood pressure (hypertension) Angina pectoris (chest pain usually caused by lack of oxygen to the heart due to clogged arteries) Changes in heart rhythm Prevention of migraine headache Hereditary tremors Hypertrophic subaortic stenosis (a condition related to exertional angina) Tumors of the adrenal gland Reduce the risk of death from recurring heart attack	Stress test EKG Blood pressure monitoring CAT scan
quinopril (Accupril) [ACE inhibitor]	High blood pressure (hypertension) Congestive heart failure	Stress test EKG Blood pressure monitoring CAT scan
randitidine HCl (Zantac)	Decrease the production of stomach acid Irritation to the stomach lining Ulcers and other gastrointestinal conditions	UGI
simvastatin (Zocor) [Cholesterol-lowering drug for people at high risk of heart disease]	LDL levels ≥ 130 Bypass surgery or angioplasty to clear clogged arteries	HDL and LDL blood tests

(*continues*)

Common Drug References (*continued*)

Drug	Conditions Treated	Diagnostic Tests
streptokinase (Streptase) [Clot-dissolving medication]	Myocardial infarction (heart attack) Pulmonary embolism	Stress test EKG Blood pressure monitoring CAT scan
tetracycline (Sumycin Panmycin) [Broad-spectrum antibiotic often used as an alternative for people who are allergic to penicillin]	Bacterial infections such as Rocky Mountain spotted fever, typhus fever, and tick fevers Upper respiratory infections Pneumonia Gonorrhea Amoebic infections Urinary tract infections Severe acne Trachoma (a chronic eye infection) and conjunctivitis (pinkeye)	Physical examination Culture Urine test Blood test if needed
theophylline (Theo-dur) [Oral bronchodilator]	Symptoms of asthma, chronic bronchitis, and emphysema	Bronchoscopy Chest radiography Chest ultrasonograph Chest X-ray Pulminary ventilation scan
tobramycin ointment (Tobradex) [Topical antibiotic]	Bacterial infections of the eye	Physical examination Culture Urine test Blood test if needed
tramadol HCl (Ultram)	Moderate to moderately severe pain	Physical examination
trimethoprim and sulfamenthoxazole (Bactrim) [Antibacterial combination drug]	Certain urinary tract infections Severe middle ear infections in children Long-lasting or frequently recurring bronchitis in adults that increases in seriousness Inflammation of the intestine due to a severe bacterial infection Traveler's diarrhea in adults *Pneumocystis jiroveci* pneumonia (also for prevention of this pneumonia in people with weakened immune systems)	Physical examination Culture Urine test Blood test if needed

Common Drug References (*continued*)

Drug	Conditions Treated	Diagnostic Tests
warfarin sulfate (Coumadin) [Anticoagulant, a blood thinner]	Prevent and/or treat a blood clot that has formed within a blood vessel or in the lungs Prevent and/or treat blood clots associated with certain heart conditions or replacement of a heart valve Aid in the prevention of blood clots that may form in blood vessels anywhere in the body after a heart attack Reduce the risk of death, another heart attack, or stroke after a heart attack	Bleeding time Platelet aggregation test Clot retraction test
zolpidem tartrate (Ambien) [Relatively new drug chemically different from other common sleep medications like Halcion and Dalmane]	Insomnia (difficulty falling asleep or staying asleep, or early awakening)	Psychological examination Physical examination

Common Pharmacology Abbreviations

aa	of each
ac	before meals
ad	right ear
as	left ear
A.U.	both ears
B.I.D.	two times a day
BP	blood pressure
cc	cubic centimeter
g, gm	gram
h.s.	at bedtime
I.M.	intramuscular
IV	intravenous
mg	milligram
mL	milliliter
mm	millimeter
npo	nothing by mouth
O.D.	right eye
O.S.	left eye
O.U.	both eyes
p.c.	after meals
P.O.	orally
p.r.n.	as needed
qam	every morning
Q.D.	once a day
Q.H.	every hour
Q.I.D.	four times a day
Q.O.D	every other day
S.L.	sublingually
stat	immediately
T.I.D.	three times a day
ud	as directed
ung	ointment

Following is a common list of lab values, the purpose for which they are used and their indication

Common List of Lab Values

Lab	Purpose	Indication
Complete blood count (CBC)	Identifies number of red and white blood cells per cubic millimeter (mm^3) of blood Evaluates cellular component of blood	Tests include white blood cell count, differential white blood cell count, red blood cell indices, mean corpuscular volume, mean corpuscular hemoglobin, mean corpuscular volume, mean corpuscular hemoglobin concentration, thrombocyte test, or platelet count.
White blood cell count and differential white blood cell count	Identify number and type of white blood cell present in blood	• ↑ is called leukocytosis and is indicative of infection, hemorrhage, trauma, malignancy, general hematologic problems, and leukemia. • ↓ is called leukopenia and is indicative of viral infection, bone marrow disorders, spleen disorders, immune problems, AIDS, and nutritional deficiencies.
Red blood cell count (RBC)	Helps to diagnose anemia and other conditions affecting red blood cells	• ↑ is called erythrocytosis (slight increase) or erythremia (excessive increase) and is indicative of overproduction of red blood cells, or a decrease in the amount of blood plasma. Dehydration, severe diarrhea, acute poisoning, and chronic lung disease can increase RBC. • ↓ is called anemia. Factors that cause anemia are decreased red blood cell production, increased red blood cell destruction, and blood loss. Diseases that causes anemia include Hodgkin's disease, leukemia, rheumatic fever, and diseases that affect bone marrow.
Hematocrit or packed cell volume (PCV)	Determines percentage of red blood cells in whole blood	• RBC/plasma = PCV • ↑ indicative of erythrocytosis or polycynthemia when increase is related to increase in actual number of red blood cells • ↓ indicative of anemia • Interfering circumstances • Age, pregnancy, gender, living in high altitudes

(*continues*)

Common List of Lab Values (*continued*)

Lab	Purpose	Indication
Mean corpuscular volume (MCV)	Describes average size of an individual red blood cell	• ↑ means red blood cells are larger than normal. Pernicious anemia is associated with macrocytic red blood cells. • ↓ means red blood cells are smaller than normal. Microcytic red blood cells are seen in iron-deficiency anemia, lead poisoning, and thalassemia.
Mean corpuscular hemoglobin concentration (MCHC)	Measures the average concentration or percentage of hemoglobin within each red blood cell	• ↑ indicative of spherocytosis, is an increase in the number of abnormal, spheric, red blood cells called spherocytes • ↓ indicates red blood cells contain less hemoglobin than normal and is classified as hypochromic anemia, which means red blood cells lack color. Iron-deficiency anemia
Erythrocyte sedimentation rate (ESR, Sed rate)	Rate at which red blood cells settle out of unclotted blood in an hour. Used to determine the progress of inflammatory diseases such as rheumatoid arthritis, rheumatic fever, and acute MI.	• ↑ due to inflammation or tissue injury; infections, malignancies, collagen vascular diseases • ↓ associated with polycynthemia vera, sickle cell anemia, and a deficiency in plasma protein fibrinogen
Platelet count	Measures amount of platelets in blood	• ↑ called thrombocythemia or thrombocytosis and is seen in malignancies, early stages of chronic granulocytic leukemia, polycynthemia vera, TB, chronic inflammatory diseases, and chronic blood loss • ↓ is called thrombocytopenia; pernicious and aplastic anemias, idiopathic thrombocytopenic purpura (ITP). Commonly seen in AIDS. Patients with platelet deficits often show signs of petechiae, bleeding from gums, nosebleeds, and gastrointestinal bleeding.
Mean platelet volume (MPV)	Shows size of platelets	• ↑ in diameter occurs in systemic lupus erythematosus, idiopathic thrombocytopenic purpura in remission, various anemias, myeloproliferative disorders, and a variety of chronic disease processes • ↓ in size associated with aplastic anemia, megatoblastic anemia, and hypersplenism

Common List of Lab Values (*continued*)

Lab	Purpose	Indication
Prothrombin time (Pro-time)	Used to diagnose coagulation problems	• ↑ indicative of deficiency in one of five coagulation factors—Vitamin K deficiency, toxic levels of vitamin A, prothrombin deficiency, hemorrhagic disease of newborns, alcoholic hepatitis, biliary obstruction, salicylate poisoning
Activated partial thromboplastin time (aPTT)	Measures efficacy of anticoagulant therapy	• Measure coagulation factors 1, 2, 5, 8, 9, 10, 11, and 12 • ↑ in heparin therapy, bleeding disorder • ↓ in extensive malignancies (excluding liver), immediately after acute hemorrhage, early stage of disseminated intravascular coagulation (DIC) disease
Thrombin time	Measures blood plasma level of fibrinogen (precursor of fibrin)	• ↓ results in absence of clot formation; indicative of multiple myeloma, and congenital abnormalities of fibrinogen
Fibrinogen assay	Measures concentration of fibrinogen in the blood	• ↑ associated with hepatitis, TB, septicemia, multiple myeloma, cancer, nephrosis, and rheumatic fever • ↓ can demonstrate genetic disorders, severe liver disease, and DIC
Factor assay test	Measures plasma concentration of specific coagulation factors	Variations from normal indentified by factors: hemophilia, von Willebrand's disease, hepatic diseases, vitamin K deficiency, liver disease, nephrotic syndrome, coronary artery disease, myeloma, hypoglycemia
Chest X-ray	Image of the chest, lungs, heart, large arteries, ribs, and diaphragm	Pneumonia, emphysema, pericarditis, pleural effusion, TB, fractures, diaphragmatic hernia, scoliosis
Mammography	Image of breast tissue	Breast cancer, fibrocystic breast disease, acute suppurative mastitis, abscess, tumors, cysts
KUB	Image of kidney, ureters, and bladder	Malformations of organ, calculi, ascites
Long bone and skull radiography	Image of bones	Fracture, tumor, infection, congenital abnormalities
Spinal radiography	Image of spine	Fracture, tumor, spondylosis, arthritic changes
Angiography	Image of vessels	X-rays of vascular system by injecting a contrast medium such as iodine can reveal thrombi, emboli, and aneurysms

(continues)

Common List of Lab Values (*continued*)

Lab	Purpose	Indication
Cholcystography	Image procedure to visualize gallbladder by administering, by mouth, a radiopaque contrast agent that is excreted by the liver	Gallstones, polyps, chronic cholecystitis
T-tube cholangiography	Image of gallbladder	Common bile duct stones, structures, tumors, bile duct cysts, anatomic variations
Barium swallow	Image study digestive system	Hiatal hernia, varices, strictures, esophageal reflux, peptic ulcer, diverticula, chalasia
Upper GI	Image of gastrointestinal area	Esophageal strictures, diverticula, varices, hiatal hernia, gastric ulcers, tumors, gastritis, inflammatory diseases
Barium enema (BE)	Image of intestines	Colon tumors, obstructions, perforations, diverticula, polyps, hernias
Urinary system radiography	Image of urinary system	• Cystography, intravenous urography, IVP, retrograde pyelography • Kidneys, ureters, bladder
Arthrography	Image of joints	Joint derangement, rotator cuff rupture, joint dislocation, arthritis, synovial abnormalities, ligament tears, cartilage disease
Myelography	Radiographic examination that uses a contrast medium to detect pathology of the spinal cord	Ruptured or herniated disks, spinal cord tumors, spinal canal obstruction
Computed tomography (CT or CAT) scan	Uses X-rays to make detailed pictures of structures inside the body	Cerebral infactions, neoplasms, hematomas, aneurysms, hemorrhages, hydrocephalus, nodules, cysts, cirrhosis of liver, lymphoma, pleural effusion, bone metastasis
Magnetic resonance imaging (MRI), nuclear magnetic resonance imaging (NMRI), or magnetic resonance tomography (MRT)	Produces images through bone tissue and fluid-filled soft tissue and is able to scan transverse, sagittal, and coronal planes of the body	Abnormalities of bones, joints, cartilage
Single-photon emission computed tomography (SPECT)	Three-dimensional imaging	Assist in evaluating organ function and structure

Common List of Lab Values (*continued*)

Lab	Purpose	Indication
Positron emission tomography (PET)	Three-dimensional imaging color images	• Assist in evaluating anatomy, physiology, and biochemistry • Most often used for heart and brain
Brain scan	Scan of brain	Rupture aneurysms, abscesses, cysts, tumors, hematomas, thrombosis, hemorrhage
Cerebrospinal fluid flow scan (cisternography)	Cerebrospinal fluid	Hydrocephalus, spinal lesions, subdural hematoma, cysts
Thyroid-stimulating hormone (TSH) test	Differentiates between primary and secondary hypothyroidism	• Primary hypothyroidism: ↓ uptake of radioactive iodine • Secondary hypothyroidism: ↑ in uptake of radioactive iodine
Parathyroid scan	Assess size, position, function, and location of parathyroid	• Differential diagnosis between hyperplasia and adenoma • Abnormal glands identified
Thallium stress test	Radionuclide scan of heart	Assess coronary perfusion, patency (unblocked) of bypass blood vessels, coronary artery disease, effectiveness of medications and angioplasty
Multigated acquisition (MUGA) scan	Radionuclide study of heart in motion to record images of heart contraction and relaxation	CHF, valvular heart disease, cardiomyopathy, and ventricular aneurysm
Lung scan	Scan of lungs	• Pulmonary perfusion and ventilation scans identify embolisms • Tumors, COPD, pneumonia, atelectasis, asthma, bronchitis, emphysema, and TB best found on chest X-ray
Gallbladder and biliary system scan	Scans gallbladder and biliary system	Chronic cholecystitis, obstruction of cystic and common bile ducts caused by gallstones and tumors
Gastrointestinal reflux scan	Scan of gastrointestinal area	Gastric reflux and pulmonary aspiration, esophageal spasms, achalasia, inability of cardiac sphincter muscle of the stomach to relax
Kidney (renal) scan	Evaluate renal structure, function, and blood flow; renal excretory function; glomerular filtration rates	Renal infarction, infection, inflammatory disease, glomerulonephritis, pyelonephritis, abscesses, cysts, thrombosis or stenosis of blood vessels, assessing kidney transplants, congenital abnormalities, size and shape of kidneys

(continues)

Common List of Lab Values (*continued*)

Lab	Purpose	Indication
Liver scan	Study size, shape, and function of liver	• Liver and spleen scans are done together because the same radionuclide is used for each study • Hepatitis, cirrhosis, ascites, hepatomegaly, benign tumors, abscesses, cystic lesions, metastatic tumor
Spleen scan	Study size, shape, and function of spleen	Abnormalities, tumors, obstructions, cancer
Scrotal (testicular) scans	Study contents of scrotal sac including testes, epididymus, and spermatic cord	Epididymus orchitis, hydrocele, varicocele, testicular and spermatic cord torsion, tumors, hematomas
Gallium-67 scan	Radionuclide studies of entire body	Lymphomas, carcinomas of gastrointestinal tract, kidneys, uterus, stomach, testicles, metastatic and primary cancers of brain, lung, liver, and bone

Ultrasonography	• Cross-sectional gray-scale imaging
	  – Converts sound wave echoes into graphs or dots that form pictures of organs or blood vessels
	• Doppler method
	  – Converts Doppler shifts in the ultrasound signal into audible sounds or colored areas on the gray scale image
		• Neonate head: hydrocephalus, cerebral hemorrhages
		• Thyroid: goiters, tumors, cysts
		• Ocular: Graves' disease, hemorrhages, detached retina
		• Breast: tumors, cysts
		• Echocardiography: stenosis, prolapse, PE, thrombi, tetralogy of Fallot
		• Intravascular: identify candidates for CABG, thrombi, atherosclerotic lesions

Electrocardiogram (EKG or ECG)	Records electrical impulses that stimulate heart to contract	Arrythmias, Wolff-Parkinson-White syndrome, pericarditis
Electroencephalography (EEG)	Records electrical activity of the cerebral cortex	Lesions, hemorrhages, infarction, glioblastoma, abscesses, seizure disorders
Electromyography (EMG)	Evaluates and records electrical activity of skeletal muscles	Muscular dystrophy, myasthenia gravis, Guillain-Barré syndrome, diabetic neuropathy
Holter monitor	Continuously records electrical activity of the heart over an extended time	Arrhythmias, bradycardia, tachycardia, atrial fibrilation, atrial flutter

Common List of Lab Values (*continued*)

Lab	Purpose	Indication
Somatosensory evoked response (SER)	Monitors neurological and sensory pathways associated with pain and touch	Multiple sclerosis, Guillain-Barré syndrome, spinal cord injuries
Electrophysiology study (EPS)	Invasive study of heart's electrical function	Identifies heart defects and arrhythmias
Spirometry	Lung capacity	Lung condition
Pulmonary perfusion	Blood flow through pulmonary vessels	Lung condition
Pulmonary diffusion	O_2/CO_2 exchange	Lung condition
Pulmonary ventilation	Air exchange with atmosphere	Lung condition
Urine analysis	Measures several different components of urine, a waste product made by the kidneys Looks at clarity, color, odor, and specific gravity	• Renal or metabolic disorders, infections, or obstructions • Bilirubin: liver or bile ducts condition • Blood: infection, trauma, bleeding in kidneys • Glucose: diabetes mellitus, Cushing's syndrome, pituitary disorder, malfunction glucose reabsorption by kidneys • Ketone: diabetes, anorexia, diet low in carbohydrate and high in fat, starvation, fasting, excessive vomiting • Nitrites: UTI, *E. coli* • pH: UTI, CRF, hyperventilation, respiratory disease • Protein: nephrosis, glomerulonephritis, pyelonephritis, polycystic kidney disease, systemic UTI, diabetes, systemic lupus erythematosus • Urobilinogen: cirrhosis of liver, acute hepatitis, pernicious and hemolytic anemia, hemorrhage • Pregnancy test: checks for presence of human chorionic gonadotropin; trophoblastic disease (malignant neoplastic disease of uterus), and breast and ovarian cancer may give positive results • Phenylketonuria (PKU) urine test: routine test on newborns to test for PKU, which can cause brain damage

(continues)

Common List of Lab Values (*continued*)

Lab	Purpose	Indication

Fecal analysis	Assists with diagnosing certain conditions affecting the digestive tract	• Physical exam of feces
		  – Color, consistency, order, shape
		  – Gastrointestinal bleeding, ulcerative colitis, diverticulitis
		• Occult blood analysis
		  – Bright red—colorectal cancer, hemorrhoids, ulcerative colitis
		  – Black and tarry—upper gastrointestinal bleeding consistent with ulcers and varices

		• Leukocyte test
		  – Leukocytes in stool with diarrhea may be bacterial diarrhea
		  – Ulcerative colitis
		• Fat test
		  – Pancreatic enzyme deficiency
		• Parasite tests
		  – Protozoa infestations = dysentery = perforation and peritonitis
		  – Hookworm = anemia
		  – Pinworm = itching of skin around anus
		  – Tapeworm = diarrhea, epigastric pain, weight loss

Endoscopy studies	Allow for observation and biopsy of internal organs	• Bronchoscopy
		  – Abscesses, tumors, blockages, foreign bodies, inflammation
		• Mediastinoscopy
		  – TB, Hodgkin's disease, lymphoma, sarcoidosis, histoplasmosis
		• Thoracoscopy
		  – Plural effusion, infection, inflammation
		• Transesophageal echocardiography
		  – Aortic dissection, cardiac tumors, cardiac emboli, cardiomyopathy, myocardial ischemia, infarction, septal defects, valvular heart disease
		• Laparoscopy
		  – Pancreatitis, cirrhosis of liver, gallstones, pancreatic cancer
		• Endoscopic retrograde cholangiopancreatography
		  – Gallstones, pancreatic stones, cholangitis, pancreatitis, tumors, cysts, strictures of biliary and pancreatic ducts

Common List of Lab Values (*continued*)

Lab	Purpose	Indication
		• Proctoscopy, sigmoidoscopy, protosigmoidoscopy – Hemorrhoids, rectal prolapse, abscesses, fissures, polyps, tumors • Colonoscopy – Colon cancer, Crohn's disease, infectious colitis • Cystoscopy – Cancer of bladder, polyps, stones, prostatic hypertrophy and prostatitis • Urodynamic studies – Sensory or motor abnormalities that alter normal muscular functioning of lower urinary tract • Pelviscopy, gynecologic laparoscopy – Endometriosis, PID, ovarian cysts, tumors, fibroids • Colposcopy – Tumors, condylomata and HPV • Culdoscopy – Ectopic pregnancy, abnormal fallopian tubes, pelvic masses • Arthroscopy – Joint fractures, torn ligaments or cartilage, arthritis, synovitis • Amnioscopy – Amniotic fluid that contains meconium staining may be indicative of fetal hypoxia • Fetoscopy – Abnormal physical defects in fetus such as neural tube defects, blood disorders such as sickle cell anemia or hemophilia and skin disorders
Blood chemistry tests	Used to assess a wide range of conditions and the function of organs	• Enzymes – Proteins produced by living cells that influence the chemical reactions of the organism – Increases indicative of cell death or destruction – Linked to specific disease processes that affect specific organs

(continues)

Common List of Lab Values (*continued*)

Lab	Purpose	Indication
		• Acid phosphatase – Enzyme present in various tissues – Highest concentration known as prostatic acid phosphatase (PAP) – ↑ indicative of metastatic prostate cancer • Prostate-specific antigen (PSA) – Found in normal prostate cells – ↑ in prostate cancer • Alanine aminotransferase (ALT) – Also known as serum glutamic pyruvic transaminase (SGPT) – Found in liver with lower concentrations in heart, muscle, and kidney – ↑ associated with liver dysfunction • Alkaline phosphatase (ALP) – Found in liver, bone, and epithelium of all bile ducts – Affected by age and gender – ↑ associated with bone diseases: Paget's disease, osteomalacia, metastatic bone cancer, rickets, sarcomas arising from bone, healing fractures • Asparate aminotransferase (AST) – Also known as serum glutamic-oxaloacetic transaminase (SGOT) – ↑ associated with MI and various liver diseases • Creatine kinase (CK) – Also known as creatine phosphokinase (CPK) – Found in heart and skeletal muscles and, to a lesser degree, brain – ↑ indicative of MI, skeletal muscle disease, and brain injury or trauma – Lactic acid dehydrogenase (LD, LDH) – Found in heart, liver, kidneys, skeletal muscle, heart, brain, and lungs – ↑ associated MI • Lipase – Produced by pancreas and assists in breakdown of triglycerides – ↑ associated with acute and chronic pancreatitis, pancreatic cancer

Common List of Lab Values (*continued*)

Lab	Purpose	Indication

		• Hormones
		  – Specialized chemical substances that are produced and secreted by endocrine cells and tissue, circulate in blood, affect the metabolic activity of specific target cells and organs
		  – ↑ or ↓ affect the function of the target cells and organs
		• Antidiuretic hormone (ADH)
		  – Manufactured by hypothalamus, secreted by posterior lobe of pituitary gland, and controls amount of H_2O reabsorbed by kidneys
		  – ↑ serum levels give rise to syndrome of inappropriate ADH secretion (SIADH) conditions marked by high levels of ADH
		    • Diseases associated include cancers of lung, thymus, pancreas, urologic tract, lymphomas, leukemia, pulmonary disease, brain tumors
		    • ↓ seen in diabetes insipidus
		• Human chorionic gonadotropin (HCG)
		  – Found in pregnant women as early as 10 days after conception
		  – ↑ ectopic pregnancy, hydatidiform mole of uterus, uterine and testicular cancers
		  – ↓ seen in threatened abortion, incomplete abortion, intrauterine fetal death
		• Cortisol
		  – Most abundant glucocorticoid hormone secreted by adrenal cortex, which plays a role in maintaining blood glucose levels, metabolizing food, functioning as anti-inflammatory agent
		  – ↑ found in Cushing's syndrome, hyperthyroidism, adrenal adenoma, overproduction of adrenocorticotropic hormone (ACTH)
		  – ↓ seen in Addison's disease, hypopituitarism, hypothyroidism, hepatitis, cirrhosis
		
		(continues)

Common List of Lab Values (*continued*)

Lab	Purpose	Indication

		• Gastrin
		  – Produced and secreted by specialized cells of stomach
		  – Aids in digestion and maintenance of stomach pH
		  – ↑ indicates Zollinger-Ellison syndrome (stomach produces excess hydrochloric acid), gastrin-producing pancreatic tumor, hyperplasia of G-cells of stomach, gastric cancer, pernicious anemia
		• Growth hormone (GH)
		  – Also known as somatotropin and somatotropic hormone (STH)
		  – Released by anterior lobe of pituitary gland and is essential for growth
		  – ↑ can lead to gigantism in children, acromegaly in adults
		  – ↓ result in premature closure of epiphyseal disks, which leads to dwarfism
		• Testosterone
		  – Responsible for sperm production
		  – ↑ in men can be caused by adrenal hyperplasia and adrenocortical or testicular tumors
		  – ↓ in males associated with cryptorchidism, hypogonadism, and Klinefelter's syndrome (XXY or XXY syndrome—condition caused by a chromosome aneuploidy [chromosome problem] causing small testicles and reduced fertility)
		• Thyroid-stimulating hormone (TSH)
		  – Secreted by anterior lobe of pituitary gland
		  – ↑ indicative hypothyroidism, thyroiditis, lack of thyroid growth or development
		  – ↓ associated with secondary hypothyroidism, hyperthyroidism, and pituitary dysfunction
		  – Stimulates thyroid to produce and secrete thyroxine, triiodothyronine, and calcitonin
		  – Thyroxine (T_4) ↑ associated with Graves' disease, Plummer's disease, thyrotoxicosis

Common List of Lab Values (*continued*)

Lab	Purpose	Indication
		— Triiodothyronine (T_3) ↑ associated with hyperthyroidism, T_3 thyrotoxicosis, thyroiditis, and thyroid tumor — Calcitonin ↑ indicative of medullary cancer of thyroid, oat cell cancer of lung, breast and pancreatic cancers, pernicious anemia • Ferritin — Storage form of iron, formed in intestine, stored in liver, spleen, and bone marrow — ↑ megaloblastic, and hemolytic anemia, alcoholism, breast cancer, Hodgkin's disease — ↓ iron-deficiency anemia, severe protein deficiency, patients undergoing hemodialysis • Transferrin test; total iron binding capacity (TIBC) — Iron in blood is bound to transferrin, a protein to transport iron — ↑ and/or ↓ of TIBC, serum iron, and transferrin saturation associated with various anemias — ↓ associated with iron-deficiency anemia

Infectious disease and immunodiagnostic blood test	Tests for various infectious diseases	• Agglutination test
		— Microhemagglutination (MHA)
		  • Clumping of RBC
		— Latex agglutination
		  • Uses latex component that allows agglutination
		— Hemagglutination inhibition test
		  • RBC prevented from clumping
		  • Positive results indicates absence of agglutination
		• Fluorescent immunoassay (FIA)
		— Direct fluorescent antibody (DFA)
		  • Antigen detection
		— Indirect fluorescent antibody (IFA)
		  • Antigen or antibody detection
		• Enzyme immunoassay
		— Enzyme immunoassay (EIA)
		  • Detect antibodies or antigens in viral or parasitic diseases
		
		(*continues*)

Common List of Lab Values (*continued*)

Lab	Purpose	Indication

		– Enzyme-linked immunosorbent assay (ELISA)
		  • Detect antibodies or antigens in viral or parasitic diseases
		• Radioimmunoassay (RIA)
		  – Identify viral diseases
		  – RIA procedures are being replaced with EIA procedures
		• Syphilis detection tests (*Treponema pallidum*)
		  – Detects reagin
		    • Reagin
		      – Antibody-like substance found in serum of individuals with syphillis
		    • Venereal Disease Research Laboratory (VDRL)
		    • Rapid plasma reagin (RPR)
		  – Detects treponemal antibodies
		    • Fluorescent treponemal antibody absorption (FTA-ABS)
		    • Microhemagglutination *Treponema pallidum* antibody (MHA-TP)
		• Lyme disease (*Borrelia burgdorferi*)
		  – Western blot assay
		  – IFA
		  – ELISA
		  – Polymerase chain reaction (PCR)
		  – Legionnaires' disease test
		  – Also known as legionellosis, Legionnaires' pneumonia, *Legionella pneumonophila*
		  – Acute airborne bacterial disease that attacks respiratory system
		  – Diagnosis
		    • IFA (test of choice)
		    • ELISA
		• Chlamydia antibody test
		  – Chlamydia infections (*Chlamydia trachomatis*) are most frequent sexually transmitted disease and most frequent cause of sterility
		  – Acute airborne bacterial disease that attacks respiratory system

Common List of Lab Values (*continued*)

Lab	Purpose	Indication

		– Diagnosis
		  • IFA
		  • PCR
		  • Complement fixation (CF) test
		    – Identifies viral antibodies (primarily) and fungal antibodies
		    – Negative result indicates absence of antibody being tested and positive indicates antibody being tested is present
		• Streptococcal antibody test
		  – Antistreptolysin O titer (ASO)
		    • Detects antibodies to streptolysin O
		    • Diagnosis
		      – Rheumatic fever, glomerulonephritis, endocarditis, scarlet fever
		  – Streptozyme
		    • Identifies antibodies to several enzymes
		  – AntiDNase B (ADB)
		    • Detects antibodies to DNase B
		    • Diagnosis
		      – Streptococcal pyoderma, streptococcal pharyngitis
		• Infectious mononucleosis test
		  – Acute viral infection caused by Epstein-Barr virus (EBV)
		  – EBV causes an increase in heterophil antibody formation, which is diagnostic for infectious mononucleosis
		• Rubella antibody test
		  – German measles
		  – Diagnosis
		    • Complement fixation
		    • ELISA
		    • Latex agglutination
		    • Hemagglutination inhibition test
		• Hepatitis A
		  – Infectious hepatitis transmitted via fecal–oral route
		  – Diagnosis via RIA and ELISA
		
		(*continues*)

Common List of Lab Values (*continued*)

Lab	Purpose	Indication
		– Acute hepatitis A • Indentifies two separate antibodies; both must be present – IgM antibodies against hepatitis A virus (IgM anti-HAV) – Total antibody against hepatitis A virus (total anti-HAV) – Chronic or convalescent stage of hepatitis A • IgG antibodies against hepatitis A virus (IgG anti-HAV) appear after increase in IgM anti-HAV and can be detected for more than 10 years • Hepatitis B – Serum hepatitis caused by hepatitis B virus (HBV) transmitted via saliva, blood and serum, semen, and vaginal fluids – Associated with occupations in frequent contact with blood and blood products – Diagnosis via RIA and ELISA • Three antigen antibody substances – Hepatitis B surface antigen (HBsAg) – Antibody to HBsAg (anti-HBc) – Hepatitis B envelope antigen (HBeAg) and antibody to HBeAg (anti-HBe) • Hepatitis C – Non-A, non-B hepatitis – Caused by hepatitis C virus and transmitted by percutaneous exposure to contaminated blood and plasma derivatives – Diagnosis via EIA • Detects anti-HCV

Common List of Lab Values (*continued*)

Lab	Purpose	Indication
		• Human immunodeficiency virus (HIV-1, HIV-2); acquired immunodeficiency syndrome (AIDS) – AIDS • Late clinical stage HIV • HIV-1 most common in the United States • HIV-2 predominantly in West Africa – Caused by hepatitis C virus and transmitted by percutaneous exposure to contaminated blood and plasma derivatives – Diagnosis • EIA • If ELISA is positive, then Western blot is performed • Herpes simplex – Herpes simplex 1 (HSV-1) • Fever blisters, cold sores – Herpes simplex 2 (HSV-2) • Sexually transmitted disease of urogenital tract – Diagnosis • EIA • IFA • Cytomegalovirus (CMV) antibody test – Human viral pathogen that belongs to herpes virus family – IFA, ELISA, and latex agglutination detect CMV-specific IgM antibody • TORCH – Pregnancy screening test for toxoplasmosis, rubella, cytomegalovirus, and herpes virus • C-reactive protein (CRP) test – CRP antibody detected to evaluate inflammatory diseases and conditions that involve tissue necrosis • Rheumatoid factor (RF) test – Rheumatoid factor is an autoantibody often found in serum of rheumatoid arthritis – Also detected in patients with lupus, hepatitis, scleroderma, subacute bacterial endocarditis, TB

(continues)

Common List of Lab Values (*continued*)

Lab	Purpose	Indication
		– Sheep cell agglutination or latex fixation test usually performed to detect rheumatoid factor • Anti-nuclear antibody (ANA) test – ANA antibody reacts against cellular nuclear material – Presence is highly indicative of systemic lupus erythematosus • Blood group – ABO grouping • Rh grouping – Detects presence of absence of Rh antigen on red blood cell membrane – Identifies blood as Rh negative or positive next to A and B antigen blood grouping
Culture and sensitivity tests	A culture is done to find out what kind of organism is causing an illness or infection. A sensitivity test checks what kind of medicine, such as an antibiotic, will work best to treat the illness or infection.	• Blood culture – *E. coli* (food poison, gastroenteritis, urinary tract infections, pneumonia, septicemia, and neonatal meningitis), *Staphylococcus epidermis* (nosocomial bacteremia), *Staphylococcus aureus* (MRSA), *Listeria monocytogenes* (food poisoning), *Neisseria meningitidis*, *Salmonella*, and *Klebsiella* (nosocomial wound infections, pneumoniae) • Cerebrospinal fluid culture – *E. coli, Staphylococcus aureus, Haemophilus influenzae* (bacteremia, pneumonia, and acute bacterial meningitis), *Pseudomonas aeruginosa, pneumococci, meningococci, streptococci* • Genitalia and anal cultures – *Chlamydia, Candida, Mycoplasma, Gardnerella vaginalis, Neisseria gonorrhoeae, Treponema pallidum, Trichomonas vaginalis* • Nose and throat cultures – *Staphylococcus epidermis* (nosocomial bacteremia), *Staphylococcus aureus* (MRSA), *Propionibacterium acnes* (acne), *Microsporum, Trichophyton, Epidermophyton* (ringworm, athlete's foot)

Common List of Lab Values (*continued*)

Lab	Purpose	Indication

		• Sputum culture
		  – *Haemophilus influenzae, Klebsiella pneumoniae, Micobacterium tuberculosis, Candida, Aspergillus, Corynebacterium diphtheriae, Bordetella pertusis*
		• Stool culture
		  – *Salmonella* (typhoid fever, paratyphoid fever, food poisoning), *Shigella* (dysentery), *Campylobacter* (food poisoning, diarrhea), *Yersinia, Staphylococcus, E. coli, Ascaris* (hookworm)

		• Wound culture – *Staphylococcus aureus, Klebsiella, Proteus, Pseudomonas* (peritonitis, endophthalmitis, septicemia and bacteremia, pneumonia), *Mycobacterium* (TB, leprosy)

Amniotic fluid and cerebrospinal fluid tests	Various tests used to determine various diagnoses	• Amniotic fluid
		  – Amniocentesis
		    • Fetal sex determination
		    • Fetal chromosome analysis
		      – Down syndrome, hemophilia, cystic fibrosis
		    • Alpha-fetoprotein and acetylcholinesterase levels
		      – Anencephaly, spina bifida, hydrocephalus
		• Cerebrospinal fluid
		  – Meningitis
		  – Encephalitis
		  – Guillain-Barré syndrome
		  – Neurosyphilis

Other body fluids	Various tests used to diagnose various conditions	• Effusion tests
		  – Excessive accumulation of fluid in body cavities lined with serous or synovial membranes
		  – Named for their associated cavities
		  – Sample obtained via needle aspiration
		• Pericardial effusion
		  – Hemorrhagic pericarditis, metastatic cancer, anueurysm, TB

(*continues*)

Common List of Lab Values (*continued*)

Lab	Purpose	Indication
		• Peritoneal effusion – Blocked thoracic lymph ducts, trauma, cirrhosis, pancreatitis, tuberculosis peritonitis • Pleural effusion – Emphysema, pneumonia, pulmonary TB, pulmonary infarction, cancer, thoracic trauma • Synovial effusion – Arthritis, gout, synovitis, osteoarthritis, degenerative joint disease • Gastric secretion analysis – Aplastic, hyperchormic and pernicious anemia, Zollinger-Ellison syndrome • Semen fertility – Decrease indicates infertility

TEST YOUR KNOWLEDGE

1. A patient is admitted with a diagnosis of pneumoconiosis. Which of the following may be used as a definitive diagnostic test?
   a. Pulmonary device test
   b. Pulmonary function test
   c. Bronchodilators
   d. Bronchoinhalers

2. A patient is admitted with chest pain. The physician wants to rule out angina pectoris. He performs an ECG. What would the ECG show?
   a. Low HDL
   b. High HDL
   c. Ischemia
   d. Increased blood flow

3. A patient is admitted with angina pectoris. Which of the following drugs may the patient be prescribed?
   a. Fosomax
   b. Procardia
   c. Premarin
   d. Codeine

4. A patient is admitted with angina pectoris. From which of the following drug groups may the patient receive his or her prescription?
   a. Calcium-channel blockers
   b. COX-2 Inhibitors
   c. Antiemetics
   d. Antidyskinetics

5. A patient is diagnosed with arthritis. Which of the following drugs might be prescribed?
   a. Robaxin
   b. Flonase
   c. Celebrex
   d. Albuterol

6. A patient is experiencing nausea from a Caribbean cruise. Which drug group might the patient receive a prescription from?
   a. GABA agents
   b. Antiadrenergics
   c. Ophthalmic prostaglandins
   d. Antiemetics

7. A pulmonary function test may be used to rule out which of the following diagnoses?
   a. Goiter
   b. Urologic pathologies
   c. Ophthalmic neurosis
   d. Bronchiectasis

8. Abnormal results in the thrombin time may be indicative of:
   a. multiple myeloma.
   b. bronchiectasis.
   c. decreased oxygen.
   d. pneumoconiosis.

9. ACE inhibitors are used to treat which condition?
   a. Asthma
   b. Diabetes
   c. Psychosis
   d. Hypertension

10. Increased plasma bilirubin levels are associated with:
    a. hemolytic anemias.
    b. neuropathy.
    c. diabetes.
    d. renal disease.

11. Because the lung tissue is spongy, the chest X-ray is:
    a. not a good radiography study to rule out pneumonia.
    b. a good radiography study to rule out pneumonia.
    c. inconsistent with diagnosing lung diseases.
    d. incapable of diagnosing lung diseases.

12. A patient with cretinism on thyroid scan would show a(n) _____ in _____ uptake.
    a. decrease; iodine
    b. increase; iodine
    c. decrease; sodium
    d. increase; sodium

13. A physician may prescribe _____ to treat patients with diabetes insipidus.
    a. SSRIs
    b. statins
    c. sulfonylureas
    d. vasopressin injections

14. An increase in the fibrinogen assay test results may indicate which condition?
    a. Hepatitis
    b. Diabetes insipidus
    c. Anemia
    d. Hypertension

15. Thiazolidinediones may be used to treat:
    a. depression.
    b. high cholesterol.
    c. diabetes mellitus.
    d. asthma.

16. Which of the following is used to treat cretinism?
    a. Potassium iodide
    b. Alpha-adrenergic blockers
    c. Biguanides
    d. Thyroid hormone replacement

17. Beta-adrenergic blocking drugs are used to treat which condition?
    a. Anxiety
    b. Premature labor
    c. Hypertension
    d. Alcoholism

18. A physician may use _____ to treat a patient with a diagnosis of urethritis.
    a. potassium
    b. antibiotics
    c. diuretics
    d. anticoagulants

19. Increased BUN levels are usually caused by inadequate excretion due to what condition?
    a. Alcoholism
    b. Cardiac arrhythmias
    c. Renal disease
    d. Liver disease

20. An abnormal intravenous pyelography (IVP) result may be obtained if the patient has a condition associated with the:
    a. heart.
    b. veins.
    c. kidneys.
    d. lungs.

21. Which of these tests is a primary screen for diabetes mellitus?
    a. Liver enzymes
    b. Fasting blood sugar test
    c. BUN
    d. ELISA

22. For which diagnosis might ampicillin, cephalosporins, and sulfonamides be prescribed?
    a. Electrolyte imbalance
    b. Crohn's disease
    c. CVA
    d. UTI

23. ACE inhibitors may be prescribed to treat which condition?
    a. Hypertension
    b. Congestive heart failure
    c. Angina pectoris
    d. High cholesterol

24. Nitroglycerin may be prescribed to treat which condition?
    a. Hypertension
    b. Congestive heart failure
    c. Angina pectoris
    d. High cholesterol

25. Beta blockers may be prescribed to treat which condition?
    a. Electrolyte imbalance
    b. Myocardial infarction
    c. Diabetes mellitus
    d. High cholesterol

26. An ECG is used to diagnose:
  a. heart conditions.
  b. renal conditions.
  c. cerebrovascular accidents.
  d. bronchospasms.

27. Epinephrine is used to treat:
  a. heart conditions.
  b. renal conditions.
  c. cerebrovascular accidents.
  d. bronchospasms.

28. A KUB is used to diagnose:
  a. heart conditions.
  b. renal conditions.
  c. cerebrovascular accidents.
  d. bronchospasms.

29. A cerebral angiography is used to diagnose:
  a. heart conditions.
  b. renal conditions.
  c. cerebrovascular accidents.
  d. bronchospasms.

30. Elevated triglyceride levels are associated with:
  a. an increased risk for atherosclerosis.
  b. a diet high in vegetable fats.
  c. non-insulin-dependent diabetes mellitus.
  d. decreased HDL in postmenopausal women.

31. An increase in blood potassium levels may be indicative of what condition?
  a. Diabetes
  b. Bronchospasms
  c. CVA
  d. Renal failure

32. _____ is not an antipsychotic drug.
  a. Thorazine
  b. Haldol
  c. Zyprexa
  d. Theophyline

33. Variations from normal in the spirometry may indicate which diagnosis?
  a. Cancer of the sigmoid colon
  b. Bronchitis
  c. Alcohol dependence
  d. Cystic fibrosis

34. Pharmacokinetics refers to a patient's _____ of medication.
  a. refusal
  b. acceptance
  c. metabolism
  d. route

35. Demerol may be prescribed for:
  a. emesis.
  b. severe pain.
  c. blocking drug absorption.
  d. inflammation.

36. Alpha-adrenergic blocking drugs stimulate:
  a. vasoconstriction.
  b. vasodilation.
  c. hunger.
  d. dreams.

37. An increase in the activated partial thromboplastin time (aPTT) indicates a:
  a. bleeding disorder.
  b. renal condition.
  c. liver condition.
  d. psychotic episode.

38. Decreased plasma BUN levels are associated with which condition?
  a. Glomerulonephritis
  b. Acute tubular necrosis
  c. Liver failure
  d. Chronic gout

39. An abnormal bronchoscopy test may indicate the presence of a(n):
  a. goiter.
  b. heart condition.
  c. ulcer.
  d. respiratory condition.

40. Hyponatremia is usually indicative of which condition?
    a. Cystic fibrosis
    b. Diabetes mellitus
    c. Diabetes incipidus
    d. Excess body water

41. NSAIDs are used to treat:
    a. asthma.
    b. hypertension.
    c. dementia.
    d. arthritis.

42. A patient diagnosed with leukocytopenia would show a(n) _____ in _____.
    a. increase; WBC
    b. increase; RBC
    c. decrease; WBC
    d. decrease; RBC

43. A patient diagnosed with leukocytosis would demonstrate a(n) _____ in _____.
    a. increase; WBC
    b. increase; RBC
    c. decrease; WBC
    d. decrease; RBC

44. SSRIs may be used to treat:
    a. hypertension.
    b. arthritis.
    c. depression.
    d. UTI.

45. Ditropan is categorized with:
    a. statins.
    b. urinary antispasmodics.
    c. sulfonylureas.
    d. ACE inhibitors.

46. Digoxin may be used to treat:
    a. an ulcer.
    b. CHF.
    c. excessive fluid retention.
    d. high cholesterol.

47. Nitroglycerin may be used to treat:
    a. an ulcer.
    b. angina.
    c. excessive fluid retention.
    d. high cholesterol.

48. Intravenous vasodilators may be used to:
    a. treat an ulcer.
    b. treat a hemorrhage.
    c. induce labor.
    d. treat malignant hypertension.

49. Which of the following may be prescribed for lowering cholesterol?
    a. Zocar
    b. Zithromax
    c. Zantac
    d. Xanax

50. Increased plasma creatinine levels are associated with:
    a. liver failure due to cirrhosis.
    b. early stages of muscular dystrophy.
    c. excessive loss of kidney function.
    d. ingestion of creosote.

Clinical Classification Systems

ICD-9-CM OFFICIAL GUIDELINE FOR CODING AND REPORTING

Conventions, general coding guidelines

   The conventions, general guidelines and chapter-specific guidelines are applicable to all healthcare settings unless otherwise indicated. The conventions and instructions of the classification take precedence over guidelines.

A. Conventions for the ICD-9-CM

   The conventions for the ICD-9-CM are the general rules for use of the classification independent of the guidelines. These conventions are incorporated within the index and tabular of the ICD-9-CM as instructional notes. The conventions are as follows:

1. Format:
   The ICD-9-CM uses an indented format for ease in reference

2. Abbreviations

   a. Index abbreviations
      NEC "Not elsewhere classifiable"
      This abbreviation in the index represents "other specified" when a specific code is not available for a condition the index directs the coder to the "other specified" code in the tabular.

   b. Tabular abbreviations
      NEC "Not elsewhere classifiable"
      This abbreviation in the tabular represents "other specified." When a specific code is not available for a condition the tabular includes an NEC entry under a code to identify the code as the "other specified" code.
      (See Section I.A.5.a., "Other" codes")
      NOS "Not otherwise specified"
      This abbreviation is the equivalent of unspecified.
      (See Section I.A.5.b., "Unspecified" codes)

3. Punctuation

   a. [ ] Brackets are used in the Tabular List to enclose synonyms, alternative wording or explanatory phrases. Brackets are used in the index to identify manifestation codes.
      (See Section I.A.6., "Etiology/manifestations")

    b. ( ) Parentheses are used in both the index and tabular to enclose supplementary words that may be present or absent in the statement of a disease or procedure without affecting the code number to which it is assigned. The terms within the parentheses are referred to as nonessential modifiers.

    c. : Colons are used in the Tabular List after an incomplete term, which needs one or more of the modifiers following the colon to make it assignable to a given category.

4. Includes and Excludes Notes and Inclusion Terms

    a. Includes: This note appears immediately under a three-digit code title to further define, or give examples of, the content of the category.

    b. Excludes: An excludes note under a code indicates that the terms excluded from the code are to be coded elsewhere. In some cases, the codes for the excluded terms should not be used in conjunction with the code from which it is excluded. An example of this is a congenital condition excluded from an acquired form of the same condition. The congenital and acquired codes should not be used together. In other cases, the excluded terms may be used together with an excluded code. An example of this is when fractures of different bones are coded to different codes. Both codes may be used together if both types of fractures are present.

    c. Inclusion terms: List of terms is included under certain four- and five-digit codes. These terms are the conditions for which that code number is to be used. The terms may be synonyms of the code title, or, in the case of "other specified" codes, the terms are a list of the various conditions assigned to that code. The inclusion terms are not necessarily exhaustive. Additional terms found only in the index may also be assigned to a code.

5. Other and Unspecified Codes

    a. "Other" codes

    Codes titled "other" or "other specified" (usually a code with a 4th digit 8 or 5th digit 9 for diagnosis codes) are for use when the information in the medical record provides detail for which a specific code does not exist. Index entries with NEC in the line designate "other" codes in the tabular. These index entries represent specific disease entities for which no specific code exists so the term is included within an "other" code.

    b. "Unspecified" codes

    Codes (usually a code with a 4th digit 9 or 5th digit 0 for diagnosis codes) titled "unspecified" are for use when the information in the medical record is insufficient to assign a more specific code.

6. Etiology/manifestation convention ("code first," "use additional code," and "in diseases classified elsewhere" notes)

    a. Certain conditions have both an underlying etiology and multiple body system manifestations due to the underlying etiology. For such conditions, the ICD-9-CM has a coding convention that requires the underlying condition be sequenced first followed by the manifestation.

    b. Wherever such a combination exists, there is a "use additional code" note at the etiology code, and a "code first" note at the manifestation code. These instructional notes indicate the proper sequencing order of the codes, etiology followed by manifestation.

    c. In most cases the manifestation codes will have in the code title, "in diseases classified elsewhere." Codes with this title are a component of the etiology/manifestation convention. The code title indicates that it is a manifestation code. "In diseases classified elsewhere" codes are never permitted to be used as first listed or principal diagnosis codes. They must be used in conjunction with an underlying condition code and they must be listed following the underlying condition.

    d. There are manifestation codes that do not have "in diseases classified elsewhere" in the title. For such codes a "use additional code" note will still be present and the rules for sequencing apply.

    e. In addition to the notes in the tabular, these conditions also have a specific index entry structure. In the index both conditions are listed together with the etiology code first followed by the manifestation codes in brackets. The code in brackets is always to be sequenced second.

    The most commonly used etiology/manifestation combinations are the codes for Diabetes mellitus, category 250. For each code under category 250 there is a use additional code note for the manifestation that is specific for that particular diabetic manifestation. Should a patient have more than one manifestation of diabetes, more than one code from category 250 may be used with as many manifestation codes as are needed to fully describe the patient's complete diabetic condition. The category 250 diabetes codes should be sequenced first, followed by the manifestation codes.

    f. "Code first" and "Use additional code" notes are also used as sequencing rules in the classification for certain codes that are not part of an etiology/manifestation combination.

    (See Section I.B.9., "Multiple coding for a single condition")

7. "And"

    a. The word "and" should be interpreted to mean either "and" or "or" when it appears in a title.

8. "With"

    a. The word "with" should be interpreted to mean "associated with" or "due to" when it appears in a code title, the Alphabetic Index, or an instructional note in the Tabular List.

    b. The word "with" in the Alphabetic Index is sequenced immediately following the main term, not in alphabetical order.

9. "See" and "See Also"

    a. The "see" instruction following a main term in the index indicates that another term should be referenced. It is necessary to go to the main term referenced with the "see" note to locate the correct code.

    b. A "see also" instruction following a main term in the index instructs that there is another main term that may also be referenced that may provide additional index entries that may be useful. It is not necessary to follow the "see also" note when the original main term provides the necessary code.

B. General Coding Guidelines

1. Use of Both Alphabetic Index and Tabular List

    a. Use both the Alphabetic Index and the Tabular List when locating and assigning a code. Reliance on only the Alphabetic Index or the Tabular List leads to errors in code assignments and less specificity in code selection.

2. Locate each term in the Alphabetic Index
    a. Locate each term in the Alphabetic Index and verify the code selected in the Tabular List. Read and be guided by instructional notations that appear in both the Alphabetic Index and the Tabular List.
3. Level of Detail in Coding
    a. Diagnosis and procedure codes are to be used at their highest number of digits available.
    b. ICD-9-CM diagnosis codes are composed of codes with three, four, or five digits. Codes with three digits are included in ICD-9-CM as the heading of a category of codes that may be further subdivided by the use of fourth and/or fifth digits, which provide greater detail.
    c. A three-digit code is to be used only if it is not further subdivided.
    d. Where fourth-digit subcategories and/or fifth-digit subclassifications are provided, they must be assigned. A code is invalid if it has not been coded to the full number of digits required for that code. For example, acute myocardial infarction, code 410, has fourth digits that describe the location of the infarction (e.g., 410.2, Of inferolateral wall), and fifth digits that identify the episode of care. It would be incorrect to report a code in category 410 without a fourth and fifth digit.
    e. ICD-9-CM Volume 3 procedure codes are composed of codes with either three or four digits. Codes with two digits are included in ICD-9-CM as the heading of a category of codes that may be further subdivided by the use of third and/or fourth digits, which provide greater detail.
4. Code or codes from 001.0 through V91.99
    a. The appropriate code or codes from 001.0 through V91.99 must be used to identify diagnoses, symptoms, conditions, problems, complaints, or other reason(s) for the encounter/visit.
5. Selection of codes 001.0 through 999.9
    a. The selection of codes 001.0 through 999.9 will frequently be used to describe the reason for the admission/encounter. These codes are from the section of ICD-9-CM for the classification of diseases and injuries (e.g., infectious and parasitic diseases; neoplasms; symptoms, signs, and ill-defined conditions, etc.).
6. Signs and Symptoms
    a. Codes that describe symptoms and signs, as opposed to diagnoses, are acceptable for reporting purposes when a related definitive diagnosis has not been established (confirmed) by the provider. Chapter 16 of ICD-9-CM, Symptoms, Signs, and Ill-defined conditions (codes 780.0–799.9) contain many, but not all codes for symptoms.
7. Conditions that are an integral part of a disease process
    a. Signs and symptoms that are associated routinely with a disease process should not be assigned as additional codes, unless otherwise instructed by the classification.
8. Conditions that are not an integral part of a disease process
    a. Additional signs and symptoms that may not be associated routinely with a disease process should be coded when present.
9. Multiple coding for a single condition
    a. In addition to the etiology/manifestation convention that requires two codes to fully describe a single condition that affects multiple

body systems, there are other single conditions that also require more than one code. "Use additional code" notes are found in the tabular at codes that are not part of an etiology/manifestation pair where a secondary code is useful to fully describe a condition. The sequencing rule is the same as the etiology/manifestation pair— "use additional code" indicates that a secondary code should be added.

b. For example, for infections that are not included in Chapter 1, a secondary code from category 041, Bacterial infection in conditions classified elsewhere and of unspecified site, may be required to identify the bacterial organism causing the infection. A "use additional code" note will normally be found at the infectious disease code, indicating a need for the organism code to be added as a secondary code.

c. "Code first" notes are also under certain codes that are not specifically manifestation codes but may be due to an underlying cause. When a "code first" note is present and an underlying condition is present the underlying condition should be sequenced first.

d. "Code, if applicable, any causal condition first," notes indicate that this code may be assigned as a principal diagnosis when the causal condition is unknown or not applicable. If a causal condition is known, then the code for that condition should be sequenced as the principal or first-listed diagnosis.

e. Multiple codes may be needed for late effects, complication codes and obstetric codes to more fully describe a condition. See the specific guidelines for these conditions for further instruction.

10. Acute and Chronic Conditions

a. If the same condition is described as both acute (subacute) and chronic, and separate subentries exist in the Alphabetic Index at the same indentation level, code both and sequence the acute (subacute) code first.

11. Combination Code

a. A combination code is a single code used to classify:
Two diagnoses, or
A diagnosis with an associated secondary process (manifestation)
A diagnosis with an associated complication

b. Combination codes are identified by referring to subterm entries in the Alphabetic Index and by reading the inclusion and exclusion notes in the Tabular List.

c. Assign only the combination code when that code fully identifies the diagnostic conditions involved or when the Alphabetic Index so directs. Multiple coding should not be used when the classification provides a combination code that clearly identifies all of the elements documented in the diagnosis. When the combination code lacks necessary specificity in describing the manifestation or complication, an additional code should be used as a secondary code.

12. Late Effects

a. A late effect is the residual effect (condition produced) after the acute phase of an illness or injury has terminated. There is no time limit on when a late effect code can be used. The residual may be apparent early, such as in cerebrovascular accident cases, or it may occur months or years later, such as that due to a previous injury. Coding of late effects generally requires two codes sequenced in the following order: The condition or nature of the late effect is sequenced first. The late effect code is sequenced second.

b. Exceptions to the above guidelines are those instances where the late effect code has been expanded (at the fourth- and fifth-digit levels) to include the manifestation(s) or the classification instructs otherwise. The code for the acute phase of an illness or injury that led to the late effect is never used with a code for the late effect.

13. Impending or Threatened Condition

    a. Code any condition described at the time of discharge as "impending" or "threatened" as follows:

    If it did occur, code as confirmed diagnosis.

    If it did not occur, reference the Alphabetic Index to determine if the condition has a subentry term for "impending" or "threatened" and also reference main term entries for "Impending" and for "Threatened."

    b. If the subterms are listed, assign the given code.

    c. If the subterms are not listed, code the existing underlying condition(s) and not the condition described as impending or threatened.

14. Reporting Same Diagnosis Code More Than Once

    a. Each unique ICD-9-CM diagnosis code may be reported only once for an encounter. This applies to bilateral conditions or two different conditions classified to the same ICD-9-CM diagnosis code.

15. Admissions/Encounters for Rehabilitation

    a. When the purpose for the admission/encounter is rehabilitation, sequence the appropriate V code from category V57, Care involving use of rehabilitation procedures, as the principal/first-listed diagnosis. The code for the condition for which the service is being performed should be reported as an additional diagnosis.

    b. Only one code from category V57 is required. Code V57.89, Other specified rehabilitation procedures, should be assigned if more than one type of rehabilitation is performed during a single encounter.

    c. A procedure code should be reported to identify each type of rehabilitation therapy actually performed.

16. Documentation for BMI and Pressure Ulcer Stages

    a. For the body mass index (BMI) and pressure ulcer stage codes, code assignment may be based on medical record documentation from clinicians who are not the patient's provider (i.e., physician or other qualified healthcare practitioner legally accountable for establishing the patient's diagnosis), since this information is typically documented by other clinicians involved in the care of the patient (e.g., a dietitian often documents the BMI and nurses often documents the pressure ulcer stages). However, the associated diagnosis (such as overweight, obesity, or pressure ulcer) must be documented by the patient's provider. If there is conflicting medical record documentation, either from the same clinician or different clinicians, the patient's attending provider should be queried for clarification. The BMI and pressure ulcer stage codes should only be reported as secondary diagnoses. As with all other secondary diagnosis codes, the BMI and pressure ulcer stage codes should only be assigned when they meet the definition of a reportable additional diagnosis (see Section III, Reporting Additional Diagnoses).

17. Syndromes

    a. Follow the Alphabetic Index guidance when coding syndromes. In the absence of index guidance, assign codes for the documented manifestations of the syndrome.

18. Documentation of Complications of Care

    a. Code assignment is based on the provider's documentation of the relationship between the condition and the care or procedure. The guideline extends to any complications of care, regardless of the chapter the code is located in. It is important to note that not all conditions that occur during or following medical care or surgery are classified as complications. There must be a cause-and-effect relationship between the care provided and the condition, and an indication in the documentation that it is a complication. Query the provider for clarification, if the complication is not clearly documented.

THE ICD-10 TRANSITION: AN INTRODUCTION[1]

    a. The ICD-9 code sets used to report medical diagnoses and inpatient procedures will be replaced by ICD-10 code sets. This fact sheet provides background on the ICD-10 transition, general guidance on how to prepare for it, and resources for more information.

    b. About ICD-10

        i. ICD-10-CM/PCS (International Classification of Diseases, 10th Edition, Clinical Modification/Procedure Coding System) consists of two parts:

            1. ICD-10-CM for diagnosis coding

            2. ICD-10-PCS for inpatient procedure coding

        ii. ICD-10-CM is for use in all U.S. healthcare settings. Diagnosis coding under ICD-10-CM uses three to seven digits instead of the three to five digits used with ICD-9-CM, but the format of the code sets is similar.

        iii. ICD-10-PCS is for use in U.S. inpatient hospital settings only. ICD-10-PCS uses seven alphanumeric digits instead of the three or four numeric digits used under ICD-9-CM procedure coding. Coding under ICD-10-PCS is much more specific and substantially different from ICD-9-CM procedure coding.

        iv. The transition to ICD-10 is occurring because ICD-9 produces limited data about patients' medical conditions and hospital inpatient procedures. ICD-9 is 30 years old, has outdated terms, and is inconsistent with current medical practice. Also, the structure of ICD-9 limits the number of new codes that can be created, and many ICD-9 categories are full.

    c. Who Needs to Transition

        i. ICD-10 will affect diagnosis and inpatient procedure coding for everyone covered by the Health Insurance Portability Accountability Act (HIPAA), not just those who submit Medicare or Medicaid claims. The change to ICD-10 does not affect CPT coding for outpatient procedures.

---

[1]Reproduced from CMS (June 2013). The ICD-10 Transition: An Introduction. http://www.cms.gov/Medicare/Coding/ICD10/Downloads/ICD10_Introduction_060413[1].pdf. Accessed March 4, 2014.

ICD-10-CM and ICD-10-PCS Official Guideline for Coding and Reporting

1. Documentation and Coding Quality
   a. Accurate coding is contingent upon complete, accurate, legible, and timely documentation.
   b. ICD-10-CM and ICD-10-PCS and CPT coding drives reimbursement and is a mechanism used to determine utilization of services and the quality of care rendered to patients.
   c. ICD-10
      i. Copyrighted by WHO
      ii. Used to code and classify mortality data from death certificates
      iii. Replaced ICD-9 for this purpose as of January 1, 1999
   d. ICD-10-CM
      i. The codes in ICD-10-CM are not currently valid for any purpose or use.
      ii. Proposed to replace ICD-9-CM Volumes 1 and 2 with implementation based on the process for adoption of standard under the Health Insurance Portability and Accountability Act of 1996
   e. ICD-10-PCS
      i. New procedure coding system developed as a replacement for ICD-9-CM, Volume 3
2. Nomenclature and Classification System
   a. Nomenclature is a list of proper names for diseases and operations; each listing may include a code number.
      i. Standard Nomenclature of Disease and Operations (SNDO)
      ii. Standard Nomenclature of Medicine (SNOMED)
      iii. Standard Nomenclature of Medicine Clinical Terminology (SNOMEDCT)
   b. Classification is a system of assigning code numbers to diseases and operations; related diseases may be grouped together.
      i. ICD-9-CM (discontinued September 30, 2014)
      ii. ICD-10 (ICD-10-CM replaced ICD-9-CM volumes 1 and 2)
      iii. ICD-10-PCS (ICD-10-PCS replaced ICD-9-CM volume 3)
      iv. ICD-O
      v. DSM-5 (*Diagnostic and Statistical Manual of Mental Disorders*)
3. Why We Code
   a. Research
   b. Reimbursement
   c. Predict Healthcare Trends
   d. Plan for Future Healthcare Needs
   e. Evaluate Use of Healthcare Facilities
   f. Study Healthcare Costs
4. ICD-10-CM and ICD-10-PCS
   a. International Classification of Disease, 10th revision, Clinical Modification
      i. The ICD-10 is copyrighted by the World Health Organization (WHO), which owns and publishes the classification. WHO has authorized the development of an adaptation of ICD-10 for the United States for U.S. government purposes. As agreed, all modifications to the ICD-10 must conform to WHO conventions for the ICD. ICD-10-CM was developed following a thorough evaluation by a Technical Advisory Panel and extensive additional consultation with physician groups, clinical coders, and others to assure clinical accuracy and utility.

b. Uses
- **i.** Translate descriptive information into numerical codes for disease, injuries, conditions, and procedures
- **ii.** Classify morbidity (sickness) and mortality (death)
- **iii.** ICD-10 code sets
    - **1.** ICD-10-CM replaced volumes 1 and 2 of ICD-9-CM.
        - **a.** Alphabetic Index of diseases
        - **b.** Alphanumeric listing of diseases by body systems
    - **2.** ICD-10-PCS replaced volume 3 of ICD-9-CM.
        - **a.** Alphabetic Index of procedures
        - **b.** Alphanumeric listing of procedures by body systems

c. ICD-10-CM Guidelines of Coding
- **i.** Uniform Hospital Discharge Data Set Terms (UHDDS)
    - **1.** Admitting diagnosis
        - **a.** Working diagnosis
    - **2.** Principal diagnosis
        - **a.** The condition established after study to be chiefly responsible for occasioning the admission of the patient to the hospital for care
    - **3.** Other diagnoses
        - **a.** Additional conditions that affect patient care
    - **4.** First-listed diagnoses
        - **a.** Term used in lieu of a principle diagnosis in an outpatient setting
    - **5.** Principal procedure
        - **a.** Performed for definitive treatment, or one that is necessary, to care for a complication
        - **b.** If more than one procedure, relates to principal diagnosis
    - **6.** Other procedures
        - **a.** Sequenced after principal procedure

d. Official Guidelines Developed by 4 Groups:
- **i.** American Hospital Association (AHA)
    - **1.** Maintains central office on ICD-10-CM
    - **2.** Approves official coding guidelines
    - **3.** Publishes coding clinic
- **ii.** American Health Information Management Association (AHIMA)
    - **1.** Certifies coders
    - **2.** Provides coding education
    - **3.** Sponsors Council on Coding and Classification and the Society for Clinical Coding
    - **4.** Approves official coding guidelines
- **iii.** Centers for Medicaid and Medicare Services (CMS)
    - **1.** Maintains the procedure classification
    - **2.** Approves official coding guidelines
- **iv.** National Center for Health Statistics (NCHS)
    - **1.** Maintains the disease classification
    - **2.** Approves official coding guidelines
    - **3.** Official ICD-10-CM coding guidelines can be found at http://www.cdc.gov/nchs/datawh/ftpserv/ftpicd10/ftpicd10.htm#guidelines

5. Format of ICD-10-CM Coding Book
- **a.** Volume 1 (Tabular List of diseases and injuries)
    - **i.** Chapter
        - **1.** Divided by conditions that affect a specific body system and conditions according to etiology

      ii. Section

         1. Groups of 3-digit categories

      iii. Category

         1. Three-digit code numbers

      iv. Subcategory

         1. Four-digit code numbers

      v. Subclassification

         1. Five-digit code numbers and the most specific code

   b. Volume 2 (Alphabetic Index of diseases and injuries)

      i. Main terms

         1. Usually identify disease conditions

      ii. Subterms

         1. Indicate site, type, or etiology for a condition or injury

      iii. Carryover lines

         1. Used when complete entry cannot fit on a single line

      iv. Code number and modifier

         1. ICD-9-CM code with modifying term (if any)

      v. Connecting word

         1. Expresses the relationship between main term or subterm, indicating an associated condition or etiology

            a. With, in, due to

  c. ICD-10-CM Conventions

  d. ICD-10-CM General Coding Guidelines

      i. Locating a code in the ICD-10-CM

         1. To select a code in the classification that corresponds to a diagnosis or reason for visit documented in a medical record, first locate the term in the Alphabetic Index, and then verify the code in the Tabular List. Read and be guided by instructional notations that appear in both the Alphabetic Index and the Tabular List.

         2. It is essential to use both the Alphabetic Index and Tabular List when locating and assigning a code. The Alphabetic Index does not always provide the full code. Selection of the full code, including laterality and any applicable 7th character can only be done in the Tabular List. A dash (-) at the end of an Alphabetic Index entry indicates that additional characters are required. Even if a dash is not included at the Alphabetic Index entry, it is necessary to refer to the Tabular List to verify that no 7th character is required.

      ii. Level of detail in coding

         1. Diagnosis codes are to be used and reported at their highest number of characters available.

         2. ICD-10-CM diagnosis codes are composed of codes with three, four, five, six, or seven characters. Codes with three characters are included in ICD-10-CM as the heading of a category of codes that may be further subdivided by the use of fourth and/or fifth characters and/or sixth characters, which provide greater detail.

         3. A three-character code is to be used only if it is not further subdivided. A code is invalid if it has not been coded to the full number of characters required for that code, including the 7th character, if applicable.

      iii. Code or codes from A00.0 through T88.9, Z00-Z99.8

         1. The appropriate code or codes from A00.0 through T88.9, Z00–Z99.8 must be used to identify diagnoses, symptoms, conditions, problems, complaints, or other reason(s) for the encounter/visit.

iv. Signs and symptoms
  1. Codes that describe symptoms and signs, as opposed to diagnoses, are acceptable for reporting purposes when a related definitive diagnosis has not been established (confirmed) by the provider. Chapter 18 of ICD-10-CM, Symptoms, Signs, and Abnormal Clinical and Laboratory Findings, Not Elsewhere Classified (codes R00-R99) contain many, but not all codes for symptoms.
  2. ICD-10-CM Official Guidelines for Coding and Reporting 2013 Page 13 of 113. Elsewhere Classified (codes R00.0–R99) contains many, but not all codes for symptoms.
v. Conditions that are an integral part of a disease process
  1. Signs and symptoms that are associated routinely with a disease process should not be assigned as additional codes, unless otherwise instructed by the classification.
vi. Conditions that are not an integral part of a disease process
  1. Additional signs and symptoms that may not be associated routinely with a disease process should be coded when present.
vii. Multiple coding for a single condition
  1. In addition to the etiology/manifestation convention that requires two codes to fully describe a single condition that affects multiple body systems, there are other single conditions that also require more than one code. "Use additional code" notes are found in the Tabular List at codes that are not part of an etiology/manifestation pair where a secondary code is useful to fully describe a condition. The sequencing rule is the same as the etiology/manifestation pair, "use additional code" indicates that a secondary code should be added.
  2. For example, for bacterial infections that are not included in Chapter 1, a secondary code from category B95, *Streptococcus*, *Staphylococcus*, and *Enterococcus*, as the cause of diseases classified elsewhere, or B96, Other bacterial agents as the cause of diseases classified elsewhere, maybe required to identify the bacterial organism causing the infection. A "use additional code" note will normally be found at the infectious disease code, indicating a need for the organism code to be added as a secondary code.
  3. "Code first" notes are also under certain codes that are not specifically manifestation codes but may be due to an underlying cause. When there is a "code first" note and an underlying condition is present, the underlying condition should be sequenced first.
  4. "Code, if applicable, any causal condition first" notes indicate that this code may be assigned as a principal diagnosis when the causal condition is unknown or not applicable. If a causal condition is known, then the code for that condition should be sequenced as the principal or first-listed diagnosis.
  5. Multiple codes may be needed for sequela, complication codes, and obstetric codes to more fully describe a condition. See the specific guidelines for these conditions for further instruction.
  6. ICD-10-CM Official Guidelines for Coding and Reporting 2013. Page 14 of 113
viii. Acute and chronic conditions
  1. If the same condition is described as both acute (subacute) and chronic, and separate subentries exist in the Alphabetic Index at

the same indentation level, code both and sequence the acute (subacute) code first.

   ix. Combination code

      1. A combination code is a single code used to classify:

        a. Two diagnoses, or a diagnosis with an associated secondary process (manifestation)

        b. A diagnosis with an associated complication

      2. Combination codes are identified by referring to subterm entries in the Alphabetic Index and by reading the inclusion and exclusion notes in the Tabular List.

      3. Assign only the combination code when that code fully identifies the diagnostic conditions involved or when the Alphabetic Index so directs. Multiple coding should not be used when the classification provides a combination code that clearly identifies all of the elements documented in the diagnosis. When the combination code lacks necessary specificity in describing the manifestation or complication, an additional code should be used as a secondary code.

   x. Sequela (late effects)

      1. A sequela is the residual effect (condition produced) after the acute phase of an illness or injury has terminated. There is no time limit on when a sequela code can be used. The residual may be apparent early, such as in cerebral infarction, or it may occur months or years later, such as that due to a previous injury. Coding of sequela generally requires two codes sequenced in the following order: The condition or nature of the sequela is sequenced first. The sequela code is sequenced second.

      2. An exception to the above guidelines are those instances where the code for the sequela is followed by a manifestation code identified in the Tabular List and title, or the sequela code has been expanded (at the fourth, fifth, or sixth character levels) to include the manifestation(s). The code for the acute phase of an illness or injury that led to the sequela is never used with a code for the late effect.

      3. See Section I.C.9. Sequelae of cerebrovascular disease

      4. See Section I.C.15. Sequelae of complication of pregnancy, childbirth, and the puerperium

      5. See Section I.C.19. Application of 7th characters for Chapter 19

   xi. ICD-10-CM Official Guidelines for Coding and Reporting 2013. Page 15 of 113

   xii. Impending or Threatened condition

      1. Code any condition described at the time of discharge as "impending" or "threatened" as follows:

        a. If it did occur, code as confirmed diagnosis.

        b. If it did not occur, reference the Alphabetic Index to determine if the condition has a subentry term for "impending" or "threatened" and also reference main term entries for "Impending" and for "Threatened."

      2. If the subterms are listed, assign the given code.

      3. If the subterms are not listed, code the existing underlying condition(s) and not the condition described as impending or threatened.

   xiii. Reporting same diagnosis code more than once

      1. Each unique ICD-10-CM diagnosis code may be reported only once for an encounter. This applies to bilateral conditions when there are no distinct codes identifying laterality or two different conditions classified to the same ICD-10-CM diagnosis code.

xiv. Laterality

    1. Some ICD-10-CM codes indicate laterality, specifying whether the condition occurs on the left, right, or is bilateral. If no bilateral code is provided and the condition is bilateral, assign separate codes for both the left and right sides. If the side is not identified in the medical record, assign the code for the unspecified side.

xv. Documentation for BMI, non-pressure ulcers, and pressure ulcer stages

    1. For the body mass index (BMI), depth of non-pressure chronic ulcers and pressure ulcer stage codes, code assignment may be based on medical record documentation from clinicians who are not the patient's provider (i.e., physician or other qualified healthcare practitioner legally accountable for establishing the patient's diagnosis), since this information is typically documented by other clinicians involved in the care of the patient (e.g., a dietitian often documents the BMI and nurses often document the pressure ulcer stages). However, the associated diagnosis (such as overweight, obesity, or pressure ulcer) must be documented by the patient's provider. If there is conflicting medical record documentation, either from the same clinician or different clinicians, the patient's attending provider should be queried for clarification.

    2. The BMI codes should only be reported as secondary diagnoses. As with all other secondary diagnosis codes, the BMI codes should only be assigned when they meet the definition of a reportable additional diagnosis (see Section III, Reporting Additional Diagnoses).

    3. ICD-10-CM Official Guidelines for Coding and Reporting 2013 Page 16 of 113

xvi. Syndromes

    1. Follow the Alphabetic Index guidance when coding syndromes. In the absence of Alphabetic Index guidance, assign codes for the documented manifestations of the syndrome. Additional codes for manifestations that are not an integral part of the disease process may also be assigned when the condition does not have a unique code.

xvii. Documentation of complications of care

    1. Code assignment is based on the provider's documentation of the relationship between the condition and the care or procedure. The guideline extends to any complications of care, regardless of the chapter the code is located in. It is important to note that not all conditions that occur during or following medical care or surgery are classified as complications. There must be a cause-and-effect relationship between the care provided and the condition, and an indication in the documentation that it is a complication. Query the provider for clarification, if the complication is not clearly documented.

xviii. Borderline diagnosis

    1. If the provider documents a "borderline" diagnosis at the time of discharge, the diagnosis is coded as confirmed, unless the classification provides a specific entry (e.g., borderline diabetes).

If a borderline condition has a specific index entry in ICD-10-CM, it should be coded as such. Since borderline conditions are not uncertain diagnoses, no distinction is made between the care setting (inpatient versus outpatient). Whenever the documentation is unclear regarding a borderline condition, coders are encouraged to query for clarification.

e. ICD-10-PCS Conventions and general coding guidelines for procedures

    i. A1

        1. ICD-10-PCS codes are composed of seven characters. Each character is an axis of classification that specifies information about the procedure performed. Within a defined code range, a character specifies the same type of information in that axis of classification.

           a. *Example:* The fifth axis of classification specifies the approach in sections 0 through 4 and 7 through 9 of the system.

    ii. A2

        1. One of 34 possible values can be assigned to each axis of classification in the seven-character code: they are the numbers 0 through 9 and the alphabet (except I and O because they are easily confused with the numbers 1 and 0). The number of unique values used in an axis of classification differs as needed.

           a. *Example:* Where the fifth axis of classification specifies the approach, seven different approach values are currently used to specify the approach.

    iii. A3

        1. The valid values for an axis of classification can be added to as needed.

           a. *Example:* If a significantly distinct type of device is used in a new procedure, a new device value can be added to the system.

    iv. A4

        1. As with words in their context, the meaning of any single value is a combination of its axis of classification and any preceding values on which it may be dependent.

           a. *Example:* The meaning of a body part value in the Medical and Surgical section is always dependent on the body system value. The body part value 0 in the Central Nervous body system specifies Brain and the body part value 0 in the Peripheral Nervous body system specifies Cervical Plexus.

    v. A5

        1. As the system is expanded to become increasingly detailed, over time more values will depend on preceding values for their meaning.

           a. *Example:* In the Lower Joints body system, the device value 3 in the root operation Insertion specifies Infusion Device and the device value 3 in the root operation Replacement specifies Ceramic Synthetic Substitute.

    vi. A6

        1. The purpose of the Alphabetic Index is to locate the appropriate table that contains all information necessary to construct a procedure code. The PCS Tables should always be consulted to find the most appropriate valid code.

    vii. A7

        1. It is not required to consult the index first before proceeding to the tables to complete the code. A valid code may be chosen directly from the tables.

viii. A8

    1. All seven characters must be specified to be a valid code. If the documentation is incomplete for coding purposes, the physician should be queried for the necessary irrformation.

ix. A9

    1. Within a PCS table, valid codes include all combinations of choices in characters 4 through 7 contained in the same row of the table. In the example below, 0JHT3VZ is a valid code, and 0JHW3VZ is *not* a valid code.

Section: 0 Medical and Surgical
Body System: J Subcutaneous Tissue and Fascia
Operation: H Insertion: Pulling in a nonbiological appliance that monitors, assists, performs, or prevents a physiological function but does not physically take the place of a body part

Body Part	Approach	Device	Qualifier
Subcutaneous Tissue and Fascia, Head and Neck V Subcutaneous Tissue and Fascia, Upper Extremity W Subcutaneous Tissue and Fascia, Lower Extremity	0 Open 3 Percutaneous	1 Radioactive Element 3 Infusion Device	Z No Qualifier
T Subcutaneous Tissue and Fascia, Trunk	0 Open 3 Percutaneous	1 Radioactive Element 3 Infusion Device V Infusion Pump	Z No Qualifier

Reproduced from CMS (2013). ICD-10-PCS Official Guidelines for Coding and Reporting: Conventions. http://www.cms.gov/Medicare/Coding/ICD10/Downloads/PCS_2013_guidelines.pdf. Accessed March 4, 2014.

    x. A10

        1. "And," when used in a code description, means "and/or."

            a. *Example:* Lower Arm and Wrist Muscle means lower arm and/or wrist muscle.

    xi. A11

        1. Many of the terms used to construct PCS codes are defined within the system. It is the coder's responsibility to determine what the documentation in the medical record equates to in the PCS definitions. The physician is not expected to use the terms used in PCS code descriptions, nor is the coder required to query the physician when the correlation between the documentation and the defined PCS terms is clear.

            a. *Example:* When the physician documents "partial resection" the coder can independently correlate "partial resection" to the root operation Excision without querying the physician for clarification.

Reproduced from CMS. (2013). ICD-10-PCS Official Guidelines for Coding and Reporting: Conventions. http://www.cms.gov/Medicare/Coding/ICD10/Downloads/PCS_2013_guidelines.pdf. Accessed March 4, 2014.

6. Conventions for the ICD-10-CM

The conventions for the ICD-10-CM are the general rules for use of fhe classification independent of the guidelines. These conventions are incorporated within the Alphabetic Index and Tabular List of the ICD-10-CM as instructional notes.

a. The Alphabetic Index and Tabular List. The ICD-10-CM is divided into the Alphabetic Index, an alphabetical list of terms and their corresponding code, and the Tabular List, a structured list of codes divided into chapters based on body system of condition. The Alphabetic Index consists of the following parts: the Index of Diseases and Injury, the Index of External Causes of Injury, the Table of Neoplasms, and the Table of Drugs and Chemicals.

See Section I. C2. General guidelines

See Section 1. C. 19. Adverse effects, poisoning, underdosing and toxic effects

b. Format and Structure. The ICD-10-CM Tabular List contains categories, subcategories, and codes. Characters for categories, subcategories, and codes may be either a letter or a number. All categories are three characters. A three-character category that has no further subdivision is equivalent to a code. Subcategories are either four or five characters. Codes may be three, four, five, six, or seven characters. That is, each level of subdivision after a category is a subcategory. The final level of subdivision is a code. Codes that have applicable seventh characters are still referred to as codes, not subcategories. A code that has an applicable seventh character is considered invalid without the seventh character. The ICD-10-CM uses an indented format for ease in reference.

c. Use of Codes for Reporting Purposes. For reporting purposes only codes are permissible, not categories or subcategories, and any applicable seventh character is required.

d. Placeholder Character. The ICD-10-CM utilizes a placeholder character "X." The "X" is used as a placeholder at certain codes to allow for future expansion. An example of this is at the poisoning, adverse effect, and underdosing codes, categories T36–T50.

Where a placeholder exists, the X must be used for the code to be considered a valid code.

e. Seventh Characters. Certain ICD-10-CM categories have applicable seventh characters. The applicable seventh character is required for all codes within the category, or as the notes in the Tabular List instruct. The seventh character must always be the seventh character in the data field. If a code that requires a seventh character is not six characters, a placeholder X must be used to fill in the empty characters.

f. Abbreviations

    i. Alphabetic Index abbreviations

        1. NEC "Not elsewhere classifiable": This abbreviation in the Alphabetic Index represents "other specified." When a specific code is not available for a condition, the Alphabetic Index directs the coder to the "other specified" code in the Tabular List.

        2. NOS "Not otherwise specified": This abbreviation is the equivalent of unspecified.

    ii. Tabular List abbreviations

        1. NEC "Not elsewhere classifiable": This abbreviation in the Tabular List represents "other specified." When a specific code is not available for a condition the Tabular List includes an NEC entry under a code to identify the code as the "other specified" code.

        2. NOS "Not otherwise specified": This abbreviation is the equivalent of unspecified.

g. Punctuation

    i. [ ] Brackets are used in the Tabular List to enclose synonyms, alternative wording or explanatory phrases. Brackets are used in the Alphabetic Index to identify manifestation codes.

    ii. () Parentheses are used in both the Alphabetic Index and Tabular List to enclose supplementary words that may be present or absent in the statement of a disease or procedure without affecting the code number to which it is assigned. The terms within the parentheses are referred to as nonessential modifiers.

    iii. : Colons are used in the Tabular List after an incomplete term which needs one or more of the modifiers following the colon to make it assignable to a given category.

h. Use of "And"

See Section I. A14. Use of the term "And"

i. Other and Unspecified codes

    i. "Other" codes. Codes titled "other" or "other specified" are for use when the information in the medical record provides detail for which a specific code does not exist. Alphabetic Index entries with NEC in the line designate "other" codes in the Tabular List. These Alphabetic Index entries represent specific disease entities for which no specific code exists so the term is included within an "other" code.

    ii. "Unspecified" codes. Codes titled "unspecified" are for use when the information in the medical record is insufficient to assign a more specific code. For those categories for which an unspecified code is not provided, the "other specified" code may represent both other and unspecified.

j. Includes Notes. This note appears immediately under a three character code title to further define, or give examples of, the content of the category.

k. Inclusion Terms. A list of terms is included under some codes. These terms are the conditions for which that code is to be used. The terms may be synonyms of the code title, or, in the case of "other specified" codes, the terms are a list of the various conditions assigned to that code. The inclusion terms are not necessarily exhaustive. Additional terms found only in the Alphabetic Index may also be assigned to a code.

l. Excludes Notes. The ICD-10-CM has two types of excludes notes. Each type of note has a different definition for use but they are all similar in that they indicate that codes excluded from each other are independent of each other.

    i. Excludes1. A type 1 Excludes note is a pure excludes note. It means "NOT CODED HERE!" An Excludes1 note indicates that the code excluded should never be used at the same time as the code above the Excludes1 note. An Excludes1 is used when two conditions cannot occur together, such as a congenital form versus an acquired form of the same condition.

    ii. Excludes2. A type 2 Excludes note represents "Not included here." An Excludes2 note indicates that the condition excluded is not part of the condition represented by the code, but a patient may have both conditions at the same time. When an Excludes2 note appears under a code, it is acceptable to use both the code and the excluded code together, when appropriate.

m. Etiology/Manifestation Convention ("Code First," "Use Additional Code," and "In Diseases Classified Elsewhere" Notes).

    i. Certain conditions have both an underlying etiology and multiple body system manifestations due to the underlying etiology. For such conditions, the ICD-10-CM has a coding convention that requires the underlying condition be sequenced first followed by the manifestation. Wherever such a combination exists, there is a "use additional code" note at the etiology code, and a "code first" note at the manifestation code. These instructional notes indicate the proper sequencing order of the codes, etiology followed by manifestation.

    ii. In most cases the manifestation codes will have in the code title, "in diseases classified elsewhere." Codes with this title are a component of the etiology/manifestation convention. The code title indicates that it is a manifestation code. "In diseases classified elsewhere" codes are never permitted to be used as first-listed or principal diagnosis codes. They must be used in conjunction with an underlying condition code and they must be listed following the underlying condition. See category F02, Dementia in other diseases classified elsewhere, for an example of this convention.

    iii. There are manifestation codes that do not have "in diseases classified elsewhere" in the title. For such codes, there is a "use additional code" note at the etiology code and a "code first" note at the manifestation code and the rules for sequencing apply.

    iv. In addition to the notes in the Tabular List, these conditions also have a specific Alphabetic Index entry structure. In the Alphabetic Index both conditions are listed together with the etiology code first followed by the manifestation codes in brackets. The code in brackets is always to be sequenced second.

    v. An example of the etiology/manifestation convention is dementia in Parkinson's disease. In the Alphabetic Index, code G20 is listed first, followed by code F02.80 or F02.81 in brackets. Code G20 represents the underlying etiology, Parkinson's disease, and must be sequenced first, whereas codes F02.80 and F02.81 represent the manifestation of dementia in diseases classified elsewhere, with or without behavioral disturbance.

    vi. "Code first" and "Use additional code" notes are also used as sequencing rules in the classification for certain codes that are not part of an etiology/mianifestation combination.
See Section I.B. 7. Multiple coding for a single condition.

n. "And." The word "and" should be interpreted to mean either "and" or "or" when it appears in a title. For example, cases of "tuberculosis of bones," "tuberculosis of joints," and "tuberculosis of bones and joints" are classified to subcategory A18.0, Tuberculosis of bones and joints.

o. "With"

    i. The word "with" should be interpreted to mean "associated with" or "due to" when it appears in a code title, the Alphabetic Index, or an instructional note in the Tabular List.

    ii. The word "with" in the Alphabetic Index is sequenced immediately following the main term, not in alphabetical order.

p. "See" and "See Also"

    i. The "see" instruction following a main term in the Alphabetic Index indicates that another term should be referenced. It is necessary to go to the main term referenced with the "see" note to locate the correct code.

    ii. A "see also" instruction following a main term in the Alphabetic Index instructs that there is another main term that may also be referenced that may provide additional Alphabetic Index entries that may be useful. It is not necessary to follow the "see also" note when the original main term provides the necessary code.

q. "Code Also" Note. A "code also" note instructs that two codes may be required to fully describe a condition, but this note does not provide sequencing direction.

r. Default Codes. A code listed next to a main term in the ICD-10-CM Alphabetic Index is referred to as a default code. The default code represents that condition that is most commonly associated with the main term, or is the unspecified code for the condition. If a condition is documented in a medical record (for example, appendicitis) without any additional information, such as acute or chronic, the default code should be code should be assigned.

Reproduced from the CDC (2014). ICD-10-CM Official Guidelines for Coding and Reporting. http://www.cdc.gov/nchs/data/icd/icd10cm_guidelines_2014.pdf. Accessed March 5, 2014.

7. General Coding Guidelines

a. Locating a Code in the ICD-10-CM

   i. To select a code in the classification that corresponds to a diagnosis or reason for visit documented in a medical record, first locate the term in the Alphabetic Index, and then verify the code in the Tabular List. Read and be guided by instructional notations that appear in both the Alphabetic Index and the Tabular List.

   ii. It is essential to use both the Alphabetic Index and Tabular List when locating and assigning a code. The Alphabetic Index does not always provide the full code. Selection of the full code, including laterality and any applicable seventh character can only be done in the Tabular List. A dash (-) at the end of an Alphabetic Index entry indicates that additional characters are required. Even if a dash is not included at the Alphabetic Index entry, it is necessary to refer to the Tabular List to verify that no seventh character is required.

b. Level of Detail in Coding

   i. Diagnosis codes are to be used and reported at their highest number of characters available.

   ii. ICD-10-CM diagnosis codes are composed of codes with three, four, five, six, or seven characters. Codes with three characters are included in ICD-10-CM as the heading of a category of codes that may be further subdivided by the use of fourth and/or fifth characters and/or sixth characters, which provide greater detail.

   iii. A three-character code is to be used only if it is not further subdivided. A code is invalid if it has not been coded to the full number of characters required for that code, including the seventh character, if applicable.

c. Code or Codes from A00.0 Through T88.9, Z00–Z99.8. The appropriate code or codes from A00.0 through T88.9, Z00–Z99.8 must be used to identify diagnoses, symptoms, conditions, problems, complaints, or other reason(s) for the encounter/visit.

d. Signs and Symptoms. Codes that describe symptoms and signs, as opposed to diagnoses, are acceptable for reporting purposes when a related definitive diagnosis has not been established (confirmed) by the provider. Chapter 18 of ICD-10-CM, Symptoms, Signs, and Abnormal Clinical and Laboratory Findings, Not Elsewhere Classified (codes R00.0–R99) contains many, but not all codes for symptoms.

 e. Conditions That Are an Integral Part of a Disease Process. Signs and symptoms that are associated routinely with a disease process should not be assigned as additional codes, unless otherwise instructed by the classification.

 f. Conditions That Are Not an Integral Part of a Disease Process. Additional signs and symptoms that may not be associated routinely with a disease process should be coded when present.

 g. Multiple Coding for a Single Condition

  i. In addition to the etiology/manifestation convention that requires two codes to fully describe a single condition that affects multiple body systems, there are other single conditions that also require more than one code. "Use additional code" notes are found in the Tabular List at codes that are not part of an etiology/manifestation pair where a secondary code is useful to fully describe a condition. The sequencing rule is the same as the etiology/manifestation pair, "use additional code" indicates that a secondary code should be added.

  ii. For example, for bacterial irrfections that are not included in Chapter 1, a secondary code from category B95, Streptococcus, Staphylococcus, and Enterococcus, as the cause of diseases classified elsewhere, or B96, Other bacterial agents as the cause of diseases classified elsewhere, may be required to identify the bacterial organism causing the infection. A "use additional code" note will normally be found at the infectious disease code, indicating a need for the organism code to be added as a secondary code.

  iii. "Code first" notes are also under certain codes that are not specifically marrifestation codes but may be due to an underlying cause. When there is a "code first" note and an underlying condition is present, the underlying condition should be sequenced first.

  iv. "Code, if applicable, any causal condition first" notes indicate that this code may be assigned as a principal diagnosis when the causal condition is unknown or not applicable. If a causal condition is known, then the code for that condition should be sequenced as the principal or first-listed diagnosis. Multiple codes may be needed for sequela, complication codes and obstetric codes to more fully describe a condition. See the specific guidelines for these conditions for further instruction.

 h. Acute and Chronic Conditions. If the same condition is described as both acute (subacute) and chronic, and separate subentries exist in the Alphabetic Index at the same indentation level, code both and sequence the acute (subacute) code first.

 i. Combination Code

  i. A combination code is a single code used to classify:

   1. Two diagnoses or

   2. A diagnosis with an associated secondary process (manifestation)

   3. A diagnosis with an associated complication

  ii. Combination codes are identified by referring to subterm entries in the Alphabetic Index and by reading the inclusion and exclusion notes in the Tabular List.

  iii. Assign only the combination code when that code fully identifies the diagnostic conditions involved or when the Alphabetic Index so directs. Multiple coding should not be used when the classification provides a combination code that clearly identifies all of the elements documented in the diagnosis. When the combination code lacks necessary specificity in describing the manifestation or complication, an additional code should be used as a secondary code.

j. Sequela (Late Effects)

   i. A sequela is the residual effect (condition produced) after the acute phase of an illness or injury has terminated. There is no time limit on when a sequela code can be used. The residual may be apparent early, such as in cerebral infarction, or it may occur months or years later, such as that due to a previous injury. Coding of sequela generally requires two codes sequenced in the following order: The condition or nature of the sequela is sequenced first. The sequela code is sequenced second.

   ii. An exception to the above guidelines are those instances where the code for the sequela is followed by a manifestation code identified in the Tabular List and title, or the sequela code has been expanded (at the fourth, fifth, or sixth character levels) to include the manifestation(s). The code for the acute phase of an illness or injury that led to the sequela is never used with a code for the late effect.
   See Section I.C.9. Sequelae of cerebrovascular disease
   See Section I.C.15. Sequelae of complication ofpregpancy, childbirth and the puerpervum
   See Section I.C.19. Application of 7th characters for Chapter 19

k. Impending or Threatened Condition

   i. Code any condition described at the time of discharge as "impending" or "threatened" as follows:

      1. If it did occur, code as confirmed diagnosis.

      2. If it did not occur, reference the Alphabetic Index to detennine if the condition has a subentry term for "impending" or "threatened" and also reference main term entries for "Impending" and for "Threatened."

   ii. If the subterms are listed, assign the given code.

   iii. If the subterms are not listed, code the existing underlying condition(s) and not the condition described as impending or threatened.

l. Reporting Same Diagnosis Code More Than Once. Each unique ICD-10-CM diagnosis code may be reported only once for an encounter. This applies to bilateral conditions when there are no distinct codes identifying laterality or two different conditions classified to the same ICD-10-CM diagnosis code.

m. Laterality. Some ICD-10-CM codes indicate laterality, specifying whether the condition occurs on the left, right, or is bilateral. If no bilateral code is provided and the condition is bilateral, assign separate codes for both the left and right sides. If the side is not identified in the medical record, assign the code for the unspecified side.

n. Documentation for BMI, Non-pressure ulcers, and Pressure Ulcer Stages

   i. For the body mass index (BMI), depth of non-pressure chronic ulcers, and pressure ulcer stage codes, code assignment may be based on medical record documentation from clinicians who are not the patient's provider (i.e., physician or other qualified healthcare practitioner legally accountable for estabhshing the patient's diagnosis), since this information is typically documented by other clinicians involved in the care of the patient (e.g., a dietitian often documents the BMI and nurses often document the pressure ulcer stages). However, the associated diagnosis (such as overweight, obesity, or pressure ulcer) must be documented by the patient's provider. If there is conflicting medical record documentation, either from the same clinician or different clinicians, the patient's attending provider should be queried for clarification.

    ii. The BMI codes should only be reported as secondary diagnoses. As with all other secondary diagnosis codes, the BMI codes should be assigned only when they meet the definition of a reportable additional diagnosis (see Section III, Reporting Additional Diagnoses).

o. Syndromes. Follow the Alphabetic Index guidance when coding syndromes. In the absence of Alphabetic Index guidance, assign codes for the documented manifestations of the syndrome. Additional codes for manifestations that are not an integral part of the disease process may also be assigned when the condition does not have a unique code.

p. Documentation of Complications of Care. Code assignment is based on the provider's documentation of the relationship between the condition and the care or procedure. The guideline extends to any complications of care, regardless of the chapter the code is located in. It is important to note that not all conditions that occur during or following medical care or surgery are classified as complications. There must be a cause-and-effect relationship between the care provided and the condition, and an indication in the documentation that it is a complication. Query the provider for clarification, if the complication is not clearly documented.

q. Borderline Diagnosis. If the provider documents a "borderline" diagnosis at the time of discharge, the diagnosis is coded as confirmed, unless the classification provides a specific entry (e.g., borderline diabetes). If a borderline condition has a specific index entry in ICD-10-CM, it should be coded as such. Since borderline conditions are not uncertain diagnoses, no distinction is made between the care setting (inpatient versus outpatient). Whenever the documentation is unclear regarding a borderline condition, coders are encouraged to query for clarification.

Reproduced from the CDC (2014). ICD-10-CM Official Guidelines for Coding and Reporting. http://www.cdc.gov/nchs/data/icd/icd10cm_guidelines_2014.pdf. Accessed March 5, 2014.

8. CPT-4 and HCPCS

  a. The Common Procedural Terminology, 4th Edition (CPT-4) was developed in 1960 by American Medical Association. Its main purpose is to standardize the classification and reporting of healthcare services to facilitate reimbursement. It describes medical, surgical, and diagnostic services and is revised and updated annually.

  b. CMS adopted CPT as level I of the Healthcare Common Procedure Coding System (HCPCS).

  c. Content of CPT
    i. Nine chapters (sections)
      1. Introduction
      2. Evaluation and management (E/M)
      3. Anesthesia
      4. Surgery
      5. Radiology
      6. Pathology and laboratory
      7. Medicine
      8. Appendices
      9. Index

ii. Section format includes section, subsection, heading, and subheading.
1. Section: surgery
2. Subsection: respiratory
3. Heading: trachea and bronchi
4. Subheading: incision
iii. Punctuation, typeface, and symbols
1. Semicolon and indention
2. Boldface type
3. Symbols
  a. Triangle △
    i. Code whose description changed
  b. Bullet •
    i. New code
  c. Sideways double triangle ▷◁
    i. New or revised text
  d. Plus +
    i. Add on codes
  e. Bull's eye ⊙
    i. Administration of conscious sedation
  f. Circle with slash ⊘
    i. Not permitted to be appended with modifier 51 multiple procedures
  g. Circle with arrow ⊛
    i. Directs coder to an AMA-published reference
iv. Modifiers
1. Used to indicate that a performed service or procedure has been altered by some specific circumstance but not changed in its definition
  a. To report only the professional component of a procedure or service
  b. To report a service mandated by a third-party payer
  c. To indicate that a procedure was performed bilaterally
  d. To report multiple procedures performed at the same session by the same provider
  e. To report that a portion of a service or procedure is reduced or eliminated at the physician's discretion
  f. To report assistant surgeon services
v. Unlisted procedures: due to advances in medicine, physicians or other healthcare professionals may perform services or procedures that have not yet been designated with a specific CPT code. Each section of the CPT book identifies an unlisted procedure code for these procedures. Use of an unlisted procedure code requires a special report or documentation to describe the service.
vi. Add-on codes: codes that describe procedures or services that must never be reported as stand-alone codes. These procedures and services are always performed in addition to the primary procedure or service and are identified by the "+" symbol.
vii. Unbundling: reporting a procedure or service using separate codes for each part of the procedure when one comprehensive code covers all the parts.
viii. Separate procedure: identified by the inclusion of the term (separate procedure) in the code descriptor. A code designated as

a separate procedure may not be reported when it is an integral component of another procedure or service.

    ix. How to use the index

        1. Main terms

        2. Subterms

        3. Code ranges

        4. Crossreferences

d. General Rules for CPT Coding

    i. Identify the procedures and services to be coded by carefully reviewing the health record documentation.

    ii. Consult the index under the main term for the procedure performed and consult any subterms under the main term.

    iii. If the term is not located under the procedure performed, check the organ or site, condition, or eponym, synonym, or abbreviation.

    iv. Note the code number(s) found opposite the selected main term or subterm.

    v. Check the code(s) or code range in the body of the CPT codebook.

        1. When a single code number is provided, locate the code in the body of the CPT codebook.

        2. When two or more codes separated by a comma are shown, locate each code in the body of the CPT codebook.

        3. When a range of codes is shown, locate the range in the body of the CPT codebook.

    vi. Read and be guided by any coding notes under the code, at the subheading, heading, subsection, or section level.

    vii. Never code directly from the index.

    viii. Assign the appropriate modifier(s) when necessary to complete the code description.

    ix. Assign the appropriate code.

    x. Continue coding all components of the procedure or service using the above steps.

e. CMS administers HCPCS, which includes two (formerly three) levels of codes.

    i. Level 1: current procedural terminology

    ii. Level 2: alphanumeric procedure and modifier codes, codes representing items, supplies, and non-physician services not covered by the CPT codes

    iii. Level 3: local procedure and modifier codes used prior to 2003. Additional Level 2 codes are used now to compensate for the loss of the Level 3 codes.

PRACTICAL APPLICATION OF YOUR KNOWLEDGE

1. History of Coding

    a. Explain the purpose of coding.

    b. Define DRGs and explain their impact on hospital reimbursement.

    c. List cooperating parties responsible for maintaining and updating ICD-10-CM.

    d. Explain APC's impact on outpatient coding.

2. Important Definitions

    a. Define principal diagnosis.

    b. Explain how complications may affect a patient's length of stay.

    c. Explain the difference between diagnostic and therapeutic procedures and its significance in determining the principal procedure.

3. Principles of CPT

   a. List the two levels of HCPCS.

   b. Explain the purpose of modifiers.

   c. Where are the guidelines for CPT found?

4. CPT Coding Terms

   Match each of the following terms with its definition:

a. Global surgical package	**d.** Separate procedures
b. Add-on codes	**e.** Comprehensive code
c. Unbundling	**f.** Starred surgical procedures

   1. ____ When this note is in parentheses in the code description, it represents services that are commonly an integral part of a more extensive procedure.

   2. ____ This term refers to the use of multiple procedure codes for a group of services or procedures that actually can be identified by one comprehensive code.

   3. ____ These items are included in the CPT code for the defined surgical service.

   4. ____ This is used to describe a procedure or service at the highest level of complexity.

   5. ____ These are codes in the CPT manual that are submitted in addition to other codes.

   6. ____ These are considered minor surgical procedures to which the global surgical package does not apply.

5. Code the following scenarios. Use ICD–10–CM for questions a–j and CPT for questions k–o.

  a. A patient with CRF due to HTN was admitted for dialysis. Hemodialysis was given.

  b. Patient was diagnosed with adenocarcinoma of the lower outer quadrant of the left breast. A mastectomy was performed 2 weeks ago. No metastasis was found. The patient is now admitted for chemotherapy.

  c. A patient was admitted with GSW to the abdomen. Exploratory laparotomy was performed and a hepatic laceration was noted and sutured without any complications.

  d. A patient with a history of a previous CVA 8 years ago with residual right hemiparesis is admitted with an acute embolic cerebral infarction. The patient has a history of CHF and receives Lasix during this admission. The patient is later transferred to rehabilitation.

  e. A female who was 39 weeks pregnant delivered a breech female infant by classical cesarean section for a low fetal heart rate (bradycardia). The cesarean section wound became an infection and the patient stayed in the hospital an additional 3 days for antibiotics.

  f. A 55-year-old male was admitted due to a traumatic brain injury resulting in subarachnoid hematoma. The patient experienced a loss of consciousness of 5 minutes. A craniotomy with evacuation of the hematoma was performed. The patient recovered without any immediate complications.

  g. A 40-year-old male with type 2 diabetes is admitted with uncontrolled glucose levels that result in ketoacidosis. (The patient also has diabetic proliferative retinopathy that will be treated as an outpatient day surgery.)

h. A preterm delivery of a single live born female by low cervical cesarean section due to mild pre-eclampsia. There was no history of hypertension prior to pregnancy. There were no postpartum complications.

i. A patient was admitted with unstable angina due to coronary artery disease (CAD). Percutaneous transluminal coronary angioplasty (PTCA) was performed with (drug-eluting) stent insertion.

j. A 34-week, preterm, 1565-gram male infant was delivered by cesarean section. The infant was ABO incompatible. The infant Coombs test was positive, which confirmed the diagnosis. The infant is jaundiced due to the ABO incompatibility. Phototherapy was started.

k. Repair of a reducible right inguinal hernia with hydrocelectomy of the spermatic cord. Patient is 5 months old and male.

l. Hand laceration (3 cm), forehead (12 cm), and neck (5 cm). The lacerations were repaired with sutures in layered closure.

m. Pars plana victrectomy with membrane peeling and panretinal photocoagulation on the left eye.

n. Orchioplexy for (bilateral) undescended testes by inguinal approach.

o. Laparoscopic cholecystectomy with intraoperative cholangiogram.

TEST YOUR KNOWLEDGE

1. Nonessential modifiers are enclosed in:
   a. braces.
   b. slanted brackets.
   c. parentheses.
   d. square brackets.

2. A late effect is a(n):
   a. disease that lasts more than a year after diagnosis.
   b. external cause of accident or injury.
   c. readmission for the same problem within 7 days of the previous admission.
   d. residual effect of an acute illness or injury.

3. The interaction of two prescribed drugs taken as directed is considered a(n):
   a. accident.
   b. poisoning.
   c. late effect.
   d. adverse effect.

4. How would a coder report a definitive procedure performed in conjunction with an exploratory laparotomy?
   a. Code both procedures, but list the definitive procedure first
   b. Code only the exploratory laparotomy
   c. Code the definitive procedure only
   d. Ask the surgeon before assigning any procedures

5. Which diagnosis is sequenced first in the following burn case: second-degree burn of the leg; third-degree burn of the wrist; and first-degree burn of the foot.
   a. Second-degree burn of the leg
   b. First-degree burn of the foot
   c. Third-degree burn of the wrist
   d. The diagnosis listed first by the attending physician

6. A system that provides a method of arranging related disease entities in groups for the reporting of statistical data is a:
   a. CPR.
   b. nomenclature system.
   c. register.
   d. classification system.

7. DRGs are part of a case-mix classification system that assigns inpatient discharges to only one DRG per episode of care. On which data elements is the assignment made?
   a. Diagnoses, procedures, patient's age, and patient's disposition at discharge
   b. Principal diagnosis and principal procedure
   c. Surgical procedure, patient's age, and patient's financial class
   d. Principal diagnosis, severity of illness, and patient's disposition at discharge

8. A coder reads a procedure note, but fails to find an appropriate CPT code that matches the procedure performed. When the bill goes out to the fiscal intermediary, a special report is prepared and sent with a(n):
   a. starred procedure.
   b. unlisted procedure.
   c. unbundled procedure.
   d. separate procedure.

9. How are brackets used in ICD-10-CM?
   a. To enclose words or numbers within volume 2
   b. To designate synonyms, alternate wordings, abbreviations, or explanatory phrases
   c. To enclose supplementary words that may or may not be present in the diagnostic statement
   d. To indicate additional codes that must be used

10. Which of the following is not a section of CPT?
    a. Surgery
    b. Psychiatry
    c. Radiology
    d. Anesthesiology

11. Probable, possible, and suspected condition(s) of patients are coded as if they exist if the condition(s) are:
    a. treated while the patient is in the hospital.
    b. not treated while the patient is in the hospital.
    c. ruled out while the patient is in the hospital.
    d. diagnosed prior to admission.

12. Key terms for using Z codes are:
    a. delivery of, possible cause, or due to.
    b. threatened to, impending case, or late effect of.
    c. admission for, history of, observation, or status.
    d. prior to, late effect of, possible, or probable.

13. If a baby is born at Hospital A and transferred to Hospital B the first day of life, the P00 code should be used by which hospital(s)?
    a. A and B
    b. A only
    c. B only
    d. Inappropriate for use by either facility

14. What is code Z34 used for?
    a. Multiple live births, delivered head first
    b. Multiple live births, cesarean section, forceps delivery
    c. Single newborn, stillborn
    d. Single live newborn, delivered head first and full term

15. A complication is a condition that:
    a. was diagnosed prior to admission to the hospital.
    b. was caused by a nosocomial infection.
    c. arises while the patient is in the hospital.
    d. is a sentinel event that is reported to The Joint Commission

16. External Causes of Morbidity codes are:
    a. sometimes used as principal diagnoses.
    b. mandatory for pregnancy determination.
    c. used voluntarily by the healthcare organization.
    d. never used as principal diagnoses.

17. When locating a term for coding a neoplasm diagnosis, one should access:
    a. the Alphabetic Index.
    b. the Tabular Index.
    c. both the Alphabetic and Tabular Indexes.
    d. the Table of Neoplasms.

18. The word "and" should be interpreted to mean "and" as well as "_____."
    a. or
    b. with
    c. see
    d. see also

19. A patient has right-side hemiplegia from a CVA last year. This year the patient is admitted and discharged for an appendicitis. How should the hemiplegia be coded?
    a. Acute hemiplegia
    b. Late-effect hemiplegia
    c. Due to CVA
    d. Not treated, therefore not coded

20. ICD-9-CM 192 code is used for malignant neoplasm of other and unspecified parts of the nervous system. Code 192.1 reads "cerebral meninges, Dura (mater), Falx (cerebelli) (cerebri)." The terms listed in parentheses are:
    a. to be coded as complications or cormorbidities.
    b. synonyms or alternative phrasing for the preceding word.
    c. supplementary words or nonessential modifiers.
    d. eponyms for the preceding word.

21. What are Z codes used to classify?
    a. Factors influencing health status and contact with health services
    b. External causes of injury and poisoning
    c. Late effects of external causes
    d. Misadventures and complications of care guidelines

22. A patient is admitted because of threatened abortion and subsequently aborted. Threatened abortion should:
    a. not be coded; code underlying condition.
    b. be coded as a late effect of the underlying condition.
    c. be coded as confirmed diagnosis.
    d. not be coded; code as complete abortion.

23. What are External Causes of Morbidity codes used to classify?
    a. Factors influencing health status and contact with health services
    b. External causes of injury and poisoning
    c. Injuries and poisonings
    d. Symptoms, signs, and ill-defined conditions

24. CMS uses which of the following as the HCPCS level 1 codes?
    a. CPT codes
    b. All ICD-9-CM codes
    c. DRGs
    d. E codes of ICD-9-CM

25. What does the filled-in dot (·) appearing to the left of a CPT code designate?
    a. Add-on code
    b. New and revised test in coding notes
    c. Code's terminology has been revised
    d. New code in the current edition

[Use of ICD-10-CM and CPT coding books are required for the remaining portion. (*Note:* Because the exams are computerized, you will not need your coding books while sitting for the national RHIA and RHIT examinations.)]

26. Immediately after delivery, a critically ill neonate receives care under the direction and supervision of a pediatrician. What is the CPT-4 code?
    a. 99468
    b. 99285
    c. 99245
    d. 99205

27. During surgery, Ms. Johnson demonstrates distress and the physician must discontinue the procedure. What modifier may be used to report that the physician discontinued the procedure?
    a. -22
    b. -52
    c. -53
    d. -57

28. Bob was treated because he had right-leg paralysis due to poliomyelitis from childhood. How is this case coded using the ICD-9 coding guidelines?
    a. 344.30, 138
    b. 344.31, 138
    c. 342.01, 138
    d. 138, 344.31

29. Bob was treated because he had right-leg paralysis due to poliomyelitis from childhood. How is this case coded using the ICD-10 coding guidelines?
    a. G83.10, A52.17, B91
    b. B91
    c. B91, A52.17
    d. G83.10

30. Bob was admitted with seizures and has a history of malignant neoplasm of the liver. Further diagnostic testing revealed metastasis of the liver cancer to the kidney. How is this case coded using the ICD-9 coding guidelines?
    a. 198.0, 780.39, 155.0
    b. V10.07, 780.39, 198.0
    c. 155.0, V10.07, 198.0, 780.39
    d. 198.0, 780.39, V10.07

31. Bob was admitted with seizures and has a history of malignant neoplasm of the liver. Further diagnostic testing revealed metastasis of the liver cancer to the kidney. How is this case coded using the ICD-10 coding guidelines?
    a. C79.00, Z85.05
    b. Z85.05
    c. C79.00, R56.9
    d. C79.00, R56.9, Z85.05

32. A 78-year-old woman is treated for severe malnutrition, percutaneous endoscopic gastrostomy. How is this case coded using the ICD-9 coding guidelines?
    a. 262, 43.11
    b. 261, 43.11
    c. 263.2, 43.11
    d. 263.9, 43.11

33. A 78-year-old woman is treated for severe malnutrition, percutaneous endoscopic gastrosomy. How is this case coded using the ICD-10 coding guidelines?
    a. E43, E45, 00H63UZ
    b. E43, 507.0, 00H63UZ
    c. E43, 00H63UZ
    d. E45, E43, 00H63UZ

34. A 13-year-old girl is admitted with sickle cell anemia with crisis. How is this case coded using the ICD-9 coding guidelines?
    a. 282.61
    b. 282.62
    c. 282.62, V13.09
    d. 282.64

35. A 13-year-old girl is admitted with sickle cell anemia with crisis. How is this case coded using the ICD-10 coding guidelines?
    a. D56.00
    b. D57.00
    c. D59.00
    d. D57.0A

36. Patient is stated to have anxiety with depression. How is this case coded using the ICD-9 coding guidelines?
    a. 300.4
    b. 300.00
    c. 300.10
    d. 300.00, 311

37. Patient is stated to have anxiety with depression. How is this case coded using the ICD-10 coding guidelines?
    a. F41.8
    b. F34.9
    c. F34.7
    d. F34.4

38. Bob is 65 years old and has aspiration pneumonia with pneumonia due to *Staphylococcus aureus*. He also has emphysema. How is this case coded using the ICD-9 coding guidelines?
    a. 507.0, 482.41, 492.8
    b. 482.41, 507.0, 492.8
    c. 482.41, 492.8
    d. 507.0, 483.31, 492.8

39. Bob is 65 years old and has aspiration pneumonia with pneumonia due to *Staphylococcus aureus*. He also has emphysema. How is this case coded using the ICD-10 coding guidelines?
    a. J69.0, J15.211; J43.9
    b. J69.0
    c. J15.211, J43.9
    d. J43.9

40. Patient has acute and chronic cholecystitis with cholelithiasis. Laproscopic cholecystectomy attempted and converted to open. How is this case coded using the ICD-9 coding guidelines?
    a. 574.10, 574.00, 51.22, 51.23
    b. 574.01, 574.10, 51.22
    c. 574.20, 51.22, 51.23
    d. 574.00, 574.10, 51.22, 51.23

41. Patient has acute and chronic cholecystitis with cholelithiasis. Laproscopic cholecystectomy attempted and converted to open. How is this case coded using the ICD-10 coding guidelines?
 a. K80.12, K64.11, 0FT44ZZ
 b. K64.11
 c. 0FT44ZZ
 d. K80.12, 0FT44ZZ

42. The patient has an acute urinary tract infection due to *E. coli*. How is this case coded using the ICD-9 coding guidelines?
 a. 599.84, 041.4
 b. 041.4, 599.0
 c. 599.0, 041.4
 d. 599.0

43. The patient has an acute urinary tract infection due to *E. coli*. How is this case coded using the ICD-10 coding guidelines?
 a. N39.0, A49.1
 b. 0FT40ZZ
 c. N39.0, A49.1, 0FT.40ZZ
 d. 0FT.40ZZ

44. Single newborn delivered at 42 weeks gestation; manually assisted delivery. How is this case coded using the ICD-9 coding guidelines?
 a. 645.11, V27.0, 73.59
 b. 645.21, V27.0, 73.59
 c. 645.21, V27.0, 73.51
 d. 650, V27.0, 73.51

45. Single newborn delivered at 42 weeks gestation; manually assisted delivery. How is this case coded using the ICD-10 coding guidelines?
 a. D48.0, Z37.0, 10E0XZZ
 b. D48.0, Z37.0
 c. D48.0
 d. 10E0XZZ

46. Bob had a recurrent internal derangement of the right knee. Physician performed a diagnostic arthroscopy of the knee. How is this case coded using the ICD-9 coding guidelines?
 a. 718.66, 80.26
 b. 718.36, 80.26
 c. 718.36, 80.16
 d. 718.66, 80.16

47. Bob had a recurrent internal derangement of the right knee. Physician performed a diagnostic arthroscopy of the knee. How is this case coded using the ICD-10 coding guidelines?
 a. M22.Z00
 b. M24.461, 0SJC4ZZ
 c. 0SJC4ZZ
 d. 0SJC4ZZ, 0SJC4ZZ

MOCK MEDICAL RECORDS

Instructions for questions 48–60:

Following are inpatient, day surgery, and outpatient observation medical records. Code the following medical records using ICD-9-CM, as well as ICD-10-CM and CPT-4 (for outpatient and day surgery records) codes.

48.

HOUSTON HEALTH CARE CENTER
History and Physical

Patient name: *Case 1*

Present complaint: Gallstones and hyperbilirubinemia

Past history:

    Pertinent surgeries: None

    Pertinent medical illness: Hypertension

    Current medications: Zestril

    Allergies: None

    Smoking: None

    Alcohol: None

Vital signs:

    Pulse: 21   Respiratory Rate: 12   Blood pressure: 140/93

General: Alert, oriented. No acute distress

Pertinent lab: Hyperbilirubinemia

HEENT: No mass or deformity

Torso/Breast: No mass or deformity

Heart: Normal rhythm, no murmur or gallop

Lungs: Clear to auscultation

Abdomen: Epigastric and RLQ pain

Pelvic/Rectal: No mass or tenderness

Extremities: No edema or tenderness

Neurological: Intact

_____

Impressions: Choledocholithiasis

Treatment and plan: Endoscopic retrograde cholangiopancreatography (ERCP)

Signature: _____ MD

H&P

HOUSTON HEALTH CARE CENTER
Procedure Note

Preoperative diagnosis: Gallstones and hyperbilirubin

Procedure: Endoscopic retrograde sphincterotomy with stone extraction

Surgeon: Dr. Xxxxx

Anesthesia: Versed, meperidine (Demerol), and benzocaine (Cetacaine)

Postoperative diagnosis: Choledocholithiasis

Drains, complications: None

Estimated blood loss: None

Findings: Choledocholithiasis

Signature: _____ MD

Procedure Note

HOUSTON HEALTH CARE CENTER

Operative Report

Preoperative diagnoses: 1. Status postendoscopic retrograde cholangiopancreaticogram with choledocholithiasis and choledochotomy
2. Cholecystitis
3. Cholelithiasis

Postoperative diagnoses: 1. Status postendoscopic retrograde cholangiopancreaticogram with choledocholithiasis and choledochotomy
2. Cholecystitis
3. Cholelithiasis

Procedure performed: Laparoscopic cholecystectomy

Anesthesia: General endotracheal anesthesia

Estimated blood loss: Minimal

Complications: None

Findings: 1. Inflamed gallbladder with mucinous, clear material
2. Multiple stones

Procedure in detail: The patient was prepped and draped in the supine position.

A small supraumbilical incision was made and carried down through the subcutaneous tissue using electrocautery. The linea alba was identified and divided. The finger was bluntly inserted through the preperitoneal space into the peritoneum. Stay sutures of #2-0 Vicryl were placed to the right and left of midline.

A Hasson trocar was passed into the abdomen, and the abdomen was insufflated with air. There were no hemodynamic changes.

Examination revealed a distended, mildly inflamed gallbladder. There were some adhesions between the liver capsule and the anterior abdominal wall.

A 10-mm trocar was placed in the upper midline and two 5-mm trocars in the right upper quadrant. The gallbladder was aspirated using a long needle. Clear material was returned. After the gallbladder was aspirated flat, it was grasped and elevated up over the liver. Some mild adhesions of the gallbladder to the duodenum were taken down, and the dissection was begun at the level of the infundibulum/cystic duct junction.

The cystic duct was easily identified, clipped twice proximally and once distally, and divided. The cystic artery was easily identified, clipped twice proximally and once distally, and divided. The gallbladder was dissected free from the underlying liver bed without entering the liver parenchyma. The gallbladder was drawn out through the umbilicus and opened on the back table. There was clear, milky, mucoid fluid with multiple stones but no evidence of any tumor. The bed was then examined, and there was no bleeding.

(continues)

Op Report

HOUSTON HEALTH CARE CENTER
Operative Report *(Continued)*

This was thoroughly irrigated and aspirated, including the Morrison pouch in the lateral aspect of the right lobe. The trocars were removed sequentially with no evidence of any bleeding. The 10-mm trocar sites were closed with #2-0 Vicryl at the fascia. All four trocar sites were closed at the skin with a running, subcuticular suture of #4-0 Vicryl after being thoroughly irrigated, and dry dressings were applied.

The patient tolerated the procedure well and had no hemodynamic oxygenation problems.

Dictated and reviewed by: _____ MD

Op Report

HOUSTON HEALTH CARE CENTER
Surgical Pathology Report

Clinical information

Preoperative diagnosis: Acute cholecystitis

Postoperative diagnosis: Same as above

Tissue

Source description: Gallbladder

Gross description:

The specimen is received in formalin in a container labeled with the patient's name, Ella Dawson, and medical record number and designated "gallbladder." It consists of an opened gallbladder measuring 10 cm in length and 5 cm in circumference. The serosa is tan-pink. The wall measures 0.2 cm in thickness.

The mucosa is unremarkable. Also present in the container are two irregular lobulated tan-yellow stones. Representative sections are submitted in cassettes A1–A3.

3 blocks, 3 H&E

Azk:Mbv

Diagnosis:

Gallbladder, cholecystectomy: Acute and chronic cholecystitis. Cholelithiasis.

Path Report

HOUSTON HEALTH CARE CENTER
Operative Note

Preoperative diagnosis: Choledocholithiasis s/p ERCP

Procedure: Laparoscopic cholecystectomy

Surgeon: Dr. Xxxxx

Anesthesia: General

Postoperative diagnosis: Cholecystitis and cholelithiasis

Drains, complications: None

Estimated blood loss: Minimal

Findings: Inflamed gallbladder; mucinous, clear material; multiple gallstones

Signature: _____ MD

Op Note

Answer Sheet for Case 1

Code this inpatient medical record using ICD-10-CM diagnoses and ICD-10-PCS procedure codes.

Principal diagnosis:

Secondary diagnoses (if any):

Principal procedure:

Other procedures (if any):

49.

HOUSTON HEALTH CARE CENTER
History and Physical

Patient name: *Case 2*

Present complaint: 28-year-old, gravida 2, para 1 with chief complaint of incompetent cervix here for cerclage insertion.

Past history:

   Pertinent surgeries: None

   Pertinent medical illness: None

   Current medications: None

   Allergies: No known allergies

   Smoking: None

   Alcohol: None

Vital signs:

   Pulse: 101   Respiratory rate: 20   Blood pressure: 131/80

General: Alert, oriented, no acute distress

Pertinent lab:

HEENT: No mass or deformity

Torso/Breast: No mass or deformity

Heart: Normal rhythm, no murmur or gallop

Lungs: Clear to auscultation

Abdomen: Gravid

Pelvic/Rectal: No mass or tenderness

Extremities: No edema or tenderness

Neurological: Intact

_____

Impressions: Incompetent cervix at 12 weeks

Treatment and plan: McDonald's cerclage insertion

Signature: _____ MD

H&P

HOUSTON HEALTH CARE CENTER
Operative Report

Procedure: McDonald's cerclage placement

Diagnosis: Intrauterine pregnancy at 12 weeks with cervical incompetence

Anesthesia: Epidural

Findings and technique: Preoperatively, her internal os was approximately 1 cm dilated. The posterior cervix was approximately 2 cm long, and the interior cervix was approximately 1 cm long. At the end of the procedure, the knot could be felt at the 12 o'clock position and the internal os was closed to digital examination.

The patient was in the dorsal lithotomy position. She had an internal and an external perineal prep and was draped for the procedure. A Mersilene band on two needles was used with one needle placed in at the 6 o'clock position and brought out at 3 o'clock, and replaced at the same position and brought out at 12 o'clock. The other needle was taken in at 3 o'clock and brought out at 9 o'clock, and then replaced and brought out at 12 o'clock position. The Mersilene band then was tied at the 12 o'clock position until the internal os was closed. It was palpable at the end of the procedure, and the two ends were cut long. The patient received perioperative antibiotics, and her heart tones were Dopplerable before the procedure. The procedure was without complications, and the patient was taken to the recovery room in stable condition.

Op Report

HOUSTON HEALTH CARE CENTER
Operative Note

Preoperative diagnosis: Incompetent cervix at 12 weeks

Procedure: Cerclage insertion

Surgeon: Dr. Xxxxx

Anesthesia: General

Postoperative diagnosis: Incompetent cervix at 12 weeks

Drains, complications: None

Estimated blood loss: None

Signature: _____ MD

Op Note

HOUSTON HEALTH CARE CENTER
Discharge Note/Discharge Order

Hospital course: Uncomplicated

Discharge instructions:

Medication: None

Activity: As tolerated

Diet: As per instructions

Follow-up: 2 weeks in office

Discharge status: Stable

Final diagnosis: Incompetent cervix at 12 weeks

Signature: _____

Discharge

Answer Sheet for Case 2

Code this inpatient medical record using ICD-10-CM diagnoses and ICD-10-PCS procedure codes.

Principal diagnosis:

Secondary diagnoses (if any):

Principal procedure:

Other procedures (if any):

50.

HOUSTON HEALTH CARE CENTER
History and Physical

Patient name: *Case 3*

Present complaint: Numbness in left hand

Past history:

    Pertinent surgeries: Right carpal tunnel release

    Pertinent medical illness: None

    Current medications: Avapro

    Allergies: None

    Smoking: Yes

    Alcohol: Yes

Vital signs:

    Pulse: 112   **Respiratory rate**: 20   **Blood pressure**: 122/80

General: Alert, oriented, no acute distress

Pertinent lab:

HEENT: No mass or deformity

Torso/Breast: No mass or deformity

Heart: Normal rhythm, no murmur or gallop

Lungs: Clear to auscultation

Abdomen: No mass or tenderness

Pelvic/Rectal: Deformed

Extremities: Left hand with numbness and decreased sensation

Neurological: Median neuropathy

Impressions: Carpal tunnel syndrome, left hand

Treatment and plan: Carpal tunnel release

Signature: _____ MD

H&P

HOUSTON HEALTH CARE CENTER
Operative Report

Preoperative diagnosis: Carpal tunnel syndrome left wrist

Postoperative diagnosis: Carpal tunnel syndrome left wrist

Operation: Decompression of medial nerve, left wrist

Surgeon: Dr. Xxxxx

Anesthesia: Bier block

Estimated blood loss: Less than 500 cc

Procedure: Under Bier block anesthesia, preparation was done with Betadine scrub, Betadine solution, and sterile draping. Curvilinear incision was made based on the lunar side of the longitudinal wrist crease and carried up to the proximal flexor wrist crease. This was carried through subcutaneous tissue. Range retractors were inserted. The median nerve was visualized using the microscope at the proximal edge of the transverse carpal ligament. The nerve was protected and, using curved dissecting scissors, the transverse carpal ligament was sectioned under direct vision. The nerve was quite compressed. After the ligament had been sectioned, the wound was closed with interrupted 5-0 nylon sutures and sterile dressings were applied. The patient tolerated the procedure well and circulation to the extremity was intact at the completion of the procedure.

Op Report

HOUSTON HEALTH CARE CENTER
Operative Note

Preoperative diagnosis: Carpal tunnel syndrome

Procedure: Carpal tunnel release, left hand

Surgeon: Dr. Xxxxx

Anesthesia: General

Postoperative diagnosis: Carpal tunnel syndrome

Drains, complications: None

Estimated blood loss: None

Signature: _____ MD

Op Note

HOUSTON HEALTH CARE CENTER

Discharge Note/Discharge Order

Hospital course: Stable

Discharge instructions:

   Medication: As per instructions

   Activity: As tolerated

   Diet: As per instructions

   Follow-up: Month

Discharge status: Discharged when criteria for discharge were met

Final diagnosis: Carpal tunnel syndrome

Signature: _____

Discharge

Answer Sheet for Case 3

Code this day surgery medical record using ICD-10-CM diagnostic and CPT-4 procedural codes.

Principal diagnosis:

Secondary diagnoses (if any):

CPT code(s):

51.

HOUSTON HEALTH CARE CENTER
History and Physical

Patient name: *Case 4*

Present complaint: R knee pain

Past history:

   Pertinent surgeries: None

   Pertinent medical illness: None

   Current medications: None

   Allergies: None

   Smoking: No

   Alcohol: No

Vital signs: Stable

General:

Pertinent lab: Normal

HEENT: No mass or deformity

Torso/Breast: No mass or deformity

Heart: Normal rhythm, no murmur or gallop

Lungs: Clear to auscultation

Abdomen: No mass or tenderness

Pelvic/Rectal: No mass or tenderness

Extremities: R knee tender medial joint

Neurological: Intact

Impressions: Torn medial meniscus

Treatment and plan: Arthroscopy

Signature: _____ MD

H&P

HOUSTON HEALTH CARE CENTER
Operative Report

Procedure: Arthroscopic partial medial meniscectomy

Diagnosis: Torn medial meniscus

Anesthesia: General

Technique: After induction with general anesthesia, a standard three-portal approach of the knee was evaluated. Mild synovitic changes were noted in all three compartments. The anterior cruciate ligament was intact, as was the lateral meniscus, and there were only slight synovitic changes in the anterior compartment. The anterior portion of the medial meniscus had a flap tear, which was debrided with an aggressive resector.

After all instruments were withdrawn, 4-0 nylon horizontal mattress stitches were used to close the wound and pressure dressings were applied. The patient was awakened and removed to the recovery room in good condition.

Op Report

HOUSTON HEALTH CARE CENTER
Operative Note

Preoperative diagnosis: Torn medial meniscus

Procedure: Arthroscopic meniscectomy

Surgeon: Dr. Xxxxx

Anesthesia: General

Postoperative diagnosis: Torn medial meniscus

Drains, complications: None

Estimated blood loss: None

Findings: Torn medial meniscus

Signature: _____ MD

Op Note

HOUSTON HEALTH CARE CENTER
Discharge Note/Discharge Order

Hospital course: Good

Discharge instructions:

    Medication: As per instructions

    Activity: As tolerated

    Diet: As per instructions

    Follow-up: 3 days

Discharge status: Stable

Final diagnosis: Torn medial meniscus, right knee

Signature: _____

Discharge

Answer Sheet for Case 4

Code this day surgery medical record using ICD-10-CM diagnostic and CPT-4 procedure codes.

Principal diagnosis:

Secondary diagnoses (if any):

CPT code(s):

52.

HOUSTON HEALTH CARE CENTER
History and Physical

Patient name: *Case 5*

Present complaint: 38-year-old, gravida 2, para 2, LMP two weeks ago, no form of birth control, currently desires permanent sterilization.

Past history:

    Pertinent surgeries: Laparoscopy 10 years ago for ovarian cyst

    Pertinent medical illness: None

    Current medications: Multivitamin

    Allergies: No known allergies

    Smoking: None

    Alcohol: None

Vital signs:

    Pulse: 70   **Respiratory Rate**: 18   **Blood pressure**: 152/95

General: Alert, oriented, no acute distress

HEENT: WNL

Torso/Breast: No mass or deformity

Heart: Normal rhythm, no murmur or gallop

Lungs: Clear to auscultation bilaterally

Abdomen: Soft, not tender

Pelvic/Rectal: Deferred to OR

Extremities: No edema or tenderness

Neurological: Grossly intact

Impressions: Multiparity desires permanent sterilization

Treatment and plan: To OR for scope bilateral tubal ligation

Signature: _____ MD

H&P

HOUSTON HEALTH CARE CENTER
Operative Report

Procedure: Scope bilateral tubal ligation using Falope rings

Diagnosis: Multiparity desiring permanent sterilization

Anesthesia: General endotracheal

Fluids: 400 cc in

Estimated blood loss: Minimal

Procedure in detail: The patient was taken to the operating room, where general anesthesia was induced without difficulty. She was placed in the dorsal lithotomy position and prepped and draped in the usual sterile fashion.

An infraumbilical incision was made with a scalpel and a 10-mm trocar was inserted through this incision until peritoneal placement was attained. This was confirmed using the low pressure of CO_2 gas. The camera was inserted and attention was then turned to the suprapubic incision site. A 5-mm trocar was inserted here without difficulty. The Falope ring applicator was then passed through this. Both tubes were identified and followed to the fimbriated ends. Approximately 3 cm from the cornua, the tube was grasped and the Falope ring was applied on both sides without difficulty. Both had good knuckle of the tube with good blanching noted. Pictures were taken. The rest of the pelvic anatomy appeared normal. The gas was evacuated from the abdomen. Both trocars were removed. The incision was closed with subcuticular 3-0 Vicryl. She tolerated the procedure well and went to the recovery room in stable condition.

Complications: None

Counts: All counts were correct.

Dictated by: _____ (Resident)

Reviewed by: _____ (Surgeon)

Op Report

HOUSTON HEALTH CARE CENTER
Operative Note

Preoperative diagnosis: Multiparity, desires permanent sterilization

Procedure: Bilateral tubal ligation with Falope rings

Surgeon: Dr. Xxxxx

Anesthesia: General

Postoperative diagnosis: Multiparity, desires permanent sterilization

Drains, complications: None

Estimated blood loss: Minimal

Signature: _____ MD

Op Note

HOUSTON HEALTH CARE CENTER
Discharge Note/Discharge Order

Hospital course: Uncomplicated

Discharge instructions:

Medication: Vicodin 1–2 tablets every 4 hours as needed

Activity: Do not attempt to make any important decision for a period of 24 hours. Do not drive for 24 hours.

Diet: Advance as tolerated when awake, alert, and oriented

Follow-up: 2 weeks in office

Discharge status: Stable

Final diagnosis: Multiparity, desires permanent sterilization s/p bilateral tubal ligation

Signature: _____

Discharge

Answer Sheet for Case 5

Code this day surgery medical record using ICD-10-CM diagnostic and CPT-4 procedural codes.

Principal diagnosis:

Secondary diagnoses (if any):

CPT code(s):

53.

HOUSTON HEALTH CARE CENTER
History and Physical

Patient name: *Case 6*

Present complaint: 25-year-old female patient with pilonidal cyst with continuous drainage, swelling, and pain

Past history:

    Pertinent surgeries: None

    Pertinent medical illness: Hypothyroidism and depression

    Current medications: Synthroid, Paxil, Zyprexan, and multivitamins

    Allergies: No known allergies

    Smoking: None

    Alcohol: None

Vital signs:

    Pulse: 86   Respiratory Rate: 10   Blood pressure: 128/80

General: Alert, oriented, no acute distress

HEENT: WNL

Torso/Breast: No mass or deformity

Heart: Normal rhythm, no murmur or gallop

Lungs: Clear to auscultation bilaterally

Abdomen: Soft, not tender

Pelvic/Rectal: WNL

Extremities: No edema or tenderness

Neurological: Grossly intact

Impressions: Patient with obvious pilonidal cyst

Treatment and plan: Pilonidal cystectomy

Signature: _____ MD

H&P

HOUSTON HEALTH CARE CENTER

Operative Report

Procedure: Pilonidal cystectomy

Diagnosis: Pilonidal cyst

Anesthesia: General endotracheal and 30 cc of 0.25% Marcaine with epinephrine as a local block

Operative findings: Small superficial subcutaneous sinus and pilonidal cyst, at midline within the buttocks.

Complications: None

Counts: All counts were correct.

Procedure in detail: The patient was taken to the operating room and placed supine on the stretcher, then subsequently induced with general anesthesia. Once the patient was orally endotracheally intubated, she was flipped into a prone position onto two rolls, with care taken not to put any undue pressure on her breasts. Once the patient was positioned in a prone position, the buttocks were spread and held with tape. The area between the buttocks was fully prepped and draped in the usual surgical sterile fashion. A lacrymal probe was used to go through a sinus that tracked into the midline and opened up at midline with a slight extension superiorly. Once the cavity was delineated, local anesthesia was injected into circumferential tissues and deep through the cyst, using 0.25% Marcaine with epinephrine, approximately 30 cc. After local anesthesia was injected, Bovie electrocautery was used to open up the sinus tracts and the edges were cauterized, to allow better drainage of the cavity. The cavity was subsequently scraped and cleaned. Once the entire cavity was fully debrided and skin edges were excised, hemostasis was achieved using Bovie electrocautery. The cavity was packed using a moist 4 × 4 and another 4 × 4 was placed on top and held in place using tape. The patient was subsequently rolled back into a supine position on the stretcher and then awoke from general anesthesia, extubated, and taken to the post-anesthesia care unit, in an alert and hemodynamically stable condition.

Dictated by: _____ (Resident)

Reviewed by: _____ (Surgeon)

Op Report

HOUSTON HEALTH CARE CENTER
Operative Note

Preoperative Diagnosis: Pilonidal cyst

Procedure: Pilonidal cystectomy

Surgeon: Dr. Xxxxx

Anesthesia: General endotracheal and 30 cc of 0.25% Marcaine with epinephrine as a local block

Postoperative diagnosis: Pilonidal cyst

Drains, Complications: None

Estimated blood loss: Minimal

Signature: _____ MD

Op Note

HOUSTON HEALTH CARE CENTER
Discharge Note/Discharge Order

Hospital course: Uncomplicated

Discharge instructions:

Dressing: Sitz baths 3 times a day and after each bowel movement. Change gauze to wound 3 times a day.

Medication: Darvocet n-100, one or two tablets by mouth, if needed for pain

Activity: Do not attempt to make any important decision for a period of 24 hours. Do not drive for 24 hours.

Diet: Resume

Follow-up: 2 weeks in office

Discharge status: Stable

Final diagnosis: Pilonidal cyst

Signature: _____

Discharge

Answer Sheet for Case 6

Code this day surgery medical record using ICD-10-CM diagnostic and CPT-4 procedure codes.

Principal diagnosis:

Secondary diagnoses (if any):

CPT code(s):

54.

HOUSTON HEALTH CARE CENTER
History and Physical

Patient name: *Case 7*

Present complaint: This is a 53-year-old man with flank pain.

History of present illness: The patient started having left flank pain in October of last year. At that time, he was seen at a local emergency room, and a CT scan demonstrated a 7-mm proximal stone in the left ureter that he was told would pass. Because the patient did not have any more pain, he did not follow up, but in December of last year he had another episode of recurrent pain, and this time a repeat CT scan demonstrated the stone had dropped to the lower part of the ureter, causing obstruction at the level of the sacroiliac joint. The patient came to me and was asymptomatic and had a negative urinalysis, but a KUB and review of his X-rays demonstrated the stone to be visible in the pelvis of the left ureter and the patient was advised to have extracorporeal shock wave lithotripsy. He has been on Flomax to prevent potential postprocedure urinary retention.

Past history:

    Pertinent surgeries: None

    Pertinent medical illness: Hypertension

    Current medications: Atenolol (Flomax) 25 mg daily

    Family history: The patient's father died at the age of 72 of unknown cause, per patient. The mother died at the age of 86 from liver cancer.

    Allergies: No known allergies

    Smoking: None

    Alcohol: None

Vital signs:

    Pulse: 70   **Respiratory Rate**: 18   **Blood pressure**: 152/95

General: The patient is well developed and well nourished in no acute distress.

HEENT: WNL

Torso/Breast: No mass or deformity

Heart: Normal sinus rhythm, no murmur or gallop

Lungs: Clear to auscultation bilaterally

Abdomen: Soft, there is no organomegaly or tenderness

(continues)

H&P

HOUSTON HEALTH CARE CENTER

History and Physical *(Continued)*

Genitourinary: There is no costovertebral angle (CVA) tenderness. The patient has a normal circumcised penis, bilateral descended normal testes, and a 15 g, benign-feeling prostate.

Extremities: No edema or tenderness

Impressions: This is a patient with an obstructing left lower third ureteral calculus admitted for extracorporeal shock wave lithotripsy (ESWL).

Signature: _____ MD

H&P

HOUSTON HEALTH CARE CENTER
Operative Report

Procedure: Left extracorporeal shock wave lithotripsy

Diagnosis: Ureteral calculus

Anesthesia: Local

Shocks: 4000 to left ureter

Flouro: 7.5

Patient's position: Prone

Procedure in detail: The primary operative procedure consisted of extracorporeal shock wave lithotripsy using the Litotron lithotripter. The patient was positioned on the treatment table. Biaxial fluoroscopy was utilized to localize the stone(s). When added, additional radiographic snapshots were utilized to assist localization. Multiple firing of the electromagnetic shock wave source as noted above was made to effect pulverization of the stone(s). Upon completion of the procedure, the patient was transferred back to the recovery room for observation.

Complications: None

Dictated and reviewed by: _____ MD

Op Report

HOUSTON HEALTH CARE CENTER
Operative Note

Preoperative diagnosis: Ureteral calculus

Procedure: Left extracorporeal shock wave lithotripsy

Surgeon: Dr. Xxxxx

Anesthesia: Local

Postoperative diagnosis: Ureteral calculus

Signature: _____ MD

Op Note

HOUSTON HEALTH CARE CENTER
Discharge Note/Discharge Order

Hospital course: Uneventful

Discharge instructions:

Medication: None

Activity: As tolerated

Diet: Advance as tolerated

Follow-up: 3 days

Discharge status: Stable

Final diagnosis: Ureteral calculus

Signature: _____

Discharge

Answer Sheet for Case 7

Code this day surgery medical record using ICD-10-CM diagnostic and CPT-4 procedure codes.

Principal diagnosis:

Secondary diagnoses (if any):

CPT code(s):

55.

HOUSTON HEALTH CARE CENTER
Face Sheet

Patient name: *Case 8*

Final diagnosis: Obscured vision after cataract extraction

Procedures: YAG laser posterior capsulotomy, right eye

Face Sheet

HOUSTON HEALTH CARE CENTER
Laser Operative Summary Report

Patient name: *Case 8*

History: Progressive loss of vision in right eye over past 4–6 months. Macular hole surgery 4 years ago and cataract surgery 3 years ago.

Medications: Levoxyl, Premarin, Lantac

Allergies: Penicillin and codeine

Physical find: Cloudy capsule right eye

Visual activity: OD 20/50 Ocular tension OD 15

Slit lamp: OD cloudy posterior capsule

Fundus: OD macular scarring

Vital signs: BP: 135/81   Pulse: 69   Mental status: Alert

Diagnosis: OD cloudy capsule

Procedure: YAG laser capsulotomy

Anesthesia: Topical

Contact lens: Yes, Abraham

Area/Pattern: OD

Parameters: 1. # Pulses: 13

2. Spot size: N/A

3. Power: 3.1 mW

4. Duration:

Complications: None

Patch: No

Return visit: 1 hour

Diet: Regular

Activity: As tolerated

Signature: _____ MD

Op Report

Answer Sheet for Case 8

Code this day surgery medical record using ICD-10-CM diagnostic and CPT-4 procedural codes.

Principal diagnosis:

Secondary diagnoses (if any):

CPT code(s):

56.

HOUSTON HEALTH CARE CENTER

History and Physical

Patient name: *Case 9*

History: This child has had recurrent ear infections over the last 4 months. He has received several courses of appropriate antibiotic therapy, to which he initially responds well but relapses soon after discontinuation of the drug. He had his first episode at the age of 5 months. The child also suffers from cough variant asthma for which he is on inhaler frequently. He has no known risk factors for otitis media, other than an older sibling having had tubes placed at the age of 2 years old.

Physical examination: Clinical examination today showed evidence of a left acute otitis media. The right ear also had an otitis media with effusion. Nose and throat were normal.

Recommendations: This child is a candidate for placement of pressure-equalizing (PE) tubes. I have discussed the procedure, its complications, and outcome with his mother, who has consented for this. I have also recommended a course of high-dose amoxicillin to cover the child in view of the presence of acute otitis media.

Signature: _____ MD

H&P

HOUSTON HEALTH CARE CENTER
Operative Report

Diagnosis: Chronic otitis media with effusion

Procedure: Myringotomy left and right with insertion of pressure-equalizing tubes left and right

Anesthesia: General mask

Estimated blood loss: Less than 1 cc

Complications: None

Condition: Satisfactory

Indication for surgery: This is a 10-month-old male with a history of recurrent otitis media not responding satisfactorily to antibiotic therapy. Clinical examination showed inflamed tympanic membranes. There was evidence of effusion behind both tympanic membranes. In addition, there was evidence of a recent acute episode of otitis media. In view of the recurrent nature of his problem, it was decided to proceed with insertion of PE tubes.

Procedure: The patient was brought to the operating room and general anesthetic was administered via a face mask. The right ear was first examined under the microscope. The external auditory canal was cleared of cerumen. An anterior inferior myringotomy was performed. A mucoid effusion was suctioned out of the middle ear and a blue Pope tympanostomy tube was inserted. The opposite ear was examined under the microscope. The external auditory canal was cleared of cerumen. An anterior inferior myringotomy was performed. Mucoid effusion was suctioned out of the middle ear and a blue Pope tympanostomy tube was inserted. No complications were encountered. Antibiotic ear drops were instilled in both ears. The patient was then handed back to the anesthesiologist in satisfactory condition and taken to the recovery room.

Dictated and reviewed by: _____ (Surgeon)

Op Report

HOUSTON HEALTH CARE CENTER
Operative Note

Preoperative diagnosis: Chronic otitis media with effusion

Postoperative diagnosis: Chronic otitis media with effusion

Procedure: Myringotomy left and right with insertion of pressure-equalizing tubes left and right

Surgeon: Dr. Xxxxx

Anesthesia: General endotracheal

Complications: None

Signature: _____ MD

Op Note

HOUSTON HEALTH CARE CENTER
Discharge Note/Discharge Order

Hospital course: Uncomplicated

Discharge instructions:

Medication: Tylenol, prn
Cortisporin 3 drops, 3 times a day for 3 days

Activity: Encourage child to rest at home the first day after surgery

Diet: Regular

Follow-up: 2 weeks in office

Discharge status: Stable

Final diagnosis: Chronic otitis media with effusion

Signature: _____

Discharge

Answer Sheet for Case 9

Code this day surgery medical record using ICD-10-CM diagnostic and CPT-4 procedural codes.

Principal diagnosis:

Secondary diagnoses (if any):

CPT code(s):

57.

HOUSTON HEALTH CARE CENTER
Face Sheet

Patient name: *Case 10*

Final diagnosis: New-onset angina, coronary artery disease
History of coronary stent insertion
History of myocardial infarction
Diabetes mellitus, history of smoking, hypertension, hypercholesterolemia

Procedures: Left heart catheterization
Selective angiogram (Judkins technique)
Left ventriculogram

Reason for admission: Left heart catheterization and selective coronary angiography.

Indications for procedure: 1. Known coronary artery disease, status post coronary angioplasty with stent insertion of the right coronary artery.
2. New-onset angina

History of present illness: This 50-year-old man with a history of a non-Q wave myocardial infarction 6 weeks ago, status post angioplasty at that time, presented back to the clinic with further worsening of his angina, and was referred for cardiac catheterization. The risks and benefits of cardiac catheterization have been discussed with the patient.

He has done relatively well since the angioplasty until recently, when he was admitted for additional problem, which was a diverticular perforation. There was a small area of ischemia on the inferior wall following the evaluation for preoperative clearance for drainage of the diverticular abscess.

He has no PND, orthopnea, or peripheral edema. However, on his last consultation he did complain of new-onset chest pain on exertion. In conjunction, the finding of coronary ischemia remains of concern in that he may have developed restenosis of his previous coronary stent. I have discussed this with the patient and he wishes to go ahead with cardiac catheterization.

Coronary artery disease risk factors: Risk factors include hypertension and hypercholesterolemia. He has a history of diabetes. No history of asthma. He has a family history of heart disease. He is an ex-smoker.

Past medical/surgical history: As described above, myocardial infarction 6 weeks ago with stenting of the right coronary artery.

Allergies: Allergic to penicillin. He denies any allergies to iodine or seafood.

(continues)

Face Sheet

HOUSTON HEALTH CARE CENTER
Face Sheet *(Continued)*

Review of systems: Unremarkable, he has no bowel disturbance or urinary tract disturbance. He has no neurological symptoms.

Current medications:

1. Lisinopril 0.5 mg qd
2. Metoprolol 50 mg bid
3. Plavix 75 mg qd
4. Aspirin 325 mg qd
5. Lipitor 10 mg qd
6. Niaspan 500 mg bid. He was noted to have an extremely low HDL in the hospital and therefore was started on Niaspan to try and raise his HDL. He appears to be tolerating all of his medications relatively well at this point in time.

Physical examination:

Vital signs:

   Blood pressure was 140/70, pulse 72 and regular

Neck: JVD flat. No carotid bruits

Heart: S_1 and S_2 normal

Chest: Clear

Abdomen: Soft and nontender

Extremities: No peripheral edema

Assessment and plan: The patient is clinically stable with no fever and is planning elective surgery for his diverticular perforation. Given the inferolateral ischemia and new-onset angina, I recommend a cardiac catheterization.

Signature: _____ MD

Face Sheet

HOUSTON HEALTH CARE CENTER
Procedure Note

Left heart cath, selective coronary (Judkins technique), and left ventriculogram

Findings: LM: Normal

            LAD: Mild disease

            Ramus: 60–65% stenosis

            CX: Mild disease

            RCA: Patent stent

Assessment and plan: Continue medical treatment and discharge after bed rest

Procedure Note

Answer Sheet for Case 10

Code this outpatient observation medical record using ICD-10-CM diagnostic and CPT-4 procedural codes.

Principal diagnosis:

Secondary diagnoses (if any):

Principal procedure:

Other procedures (if any):

CPT code(s):

58.

HOUSTON HEALTH CARE CENTER
History and Physical

Patient name: *Case 11*

Present complaint: Tonsillitis

Present illness: 12-year-old male with recurrent episodes of acute tonsillitis

Review of systems: Negative

Past history: Negative

Allergies: NKA

Current medication: None

Physical examination:

Vital signs:

   Pulse: 84   **Respiratory Rate**: 16   **Temperature**: 98°F

   Age: 12   **Sex**: M

General: No acute distress

HEENT: PERRL, TM's nl, tonsils +3 enlarged with deep crypts

Chest and lungs: Clear

Heart: R R + R

Abdomen: Soft

Pelvic/Genitalia: defer

Neurological: WNL

Extremities: No edema

Impressions: Chronic tonsillitis

Treatment and plan: Tonsillectomy, possible adenoidectomy

Signature: _____ MD

H&P

HOUSTON HEALTH CARE CENTER
Operative Report

Preoperative diagnosis: 1. Chronic nasal obstruction
2. Chronic tonsillitis
3. Adenoid hypertrophy

Postoperative diagnosis: 1. Chronic nasal obstruction
2. Chronic tonsillitis
3. Adenoid hypertrophy

Procedures performed: Tonsillectomy and adenoidectomy

Anesthesia: General

Complications: None

Estimated blood loss: 5 cc

Indications and findings: This 12-year-old has had recurrent episodes of pharyngitis as well as chronic nasal obstruction. He is totally unable to breathe through his nose.

Findings at the time of surgery included very small tonsils, but a very large adenoid pad in the nasopharynx that obstructed the air flow through his nose. There was also pus in the nasal cavities. The adenoidectomy was accomplished by using a suction cautery.

Description of procedure: The patient was taken to the operating room and was placed on the table in the supine position. He was put to sleep under general anesthetic and intubated. The table was then turned for the procedure.

Using a Crowe-Davis mouth gag in place, the nasopharynx was first inspected. This was accomplished by passing a red rubber catheter through the nose and retracting the soft palate. Upon inspection, it was clear that the adenoid tissue was very enlarged. Using a suction cautery, this was substantially reduced. Also, the nose was irrigated copiously with cold saline to flush out all of the pus. Any bleeding in the nasopharynx was stopped with the electrocautery.

Attention was then turned to the tonsils, which were both rather small. The right tonsil was removed. The left tonsil was cauterized. The airway was good. There was no bleeding. The patient was then awakened in the operating room, extubated, and taken to the recovery room.

Dictated and reviewed by: _____ (Surgeon)

Op Report

HOUSTON HEALTH CARE CENTER
Operative Note

Preoperative diagnosis: Chronic tonsillitis

Postoperative diagnosis: 1. Chronic nasal obstruction
2. Chronic tonsillitis
3. Adenoid hypertrophy

Procedure: Tonsillectomy and adenoidectomy

Surgeon: Dr. Xxxxx

Anesthesia: General

Drains, complications: None

Estimated blood loss: 5 cc

Findings: Chronic nasal obstruction; chronic tonsillitis; adenoid hypertrophy

Signature: _____ MD

Op Note

HOUSTON HEALTH CARE CENTER
Discharge Note/Discharge Order

Diagnosis: 1. Chronic nasal obstruction
2. Chronic tonsillitis
3. Adenoid hypertrophy

Procedure: Tonsillectomy and adenoidectomy

Diet: Clear liquid; advance as tolerated

Activity: At liberty

Discomfort: Tylenol with codeine elixir 3 tsp/po q 4 prn. Amoxil 250 mg po bid

Follow-up: In 2 weeks

Condition at discharge: Stable

Signature: _____

Answer Sheet for Case 11

Code this day surgery medical record using ICD-10-CM diagnostic and CPT-4 procedural codes.

Principal diagnosis:

Secondary diagnoses (if any):

CPT code(s):

59.

HOUSTON HEALTH CARE CENTER
History and Physical

Patient name: *Case 12*

Present complaint: Undescended testicles

Present illness: 13-year-old male with undescended testicles and urinary incontinence

Review of systems: Negative

Past history: Reactive airway disease

Past surgical history: Newborn circumcision

Allergies: NKA

Current medication: Rhinocort

Physical examination:

Vital signs:

   Pulse: 84   Respiratory Rate: 16   Temperature: 98°F

   Age: 13   Sex: M

General: No acute distress

HEENT: Normal

Chest and lungs: Clear to auscultation bilaterally

Abdomen: Soft, nontender

Pelvic/Genitalia: Circumcised, bilateral testes with external ring in scrotum

Neurological: Nonfocal

Extremities: Normal

Impressions: Bilateral undescended testes

Treatment and plan: Bilateral orchiopexy

Signature: _____ MD

H&P

HOUSTON HEALTH CARE CENTER

Operative Report

Preoperative diagnosis: Undescended testicles

Postoperative diagnosis: Undescended testicles

Procedures performed: Bilateral orchiopexy

Anesthesia: General

Complications: None

Procedure in detail: After anesthesia was administered, the patient was prepped and draped in sterile fashion and placed in the supine position. We made small inguinal incisions on both sides, dissected down the external oblique fascia, and opened at the external ring. The testes were low in the canal. They were mobilized and brought up into the wound. The gubernacular and lateral attachments were then divided. The testes were then mobilized back into the ring. A closed processus vaginalis was present on each side, and this was dissected from the cord structure and transected to further lengthen the cord vessels.

The tunica was then opened over the testes. The appendix testis and appendix epidymidis was present on the left side. No appendages were on the right. Both testes were very small. The left testis measured about 9 mm and the right 8 mm, but the volume of the testes was also reduced. The epididymal attachments were normal.

A Dartos pouch was created in the usual way. The testes were brought down to the pouch and secured there with Vicryl suture. Both incisions were closed with absorbable suture. Steri-Strips were placed across the incisions. The patient tolerated the procedure well.

Dictated and reviewed by: _____ (Surgeon)

Op Report

HOUSTON HEALTH CARE CENTER
Operative Note

Preoperative diagnosis: Undescended testicles

Postoperative diagnosis: Undescended testicles

Procedure: Bilateral orchiopexy

Surgeon: Dr. Xxxxx

Anesthesia: General

Drains, complications: None

Findings: Undescended testicles

Signature: _____ MD

Op Note

HOUSTON HEALTH CARE CENTER
Discharge Note/Discharge Order

Diagnosis: Undescended testicles

Procedure: Bilateral orchiopexy

Diet: Regular

Activity: No straddle toys or bicycle riding

Discomfort: Tylenol with codeine 5–10 mL po q 4 as needed for pain

Follow-up: In 3 weeks

Condition at discharge: Stable

Signature: _____

Discharge

Answer Sheet for Case 12

Code this day surgery medical record using ICD-10-CM diagnostic and CPT-4 procedural codes.

Principal diagnosis:

Secondary diagnoses (if any):

CPT code(s):

60.

HOUSTON HEALTH CARE CENTER
Face Sheet

Patient name: *Case 13*

Final diagnosis: Screening for colon cancer
Family history of colon cancer

Procedures: Colonoscopy

Face Sheet

HOUSTON HEALTH CARE CENTER

History and Physical

Present complaint: Family history of colon cancer

Past history: None

Current medications: None

Allergies: NKA

Smoking or drinking: No

Physical examination:

    General: Alert

    HEENT: No mass or deformity

    Torso/Breast: No mass or deformity

    Heart: Normal rhythm

    Lung: Clear to auscultation

    Abdomen: No mass or tenderness

    Extremities: No edema or tenderness

Neurological: Intact

Impression: Family history of colon cancer

Treatment and plan: Colonoscopy

Signature: _____ MD

H&P

HOUSTON HEALTH CARE CENTER
Procedure Note

Preoperative diagnosis: Family history of colon cancer

Postoperative diagnosis: Colon polyps

Procedure: Colonoscopy with polypectomy

Medications: Demerol 50 mg; Versed 2.0

Findings: 4-mm polyp at sigmoid

Pathology results: Tubular adenoma with villious component

    Follow up biopsy results in 1–2 weeks

    Repeat colonoscopy in 2–3 years

Signature: _____ MD

Procedure Note

HOUSTON HEALTH CARE CENTER

Discharge Note/Discharge Order

Hospital course: Stable

Discharge instructions:

Medication: None

Activity: As tolerated

Diet: As per instructions

Follow-up: 1–2 weeks

Discharge status: Discharged when criteria met

Final diagnosis: Colon polyp

Signature: _____

Discharge

Answer Sheet for Case 13

Code this day surgery medical record using ICD-10-CM diagnostic and CPT-4 procedural codes.

Principal diagnosis:

Secondary diagnoses (if any):

CPT code(s):

Organization and Management: Human and Financial Resources

© saicle/ShutterStock, Inc.

1. Management
  a. Defined
    i. People who get things done through other people; contrasted with people who actually do the work
    ii. Process of coordinating individual and group actions toward the accomplishment of organizational goals in a manner that is acceptable to the larger social cultural system
    iii. Process of planning, organizing, and leading the activities of an organization
  b. What Managers Do
    i. Get things done through other people
    ii. Have and use authority to get things done
    iii. Communicate
    iv. Solve problems
    v. Provide direction
  c. Mintzberg's Managerial Roles (Table 9-1)
  d. Levels of Management
    i. Supervisory
      1. Oversee the organization's efforts at the staff level and monitor the effectiveness of everyday operations and individual performance against established standards
      2. Ensure that the organization's human assets are used effectively and that its policies and procedures are carried out consistently
    ii. Middle
      1. Primarily concerned with facilitating the work performed by supervisory and staff-level personnel as well as by executive leaders
      2. Develop, implement, and revise the organization's policies and procedures, under the direction of executive managers
      3. Execute the organizational plans developed at the board and executive levels
      4. Provide the operational information that executives need to develop meaningful plans for the organization's future

Table 9-1 Mintzberg's Managerial Roles	
Managerial Activities	**Related Roles**
Interpersonal	Figurehead
	Liaison
	Leader
Informational	Monitor
	Disseminator
	Spokesperson
Decisional	Entrepreneur
	Disturbance handler
	Resource allocator
	Negotiator

Data from Abdelhak, M., Grostick, S., & Hanken, M. A. (2012). *Health information: Management of a strategic resource*. St. Louis: Saunders Elsevier and Montana, P., & Charnov, B. (2008). *Management*. Hauppauge: Barron's Educational Series.

iii. Executive management
1. Hired by the board, or by the chief executive officer with board approval
2. Responsible for working with the board to set the organization's future direction and establish its strategic plan
3. Ensures that the organization uses its assets wisely, fulfills its current mission, and works toward achieving a meaningful vision for the future
4. Oversees broad functions, departments, or groups of departments
5. Establishes the policies of healthcare organizations and leads their quality improvement and compliance initiatives
6. Works with community leaders to make sure that the healthcare organization contributes to the well-being of the community it serves
7. Titles include
   a. Chief executive officer
   b. President
   c. Executive vice president
   d. Senior vice president
   e. Vice president
   f. Director

iv. Board of governors or board of directors
1. Ultimately responsible for the operation of the healthcare organization
2. Final authority in setting the organization's strategic direction, mission, and vision and general philosophy and ethical base
3. Represents the interests of the organization's owners
   a. Types of owners
      i. Federal government
      ii. State government
      iii. Local government

        iv. Investment group

        v. Educational institution

        vi. Religious organization

        vii. Public group

           1. Stockholders elect board members.

           2. In for-profit entities, investors purchase stock on stock exchanges and receive a share of the profits.

        viii. Private group

           1. Board members are appointed.

           2. May operate as not-for-profit charitable organizations

      4. Consist of chairperson and 10 to 20 board members

e. Landmarks in Management as a Discipline

    i. Scientific

      1. Earliest attempt to study management in a scientific manner, emphasizing worker efficiency achieved through the "one right way" to perform a task, as determined by the expert who possesses a scientific understanding of the work achieved by methodic study

      2. Max Weber (1864–1920): proposed organizations become bureaucracies

      3. Frederick Taylor (1856–1915): attempted to study management scientifically by conducting time and motion studies

      4. Henry Gantt (1861–1919): developed charting method (Gantt chart) that is still used for project management

    ii. Administrative

      1. To compensate for scientific management's exclusion of senior management, administrative management argued that management was a profession and could be learned.

      2. Henri Fayol (1841–1925): identified five management functions and 14 principles (see Table 9-2)

        a. Planning

        b. Organizing

        c. Leading (directing)

        d. Controlling

    iii. Humanistic

      1. Focused on how to treat employees

      2. Initiated the human relations movement

      3. Hawthorne effect

        a. Experiment conduct by Mayo and Roethlisberger from 1924 to 1932 to test the effect of lighting level in the workplace on productivity

        b. Concluded positive attention and human relations improved performance

    iv. Human resources management

      1. Abraham Maslow (1908–1970): suggested hierarchy of needs to help explain behavior and provide guidance for managers on how to better motivate workers

        a. Physiological needs

        b. Safety

        c. Social belonging

        d. Self-esteem

        e. Self-actualization or creativity needs

Table 9-2 Fayol's 14 Principles of Management

Principle	Description
Specialization of labor	Work allocation and specialization allow concentrated activities, deeper understanding, and better efficiency.
Authority	The person to whom responsibilities are given has the right to give direction and expect obedience.
Discipline	The smooth operation of a business requires standards, rules, and values for consistency of action.
Unity of command	Every employee receives direction and instructions from only one boss.
Unity of direction	All workers are aligned in their efforts toward a single outcome.
Subordination of individual interest	Accomplishing shared values and organizational goals takes priority over individual agendas.
Remuneration	Employees should receive fair pay for work.
Centralization	Decisions are made at the top.
Scalar chair	Everyone is clearly included in the chain of command and line of authority from top to bottom of the organization.
Order	People should clearly understand where they fit in the organization, and all people and material have a place.
Equity	People are treated fairly, and a sense of justice should pervade the organization.
Tenure	Turnover is undesirable, and loyalty to the organization is sought.
Initiative	Personal initiative should be encouraged.
Espirit de corps	Harmony, cohesion, teamwork, and good interpersonal relationships should be encouraged.

Data from Fayol, H. (1917). Administration Industrieel et Generale, trans. C. Storrs, General and Industrial Management. Pitman, 1949.

2. Douglas McGregor (1906–1964): recognized the shift in conceptual models from assumptions that workers were incapable of independent action to beliefs in their potential and high performance
   a. Theory X
      i. Presumes workers inherently dislike work and avoid it.
      ii. Employees have little ambition and mostly want security.
      iii. Managerial direction and control are necessary.

      b. Theory Y

          i. Assumes work is as natural as play.

          ii. Motivation could be both internally and externally driven.

          iii. Under the right conditions, people will seek responsibility and be creative.

  v. Operations management: developed out of need to better understand how products and services could be manufactured and delivered

    1. Forecasting: previous conditions are projected into the future.

    2. Linear programming: used to identify an optimal decision, given a set of planned constraints or limited resources.

    3. Break-even analysis: helps planners determine the level of sales at which total revenues equal the total costs. Revenues beyond that are profit.

    4. Queuing theory: mathematical theory for determining the flow of customers or for designing optimal wait times for services.

    5. Simulation and inventory modeling: based on computerization and systems concepts. Key components and processes of a system are represented in a computer model so that planner can experiment with different operating strategies and designs to get the best results before committing to their actual implementation.

    6. PERT

      a. Allows large, long-term, and complex projects to be shown graphically in order to clarify critical task sequences, potential bottlenecks, and the time required for them.

      b. For complex situations, computer decision support can help explore and optimize decisions.

  vi. Contemporary management

    1. Peter Drucker (1909–2005)

      a. Formulated practice of strategy by integrating formulation, tactical planning, and budgeting into a single system of management

      b. Elaborated on the technique of management by objectives (MBO), in which clear target objectives could be stated and measured and could direct behavior

         i. Four elements

            1. Top management plans and sets goals

            2. Managers with subordinates set individual objectives related to organizational goals

            3. Autonomy in the means of achieving objectives

            4. Regular review of performance in obtaining objectives

    2. W. Edwards Deming (1900–1993)

      a. Focused on quality improvement instead of quotas, because workers spent too much time trying to look good or protect themselves by seeking short-term objectives and ignoring long-term and critical outcomes

      b. Total quality management (TQM)

         i. Purported to overcome the limitations of MBO

         ii. Offered a way to build in high performance by maximizing employee potential and continuous improvement of process

f. Basic Components of Management

  i. Effectiveness

    1. Ensures that the utilization of resources accomplishes the objectives (products or services)

      2. Effectiveness is a product of productivity, performance, and efficiency.
- **ii.** Functions
  - **1.** Planning
  - **2.** Organizing
  - **3.** Directing (leading)
  - **4.** Controlling
- **iii.** Resources
  - **1.** External
    - **a.** Human resources
    - **b.** Money
    - **c.** Materials
    - **d.** Machinery
  - **2.** Internal
    - **a.** Creativity
    - **b.** Coordination
    - **c.** Cooperation
    - **d.** Communication
    - **e.** Common sense
- **iv.** Objectives
  - **1.** Something toward which effort is directed
  - **2.** Purposes to be achieved
  - **3.** Direct an organization in the face of change
- **g.** Functions of Management (Planning, Organizing, Directing, Controlling)
  - **i.** Planning
    - **1.** Choose a destination, evaluate alternatives, and decide the specific course
    - **2.** Determine what work must be done
    - **3.** Define roles and mission
    - **4.** Most important of management functions
    - **5.** To plan effectively managers must:
      - **a.** Understand the mission and vision of the organization
      - **b.** Work-group goals should be measurable, reflect organizational and personal priorities, and be challenging yet attainable.
      - **c.** Goals should be flexible and capable of responding to changing conditions.
    - **6.** In planning, managers perform the following:
      - **a.** Define objectives
      - **b.** Set courses of action
      - **c.** Arrange matters in advance
      - **d.** Determine what work must be done
      - **e.** Define role and mission
    - **7.** Planning involves:
      - **a.** Choosing a destination
      - **b.** Evaluating alternative routes
      - **c.** Deciding on the specific course to reach the chosen destination
    - **8.** Stages of planning
      - **a.** Setting the stage: a period to gather data to understand the environment facing the organization and its individual parts
      - **b.** Setting goals
        - **i.** Goal is a long-range aim, a destination to which the organization commits itself. Goals tend to be general,

        unqualified statements that describe the outcome or attribute the organization seeks to achieve.

    ii. Goals should:

        1. Be specific

        2. Reflect organizational priorities and personal priorities

        3. Be measurable

        4. Be challenging yet attainable

        5. Relate to critical success factors

c. Plan development

    i. Mission statement: organization's overall purpose and philosophy

    ii. Strategic planning: philosophical analysis of what the organization is (its mission), what it hopes to be (its vision), and innovative ways of achieving the type of future that will ensure the organization's survival and effectiveness

    iii. Long-range plans: shorter term than strategic plans (typically 1–5 years)

    iv. Tactical planning: operational and budgetary planning designed to accomplish immediate and short-term plans

        1. Operational plans: 1 year or less, day to day, time, talent, tasks

        2. Intermediate: programmatic plans of 1 year or less

        3. Short-range: includes financial and budgetary planning

d. Implementation

    i. Planning flexibility: a good plan can be altered easily and adjusted in light of change.

    ii. Contingency plan: plans that take into account conditions different from those assumed to provide the foundation for the primary plan.

    iii. Paradox of planning: the areas in which plans are most likely to be inaccurate are the areas in which they are most needed, and the areas in which plans are most accurate are those in which they are less essential.

e. Feedback or review

    i. Control necessary to ensure that plans meet the goals established early in the process; emphasis is on the result and whether activities are proceeding according to plan.

    ii. MBO is a systematic and organized approach that allows management to focus on achievable goals and to attain the best possible results from available resources; it involves participative goal setting and evaluation based on results.

9. Approaches to planning

  a. Gap analysis answers the questions

    i. Where are we today?

    ii. Where do we want to go?

    iii. How are we going to get there?

  b. SWOT is an organization's review of its:

    i. Strengths

    ii. Weaknesses

    iii. Opportunities

    iv. Threats

10. Tools related to the planning function
   a. Policies: general broad guidelines to action that relate to goal attainment and translate overall objectives into comprehensible and practical terms; should be consistent; require judgment but not complex interpretation
   b. Procedures: plans for action; a series of related steps designed to accomplish a specific task; developed to define the task clearly, achieve uniformity of practice, and facilitate training
   c. Rules: plans that depict a required prohibited course of action accurately; require no decision making or interpretation but rather require or limit specific action authoritatively and officially
   d. Objectives: more specific statements that define the expectations or outcomes given by the goal statement
      i. Routine objectives: ongoing, continue from year to year
      ii. Innovative objectives: involve solving a special problem, a new project, or similar nonrecurrent assignment
      iii. Improvement objectives: require continuous performance improvement
   e. Standards: measures established to serve as criteria or levels of reference for determining the accomplishment of objectives
ii. Organizing
   1. Defined as distributing or allocating resources toward the accomplishment of the objectives of the defined plan
   2. Classifying and dividing the work into manageable units
   3. Has a formal and an informal structure
   4. Staffing
      a. Determining the requirements for ensuring the availability of personnel to perform the work
      b. Selecting personnel and appointing people to organizational positions
      c. Developing personnel to provide opportunities for people to increase their capabilities in line with organizational needs
      d. Determining personnel needs; analyzing the work for personnel capabilities required
   5. Components of organization
      a. Organizational chart: a schematic representation of the manner in which work is arranged and related so it can be performed
      b. Responsibility: the obligation of an individual to carry out assigned tasks to the best of his or her abilities; two major types of relationship responsibility
         i. Line: positions that have direct responsibility for accomplishing the objectives of an organization
         ii. Staff: positions that assist and advise the manager in accomplishing objectives
      c. Authority: the right given to each position holder to command the behavior for which the position is responsible
      d. Unity of command: states that an employee should have one and only one immediate boss
      e. Span of control: the number of immediate subordinates a manager can manage effectively
      f. Scalar principle: chain of command; the authority flows down the chain of command from the top to the lowest level

      g. Accountability: the obligation to account for the results expected

      h. Delegation: act of passing one's rights or authority to another so as to prohibit or require actions on the part of another; the conveyance of responsibility and authority from superior to subordinate

iii. Directing (Leading)

    1. Leading: stimulating members to meet objectives; getting all members of a work group to contribute effectively and efficiently to the achievement of the organization's objectives

    2. Bringing about the human activity required to accomplish objectives

    3. Assigning: charging individual employees with job responsibilities or specific tasks to be performed

    4. Motivating: influencing people to perform in a desired manner

    5. Communicating: achieving effective flow of ideas and information in all desired directions

    6. Coordinating: achieving harmony of group effort toward the accomplishment of individual and group objectives

    7. Centralization: only limited amount of authority is delegated; provides closer control of operations, uniformity of policies, procedures, practices

    8. Decentralization: significant amount of authority delegated to lower levels of organization; enables faster decision making without resorting to higher-level consulting; excellent training experience for promotion to higher-level management; may result in decisions better adapted to local conditions

    9. Flow charting: used to collect information on the steps of work process and to analyze and improve the process; identifies problems; helps eliminate duplication, workstation travel time, delays

iv. Controlling

    1. Tools or methods that help a supervisor measure the progress of work against performance standards with sufficient time to take corrective action if there are deviations; tools must be measurable, economical, and timely.

    2. Ensuring the effective accomplishment of objectives; clear objectives include:

      a. An action verb that describes an observable performance

      b. Conditions under which the action is to occur

      c. Statement of the standard or quality of performance (or competency) that is acceptable

      d. Time limits for completion of the action

    3. Establishing standards: devising a gauge of successful performance in achieving objectives

    4. Measuring performance

      a. Assessing actual versus planned performance

      b. Feedback mechanism for planning

      c. Determines whether planning has been effective and takes steps to ensure goals

      d. Assess employee performance

5. Corrective action
   a. Bringing about performance improvement toward objectives
   b. Detecting and correcting significant variations in the results obtained from planned activities by means of variance analysis
      i. Determines cause of deviation (deviation is the gap between actual performance and the established standard for that performance)
      ii. Review of deviation from standards found from monitoring
      iii. Financial planning
6. Requirements for controlling
   a. An understanding of what is necessary to meet standards defined in objectives and goals
   b. Monitoring to determine actual performance and compare it to the expected performance
   c. Mechanism to ensure that adequate resources exist to meet standards and take corrective action
7. Four basic steps to controlling
   a. Establish standards of performance: standards are criteria for determining the characteristics of acceptable performance and progress, utilizing scientific methods, simulation, past performance record, benchmarking
   b. Use controls to compare actual performance with standards
   c. Determine causes of deviation from standards
   d. Correct deviations from plans, standards, and expectations
8. Productivity: measures of the number of items created or the number of services accomplished per staff hour that meet established levels of quality; e.g., an employee coded 10 records in one hour, and 9 records were coded with 100% accuracy; therefore, the coder had a productivity of 9 or 90%.
9. Quality and quantity monitors (see Table 9-3)

Table 9-3 Quality and Quantity Monitors

Quality	Quantity
Direct inspection	Employee-reported volume log
Checklist	Stopwatch or time and motion studies
Questionnaire	Work sampling
Benchmarking	
Work simplification	

h. Role of Supervisor in Management

    i. Oversees the organization's efforts at the staff level, monitors the effectiveness of everyday operations, and measures individuals' performances against established standards

    ii. Supervisor

        1. Works in small groups

        2. Hands-on functions

        3. Staff training, recruitment, and retention

        4. Directs, schedules, and monitors daily work

        5. Revises procedures

        6. Conducts performance reviews

        7. Has advanced technical skills

i. Change Management

    i. The management of change within the organization

    ii. Organizational development: process of an organization reflecting on its own processes and consequently revising them for improved performance

    iii. Change agent

        1. Specialist in organizational development who facilitates the change brought about by the innovation

        2. Stages of change agents' work

            a. Scouting

            b. Entry and contracting

            c. Diagnosis or data gathering and feedback

            d. Planning

            e. Implementation

            f. Evaluation

            g. Termination

    iv. Stages of change

        1. Kurt Lewin's model (three stages)

            a. Unfreezing

                i. Presenting the discrepancies between the status quo and the desired goals

                ii. Creates a state of cognitive dissonance, which is an uncomfortable awareness of two incompatible perceptions or beliefs

                iii. Motivates the person to resolve dissonance, usually by changing the situation to make the perceptions congruent

            b. Moving to the new desired state for the organization

            c. Refreezing: new barriers are reinforced to become as stable and institutionalized as the previous status quo was.

        2. Elizabeth Kübler-Ross's stages of grief

            a. Shock and denial

            b. Anger and resentment

            c. Bargaining and negotiation

            d. Depression and despair

            e. Acceptance and reorientation

2. Leadership

    a. Multiple Aspects

        i. The interpersonal influence directed toward attainment of a specific goal or goals

        ii. Ability to inspire and influence others; process of influencing the behavior of group members

      iii. The process by which one individual influences others to accomplish goals

      iv. Takes the part of a manager who influences subordinates to accomplish desired goals within a business organization

      v. Art of mobilizing others to want to struggle for shared aspirations

b. Characteristics of Effective Leadership

      i. A strong drive for responsibility and devotion to completing tasks

      ii. Persistent in the pursuit of established goals

      iii. Innovation and originality in problem solving and decision making

      iv. Self-confident; strong personal identity

      v. Exercise initiative and make things happen

      vi. Willing to accept the consequences of actions

      vii. Deals effectively with stress and willing to tolerate frustration

      viii. Ability to influence the actions of others

c. Leadership Practices

      i. Empower and motivate others

      ii. Recognize valuable ideas

      iii. Serve as a symbol of the work group's identity

      iv. Create a vision

      v. Renew the tangible (including people) and intangible resources

      vi. Network externally to promote data/information dissemination to customers

      vii. Demonstrate credibility to maintain trust

      viii. Listen and keep in touch internally and externally with regard to the organization

      ix. Maintain a standard of excellence

d. Leadership Styles

      i. Bureaucratic: derives authority from the organization's set of rules and regulations; leads through reliance on rules and regulations and on formal grant of authority derived from higher levels of management

      ii. Laissez-faire: free reign or hands-off management; most successful in highly professional setting with knowledge-based workers who have a high sense of professional commitment

      iii. Democratic: utilizes a decision-making process that allows others to participate and takes others' opinions into consideration

      iv. Autocratic

          1. Rules with unlimited authority and undisputed power; monarch

          2. Efficiency results from arranging work so that human elements have little effect

          3. Usually practiced by formal leaders who use their positions as the way to influence the behavior of others

      v. Transactional: strives to create an efficient workplace by balancing task accomplishment with interpersonal satisfaction

      vi. Transformational: promotes innovation and organizational change; charismatic or has ability to inspire and motivate people beyond what is expected with exceptionally high levels of commitment

e. Types of Power

      i. Reward: ability to withhold or provide rewards for performance

      ii. Expert: leader has knowledge or expertise that is of value

      iii. Referent: personal characteristics that are appealing to the constituency, and the constituency follow out of admiration, charismatic impact, or the desire to be like the leader

      iv. Legitimate: comes from the authority of one's rank and position in the chain of command

      v. Coercive: utilizes punishment to maintain control

      vi. Information: persuasive content of the message, apart from personal characteristics of messenger

      vii. Representative: followers democratically delegate power to the leader for the purpose of representing their interests and making decisions on their behalf

3. Communication

  a. Transference of understanding between two parties (individual or organizations); may be verbal, nonverbal, or written

  b. Understanding the Communication Process

      i. Who is speaking

      ii. Message content

      iii. Medium of transmission

      iv. Context of letter, written inquiry, or spoken message

      v. Consequences of interaction

  c. Nonverbal Communication

      i. Movements and gestures

      ii. Expressions

      iii. Dress

      iv. Silence (people may not speak, yet ideas are exchanged)

      v. Gestures vary from one culture to another and may affect communication

  d. Communication Model

      i. Sender: originator of a stimulus (message)

      ii. Encoding: act that begins the communication process

      iii. Decoding: process of understanding the message

      iv. Filtering: altering of a message as it passes through the personalities of either the sender or the receiver

      v. Receiver: one who receives the message

      vi. Noise: anything that changes or interferes with the message but is not part of either the receiver or the sender

      vii. Feedback loop: connects the receiver and the sender; by evaluating feedback, the sender can gain valuable insight into the way the message is being received.

  e. Communication Process Model

      i. Downward (e.g., to subordinates)

      ii. Laterally (e.g., to colleagues)

      iii. Diagonally (e.g., from superior to subordinate outside of department)

      iv. Upward (e.g., to superior)

  f. Barriers to Communication

      i. Message overload

      ii. Message complexity

      iii. Personal distortion mechanisms

         1. Inattention

         2. Premature evaluation

         3. Lack of a common vocabulary

      iv. Psychological distortion mechanisms
         1. Rationalization
         2. Denial
    g. Rules for Effective Interpersonal Communication
      i. Be clear and concise
      ii. Use vocabulary that is common to the individual or group
      iii. Check to make sure the message was received clearly and accurately
      iv. Try not to communicate in great haste
      v. Listen to others
      vi. Keep a written record of communication
    h. Listening Skills
      i. Avoid distractions
      ii. Evaluate the sender, and make adjustments for a different frame of reference
      iii. Seek to sort out the major theme and key points of the message to reduce the amount of information that must be retained
      iv. Consider factors surrounding the message to learn its full meaning
      v. Seek further clarification if needed
      vi. Respond to the message thoughtfully

4. Conflict
  a. Disagreement within the organizational setting between two or more parties, or between two or more positions, regarding how to best attain the organization's goals
  b. Sources of Conflict
    i. Differences in goals
    ii. Resource competition
    iii. Communication failure and misinterpretation of information
    iv. Disagreement over performance standards
    v. Organizational structure incongruities
  c. Strategies for Managing Group Conflict
    i. Avoidance
    ii. Smoothing
    iii. Dominance or power intervention
    iv. Compromise
    v. Confrontation
  d. Strategies for Resolution
    i. Know background of conflict
    ii. Evaluate background of those in the conflict
    iii. Analyze the relationship between conflicting parties
    iv. Realize the benefits to be derived from resolving conflict

5. Solving Problems
  a. Making a choice between two or more alternatives
  b. Styles of Decision Making
    i. Problem avoider: ignores signals of possible problem eruption
    ii. Problem solver: solves problems
    iii. Problem seeker: actively looks for opportunities to plan, anticipate, and solve possible problems before they occur
  c. Decision making is a systematic way of solving problems.
  d. Decision-Making Process
    i. Define the real problem, after awareness of the symptoms
    ii. Set criteria for making the decision while analyzing available information

     iii. Generate relevant alternative solutions to the problem
     iv. Analyze and evaluate these alternatives
     v. Select the best alternatives for a solution
     vi. Implement the chosen alternatives
     vii. Monitor and evaluate the decision's effectiveness
  e. Problem-Solving Techniques
     i. Multidimensional approach
      1. Define problem by determining the magnitude of problem and writing a problem statement
      2. Assess the context by determining your authority to act and identifying whom to involve
      3. Weigh the alternatives
       a. Gather information about causes and solutions
       b. Identify criteria for evaluating alternatives
       c. Generate and rate alternatives and select best solution
      4. Create an implementation plan
       a. Evaluate and assign resources
       b. Identify implementation activities and completion dates
       c. Identify whom to inform
     ii. Brainstorming: maximizes ideas and generates alternatives
     iii. Nominal group technique
      1. Generate possible solutions in writing
      2. Present ideas to group
      3. Rank ideas anonymously
     iv. Delphi technique
      1. Elicit group input while controlling for bias and distortion
      2. Group members never meet, and their responses to the questionnaire are anonymous.
      3. Identify future trends
  f. Work-Group Dynamics
     i. Formal
      1. Those designated by and sanctioned by the organization
      2. Groups adhere to the scalar principle of organizational power.
      3. Receive legitimacy from the organization itself
      4. Communication flows according to organizational design.
     ii. Informal
      1. Created by the employees themselves
      2. Not sanctioned by the organization
     iii. Basic group forms
      1. Functional
      2. Task
      3. Interest
      4. Peer
      5. Committees
       a. Formal groups created by organization
       b. Have a specific purpose
       c. Structure
       d. Committee chairperson and members

6. Human Resources Management (HRM)
  a. Human resources planning is proactive and improves utilization of resources by providing a planned method of matching personnel with organizational or departmental goals and objectives; it ensures long-term health of the organization's human assets.

b. Effective human resources planning can prevent termination or layoffs and provide directives for recruitment and training.

c. Human resources planning assures that manager can overcome both external and internal challenges.

d. Human resources activities should be performed with the organization's unique mission, culture, size, and structure in mind and take into consideration the greater social, political, legal, economic, technological, and cultural environments in which it operates.

e. Contributes to success of organization by enhancing its productivity, quality, and service

f. Ensures compliance with legal and regulatory requirements

   i. The Joint Commission (TJC): voluntary accreditation

   ii. Occupational Safety and Health Act (OSHA): ensures safe and healthy work environment

   iii. National Labor Relations Act (NLRA, also called Wagner Act): gives employees right to collective bargaining and outlaws unfair labor practices

   iv. Healthcare amendments to the NLRA: extend the coverage and protection of the NLRA to employees of nonprofit hospitals and other healthcare organizations

   v. Labor Management Relations Act (Taft–Hartley Act): outlaws unfair labor practices by unions

   vi. Labor Management Reporting and Disclosure Act: forces unions to represent their members' interests properly

   vii. Civil Rights Act (Title VII): prohibits discrimination based on race, color, religion, sex, or national origin, and ensures equal employment opportunity

   viii. Vietnam Era Veterans' Readjustment Assistance Act: affirmative efforts to provide employment for qualified disabled veterans and veterans of the Vietnam era

   ix. Age Discrimination in Employment Act: protects employees between the ages of 40 and 70

   x. Americans with Disabilities Act: outlaws discrimination against people with disabilities and requires reasonable accommodations for them in the workplace

   xi. Family and Medical Leave Act (FMLA): grants unpaid leave and provides job security to employees who must take time off for medical reasons for themselves or family members

   xii. Pregnancy Discrimination Act: extends Title VII (of the Civil Rights Act of 1964) prohibitions against discrimination based on gender by broadening the definition to include pregnancy status, childbirth, and related medical conditions

   xiii. Employee assistance program (EAP)

   xiv. Termination including retirement and layoffs

   xv. Counseling and discipline

   xvi. Grievance procedures

   xvii. Employee and labor relations, including policy development and employees' rights and privacy protection

   xviii. Employee health, security, and safety

   xix. Compensation and benefits

   1. Wage and salary administration

   2. Payroll systems

        3. Performance incentive program

        4. Employee benefit program

   xx. Employee development

        1. Orientation

        2. Training

        3. Career development

        4. Performance evaluation

        5. Retention of valuable employees

        6. Alternative staffing structures (flextime, job sharing, home-based work, outsourcing)

   xxi. Staffing and selection

        1. Recruitment: process of finding, soliciting, and attracting new employees

        2. Screening and staff selection

        3. Job analysis, design, and process engineering

            a. Job evaluation provides a formal procedure to determine relative worth of each position in the organization.

            b. Tools used to evaluate jobs include job ranking, job grading, factor comparison, and point system.

        4. Job description elements

            a. Date

            b. Author

            c. Organization

            d. Job grade or classification

            e. Supervisory relationships

            f. Job status

            g. Job summary

            h. Essential functions, duties, and activities

            i. Job specifications

            j. Working conditions

g. Role of Health Information Professionals in Human Resources

   i. Staffing structures and work scheduling

   ii. Write job or position descriptions

   iii. Establish performance standards

        1. Set for both quantity and quality

        2. Should be objective and measurable

   iv. Develop policies and procedures

        1. Policy: statement about what an organization or department does

        2. Procedure: describes how work is done, how it is related to a department's policies, and how policies are carried out

   v. Recruit, select, and hire staff

   vi. Orientation of new employees: introduce new staff to the mores, behaviors, and expectations of the organization

   vii. Training and development

        1. Teach staff specific skills, concepts, or attitudes

        2. Ongoing in-service education to teach staff about skills, facts, attitudes, and behaviors, largely through internal programs

        3. Continuing education facilitates the efforts of staff members to remain current in the knowledge base of their trade or profession through external programs and meeting external standards.

        4. Career development continuously expands the capabilities of staff beyond a narrow range of skills toward a more holistically prepared person.

        viii. Empowerment of staff

        ix. Performance reviews

        x. Counsel and discipline staff

        xi. Conflict and grievance resolution

        xii. Maintain employee records

7. Strategic Management

  a. Strategy is a course of action designed to produce a desired outcome.

  b. Skills of Strategic Managers

    i. Monitor trends

    ii. Reflect on how trends may affect the future

    iii. Consider how changes in one area may affect changes in other areas

    iv. Set a course for change and help others visualize it

    v. Coach others to be partners in advancing a change agenda

    vi. Implement plans effectively

    vii. Question the status quo

  c. Elements of Strategic Management

    i. Vision

    ii. Issues

    iii. Goals

    iv. Strategies

    v. Tactics

    vi. Measure the results

8. Project Management

  a. Application of knowledge, skills, tools, and techniques to project activities so as to meet project requirements

  b. Concerned with completing a project within the expected cost and timeline with high-quality results

  c. A project team is responsible for task execution on project activities, resulting in an end product.

  d. Project team manager functions

    i. Set the project expectations

    ii. Create the project plan and recruit the project team

    iii. Manage and control project

    iv. Recommend plan revisions

    v. Execute change control

    vi. Prepare, document, and communicate project information

  e. Project Management Process

    i. Project definition

      1. Determine project scope and define project deliverables

      2. Estimate the project schedule and cost

      3. Prepare the project proposal

    ii. Project planning

      1. Identify project activities

      2. Construct the project network

        a. Determine dependencies among tasks

        b. Utilize a project schedule to determine when particular tasks can begin and when they are scheduled to end

      3. Estimate activity duration and work effort

      4. Conduct risk analysis and put contingencies in place for all risks

    iii. Project implementation

      1. Hold a kickoff meeting

      2. Perform project tasks and produce deliverables

    3. Track progress and analyze variance
    4. Establish change control
    5. Communicate project information
    6. Prepare the final report
    7. Celebrate success
  f. Project Management Life Cycle (see Table 9-4)
9. Work Design and Performance Improvement
  a. Associated with designing, redesigning, and implementing effective and efficient work processes within an organization
  b. Components of work processes and the development and use of performance standards and various methodologies in performance improvement
  c. Methods of Work Division
    i. Staffing involves determining the type and number of employees needed and what kind of work schedule is needed.
    ii. Work division
      1. Serial work division: consecutive handling of tasks or products by individuals who perform a specific function in sequence
      2. Parallel work division: concurrent handling of tasks
      3. Unit work division: simultaneous assembly, in which everyone performs a different specialized task at the same time
    iii. Work distribution analysis is used to determine whether a department's current work assignments and job content are appropriate.

Table 9-4 Project Management Life Cycle

Cycle	Description
Project definition	This process will determine the project objectives, activities, assumptions, high-level cost estimates, and anticipated schedule.
Planning and organization	A detailed project plan delineates the tasks to be performed, the resources necessary for each task, and the estimated task duration, start, and finish. The project team is established.
Tracking and analysis	By tracking project progress and analyzing it against the original plan, the project manager is able to determine when the project is not moving forward as planned.
Project revisions	When the analysis reveals project deviations, the plan may need to be modified to meet the project objectives.
Change control	This is the process of managing change request to the original project definition.
Communication	This process occurs throughout the project life cycle. Project information is collected from and disseminated to all stakeholders.

iv. Work scheduling ensures:
1. A core of employees on duty at all times when services must be provided
2. A pattern of hours to be worked and days off that employees can be reasonably sure will not be changed except in extreme emergencies
3. Fair and just treatment of all employees with regard to hours assigned

v. Management of work procedures
1. Job procedure: a structured, action-oriented list of sequential steps involved in carrying out a specific job or solving a problem
2. Procedure manual: compilation of all procedures used in a specific unit, department, or organization

vi. Work environment
1. Addresses space, equipment, aesthetics, and ergonomics
2. Work flow
   a. The established path along which tasks are sequentially completed by any number of staff to accomplish a function
   b. Well-designed work flow is critical to achieving optimal efficiency and productivity.
3. Space and equipment
   a. Workspace design can influence morale, productivity, and job satisfaction.
   b. Should address
      i. Physical environment
      ii. Office space utilization
      iii. Furniture and equipment
      iv. Space-planning techniques, guidelines, and standards
   c. Four types of office space needed
      i. Private office space
      ii. General office space
      iii. Service area
      iv. Storage area
4. Aesthetics
   a. Aesthetics of physical environment have great physiological and psychological effects on employees.
   b. Elements
      i. Lighting: sufficient brightness, exposure to natural light.
      ii. Color of walls and furniture: influences how employees feel.
      iii. Auditory impacts: music and sound incorporated into work environment may improve working conditions and relieve both mental and visual fatigue.
      iv. Temperature, moisture content, circulation: at least 2000 cubic feet per person per hour should be circulated to maintain a healthy respiratory atmosphere, and a range of 68 to 72 degrees Fahrenheit is generally acceptable.
5. Ergonomic management
   a. Assesses employee workspace for comfort and safety
   b. Educates staff on how to care for themselves to reduce injuries and discomfort

d. Performance and Work Measurement Standards

    i. Work is the task to performed; performance is the execution of the task.

    ii. Managers must determine what work is to be done, what performance standards are achievable and appropriate, and how to measure performance, and then monitor work for variance from the standard.

    iii. A standard is a performance criterion established by custom or authority with the purpose of assessing factors such as quality, productivity, and performance.

        1. Communicated to staff via rules, polices, regulations, job descriptions, verbal confirmation

        2. Criteria for setting effective standards

            a. Understandable

            b. Attainable

            c. Equitable

            d. Significant

            e. Legitimate

            f. Economical

        3. Qualitative and quantitative standards

            a. Qualitative standards specify quality levels such as accuracy and error rate; also referred to as service.

            b. Quantitative standards specify level of measurable work expected for a specific function; also referred to as productivity.

        4. Key indicator: live (versus retroactive) measurement thresholds that alert a department to its level of competent customer service

            a. Complaints

            b. Surveys to access accreditation, legal, or regulatory standards the organization has failed to meet in one or more areas

        5. Developing standards

            a. Benchmarking

                i. Based on research into the performance of similar organizations and programs or on standards established by national or local sources

                ii. Steps in benchmarking

                    1. Identify peer organization that has outstanding performance

                    2. Study the best practices within that organization

                    3. Act to implement those best practices

            b. Work measurement

                i. Process of studying the amount of work accomplished and the amount of time it takes to accomplish it

                ii. Supports manager to

                    1. Set production standards

                    2. Determine staff requirements

                    3. Establish incentive pay

                    4. Determine direct costs by function

                    5. Compare performance standards

                    6. Identify activities for process/method improvement

                iii. Accomplished through

                    1. Analysis of historical data

                    2. Employee self-logging (time ladder, volume logs)

        3. Measurement (stopwatch to record time to complete task)

        4. Work sampling (random sample of observations of work)

6. Performance measurement

  a. The process of comparing the outcomes of an organization, work unit, or employee to established performance plans and standards

  b. The results of performance measurement process are expressed as percentages, rates, ratios, averages, and other quantitative assessments.

  c. Performance controls

    i. Specific monitors (controls) are established by the manager and outcome data are collected.

    ii. Outcome data are then analyzed to determine the extent to which actual performance corresponds to the performance expectations established during the planning process.

    iii. Effective monitoring criteria include flexibility, simplicity, economy, timeliness, and focus on exceptions.

  d. Variance analysis: analysis of the performance factors involved in the work (people, supplies, equipment, and money) helps determine needed changes.

  e. Assessment of employee performance

    i. Monitor and measure outcomes and performance

    ii. Compare performance to established goals and standards

    iii. Evaluate variance and develop action plan

    iv. Take appropriate action

  f. Principles of performance improvement: determine why actual output varies from expected output and then take actions to increase the effectiveness, efficiency, and adaptability

  g. Performance improvement methodologies

    i. System analysis and design

      1. Determine need for the system and the system requirements

      2. Analyze system requirements

      3. Propose system design or redesign

      4. Evaluate the proposed system

      5. Implement the system

      6. Conduct ongoing evaluation and maintenance

      7. Use basic tools of system analysis (work distribution chart, movement diagram, flow process chart)

    ii. Continuous quality improvement (CQI)

      1. Constancy of variation

      2. Importance of data

      3. Vision and support of executive leadership

      4. Focus on customers

      5. Investment in people

      6. Importance of team

      7. Improvement model utilizing FOCUS-PDCA

        a. Find a process to improve

        b. Organize a team

     c. Clarify the knowledge
     d. Understand causes of variation
     e. Select process of improvement
     f. Plan, Do, Check, Act
    8. CQI techniques and tools
     a. Brainstorming: generates a large number of creative ideas
     b. Affinity grouping: allows team to organize and group similar ideas together
     c. Nominal group technique (NGT): brings agreement about an issue or an idea that the team considers most important by ranking ideas according to importance
     d. Multivoting technique: variation of NGT in which team members rate the issue using a distribution of points or colorful dots
     e. Root cause analysis: fishbone diagram
     f. Pareto chart: ranking of multi-voting and nominal group process displayed visually from highest to lowest
     g. Force field analysis: visual display of data generated through brainstorming
     h. Check sheet: data collection tool that permits recording and compiling observations or occurrences
     i. Scatter diagram: data analysis tool used to plot points of two variables suspected of being related to each other in some way
     j. Histogram: data analysis tool used to display frequencies of response
     k. Run chart: displays data points over a period of time
     l. Statistical process control chart: plots points over time to demonstrate how a process is performing
   iii. Reengineering
    1. Focuses on the potential revamping of the entire process to achieve improvement
    2. Expectations of reengineering
     a. Increased productivity
     b. Decreased costs
     c. Improved quality
     d. Maximized revenue
     e. More satisfied customers

10. Financial Management
  a. Definitions
   i. Financial data: individual elements of organizational financial transactions
   ii. Financial transaction: the exchange of goods or services for payment or the promise of payment
   iii. Asset: items or resources that belong to the organization and have a future value
   iv. Liabilities: amounts owed to various creditors and vendors
   v. Revenue: the monies received for services provided
   vi. Expenses: the cost to provide a service

    vii. Equity: the difference between revenues and expenses
    viii. Profit: money received from the payer less the actual cost to complete the service, assuming the cost is less than the cash received
    ix. Accounting
        1. Process of recording, summarizing, and reporting the business history of a firm
        2. Involves the collection, recording, and reporting of financial data
            a. The benefits of the financial data should exceed the cost of obtaining them.
            b. The data must be understandable.
            c. The data must be useful for making decisions.
        3. Six concepts of accounting activity
            a. Entity
            b. Going concern
            c. Stable monetary unit
            d. Time period
            e. Conservatism
            f. Materiality
        4. Principles of accounting
            a. Reliability
            b. Cost
            c. Revenue
            d. Matching
            e. Consistency
            f. Disclosure
b. Financial Accounting
    i. Authorities
        1. Financial Accounting Standards Boards
        2. Securities and Exchange Commission
        3. Centers for Medicare and Medicaid Services
        4. Internal Revenue Service
    ii. Financial statements
        1. Balance sheet: snapshot of the accounting equation at a point in time

$$\text{Assets} - \text{Liabilities} = \text{Owner's Equity}$$

        2. Income statement
            a. Shows the difference between revenues and expenses
            b. Shows the results of operations and other activities affecting the profits of the firm

$$\text{Profit (Operating Income)} = \text{Revenue} - \text{Expenses}$$

        3. Cash flow statement
            a. Shows changes in the cash and cash equivalent balances of a company for a specific fiscal period
            b. Begins with the net income of the company and then makes a series of adjustments to convert to a cash basis
            c. Cash flow results from three activities:
                i. Operating
                ii. Investing
                iii. Financing

4. Analyzing financial statements
  a. Liquidity ratios
    i. To evaluate current debt-paying and operating ability
    ii. Cash and nearness to cash

Working Capital = Current Assets – Current Liabilities

$$\text{Current Ratio} = \frac{\text{Current Assets}}{\text{Current Liabilities}}$$

$$\text{Quick Ratio} = \frac{\text{Quick Assets}}{\text{Current Liabilities}}$$

  b. Efficiency ratios
    i. Show how efficiently a company uses its assets
    ii. How quickly accounts receivable are collected
    iii. How quickly inventories are converted to cash
    iv. Accounts receivable turnover determines the average collection period for accounts.
    v. Debt to equity ratio indicates what proportion of equity and debt the company is using to finance its assets.

$$\text{Accounts Receivable Turnover} = \frac{\text{Net Credit Sales}}{\text{Average Accounts Receivable}}$$

$$\text{Debt to Equity Ratio} = \frac{\text{Long Term Debt}}{\text{Stockholdler's Equity}}$$

  c. Profitability ratios
    i. Useful in evaluating the company's operating performance
    ii. Profit margin shows how much of the sales dollars end up as profit for the company.

$$\text{Profit Margin} = \frac{\text{Net Income}}{\text{Net Sales}}$$

5. Inventory and depreciation
  a. Inventory
    i. Valuing products in inventory that are acquired at different prices or costs
    ii. First in, first out (FIFO)
    iii. Last in, first out (LIFO)
  b. Depreciation determines how to account for a long-term asset being used up over its useful life.
6. Investment decisions
  a. Compounding: value of investment is determined by length of time the investment is in place.
  b. Discounting: opposite of compounding; determines how much one must invest today at a compound interest rate of x to receive a given amount at the end of n years
  c. Rate of return
    i. Annual net inflows or outflows are averaged over the project's life for each project.
    ii. The asset value of investment value is averaged over the life of the project as well.
    iii. The asset value is depreciated on a straight-line basis for the life of the program.

       d. Payback period: how long it will take to get initial investment back for a project

       e. Net present value: difference between the present value of the investment cash outflow required for a project and the present value of future net free cash inflow from a project

  c. Budgets

    i. Numeric documents that translate the goals, objectives, and action steps into forecasts of volume and monetary resources needed

    ii. Budgets are planned and prepared consistent with the strategic plan.

$$\text{Actual Dollars Spent} - \text{Dollars Budgeted} = \text{Variance}$$

$$\frac{\text{Actual Dollars Spent} - \text{Dollars Budgeted}}{\text{Dollars Budgeted}} \times 100 = \text{Variance Percentage}$$

    iii. Types of budgets

      1. Statistics budget

        a. Historical data are used to predict the future and plan the budget.

        b. Historical data include discharges by services, payer type, DRG, length of stay by DRG, diagnosis, procedures, ambulatory visits, type and number of home health visits, and number of emergency room visits.

      2. Operating budget: managers predict cost of labor, supplies, and other expenses to support work volume of a particular department.

      3. Master budget: consolidation of all operating budgets

      4. Rolling budget: a budget established at the beginning of an accounting period is continually amended to reflect variances that arise due to changing circumstance.

      5. Flexible budget: predicated on volume; supplies, labor, and other variable expenses are budgeted in proportion to the anticipated volume.

      6. Zero-based budget: requires management to justify all activities performed by a department before allocating any funding

      7. Capital budget

        a. Planning for capital equipment acquisitions and renovations

        b. Incorporates long- and short-term operating needs as they relate to equipment

        c. Capital equipment usually has a cost in excess of a stated amount (e.g., $500), a useful life of more than 1 year, and is tagged for tracking with an identifying number.

  d. Reimbursement Methodologies

    i. Facility must be able to evaluate the underlying cost of providing services and to compare its actual reimbursements to the potential reimbursements based on charges.

    ii. All individual patient charges are captured in the patients' accounts.

    iii. Charges and underlying costs of the services provided are maintained in a database called a chargemaster.

      1. Chargemaster is a database that collects information on all of the goods and services the facility provides to patients.

      2. Used to facilitate charge capture by centralizing and standardizing charge data within the facility

e. Payment for Healthcare Services (Table 9-5)

    i. Historical aspects of healthcare in the United States have led to the third-party payer concept.

        1. A third party (insurance company) pays for services provided by the healthcare organizations or practitioners to the insured.

        2. The payer often receives premium payments from the insured's employer.

        3. Federal and state governments also cover or insure non-employees in Medicare and Medicaid programs.

        4. Reimbursement has extended beyond hospital providers to home health agencies, skilled nursing facilities, outpatient departments, ambulatory surgery centers, and rehabilitation facilities.

f. Cost Allocation Methods

    i. Step-down method

        1. Supported by Medicare in its cost-reporting requirements.

        2. Indirect departments that receive the least amount of service from other indirect departments and provide the most service to other departments have their costs allocated first.

        3. Allocation is based on the ratio of services provided to each department or some other basis such as square footage, employees, or worked hours.

Table 9-5 Types of Payment for Healthcare Services in the United States	
Time Period	**Method of Payment**
Prior to 1930s	Direct out-of-pocket remuneration
After 1930s	Establishment of insuring agents that served as forerunners for Blue Cross and other insurance companies Growth in number of hospitals as consumers demanded more services for premiums paid
Mid-1960s	Government-subsidized Medicare Further encouraged hospitals to provide services without regard to cost due to Medicare reimbursement for services
1982	Tax Equity and Fiscal Responsibility Act mandated a prospective payment system (PPS), resulting in the implementation of DRGs
Present	Various reimbursement methods currently in use, including prenegotiated amounts, reimbursement based on a discount on billed charges, per diem payments, reimbursement based on audited costs, DRGs, ambulatory care groups, resource utilization groups, and payment for services at billed or full charges

    ii. Double-distribution method

       1. Similar to step-down

       2. Assumes that the allocation of cost cannot be linear and that some indirect departments need to be allocated or distributed to less commonly dispersed or distributed departments before the costs of these departments are fully allocated

    iii. Simultaneous-equations methods

       1. Also known as algebraic or multiple apportionment method

       2. Permits multiple allocations to occur through sophisticated mathematical software and the use of simultaneous mathematical equations

g. Role of the Health Information Professional in the Budgeting Process

    i. Responsible for identifying and recording the appropriate clinical codes to describe the patient's interaction with the organization

    ii. Assure timely and accurate coding

    iii. Aggregate and maintain documentation that supports reimbursement

    iv. Communicate budgetary requirements

    v. Develop and maintain the department budget and understand what caused variation or variance from the budget

PRACTICAL APPLICATION OF YOUR KNOWLEDGE

1. Management
    a. Describe the basic components of management.
        i. Effectiveness

        ii. Functions

        iii. Resources

        iv. Objectives

    b. Define and give examples of each management function.
        i. Planning

        ii. Organizing

iii. Directing (Leading)

iv. Controlling

c. Match each statement with the correct management function.
(Planning = P, Organizing = O, Directing = D, Controlling = C)

i. _____ Manager meets with his staff weekly to give orders and encourage suggestions.

ii. _____ Supervisor of release of information (ROI) gives assignments to staff.

iii. _____ Manager sets the short range goals for the department.

iv. _____ The director of health information delegates a project to a subordinate.

v. _____ Manager makes a "to-do" list for the day.

vi. _____ Manager praises employee for doing a good job with a project.

vii. _____ Main file supervisor trains filing clerk on terminal digit order.

viii. _____ Subsequent to performing benchmarking, a supervisor sets productivity standards.

ix. _____ Supervisor motivates staff to work weekends.

x. _____ Director sets goals and timeline for completion.

xi. _____ Coding supervisor hires three analysts.

xii. _____ The management teams restructure the staff and their duties.

xiii. _____ The supervisor establishes a sequence of actions to follow in reaching the objectives of the barcoding project.

xiv. _____ The CEO of the facility defines the mission of the organization.

xv. _____ The supervisor of record processing disciplines an employee for tardiness.

d. Using the following table, develop and write supervisor job duties that correspond to the appropriate management function.

Supervisor Job Duties

Planning	Organizing

Directing (Leading)	Controlling

e. Define the following terms and identify to which management function (planning, organizing, directing, or controlling) they correspond.

    i. Strategic plan

    ii. Operational plan

    iii. Policy

    iv. Procedure

    v. Goal

    vi. Rule

    vii. Objectives

    viii. Mission statement

ix. Authority

x. Lines of authority

xi. Delegation

xii. Unity of command

xiii. Span of control

xiv. Scalar principle

xv. Staff

xvi. Line

f. Evaluate centralization and decentralization issues.
  i. Centralization

  ii. Decentralization

g. Define productivity and describe the various types of quality and quantity monitors.

h. Discuss motivation and the basic theories of motivation.

i. Discuss the role of supervisors.

j. Compare and contrast the definitions of management and leadership.
  i. Management

  ii. Leadership

2. Leadership

a. Differentiate among the approaches to leadership theories.

   i. Classical approaches

   ii. Behavioral approaches

b. Define and contrast the following:

   i. Theory X

   ii. Theory Y

   iii. Theory Z

c. Match the following statements with the correct McGregor management theory. (Theory X = X, Theory Y = Y)

   i. _____ People are naturally lazy, and they prefer to do nothing.

   ii. _____ People work mostly for money and status rewards.

   iii. _____ The main force keeping people productive in their work is the fear of being demoted or fired.

   iv. _____ People are naturally active, and they set goals and enjoy striving.

   v. _____ People are naturally dependent upon leaders.

   vi. _____ People seek many satisfactions in work.

   vii. _____ People understand and care about what they are doing and can devise and improve their own methods of doing work.

    viii. _____ People need a sense that they are seen as capable of assuming responsibility and self-correction.

    ix. _____ People seek to give meaning to their lives by identifying with nations, communities, causes, and unions.

    x. _____ People have little concern beyond their immediate and material interest.

    xi. _____ People need to be encouraged and assisted.

    xii. _____ People need to be told, shown, and trained in proper methods of work.

    xiii. _____ People appreciate being treated with courtesy.

    xiv. _____ People crave genuine respect from their fellow humans.

    xv. _____ People constantly grow, and it is never too late to learn.

d. Discuss the various leadership styles.
    i. Bureaucratic

    ii. Laissez-faire

    iii. Democratic

    iv. Autocratic

e. Match the following with the correct leadership styles. (Bureaucratic = B, Laissez-faire = L, Democratic = D, Autocratic = A)

    i. _____ The president of the institution allows all five of his vice presidents free reign in managing their respective departments.

    ii. _____ The supervisor allows the employees to participate in deciding which filing system to utilize.

iii. _____ An employee wears sandals to work. The supervisor sends the employee home because the rule states, "Employees must wear hard-toed shoes."

iv. _____ When an employee offers suggestions for a more efficient department, the director states he will incorporate only those ideas that he thinks are best.

v. _____ During the holiday season, the supervisor arranged the main file room job duties so that the work would continue to be performed regardless of the employees utilizing their vacation.

vi. _____ The director of health information exerts minimum effort in the supervision of her assistants.

vii. _____ The manager disciplined his staff for not precisely following the policy and procedure about release of information.

viii. _____ The CEO has an organization-wide meeting to obtain the ideas of the entire staff concerning optimizing financial resources.

f. Discuss the following types of power.
  i. Reward

  ii. Expert

  iii. Referent

  iv. Legitimate

  v. Coercive

  vi. Information

  vii. Representative

3. Communication

    a. Utilizing the communication model, identify the encoding, filtering, noise, decoding, and feedback in the following scenario. Also, how could the listening process be improved?

        i. The manager of ROI is training a new employee on telephone etiquette and taking telephone requests for release of information. The employee asks the manager follow-up questions for clarification of the procedure. The ROI office has a waiting area where authorized users make record requests. Within the ROI office, there are two photocopy machines, four telephone lines, and five physically active employees.

4. Problem Solving

    a. Using the decision-making process and the multidimensional approach to problem solving, determine a solution to the following.

        i. As supervisor, you are responsible for assuring that productivity is not jeopardized during the holiday season. Three out of five of your employees have requested to utilize 1 week of vacation time during the holiday season. All three employees must utilize their vacation time within this year or they will lose these hours.

Decision-Making Process	Multidimensional Approach

5. Human Resources Management

    a. You own a release of information company with 10 employees. Due to the expansion of your business, you need to hire an additional employee. One candidate for the position is 6 months pregnant. You decide not to hire her based upon the demands of the job and her pregnancy condition. She reports you to the EEOC. How do you defend your decision?

    b. List and describe 10 legal and/or regulatory requirements that have affected human resources management.

    c. What should be the result of job analysis?

    d. Explain the elements of a job description.

    e. List major activities in the recruitment process.

    f. Discuss employee counseling and discipline.

    g. What is the health information practitioner's role in training and development?

6. **Strategic Management**

    a. Discuss necessary skills of a strategic manager.

    b. Describe the elements of strategic management.

7. **Project Management**

    a. What is project management?

    b. Discuss the steps in the project management life cycle.

8. **Work Design and Performance Improvement**

    a. The number of sick-leave days taken for the main file area has increased by 50% from the previous year. The major complaints by the employees have been back strain. What steps might the manager implement to decrease the number of sick days taken by employees?

    b. Define benchmarking and describe why it is used.

c. Differentiate between brainstorming and the nominal group process.

d. Discuss the importance of the work environment on employee production.

e. Given the following scenario, design a workflow diagram for optimal productivity.
    i. The health information department of a 150-bed hospital has 8 employees. The average length of stay is 3 days, with an average of 1201 discharges per month. The hospital uses a serial-unit record and TDO filing system. The department has one manager, one coder, one analysis clerk for the physician completion area, one assembly clerk, one statistician, one release of information clerk, and two main file clerks.

9. Financial Management

    a. Why do health information managers need to know about budgetary terms, processes, and types of budgets?

    b. How does the health information practitioner contribute to the master budget?

    c. List the major functional areas in financial accounting.

    d. How do healthcare institutions get paid for services provided to patients and/or clients?

    e. Explain the role of the health information professional in the budgeting process.

    f. Describe various cost allocations methods.

10. Computation of Management and Personnel Problems

    a. It takes approximately 20 minutes to assemble and analyze a chart for deficiencies. If there are 16,020 discharges for the month, how many personnel hours are needed for this volume of work?

b. A coding supervisor at Count General Hospital needs to determine the number of full-time equivalents (FTEs) necessary to code 750 discharges per week. It takes an average of 15 minutes to code each record and each coder will work 40 hours per week. How many FTEs are required?

c. All employees are to get a 3% increase in pay at the beginning of the new fiscal year, which is July 1. Employees will also get a 7.5% merit increase on their anniversary. The director of the health information department currently makes $102,000 per year. What will her salary be as of August 25 next year, which is her anniversary date?

d. The director of health information is contemplating purchasing or leasing a new scanning system. The director calculates the payback period and rate of return on investment. The facility's required payback period is 4 years with a required rate of return of 30%. If the equipment costs $140,000 and generates $40,000 per year in savings, what would the payback period for this equipment be?

e. In a health information department, the coding staff earns and works the following hours. What is the routine (40 hours/week) cost of staffing the coding area of this health information department?

Employee	# Hours Worked per Week	Hourly Wage
Coder A	45	$45
Coder B	40	$43
Coder C	49	$48
Coder D	36	$41.50

TEST YOUR KNOWLEDGE

Use the following table for questions 1–2.

Employee	June 20xx	August 20xx
Irma	95%	98.5%
Casandra	94%	89%
Bunmi	98.2%	100%
Shirlyn	92.4%	98.3%

Productivity of four employees was calculated as follows:

1. Which employee has shown the most improvement?
   a. Irma
   b. Casandra
   c. Bunmi
   d. Shirlyn

2. Which employee needs to be counseled concerning her productivity?
   a. Irma
   b. Casandra
   c. Bunmi
   d. Shirlyn

3. As the supervisor of the birth certificate process, you conduct a monthly review of the birth certificates processed versus the certificates returned from the Bureau of Vital Statistics. Based on your review, a total of 468 birth certificates were filed and 12 were returned. What is the accuracy of processing birth certificates?
   a. 85.9%
   b. 94.4%
   c. 97.4%
   d. 100%

4. You have owned and managed a transcription company for just over 4 years with great efficiency. You have six employees, including two sales associates and four transcribers. Occasionally an employee tries to suggest changes, but you have success with the present system and you tell them to just follow the established procedures. What is your style of management?
   a. Democratic
   b. Laissez-faire
   c. Participatory
   d. Autocratic

5. Each procedure should indicate how it is related to a department's:
   a. rules.
   b. objectives.
   c. policies.
   d. standards.

6. The production of a coder has been consistently lower than the others. You suspect he is not efficient with his time. Which tool would most accurately measure his production?
   a. Work sampling
   b. Production time study
   c. Time log
   d. Standard time data

7. _____ power is based on a follower's perception that an influencer has the capacity to administer some favorable incentive.
   a. Coercive
   b. Reward
   c. Legitimate
   d. Expert

8. Which management function involves scheduling, budgeting, and selecting and setting objectives?
   a. Planning
   b. Organizing
   c. Directing
   d. Controlling

9. James is the director of HIM and Linda is his manager of the main file room. James sees one of Linda's subordinates give a medical record to a physician without following the proper procedure. James immediately goes to Linda to have her correct the clerk and the situation. To which organizational principle is James adhering?
   a. Organizational function
   b. Scalar principle
   c. Span of control
   d. Unity of command

10. The workflow in a department is complicated and congested. To study and correct the situation, which technique is the manager most likely to use?
   a. Flow process chart
   b. Movement diagram
   c. Work distribution chart
   d. Procedure flow chart

11. You own a transcription company with 13 employees. Due to the decrease of your business, you need to dismiss 2 employees. To assure that you abide by federal regulations, you determine the 2 employees to be dismissed based upon their:
   a. age.
   b. productivity.
   c. war-time service.
   d. salary.

12. A supervisor of quality improvement exerts _____ authority when she directs an employee in her section.
   a. functional
   b. line
   c. coercive
   d. staff

13. A process of allocating the cost of non-patient-revenue-generating departments to patient-generating departments can be accomplished through which method?
   a. Step-down
   b. Single distribution
   c. Double indemnity
   d. Math equations

14. The major advantage of written communication is the:
   a. fact that the message can be reinforced by other communication.
   b. opportunity to not receive feedback.
   c. ability to get the message across clearly and without interpretation.
   d. opportunity to develop the message carefully prior to dissemination.

15. Procedures provide for _____ in performing the task.
   a. flexibility
   b. guidelines
   c. standardization
   d. examples

16. A Gantt chart is useful in which of the following management activities?
   a. Scheduling
   b. Recruitment
   c. Purchasing
   d. Workflow

17. A hospital has been in operation for 4 years. It has an average of 18,000 admissions a year. The facility has expanded and expects 24,000 admissions next year. There are 6000 linear feet of filing space available, and half has been used. The facility experienced a 38% readmission rate and expects a 40% future readmission rate. If this is a unit record system, how many new file folders will be needed for next year?
a. 9600
b. 14,400
c. 14,880
d. 33,600

18. The director of the HIM department is preparing a training manual for specific functional areas in the department. What should be the determining factor for providing training?
a. Length of employment
b. Cost of training
c. Educational levels
d. Functional area objectives

19. A billing clerk is working 1 hour each day before clocking in at her scheduled start time. She explains that the workload is massive and to keep current, she must start work early. Because she has not been compensated for her hours worked, what federal regulation is being violated?
a. National Labor Relations Act
b. Labor Management Reporting and Disclosure Act
c. Civil Rights Act
d. Fair Labor Standards Act

20. A hospital averages 72 discharges per day. Coders must average 27 records per day. How many full-time coders does the department need?
a. 2
b. 3
c. 4
d. 5

21. What statement best defines management?
a. Management is getting things done by using the function of management.
b. Management is the art of getting things done through people.
c. Management is getting things done through systems.
d. Management is working through and with systems.

22. Positions of authority that advise and recommend a course of action are called:
a. line authority.
b. authority.
c. advisory authority.
d. staff authority.

23. Positions that have authority to direct the tasks of subordinates are called:
a. line authority.
b. authority.
c. staff authority.
d. direct line authority.

24. According to Henry Mintzberg, all are considered managerial roles *except*:
a. interpersonal activity.
b. editing activity.
c. decisional activity.
d. informational activity.

25. In providing orientation to a new employee, you inform her that her immediate supervisor is Kimberly Smith, the record completion supervisor. This is what principle of management?
a. Scalar chain
b. Unity of direction
c. Order
d. Unity of command

26. Introducing a new employee to the organizational structure and illustrating how the person contributes to the objectives of the department is what principle of management?
a. Scalar chain
b. Unity of direction
c. Order
d. Unity of command

27. There is a staff of 20 people in record completion. The manager organizes them in groups of 4 and assigns each team to a group of physicians to assist them in completing patient records. This is an example of organizing work by:
    a. customer.
    b. project.
    c. territory.
    d. product.

28. An organization chart identifies all of the following *except*:
    a. line of authority.
    b. responsibilities.
    c. wages and benefits.
    d. span of control.

29. The organizing function involves:
    a. defining roles.
    b. budgeting.
    c. motivating.
    d. structuring.

30. A tool used to analyze manual operations and steps in a work process is called a(n) _____ chart.
    a. organization
    b. flow process
    c. work process
    d. work distribution

31. Delegating authority:
    a. is not recommended by good leaders.
    b. frees the team leader to focus on more important and complex assignments.
    c. decreases the leader's productivity.
    d. delays decision making.

32. To classify work into manageable units is to:
    a. plan.
    b. control.
    c. direct.
    d. organize.

33. Development of goals for the future year and the development of a plan for professional development are elements of an:
    a. employee's job description.
    b. employee's handbook.
    c. employee's performance review.
    d. employee's discipline record.

34. Space costs, rent, and salaries of management team are considered:
    a. fixed costs.
    b. controls.
    c. variable costs.
    d. revenue.

35. Determining whether plans or goals are being achieved can be defined as:
    a. planning.
    b. organizing.
    c. controlling.
    d. directing.

36. Directing includes all of the following *except*:
    a. leading.
    b. actuating.
    c. taking corrective action.
    d. communicating.

37. Choose the best order for the steps in problem solving.
    a. Define problem; generate alternatives; implement alternatives; analyze problem
    b. Define problem; analyze the root of the problem; generate alternatives; implement alternatives; evaluate
    c. Analyze root of problem; generate alternatives; select best alternative; implement alternatives; evaluate
    d. Define problem; analyze the root of the problem; generate alternatives; select best alternative; implement alternatives; evaluate

38. _____ power occurs when the follower perceives that the leader has valuable knowledge.
    a. Coercive
    b. Reward
    c. Referent
    d. Expert

39. Power based on a follower's desire to identify with a charismatic leader is _____ power.
    a. coercive
    b. reward
    c. referent
    d. expert

40. A statement of the organization's overall purpose and philosophy is called the:
    a. mission statement.
    b. value statement.
    c. strategic plan.
    d. statement of objectives.

41. A tool used to determine the amount of time workers are spending on a task is called a:
    a. flow process chart.
    b. movement diagram.
    c. work distribution chart.
    d. PERT chart.

42. The ideal office temperature is about _____ degrees Fahrenheit.
    a. 70
    b. 60
    c. 65
    d. 50

43. A tool used to identify alternative courses of action for problem solving is called a:
    a. flow process chart.
    b. movement diagram.
    c. work distribution chart.
    d. decision tree.

44. A method to establish standards that involves comparison of one organization's performance with another organization is called:
    a. stop watch studies.
    b. work sampling.
    c. benchmarking.
    d. monitoring.

45. A grievance policy should do all of the following *except*:
    a. state the goals and purpose of the process.
    b. communicate critical time limits.
    c. exclude employees on probation.
    d. describe each stage of the process.

46. A human resources tool that depicts visually who is able to fill projected vacant positions is known as a:
    a. replacement chart.
    b. staffing table.
    c. resources audit.
    d. job analysis.

47. Interpersonal influence directed toward attainment of a specific goal or goals can be defined as:
    a. planning.
    b. leadership.
    c. management.
    d. delegation.

48. The feedback mechanism is considered to be:
    a. planning.
    b. controlling.
    c. organizing.
    d. directing.

49. The 85/15 rule of total quality management proposes:
    a. 85% of work problems are the result of faulty systems rather than unproductive people.
    b. 85% of work problems are the result of unproductive people rather than faulty systems.
    c. 85% of work problems are the result of bad management rather than faulty systems.
    d. 85% of work problems are the result of faulty systems and bad management.

50. Which theory suggests that in the right conditions people will seek responsibility and be creative?
    a. Theory X
    b. Theory Y
    c. Theory of motivation
    d. Maslow's need theory

References

© saicle/ShutterStock, Inc.

Abdelhak, M., Grostick, S., & Hanken, M. A. (2012). *Health information: Management of a strategic resource.* St. Louis, MO: Saunders Elsevier.

Acosta, R. *Pharmacology for health professions.* (2012). Philadelphia, PA: Lippincott, Williams and Wilkins.

Agency for Healthcare Research and Quality. (2003). AHRQ quality indicators: Guide to patient safety and indicators. http://www.qualityindicators.ahrq.gov/modules/psiresources.aspx

Agency for Healthcare Research and Quality. (2011). Health information privacy and security collaboration.

Agency for Healthcare Research and Quality. (n.d.). Collection: National Hospital Inpatient Quality Measures. http://www.qualitymeasures.ahrq.gov/browse/by-organization-indiv.aspx?objid=25813

Agency for Healthcare Research and Quality. (n.d.). Health information technology. http://healthit.ahrq.gov/portal/server.pt

AHIMA. (2011). Fundamentals of the legal health record and designated record set. *Journal of AHIMA 82*(2):44–49.

AHIMA e-Discovery Task Force. (2008). Litigation response planning and policies for e-Discovery. *Journal of AHIMA 79*(2):69–75.

American Health Information Management Association. (2011, August). Retention and destruction of health information. Appendix C: AHIMA's recommended retention standards. http://library.ahima.org/xpedio/groups/public/documents/ahima/bok1_049250.hcsp?dDocName=bok1_049250

American Health Information Management Association. (n.d.). Cognitive levels. http://www.ahima.org/certification/cognitive

American Health Information Management Association. (n.d.). Commission on Certification for Health Informatics and Information Management (CCHIM) candidate guide: Appendix G and H. http://www.ahima.org/~/media/AHIMA/Files/Certification/Candidate_Guide.ashx

American Hospital Association. (2006). Resources. http://www.aha.org/aha/issues/Quality-and-Patient-Safety/background.html.

Barton, P. (2010). *Understanding U.S. health services system.* Arlington, VA: AUPHA.

Brodnik, M. Rinehart-Thompson, L., & Reynolds, R. (2013). *Fundamentals of law for health informatics and information management.* Chicago, IL: AHIMA.

Brown, F. (2012). *ICD-9-CM coding handbook with answers*. Atlanta, GA: Health Forum, Inc.

Centers for Disease Control and Prevention. (n.d.). http://www.cdc.gov/osels/ph_surveillance/nndss/phs/infdis2011.htm

Centers for Disease Control and Prevention. (2011). Nationally notifiable infectious diseases, United States 2011.

Centers for Disease Control and Prevention. (2014). CD-10-CM official guidelines for coding and reporting. http://www.cdc.gov/nchs/data/icd/icd10cm_guidelines_2014.pdf

Centers for Medicare and Medicaid Services. (n.d.). http://www.cms.gov

Centers for Medicaid and Medicare Services. (2012, August). Stage 1 vs. Stage 2 comparison table for eligible hospitals and CAHs. https://www.cms.gov/Regulations-and-Guidance/Legislation/EHRIncentivePrograms/Downloads/stage1vsStage2CompTablesforHospitals.pdf

Centers for Medicaid and Medicare Services. (2013, June). The ICD-10 transition: An introduction. http://www.cms.gov/Medicare/Coding/ICD10/Downloads/ICD10_Introduction_060413[1].pdf

Centers for Medicaid and Medicare Services. (2013). ICD-10-PCS official guidelines for coding and reporting: Conventions. http://www.cms.gov/Medicare/Coding/ICD10/Downloads/PCS_2013_guidelines.pdf

Department of Health and Human Services. (2009). HIPAA Administrative Simplification Enforcement.

Department of Health and Human Services. (2012). Hospital Compare. http://www.hospitalcompare.hhs.gov

Department of Health and Human Services & Centers for Medicare and Medicaid. (2013). Hospital quality initiatives: HCAHPS patient's perspective of care survey. http://www.cms.hhs.gov/HospitalQualityInits/30 HospitalHCAHPS.asp#TopOfPage

Dimick, C. (2009). Who has rights to a deceased patient's records? AHIMA blog post. August 4.

Donabedian, A. (1980). *Explorations in quality assessment and monitoring: Volume 1*. Chicago, IL: Health Administration Press Edition.

Donabedian, A. (2005). Evaluating the quality of health care. http://en.wikipedia.org/wiki/AvediDonabedian

Dougherty, M. (2001). Practice brief: Accounting and tracking disclosures of protected health information. *Journal of AHIMA* 72(10):72E–72H.

Fenton, S., & Biedermann, S. (2014). *Introduction to healthcare informatics*. Chicago, IL: AHIMA.

Glandon, G., Smaltz, D., & Slovensky, D. (2014). *Information systems*. Arlington, VA: AUPHA.

Green, M., & Bowie, M. J. (2010). *Essentials of health information management*. Clifton, NJ: Thompson Delmar Learning.

Health information management services (HIMS): Retention of patient records. (n.d.). http://www.visn2.va.gov/hims/patientrecord.asp

HealthIT.gov. (n.d.). EHR incentives and certification: Meaningful use definition and objectives. http://www.healthit.gov/providers-professionals/meaningful-use-definition-objectives

Horton, L. (2012). *Calculating and reporting healthcare statistics*. Chicago, IL: AHIMA.

ICD-10-CM official guidelines for coding and reporting. (2013). http://www.cdc.gov/nchs/data/icd10/10cmguidelines_2013_final.pdf

ICD-10-PCS official guidelines for coding and reporting. (2013). http://www.cms.gov/Medicare/Coding/ICD10/Downloads/pcs_2013_guidelines.pdf

Joint Commission. (2006). Introduction to the National Patient Safety Goals. http://www.jointcommission.org/PatientSafety/NationalPatientSafety Goals/npsg_intro.htm

Joint Commission. (2010). *Comprehensive Accreditation Manual for Hospitals.*

Kuehn, L. (2012). *Procedural coding and reimbursement for physician services.* Chicago, IL: American Health Information Management Association.

LaTour, K., Eichenwald-Maki, S., & Oachs, P. (2013). *Health information management concepts, principles and practice.* Chicago, IL: AHIMA.

Leon-Chisen, N. (2014). *ICD-10-CM and ICD-10-PCS coding handbook with answers.* Chicago, IL: AHA.

McCormick, K., & Gugerty, B. (2013). *Healthcare information technology exam guide for CompTIA healthcare IT technician and HIT Pro certification.* New York, NY: McGraw-Hill.

McWay, D. (2010). *Legal and ethical aspects of health information management.* Albany, NY: Delmar.

Moini, J. (2013). *Focus on pharmacology: Essentials for health professionals.* Boston, MA: Pearson.

Moisio, M., & Moisio E. (1998). *Understanding laboratory and diagnostic tests.* Albany, NY: Delmar.

Montana, P., & Charnov, B. (2008). *Management.* Hauppauge, NY: Barron's Educational Series.

Nanji, K. C., Rothschild, J. M., & Salzberg, C. (2011). Errors associated with outpatient computerized system. *Journal of the American Medical Informatics Association, 18,* 767–777.

National Committee for Quality Assurance. (2013). Improving care. http://www .ncqa.org/portals/0/ACO_FAQs_updates_11-15-12pdf

National Committee for Quality Assurance. (n.d.). Accreditation programs. http://www.ncqa.org/Programs/Accreditation.aspx.

National Quality Forum. (2013). Mission and Vision. http://www.qualityforum .org/About_NQF/Mission_and_Vision.aspx

The Office of the Federal Register (OFR) of the National Archives and Records Administration (NARA), and the U.S. Government Printing Office (GPO). 45 CFR Parts 160. *Federal Register 14*(209):56m–56U.

Osborn, C. E. (2006). *Statistical applications for health information management.* Sudbury, MA: Jones and Bartlett.

Peden, A. (2012). *Comparative health information management.* Clifton Park, NJ: Delmar, Cengage Learning.

Ring, D. C., Herndon, J. H., & Meyer G. S. (2010). Case 34-2010: A 65 year old with an incorrect operation on the left hand. *New England Journal of Medicine, 363,* 1950–1957.

Safian, S. (2010). *The Complete Procedure Coding Book.* Boston, MA: McGraw-Hill.

Sayles, N. (2013). *Health information management technology.* Chicago, IL: AHIMA.

Sayles, N., & Trawick, K. (2010). *Introduction to computer systems for health information technology.* Chicago, IL: AHIMA.

Shaw, P., Elliott, C., Isaacson, P., & Murphy, E. (2012). *Quality and performance improvement in health care.* Chicago, IL: AHIMA.

Spath, P. (2014). *Introduction to healthcare quality management.* Arlington, VA: AUPHA.

Sultz, H., & Young, K. (2010). *Health care USA: Understanding its organization delivery.* Sudbury, MA: Jones and Bartlett.

Tabor, L., Torda, P., Thomas, S., & Zutz, J. (n.d.). Measuring quality in the early years of health insurance exchanges. http://www.ncqa.org/Portals/0/ Newsroom/AJMC_13Mar.pdf

Tan, J., & Payton, F. C. (2010). *Adaptive health management information systems: Concepts, cases, and practical applications.* Sudbury, MA: Jones and Bartlett.

The Joint Commission (2013). *2014 hospital accreditation standards.* Chicago, IL: TJC.

Thibodeau, G. & Patton, K. (2010). *The human body in health and disease.* St. Louis, MO: Mosby Elsevier.

Thomas, E. J., & Brennan, T. A. (2000). Incidence and types of preventable adverse events in elderly patients: Population based review of medical records. *British Medical Journal,* 741–744.

Turley, S. (2010). *Understanding pharmacology for health professionals.* Boston, MA: Pearson.

Answer Key

© saicle/ShutterStock, Inc.

CHAPTER 2

1. **D** Abdelhak 14, 49–50; Sayles 8; LaTour 11
2. **C** Abdelhak 486; Sayles 439; LaTour 290–291; LaTour 371
3. **D** Horton 14

$$\frac{10}{15} \times 100 = 66.6 = 67\%$$

4. **B** Abdelhak 111; LaTour 253
5. **A** Abdelhak 101, 128; Sayles 463; LaTour 367
6. **D** Abdelhak 107; Sayles 346; LaTour 278
7. **A** Abdelhak 6–9; Sayles 653; LaTour 14
8. **C** Abdelhak 131; Sayles 365; LaTour 698
9. **B** Abdelhak 111–112
10. **D** Abdelhak 123; LaTour 195
11. **C** Johns 769–770; LaTour 199
12. **B** Abdelhak 108; LaTour 176
13. **D** Abdelhak 126–130, 351; LaTour 193–194
14. **A** Abdelhak 118; LaTour 186
15. **C** LaTour 201–202
16. **A** LaTour 177
17. **A** Abdelhak 270; LaTour 182
18. **B** Abdelhak 114; Sayles 88–92; LaTour 250
19. **C** Abdelhak 113; Sayles 93; LaTour 251
20. **B** Abdelhak 9–10; Sayles 206
21. **A** Abdelhak 120; Sayles 39–43
22. **D** Sayles 333; LaTour 270–271
23. **B** Abdelhak 135; Sayles 264; LaTour 251
24. **D** Abdelhak 113–114; Sayles 672–673; LaTour 24–25
25. **D** Abdelhak 113; Sayles 93–95; LaTour 251
26. **A** Abdelhak 133; Sayles 604–605; LaTour 266
27. **B** Abdelhak 130; Sayles 350; LaTour 263–264
28. **C** Abdelhak 87; Sayles 439; LaTour 370–371

29. **A** Abdelhak 13; Sayles 104; LaTour 244
30. **C** Abdelhak 208; Sayles 343; LaTour 123 and 406
31. **D** Sayles 5
32. **C** Sayles 343; LaTour 671
33. **B** Horton 144–146

$$\frac{(134 \times 100)}{3489} = 3.84\%$$

34. **D** Sayles 336–340

$$517 \times 1.8 = 930.6 \qquad 36 \times 7 = 252 \qquad \frac{930.6}{252} = 3.69 = 4$$

Note: Since you cannot purchase 3.69 shelves, you must purchase 4.

35. **C** Abdelhak 34–36; Sayles 254; LaTour 35
36. **B** Abdelhak 145; Sayles 239; LaTour 419
37. **A** Abdelhak 6; Sayles 653; LaTour 14
38. **D** Abdelhak 11; Sayles 155; LaTour 199
39. **D** Abdelhak 12; Sayles 85; LaTour 721
40. **C** Abdelhak 9–13; Sayles 656; LaTour 16
41. **C** Abdelhak 13; Sayles 264–265; LaTour 16
42. **C** Abdelhak 18–21; Sayles 673; LaTour 39
43. **A** Abdelhak 17
44. **D** Abdelhak 18–20
45. **B** Abdelhak 46–47; Sayles 44; LaTour 670
46. **D** Abdelhak 20; Sayles 672–673; LaTour 23–24
47. **B** Sayles 676
48. **A** Abdelhak 21–22
Note: All relevant TJC standards should be upheld.
49. **D** Sayles 672–673
50. **D** Abdelhak 27; Sayles 241; LaTour 30

CHAPTER 3

1. **B** Brodnik 99
2. **D** Brodnik 340
3. **B** Brodnik 231
4. **A** Brodnik 96
5. **A** Brodnik 36
6. **C** Brodnik 38
7. **D** Brodnik 189
8. **C** Brodnik 103
9. **B** Brodnik 46
10. **A** Brodnik 233
11. **B** Brodnik 93
12. **D** Brodnik 351
13. **D** Brodnik 342
14. **B** Abdelhak 286
15. **A** Brodnik 137
16. **C** Brodnik 334
17. **C** Brodnik 329
18. **D** Brodnik 87–88
19. **A** Brodnik 87

20. **B** Brodnik 165
21. **A** Brodnik 22
22. **C** Brodnik 33
23. **A** Brodnik 87
24. **B** Brodnik 193
25. **C** Brodnik 364
26. **B** Brodnik 332
27. **B** Brodnik 233
28. **A** Brodnik 233 and 338
29. **D** Brodnik 362–363
30. **D** Brodnik 241
31. **C** Abdelhak 526
32. **D** Brodnik 241
33. **A** Brodnik 227
34. **B** Brodnik 227–228
35. **B** Brodnik 219–220
36. **C** Brodnik 35
37. **A** Brodnik 33 and 87
38. **A** Brodnik 186
39. **A** Brodnik 238
40. **A** Brodnik 238
41. **B** Brodnik 37
42. **D** Brodnik 37
43. **C** Brodnik 235
44. **D** Brodnik 149
45. **D** Brodnik 149 and 199
46. **D** Brodnik 4
47. **C** Brodnik 188
48. **A** Brodnik 335
49. **B** Brodnik 333
50. **D** Brodnik 337

CHAPTER 4

1. **C** Abdelhak 379; Horton 38; LaTour 487; Sayles 482

$$\frac{6705}{31} = 218$$

2. **D** Abdelhak 379; Horton 34–38; LaTour 487; Sayles 482

$$\frac{6750 + 7130 + 7470}{90} = 237$$

3. **B** Abdelhak 366; Horton 177; LaTour 489; Sayles 486

$$\frac{6615 + 6082 + 5668}{910 + 889 + 894} = 6.8$$

4. **C** Horton 46; Abdelhak 379; LaTour 488; Sayles 483

$$\frac{(6750 + 7130 + 7470) \times 100}{(31 \times 250) + (28 \times 250) + (31 \times 300)} = 88.8\%$$

5. **D** Abdelhak 368; LaTour 520; Sayles 542; Horton 184
6. **A** Abdelhak 379; Horton 32; LaTour 486; Sayles 480

7. D   Abdelhak 371; Horton 90; LaTour 90; Sayles 492

$$\frac{(7+1+1)\times 100}{237} = 3.79\%$$

8. B   Abdelhak 376; Horton 95–113; LaTour 493–494; Sayles 494–495

$$\frac{(3+1+1)\times 100}{7+1+1} = 55.56\%$$

9. C   Abdelhak 376; Horton 95–113; LaTour 493–494; Sayles 494–495

$$\frac{(3+1+1)\times 100}{7+1+1-1} = 62.50\%$$

10. A   Abdelhak 371; Horton 94; LaTour 492; Sayles 492

$$\frac{2\times 100}{114+2} = 1.72\%$$

11. D   Abdelhak 376; Horton 95–113; LaTour 493–494; Sayles 494–495

$$\frac{(3+1+1+1+3)\times 100}{7+1+1-1+1+3} = 75.00\%$$

12. C   Abdelhak 366, LaTour 528

13. A   Abdelhak 387; LaTour 517–519; Horton 175

14. A   Abdelhak 391

15. C   Abdelhak 371; Horton 74; LaTour 492; Sayles 492

$$\frac{(5\times 100)}{(225+5)} = 2.17\%$$

16. A   Abdelhak 368; Latour 520; Sayles 542; Horton 184

$$15 - 5 - 5 - 5 = 0$$

17. B   Abdelhak 389; LaTour 549

18. D   Abdelhak 371; Horton 90; LaTour 490–493; Sayles 492

$$\frac{(3\times 100)}{163} = 1.84\%$$

19. A   Abdelhak 371; Horton 74; LaTour 492; Sayles 492

$$\frac{(72\times 100)}{(980+72)} = 6.84\%$$

20. B   Abdelhak 376; Horton 95–113; LaTour 493–494; Sayles 494–495

$$\frac{(10\times 100)}{52} = 19.23\%$$

21. A   Abdelhak 379; Horton 38; LaTour 487; Sayles 482

$$\frac{(9901+331)}{30} = 341.06 = 341$$

22. A   Abdelhak 368; LaTour 520; Sayles 542; Horton 184

$$87 - 13 - 13 - 13 = 48$$

23. B   Abdelhak 387; LaTour 517–519; Horton 175

$$\frac{(8+9)}{2} = 8.5$$

24. C   Abdelhak 366; Horton 177; LaTour 489; Sayles 486

$$\frac{(1+3+3+4+5+7+8+9+10+11+13+17+21+25)}{14} = 9.78 = 9.8$$

25. C   Abdelhak 379; Horton 38; LaTour 489; Sayles 486

$$\frac{(20+3+17+3+4+25+8+7+13+10+5+11+9+21+1)}{15} = 10.46 = 10.5$$

26. C Abdelhak 376; Horton 95–113; LaTour 493–494; Sayles 494–495

$$\frac{(13 \times 100)}{(20 - 1)} = 68.42\%$$

27. B Abdelhak 371; Horton 90; LaTour 490–494; Sayles 492

$$\frac{(20 \times 100)}{1244} = 1.607 = 1.61\%$$

28. D Abdelhak 379; Horton 38; LaTour 487; Sayles 482

$$\frac{1113}{30} = 37.1 = 37$$

29. B Abdelhak 366; Horton 177; LaTour 489; Sayles 486

30. D Sayles 525, Horton 210

31. D Abdelhak 366; Horton 177; LaTour 489; Sayles 486

$$(1 \times 105) + (209 \times 3) + (311 \times 2) = 1354; \quad \frac{1354}{(1 + 209 + 311)} = 2.59 = 2.6$$

32. D Abdelhak 389; LaTour 549

33. B Abdelhak 379; Horton 38; LaTour 487; Sayles 482

$$\frac{(498 + 606)}{365} = 3.03 = 3$$

34. C Abdelhak 366; Horton 177; LaTour 489; Sayles 486

$$\frac{(4355 + 202 + 3998 + 300)}{(500 + 150) + (600 + 205)} = 6.08 = 6.1$$

35. D Abdelhak 379; Horton 38; LaTour 387; Sayles 482

$$\frac{(4001 + 235 + 4500 + 268)}{365} = 24.6 = 25$$

36. A Abdelhak 371; Horton 75; LaTour 492; Sayles 492

$$\frac{(1 + 2) \times 100}{(173 + 199)} = .806 = .81\%$$

37. B Abdelhak 379; Horton 46; LaTour 488, Sayles 483

$$\frac{(4001 + 235 + 4500 + 268)}{(500 \times 151) + (512 \times 214)} \times 100 = 4.865 = 4.87\%$$

38. D Abdelhak 379; LaTour 488; Sayles 483

39. B Abdelhak 371; Horton 74; LaTour 492; Sayles 492

$$\frac{(3 + 5 + 1 + 3) \times 100}{(183 + 189 + 3 + 5 + 1 + 3)} = 3.125 = 3.13\%$$

40. A Abdelhak 371; Horton 90; LaTour 490–492; Sayles 492

$$\frac{(72 \times 100)}{(980 + 72)} = 6.84\%$$

41. C Abdelhak 366; Horton 177; LaTour 489; Sayles 486
(June 30 – June 28 = 2) + July 1, 2, 3, 4, 5, 6, 7, 8 = 2 + 8 = 10

42. C Abdelhak 379; Horton 38; LaTour 487; Sayles 482
(June 28 + 29 + 30 = 3)

43. A Abdelhak 366; Horton 177; LaTour 489; Sayles 486
Note: Patient was still in-house; thus, no discharge days.

44. B Abdelhak 379; Horton 38; LaTour 487; Sayles 482
July 8 – July 1 = 7

45. A Abdelhak 379; Horton 38; LaTour 487; Sayles 482

$$\frac{14,942}{31} = 482$$

46. B Abdelhak 388; LaTour 520; Sayles 542
$98 + 6 + 3 = 107$

47. B Abdelhak 393–394; LaTour 536–537; Horton 189–190
$.918506 \times .918506 = .84365 = .843$

48. C Abdelhak 396; Horton 256
$$\frac{16}{2} = 8$$

49. D Abdelhak 387; LaTour 517–519; Horton 175
$$\frac{(79 + 82 + 78 + 81 + 87 + 92 + 99 + 79 + 80 + 84)}{10} = 84.1$$

50. B Abdelhak 392; Horton 242, 255–256
Note: Reject null hypothesis because the p-value ($5.06887E^{-8}$) is less than the alpha level, which was set at .05.

CHAPTER 5

1. C Abdelhak 463; Shaw XXV
2. A Abdelhak 463
3. C Abdelhak 468
4. C Shaw 333
5. A Shaw 330
6. C Shaw 333
7. D Shaw 18
8. D Abdelhak 474
9. C Abdelhak 549
10. D Abdelhak 667
11. D Shaw 325
12. D Abdelhak 521; Shaw 427
13. B Abdelhak 132 and 428; Shaw 131
14. D Shaw 325
15. C Shaw 113
16. D Abdelhak 473
17. A Abdelhak 6
18. A Abdelhak 549
19. C Shaw 432
20. C Abdelhak 548
21. D Abdelhak 463
22. A Abdelhak 454
23. C Abdelhak 453
24. B Abdelhak 446
25. C Abdelhak 457
26. C Abdelhak 474
27. A Abdelhak 453
28. D Adbelhak 520
29. B Abdelhak 453
30. B Abdelhak 8; Shaw 37
31. B Abdelhak 382
32. A Abdehalk 635
33. A Critical pathways; Shaw 140
34. C Abdelhak 468

35. D Abdelhak 468
36. A Abdelhak 467
37. A Abdelhak 466
38. D Shaw 429
39. B Abdelhak 467
40. C Abdelhak 444
41. D Abdelhak 522
42. C Shaw 115
43. C Abdelhak 37
44. C Abdelhak 475
45. B Abdelhak 444
46. D Abdelhak 470
47. A Abdelhak 9
48. C Abdelhak 468
49. D Abdelhak 468
50. A Shaw 432

CHAPTER 6

1. B Abdelhak 37–38; LaTour 90; Sayles 5 and 912
2. A Abdelhak 368
3. D Abdelhak 157; LaTour 94–95; Sayles 854
4. A Abdelhak 199, LaTour 125; Sayles 915
5. C Abdelhak 157; LaTour 94–95; Sayles 854
6. C Abdelhak 260; LaTour 93; Sayles 925
7. C Abdelhak 185
8. D Abdelhak 288
9. B Abdelhak 308–309; Sayles 993
10. C Abdelhak 281

$$\frac{(2500 \times 3072)}{1024} = 7500\text{k}$$

11. B Abdelhak 69; LaTour 117; Sayles 129
12. B Abdelhak 277
13. D Abdelhak 270; Sayles 876
14. D Abdelhak 310; Sayles 860
15. E Abdelhak 263
16. D Abdelhak 278
17. B Abdelhak 157; LaTour 94–95; Sayles 854
18. A Abdelhak 277; Sayles 964–966
19. C Abdelhak 273, Sayles 912
20. A Abdelhak 273, Sayles 912
21. C Abdelhak 275
22. D Abdelhak 270, Sayles 876
23. C Abdelhak 157; LaTour 94–95; Sayles 854
24. B Abdelhak 186–187
25. B Abdelhak 302
26. A Abdelhak 281
27. A Abdelhak 194; LaTour 89–90
28. C Abdelhak 161
29. B Abdelhak 161
30. D Abdelhak 155

31. A Abdelhak 161
32. C Abdelhak 196
33. C Abdelhak 268
34. A Abdelhak 187; LaTour 86
35. D Abdelhak 186; Sayles 879
36. B Abdelhak 187; Sayles 879
37. C Abdelhak 187; Sayles 879
38. A Abdelhak 203
39. B Abdelhak 180
40. D Abdelhak 293; LaTour 93–94; Sayles 925
41. B Abdelhak 157; LaTour 94–95; Sayles 854
42. C Abdelhak 271
43. A Abdelhak 272–273
44. B Abdelhak 275
45. C Abdelhak 334; LaTour 139 and 791
    Note: In year 3, changing to new system saves $1500.
46. A Abdelhak 332–335
47. C Abdelhak 332–334
48. D Abdelhak 276; Sayles 854–855
49. D Abdelhak 335–337; LaTour 878
50. B Abdelhak 276–277, 279; Sayles 854–855, 923

CHAPTER 7

1. B Thibodeau and Patton 468–470
2. C Thibodeau and Patton 400
3. B Moini 365
4. A Moini 374
5. C Moini 245
6. D Moini 490
7. D Thibodeau and Patton 454
8. A Moisio 99–100; Thibodeau and Patton 357–358
9. D Moini 12
10. A Moisio 51–53; Thibodeau and Patton 353
11. B Moisio 238; Thibodeau and Patton 96
12. A Thibodeau and Patton 322
13. D Moini 437 and 455
14. A Moisio 100–101; Thibodeau and Patton 506
15. C Moini 442–443
16. D Thibodeau and Patton 322
17. C Moini 379
18. B Moini 184
19. C Moisio 53–54; Thibodeau and Patton 560
20. C Moisio 256; Thibodeau and Patton 560
21. B Thibodeau and Patton 329
22. D Thibodeau and Patton 558
23. A Thibodeau and Patton 408
24. C Thibodeau and Patton 381
25. B Thibodeau and Patton 381
26. A Moisio 360–361; Thibodeau and Patton 383
27. D Moini 12–13, 309
28. B Moisio 240; Thibodeau and Patton 548–549

29. **C** Moisio 244–249; Thibodeau and Patton 251
30. **A** Moisio 46–47, 50–51; Thibodeau and Patton 400–401
31. **D** Moisio 32–40; Thibodeau and Patton 559–560
32. **D** Thibodeau and Patton 477
33. **B** Moisio 365; Thibodeau and Patton 474
34. **C** Moini 517
35. **B** Moini 247
36. **B** Moini 536
37. **A** Moisio 98–99; Thibodeau and Patton 347
38. **C** Moisio 54; Thibodeau and Patton 505
39. **D** Moisio 303–304; Thibodeau and Patton 87–88
40. **D** Moisio 33; Thibodeau and Patton 579
41. **D** Moini 241
42. **C** Moisio 10; Thibodeau and Patton 356
43. **A** Moisio 10; Thibodeau and Patton 356
44. **C** Thibodeau and Patton 242
45. **B** Thibodeau and Patton 558
46. **B** Moini 388
47. **B** Moini 362
48. **D** Moini 386
49. **A** Moini 393
50. **C** Moisio 54–55; Thibodeau and Patton 548

CHAPTER 8

1. **C** Brown 15
2. **D** Brown 43–44
3. **D** Brown 337–339
4. **C** Brown 49–50
5. **C** Brown 331–334
6. **D** Abdelhak 201–202
7. **A** Abdelhak 203
8. **B** Safian 296
9. **B** Brown 16
10. **B** Safian 36
11. **A** Brown 22–23
12. **C** Brown 64–66
13. **B** Brown 64
14. **D** Brown 207
15. **C** Brown 345
16. **D** Brown 63 and 310
17. **D** Brown 289–290
18. **A** Brown 17
19. **B** Brown 263–264
20. **C** Brown 15
21. **A** Brown 64
22. **C** Brown 226
23. **B** Brown 310–311
24. **A** Abdelhak 203
25. **D** Safian 40
26. **A** Safian 108
27. **C** Kuehn 100

28. A Brown 83–84
29. D Brown 371–387
30. C Brown 101
31. B Brown 122
32. C Brown 109
33. B Brown 143
34. B Brown 161–162
35. B Brown 83
36. A Brown 207
37. A Brown 197
38. A Brown 143
39. A Leon-Chisen 227
40. D Brown 161–162
41. D Leon-Chisen 250
42. C Brown 83
43. C Leon-Chisen 262
44. A Brown 207
45. A Leon-Chisen 314–317
46. B Brown 197
47. B Leon-Chisen 298

48. Patient admitted with gallstones and increased bilirubin. Has a history of hypertension and takes Zestril. Patient had an ERCP with ERS and stone extraction from the bile duct, preceded by a laparoscopic cholecystectomy. Final diagnosis is choledochelithiasis of gallbladder and bile duct with acute and chronic cholecystitis.
ICD-9-CM codes: 574.80, 401.9, 51.23, 51.85, 51.88 (Brown 161–162); ICD-10-CM and CPT-4 codes: K80, 1120, I10 (Leon-Chisen 203–204)

49. 28 year old G2P1 with cervical cerclage for incompetent cervix at 12 weeks.
ICD-9-CM codes: 654.53, 67.59 (Brown 211–212, 215); ICD-10-CM and CPT-4 codes: O34.511 (Leon-Chisen 243, 259)

50. Patient admitted for median neuropathy. Carpal tunnel syndrome of the left hand for carpal tunnel release.
ICD-9-CM codes: 354.0, 04.43, 64721-LT (Brown 131); ICD-10-CM and CPT-4 codes: G56.00 (Leon-Chisen 191)

51. Patient admitted with torn medial meniscus for arthroscopic partial medial meniscectomy of the right knee.
ICD-9-CM codes: 836.0, 80.6, 29881-RT (Brown 322); ICD-10-CM and CPT-4 codes: S83.211A (Leon-Chisen 365)

52. 38 year old admitted for sterilization by scope BTL.
ICD-9-CM codes: V25.2, 66.29, 58671 (Brown 219–221); ICD-10-CM and CPT-4 codes: Z30.2 (Leon-Chisen 263)

53. Patient admitted with pilonidal cyst for pilonidal cystectomy.
ICD-9-CM codes: 685.1, 244.9, 311, 86.21, 11770 (Brown 188–190); ICD-10-CM and CPT-4 codes: L05.91, E03, 9 (Leon-Chisen 233–235)

54. Patient admitted with obstructing ureteral calculus. Has a history of HTN and takes Atenolol 25 mg. daily. Admitted for ESWL.
ICD-9-CM codes: 592.1, 401.9, 98.51, 50590-LT (Brown 173); ICD-10-CM and CPT-4 codes: N20.1, I10 (Leon-Chisen 214)

55. Cloudy posterior capsule after cataract extraction, admitted for YAG laser posterior capsulotomy of the right eye.
ICD-9-CM codes: 366.53, 13.64, 66821-RT (Brown 133–135); ICD-10-CM and CPT-4 codes: H26.491 (Leon-Chisen 171)

56. 10 month old with recurrent otitis media of the both ears admitted for myringotomy with insertion of pressure-equalizing tubes in both ears. ICD-9-CM codes: 381.3, 20.01, 20.01, 69436-50, 69990 (Brown 136–137); ICD-10-CM and CPT-4 codes: H65.411 (Leon-Chisen 172–173)

57. 50 year old with history of MI 6 weeks ago admitted for new onset angina. He is status post PTCA at time of MI, but admitted for preoperative workup for future repair of diverticular perforation of the large intestine. Left heart cath, selective coronary angiography, left ventriculogram. ICD-9-CM codes: 414.01, 413.9, 410.72, v45.82, 562.10, 401.9, 272.0, v17.3, v15.82, 37.22, 88.56, 88.53, 93510, 93543, 93545, 93555, 93556 (Brown 254–260); ICD-10-CM and CPT-4 codes: I25.111, I214, Z95.5, K57.30, I10, E780, Z82.49, Z87.891 (Leon-Chisen 298–301)

58. A 12 year old admitted with chronic tonsillitis and adenoid hypertrophy for tonsillectomy and possible adenoidectomy. ICD-9-CM codes: 474.00, 478.1, 28.3, 42821 (Brown 141); ICD-10-CM and CPT-4 codes: I35.01, J348.1 (Leon-Chisen 177)

59. A 13 year old admitted with undescended testicles for bilateral orchiopexy. ICD-9-CM codes: 752.51, 62.5, 62.5, 54640-50 (Brown 236); ICD-10-CM and CPT-4 codes: 253.10 (Leon-Chisen 283)

60. If patient is admitted for screening colonoscopy, V76.51 or A12.11 (ICD-9-CM or ICD-10-CM respectively) should be principal followed by any findings. ICD-9-CM codes: V76.51, V16.0, 211.3, 45.42, 45385 (Brown 157–158); ICD-10-CM and CPT-4 codes: A12.11, Z13.811 (Leon-Chisen 191–192)

CHAPTER 9

1. D Abdelhak 619; Horton 138; LaTour 814–816
98.3% − 92.4% = 5.9% production increase
2. B Abdelhak 619; Horton 138; LaTour 814–816
94% − 89% = 5% production decrease
3. C Abdelhak 619; Horton 138; LaTour 814–816

$$468 - 12 = \frac{456}{468} \times 100 = 97.4\%$$

4. D Abdelhak 559–560; LaTour 700
5. C Abdelhak 696 LaTour 724; Sayles 1088
6. A Abdelhak 619; LaTour 809–810
7. B Abdelhak 564; LaTour 690–691
8. A LaTour 686; Sayles 1111
9. D Abdelhak 634–635; LaTour 686; Sayles 1078
10. B Abdelhak 625; LaTour 697
11. B Abdelhak 619–623; LaTour 807; Sayles 546
12. B LaTour 750; Sayles 1091
13. A Abdelhak 679–680; LaTour 782
14. D LaTour 697
15. C Abdelhak 646; LaTour 804; Sayles 1083
16. A Abdelhak 640; LaTour 685
17. B LaTour 274
24,000 − 40% (9600) = 14,400
18. D Abdelhak 607; LaTour 740
19. D Abdelhak 578; LaTour 722; Sayles 835

20. **B**   Abdelhak 619; Horton 138

$$\frac{72}{27} = 2.66$$

Note: The answer is 3 employees.

21. **B**   LaTour 689; Sayles 460
22. **D**   LaTour 690
23. **A**   LaTour 690
24. **B**   LaTour 690–691
25. **D**   LaTour 690
26. **C**   LaTour 690–691
27. **A**   Abdelhak 614–615
28. **C**   Abdelhak 634–635
29. **D**   Abdelhak 634–635; LaTour 690
30. **B**   Abdelhak 623–625
31. **B**   Sayles 1100–1101
32. **D**   Abdelhak 614; LaTour 690
33. **C**   LaTour 735; Sayles 73
34. **A**   LaTour 781
35. **C**   Abdelhak 676; LaTour 686
36. **C**   LaTour 783
37. **D**   LaTour 695
38. **D**   LaTour 690
39. **C**   LaTour 690
40. **A**   LaTour 690
41. **C**   LaTour 801
42. **A**   Abdelhak 654
43. **D**   Abdelhak 627
44. **C**   Abdelhak 462 and 621
45. **C**   Abdelhak 603
46. **A**   Abdelhak 584–585
47. **B**   Abdelhak 559
48. **B**   LaTour 691–692
49. **A**   LaTour 687
50. **B**   LaTour 687

Index

parathyroid scan, 319
Pareto chart, 155, 155*f*, 206, 459
paroxetine HCl (Paxil), 310
passwords, 273
patient assessment instrument (PAI), 50
patient, defined, 33
patient medical record, 276
patient payment methods, 47–48, 463, 463*t*
   insurance, 463
Patient Protection and Affordable Care Act
   (PPACA), 53–54, 103
patient rights, 233
Patient Self-Determination Act, 36, 84*t*
patient-flow management system, 288
Paxil, 310
payer, defined, 33
PCV. *See* packed cell volume
PDAs. *See* personal digital assistants
PDCA system. *See* plan, do, check, act
   system
Pearson correlation coefficient, 159, 161*f*
peer review, 218
   protection, 237
Peer Review Organizations (PROs), 192,
   193, 217
Pennsylvania Hospital, 190
performance improvement, legal
   implications of, 236–237
pericardial effusion, 333
peritoneal effusion, 334
personal digital assistants (PDAs), 274
PERT charts, 202, 441
PET. *See* positron emission tomography
pharmacology abbreviations, 314
Phenergan, 311
phenobarbital sodium (Bellatal, Luminal),
   310
PHI. *See* protected health information
physical data model, 265
physician index, 30
pie chart, 153, 154*f*, 206
Pitocin, 309
plan, do, check, act (PDCA) system, 200,
   211–213, 212*f*, 458
platelet count, 316
Platinol, 305
pleural effusion, 334
point-of-service plan, 48
portable and hand-held terminals, 27
positron emission tomography (PET), 319
potassium (K-Dur), 310
power, types of, 448–449
PPACA. *See* Patient Protection and
   Affordable Care Act
PPOs. *See* preferred provider organizations
PR. *See* prevalence rate
preadmission review, 219
precision as characteristic of data quality,
   22
prednisone (Deltasone), 310
preferred provider organizations (PPOs),
   48, 53
Pregnancy Discrimination Act, 452
prepaid health plan (insurance), 47–48

president, role of, 75
pressure ulcer stages, 344–345
prevalence rate (PR), 165–166
prevention, levels of, 165
primary patient record, 33
primary prevention, 165
Prinivil, 308
privacy
   definition of privacy, 272*t*
   practices, notice of, 109*f*–112*f*, 117
   RHIA competency statements, 4
Privacy Act of 1974, 84*t*, 272
Privacy Rule, 86, 89, 193
private law, 73
privileged communication, 80
problem solving, 450–451
Procardia XL, 309
procedure index, 30
product instructions, 1–9
product line management, 40
professional standards review
   organizations (PSROs), 217
profitability ratios, 461
programming languages, 262, 275
progress notes, 16–17
project management, 4, 202, 454–455, 455*t*
   phases of, 218–219
promethazine HCL (Phenergan), 311
proportions, 157
Propoxy, 311
propoxyphene (Darvon, Darvocet-N,
   Propoxy), 311
PROs. *See* Peer Review Organizations
prospective payment, 49–51
prospective research, 166
prostate-specific antigen (PSA), 324
protected health information (PHI), 87, 89
prothrombin time (pro-time), 317
pro-time. *See* prothrombin time
Proventil, 303
providers, defined, 33
Prozac, 306
PSA. *See* prostate-specific antigen
PSROs. *See* professional standards review
   organizations
public law, 73–74
pulmonary diffusion, 321
pulmonary perfusion, 321
pulmonary ventilation, 321
punctuation, ICD-9-CM guidelines, 339–340

Q

QAPI. *See* quality assessment and
   performance improvement
QIOs. *See* quality improvement
   organizations
qualitative analysis, 21–22
qualitative standards, 457
quality assessment, 190
quality assessment and performance
   improvement (QAPI), 229
quality assurance, 190
quality control, 190

retention schedule, 29
retrospective research, 166
retrospective review, 219
revenue cycle, 52
    RHIT competency statements, 8
RF test. *See* rheumatoid factor test
RFIT. *See* registered health information technician
RHA. *See* registered health information administrator
rheumatoid factor (RF) test, 331–332
RIA. *See* radioimmunoassay
risk factor, 165
risk management, 219–222
risks, avoidance of, 236
rolling budget, 462
root cause analysis, 190, 459
RR. *See* relative risk
rubella antibody test, 329
run chart, 206, 459

S

safety, 190
SAMHSA. *See* Substance Abuse and Mental Health Services Administration
sampling error, 157
Sandimmune Neoral, 305
scanned entry devices, 27
scatter diagrams, 155, 156*f*, 206, 459
SCHIP. *See* State Children's Health Insurance Program
scientific management, 439
scrotal (testicular) scans, 320
SDLC. *See* system development life cycle
secondary health information data sources, 30–31
secondary patient record, 33
secondary prevention, 165
Security Fundamentals for Health Information, 272
security, information, 272–273
    Internet, 275
    RHIA competency statements, 4
security of health records, 81–82
Security program, 272–273
Security Rule, 90, 116
sed rate, 316
"see also" instruction, 341
"see" instruction, 341
selective serotonin reuptake inhibitors (SSRIs), 306, 310
semen fertility, 334
sentinel events, 190, 222
sequela code, 350
SER. *See* somatosensory evoked response
serial numbering, 27
serial-unit numbering, 27
server-based DBMS, 267
SGML. *See* Standard Generalized Markup Language
Shewhart, Walter, 200
simultaneous-equations methods, 464
simvastatin (Zocor), 311

single-photon emission computed tomography (SPECT), 318
skilled-nursing facilities (SNFs), 42
sleep medication, 313
smart cards, 274
SNFs. *See* skilled-nursing facilities
SOAP format for progress notes, 16–17
Social Security Act, 35, 53
soft skills, word, 10–11
software, 259, 261, 273
somatosensory evoked response (SER), 321
source-oriented health record, 16
sources of law, 74
space management, 28
SPECT. *See* single-photon emission computed tomography
speech recognition, 274
spinal radiography, 317
spirometry, 321
spleen scan, 320
sputum culture, 333
SSRIs. *See* selective serotonin reuptake inhibitors
staffing, 444
standard deviation, 157–158
Standard Generalized Markup Language (SGML), 275
State Children's Health Insurance Program (SCHIP), 49
state court systems, 75, 76*t*
statistical process control chart, 459
statistics
    for accreditation compliance, 147
    budget, 462
    comparative use of, 147
    data presentation, 152–156
    defined, 147
    facilities that maintain, 148
    health care agencies using, 147–148
    health information practitioner's role with, 148
    on hospital services, 149–152
    level of significance, 163
    measures and tests, 156–164
    normal distribution, 158–159
    planning with, 147
    purposes of, 147
    RHIA competency statements, 3
    test of significance, 159–164
    variability, measures of, 157–158
    vital statistics, 148–149
statute of limitations, 82
    on record retention, 29
statutes, affecting healthcare systems, 74
step-down method, 463
stool culture, 333
storage requirements
    calculation of, 29
    image-based records storage, 29–30
    record retention, 29
storyboards, 206
straight numeric filing, 28
strategic information system planning, 262